The Reorganisation of
British Local Government

The Reorganisation of British Local Government

Old Orthodoxies and a Political Perspective

JOHN DEARLOVE
Lecturer in Politics, University of Sussex

CAMBRIDGE UNIVERSITY PRESS
CAMBRIDGE
LONDON · NEW YORK · MELBOURNE

Published by the Syndics of the Cambridge University Press
The Pitt Building, Trumpington Street, Cambridge CB2 1RP
Bentley House, 200 Euston Road, London NW1 2DB
32 East 57th Street, New York, NY 10022, USA
296 Beaconsfield Parade, Middle Park, Melbourne 3206, Australia

First published 1979

Printed in Great Britain by
Anchor Press Limited, Tiptree, Essex.

Library of Congress Cataloguing in in Publication Data
Dearlove, John.
The reorganisation of British local government.
Includes bibliographical references and index.
1. Local government — Great Britain. I. Title.
JS3095 1979.D4   352.041   78—18092
ISBN 0 521 22341 5 hard covers
ISBN 0 521 29456 8 paperback

Contents

To the extent that social science accepts more or less uncritically the definition of its problems as set by tradition and current folk-assumptions, and views its role as the description and analysis of situations so defined, it forfeits thereby, if these problems are wrongly defined, its chief opportunity to contribute to the 'emancipation from error' . . . And it is precisely the role of the social sciences to be troublesome.　　　　　　　(Lynd, 1939, pp. 122, 181)

Preface

This book had its origins in a talk I gave to the Institute of Local Government Studies, Birmingham University, in 1973, and people from the Institute have continued to help my work with information and ideas. John Stewart, Bob Hinings, Rod Rhodes, Stewart Ranson, and Kieron Walsh have all given me their time, but particular thanks must be extended to Royston Greenwood, who put me up when I was working in the Institute's Library and read a lengthy first draft of what later became Chapter 5. I spent the academic year 1974—5 in America as a Senior Guest Scholar under the Fulbright Program. The City University of New York, Brooklyn College, and the New York Public Library, in providing me with the opportunity to study and teach American local politics, also extended my understanding of the reorganisation of British local government. Once back in England I continued my research rather more systematically and was helped in this by a grant from the Nuffield Foundation which enabled me to travel to talk to people in local government and to work regularly in London libraries, especially at the Royal Institute of Public Administration. The Inter-Library Loans Service and the Documents Section at the University of Sussex were almost too effective in providing me with more material, and at a critical point the University granted me a term's paid leave. Stephen Yeo, Donald Winch, John Solomos, Tim Young, Mick Dunford, and Alan Cawson are all friends from Sussex who have helped me, and the final manuscript was typed by Jane Thurlow and Julia Hart before being subjected to Martin Minogue's stylistic scrutiny.

Over the years I presented aspects of my argument in papers to Jim Sharpe and Ken Newton's seminar at Nuffield College, Oxford; to the State Expenditure Group of the Conference of Socialist Economists; and to the Local Politics Group of the Political Studies Association.

Preface

Not surprisingly, the book is very much a product of this background and it is unlikely to be seen as adequate by any of those who have helped it along. On the one hand, people intimately involved in local government and its reorganisation will probably see the study as too cavalier and political, and in need of more caution and detailed empirical work into the complexity and variety of different local situations. On the other hand, people especially interested in theory and the place of local government in the national political economy may well be frustrated by my theoretical eclecticism and by the laborious citation of a mass of material and detail. I am not seeking to make a pre-emptive strike when I say that I recognise that both perspectives have a point. I have tried to find a balance between 'facts' and 'theory' but there is a need for more work at both levels. Although I see the argument I have advanced as providing a better understanding of reorganisation than any currently available in the literature, many of my unvarnished statements are best regarded as questions for further research than as firm conclusions to which I am totally committed.

Brighton, April 1978

I

Old Orthodoxies and Towards a Political Perspective

1. Old Orthodoxies

Orthodoxy means not thinking — not needing to think. Orthodoxy is unconsciousness. (George Orwell, *1984*)

What the Traditional Orthodoxy, and similar doctrines, need above all else is criticism . . . It tends to stagnate when faced only with the unanimous support of the graveyard. (Bulpitt, 1972, p.302)

English local government was substantially reorganised in the nineteenth century. When that century opened 'the term "local government" had not yet been adopted to describe the various administrative bodies which, under a sovereign Parliament, governed the towns and villages of England', but when it closed 'the whole field of internal administration, if we except the City of London, . . . lay under the control of popularly elected bodies' (Keith-Lucas, 1952, p.221; Redlich, 1903, vol. 1, p.213). However, the ink scarcely had time to dry on the reorganising statutes before experts began diagnosing faults and offering prescriptions for further change. But local authority associations could not agree, and no government was really eager to push an issue which seemed to promise more political costs than benefits (Brand, 1974; Isaac-Henry, 1975). Therefore the overall structure 'remained basically unchanged' and 'between 1945 and 1964 virtually no changes took place at all' (Lipman, 1949, p.167; Stanyer, 1970, p.16). The two commissions established by the 1958 Local Government Act operated under a 'procedure [that] was long drawn out . . . and ineffective' and offered 'limited scope' for change (Thornhill, 1971, p.11; Sharpe, 1965, p.21). It 'merely tinkered with the problem' and the result was 'a great deal of hard work over ten years — and not a great deal achieved' (Crossman, 1975, p.440; Sharp, 1969, p.48).

During the 1966—70 Labour Government there were more

serious moves to reorganise local government. Lord Redcliffe-Maud, an expert on local government, first chaired a committee concerned with the management of local government before moving on to chair the Royal Commission on Local Government in England, which was required 'to consider the structure of local government in England, outside Greater London, in relation to its existing functions; and to make recommendations for authorities and boundaries, and for functions and their division, having regard to the size and character of areas in which these can be most effectively exercised and the need to sustain a viable system of local democracy'. The Labour Government did not survive to implement change, but the incoming Conservative administration quickly tackled the boundary problem and the 1972 Local Government Act redrew the basic map of local government with a vengeance, replacing some 1,300 directly elected local authorities in England with just 401 authorities.

'A striking feature' of much of the criticism of local government has been this 'obsession with what is sometimes called the area problem' (Chester, 1954, p.2). Even so, 'there was a growing feeling inside local government (and outside too) that reorganisation of areas and functions was not enough' (Sharp, 1969, p.30; Morton, 1970, p.104). If nothing else, therefore, 'solving' the boundary problem served to put the management problem at the very top of the reorganisation agenda. The Royal Commission on Local Government in England (1969, vol. 1, p.123) felt 'certain that the new authorities will have to make far-reaching changes in traditional organisation and methods of work . . . Arrangements to ensure a corporate . . . view must be an integral part of an authority's organisation', and further advice on what local authorities should do flowed down in official reports and circulars and in the writings of academics. In addition, there has been an important push towards the introduction of neighbourhood councils and public participation in planning, and there has been renewed interest in reorganising the basis of local government finance. What sense can we make of all these changes?

It is important to realise that it is only the *implementation* of reorganisation that is novel. There is a chain of concern about local government which stretches right back into the nineteenth century. The members of the Maud Committee on the Management of Local Government 'thought in terms of the clichés of the conventional wisdom about local government' (Stanyer, 1970A, p.56); the later Redcliffe-Maud Commission did the same thing (Stanyer, 1973, pp.105—6); and we can find the 'foundations' of the Herbert Commission's 'thinking' on local government in Greater London 'in its affirmation of the traditional values of local self-government . . . Hardly a word would have failed to win the approval of J. S. Mill' (Self, 1962, p.159). In other words, there is a body of 'traditional wisdom about local government' (Richards, 1973, p.47) and a well-established discourse about practically all the contemporary problems. This conditions and limits the conventional debate. The tradition is made up of simple statements that purport to describe and explain how local government works; to diagnose the faults; and to suggest reforms which will lead to a better system characterised by democracy, efficiency, effectiveness, and co-ordinated rationality. These statements may be termed 'orthodoxies' and they are distinguished by three defining characteristics.

1 They are *widely shared and long-established.*
2 Because of this they are *rarely questioned* — or where they are questioned the critique rarely poses any fundamental challenge because it invariably comes from within the confines of the wider tradition emphasising currently neglected aspects of it.[1]
3 Even where the statements purport to offer a description and explanation they are *not based on any solid research* into the practice and behaviour of local authorities.

These three defining characteristics interact with each other in a thoughtless vicious circle. Precisely because we are dealing with statements which are regarded as true and as embodying just plain common-sense, it is seen as quite superfluous to explore them and subject them to any sort of critical questioning based on empirical enquiry and theorising. However, it is precisely the *absence* of sustained and rigorous critical enquiry consciously located outside the assumptions of the orthodoxies that has enabled them to survive and remain unquestioned.

These orthodoxies are not just entrenched in official reports, since they also pervade the academic literature of discussion. It is

---

1 For example, that orthodox rule of reform which has pointed to the need for larger local authorities to increase efficiency has been subjected to a romantic critique which is uncritical of the democracy of small authorities and the established system (see especially Rees, 1971).

one thing for politicians to slip uncritically into a tired and easy acceptance of a tradition of debate, and 'we must not expect too much from reforming committees in the way of logical analysis' (Self, 1971, p.269). But it is quite another matter for social scientists to follow this same course. For us to suspend decent research, criticism, and even independent and serious thought is a denial of the possibilities of our position and our claim to scholarship and science.[2] Why has this happened?

At the simplest level the same vicious circle is at work. The reluctance to theorise about the institutions of local government (Sancton, 1976; Sharpe, 1970; MacKenzie, 1961) and the poor quality of much research are both *effects* and *causes* of the existence and survival of the orthodoxies. In addition, the nature of academic life can easily inhibit scepticism. We enter the academic life working on a thesis under the guidance of an old master of the subject, and after entry the need for mutual survival encourages the unspoken convention which prevents dog eating dog (Mills, 1967, p.297; Lynd, 1939, p.118). It is easier to stay in the intellectual fold. You are listened to uncritically because you speak the right language, and the reduced need for thought gives you more time to write which increases the possibility of your own promotion. Not only are textbooks designed to articulate the consensus, but the fact that any manuscript has to run the gauntlet of senior figures who are likely to have risen to prominence on the strength of their ability to embellish the conventional wisdom serves to hinder the publication of critical work. Disciplinary divisions and the pressure to specialise narrows 'the scope of scientific analysis' (Meynaud, 1963, p.17), inhibit vision and imagination, and constitute a barrier to understanding by making intellectually difficult a full appreciation of the wide economic and historical context.[3] Of course, these remarks could apply to most disciplines, but the administrative focus of those who have studied local government has further encouraged the continuance of analysis within the confines of conventional wisdom. The very importance of local government, the possibility of its being reorganised from the top down, and the pressure on all of us to be practical and constructive (Bailey, 1975, p.2; Redcliffe-Maud

2 I agree with Christian Bay (1972, p.90) that 'political science education must aim at liberating the student from the blinders of the conventional wisdom'.
3 Harvey (1973, pp.147–52) even claims that a disciplinary focus involves theoretical formulations that are oriented to the preservation of the status quo.

in Wood, 1976, p.7; Simmie, 1974, p.203), have also done much
to institutionalise a reformist perspective. This orientation not
only assumes away the whole problem of the relationship between
social scientists and government, but it is also at the core of bad
research and poor theory.[4] There are two rather distinct traditions
of academic work on local government that display this perspective.
First, and of particular relevance to the boundary problem, the
older literature of local government studies displays a keen commitment to local self-government. This commitment has encouraged an
optimistic reliance on prescriptive liberal theories of representative
government to explain the practice of local government, and it
has served to inhibit the development of empirically based theories
more carefully attuned to the reality, and not the ideology, of the
local situation today. Second, and of particular relevance to the
management problem, we are now witnessing the rise of urban
policy science. Academics are prepared to deny their own freedom
of enquiry, not because of any old-fashioned and overt commitment to a particular value, but because professional and institutional stakes encourage an alignment with those of power on the
basis of a problem-solving orientation that is politically feasible.[5]
A close involvement with local government officers is a key feature
of this work. This leads to an understanding of *their* problems
which means that the academic 'tends to lose his moral autonomy'
(Mills, 1970, p.199) in the concern to engage in 'responsible'
debate. Whether from a public administration or a policy science
perspective, most academics who have concerned themselves with
the reorganisation of local government have been an integral
part of the reform tradition and therefore party to the orthodox
debate. From this perspective, reorganisation is taken on its own
terms at the level of its public face and ideology as being solely
about increasing democracy, efficiency, and effectiveness in the
general effort to create better government in the public interest.
Critique is absent. Because reorganisation is seen as apolitical and
neutral reform, those who are within the tradition cannot conceive
of the possibility of *any* criticism except that which is political,

4 There is little practical point in a reforming academic confronting the orthodoxies,
  as when evidence is presented which does challenge their validity it is quite likely
  that the evidence and the academic will be regarded as suspect and questionable —
  even unBritish — and the orthodoxy will continue to stand intact, bruised but sur-
  viving to be legitimised by something less dangerous than the vulgarity of hard and
  unyielding fact.
5 Lowi (1972, p.32) is among many who recognise the 'conservative' implications of
  this particular stance.

irrational, or parochial, and so quite beyond the pale of reasoned consideration. If academic books about reorganisation do not embody their author's own proposals for 'reform', then they are usually content to describe the proposals of others and blandly present the debate. There is no study which discusses the various facets of reorganisation as they relate to each other; which sees reorganisation as about who will control and benefit from local government; and which seeks to understand it all by looking at it in the context of the developing political economy. At its most basic, there is no study which looks at reorganisation from *outside* the British tradition of debate, and even the assessments[6] of the effects of reorganisation are of limited value.

Because of the general state of the literature any study of reorganisation must begin with a massive intellectual ground-clearing operation.

1 Recognise the entrenchment of orthodoxies and the tradition of debate about local government and its reorganisation.

2 Set down the tradition, the orthodoxies, and the languages of discussion about local government.[7]

3 Do not treat the orthodoxies as true. Make them the object of serious study. Question them and confront them with evidence which sits uneasily within the framework of thinking which they provide. Regard them as hypotheses to be tested in the soil of research about local government. This involves two questions. First, is there evidence to support the orthodoxies, and is it put forward? Second, and at a tougher level, is there evidence which challenges and contradicts them, and does it provide the basis for a different conceptualisation of local politics from that which revolves around the

6 There are a number of assessments of the success or failure of the reorganisations that have been designed to solve the boundary problem, and particular attention has centred on the reorganisation of London Government that took place in 1963. None of the assessments are of such intellectual weight. On the reorganisation following the 1972 Act, see Buxton, 1973, p.260; Sharpe, forthcoming; Committee of Inquiry into Local Government Finance, 1976, p.25; Lee, Wood, Solomon and Walters, 1974; Redcliffe-Maud and Wood, 1974, pp.52–7; Labour Party, 1977. On the reorganisation of London Government, see Royal Commission on Local Government in England, 1969, Research Study 1; Wistrich, 1972, Ch. 10; Rhodes, 1972; Hart, 1968A; Foley, 1972, pp.44, 179.

7 Anyone embarking on this sort of task can surely take a grain of comfort from Greenleaf's observation that 'a political tradition is not really too tricky a thing to get to know, at least in academic terms' (1975, p.28). Moreover to proceed in this way in an area which is enmeshed in public debate minimises the likelihood of one's own ideological entrapment (Strauss, 1967, pp.83, 94–5).

orthodox models of democracy, central control, and departmentalism?

The fact that the traditional literature of local government studies is in the reformist mould and committed to the conventional wisdom means that I am involved in its critique. (See also Stanyer, 1967; 1970, pp.42–70; 1976; Thornhill, 1971, pp.28–30; Gyford, 1976; Rhodes, 1975; Cox, 1976, p.44.). However, my critique goes beyond the usual claim that the literature is all too narrowly legalistic and institutional, since I am also concerned to deal with the ideological implications. In addition, I am not using this critique as a springboard to make a case for the new urban political science as do most critics, since I do *not* consider that this newer body of work is of much help in providing the basis for a richer political understanding of reorganisation. Even so, I do see an important place for this newer work, and in the parts of my study devoted to a critical consideration of the orthodoxies I will be leaning heavily on the literature of research, description and explanation which has grown up with the 'maturation of urban political science' (Young, 1975A, p.xiii): without it the task of challenging and questioning the orthodoxies would have to be very much more speculative.[8]

In the body of this book I will show that the traditional models that are at the centre of the descriptions and explanations of local government are grossly deficient. Whole areas of local politics go unnoticed and are left unexplored,[9] and, worse still, aspects are misrepresented because the values integral to the reformist perspective intrude themselves unchecked into empirical enquiry, so that pressing facts are bent and twisted to fit into the confines of outworn theories. There is a stubborn resistance to seeing the local political world as it is. Much of this work has to be seen as ideological, since the orthodox statements hang together to provide us with a partial view of local government as it is, and the reorganisation proposals embody a particular view of how it

8 'Authentic scientific knowledge cannot by itself prevent orthodoxy, but it can ameliorate some of the potential deceptions of consensual myths by confronting them with conclusions which are more validly contingent upon empirical reality' (Melanson, 1972, p.493).

9 There has been a limited concern with the implementation of policies and their outcome and impact on the public. The official literature has yet to pay any serious attention to the setting of local government in the context of the more informal pattern of local politics, and although academics are beginning to study this virtually no one has chosen to situate local government *and* local politics in the wider political economy. Case studies of local policy-making tend to be isolated and ahistorical.

should be. The orthodox models of local politics, if they are not overtly presenting us with the 'democratic' view from the top, only serve to 'arrest . . . social thought at inadequate and superficial concepts' (Blackburn, 1972, p.10). Local government as it should be is presented as in the public interest, at the end of the rainbow of reform. However, not only are aspects of the local political utopia impossible to implement, but advocates of reorganisation have been intent on relocating local political power away from the working class. Reformism and a positive involvement with government is grounded in an unconscious acceptance of liberal ideology both as regards the role of the state and the role of knowledge in a democratic polity. Such a stance rests on the view that the state is neutral and open to good advice, and on the idea that social scientific information will somehow produce better reorganisation. These views strongly support the basic political status quo since they do not admit the possibility that the state might not be neutral but works in the essential interests of the few, and they do not really provide for our knowledge being made available to those who seek to push for change from below on the basis of an open attack on facets of the state apparatus (Erwin, 1973; Fainstein and Fainstein, 1972). This positive orientation to reform involves 'presenting the given political system as the only possible one', and in doing this it 'serves the interests of those groups who profit most from the system' (Mueller, 1973, p.110). It cannot be doubted that academic work on local government reorganisation has done much to legitimise both the intellectual standing of the orthodoxies and the thrust of reorganisation itself.

I mentioned a little earlier that my critique of the traditional literature of local government studies did not lead to my going on to embrace wholeheartedly the new urban political science, for although this literature can help us dispose of some orthodox Aunt Sallies, it does not help us to develop a political perspective on reorganisation. It is far too soon to provide a definitive assessment of this new mode of work, but there are dangers within it. The admirable concern to engage in rigorous and systematic research is not always matched by, and can easily occur at the expense of, any real concern to deal with the troubling big questions involved in a proper consideration of reorganisation. The big issues of reorganisation are not easily amenable to empirical enquiry on the basis of atheoretical case studies alone. The study of reorganisation also forces to the fore values; the problem of objectivity, and the study of institutions, which this newer work either seeks to avoid or sees as irrelevant. The traditional literature can even now stand accused of displaying an unwarranted dogmatism, but practitioners of urban political science may one day come to be seen as socially irrelevant and irresponsible. Their overt lack of concern with what ought to be, their scientific question begging and opting out, and their concern to see all sides of a problem inhibits action, aligns them covertly with the status quo, and prevents their exploring their own ideological stance (Andreski, 1974, pp.124—5; Connolly, 1967).

A large part of this book will, then, be concerned with the case for, the approach to, and the discussion of reorganisation. Chapters 2, 3, 5 and 6 set down and explore the limitations of our 'taken-for-granted knowledge' about local government and its reorganisation (Bailey, 1975, p.20). I question, challenge, and am generally sceptical about the orthodox descriptions, explanations, diagnoses and prescriptions. This exercise carries within itself two additional points of interest. First, I will also be involved in the presentation of my own (still ill-formed) view of local politics, which, at its simplest level, I recognise as giving substance to the view from below — the view from the outsiders to power and decision-making, be they inside or outside the council chamber. Second, I hope that this essentially negative part of my study will also be seen as of interest in so far as it provides some sort of commentary on the state of the academic literature on local government. Most centrally I am engaged in a critique of the traditional literature of local government studies and the newest literature on urban policy science, but there is also a more guarded critique of urban *political* science as well. My concern to challenge the orthodoxies involves a dynamic between them and empirical enquiry which not only carries a plea for more research but could also involve a sort of synthesis between the old and the new study of local government, with potential benefits for both traditions of work. Those who wish to continue in the 'practical' and relevant tradition of formulating 'realistic' proposals for change should recognise that to do so on the basis of tired, unproved orthodoxies and unrecognised ideologies is indefensible. Prescriptions, assessments, and diagnoses must surely be adjusted to a very different reality from that which is conventionally identified, described, and explained. It is no longer possible to ignore dealing empirically with a reality which has been defined as bad and capable of change, simply on the basis of common-sense hunches grounded in outworn theories. At the same time, those more committed to empirical research should display a keener sensitivity to the subject matter of enquiry and push into the bigger questions, even if this does involve a less sophisticated research methodology.

2. And Towards a Political Perspective

To raze the simplified conceptual structures erected by one's predecessors is not only a frolic for the young in spirit, but also a necessary step toward the discovery of truths that have eluded scholars in the past.   (Fesler, 1957, p.139)

Would be working men town councillors found themselves hampered in that most of the council and committee meetings were held in the morning and afternoon; evening meetings of the local governing body naturally became one of the planks of the platform of the Crewe Branch of the ILP, founded in 1894 . . . The first Labour town councillor took his seat in November 1902.
                                        (Chaloner, 1950, pp.166–7)

A critical consideration of the orthodoxies on local government and its reorganisation is not the same as a critical consideration of the reality of reorganisation itself, and demolishing the literature does not tell us much about the political implications of re-organisation. Some may take the view that I should ignore the traditional debate, but there are two reasons why I would reject this advice. First, if you want to have an impact on the debate – especially if you want to change its whole tone and direction – then you must recognise that debate before going on to persuade people to abandon the restraints which it imposes. Second, a knowledge of the debate contains lessons pointing to pitfalls we should avoid. The ideological implications *and* the intellectual limitations of a reformist orientation, and an unthinking acceptance of the tradition of debate all highlight the need for us to adopt a less narrow perspective where we engage in questioning, research, and wider reading, and try to transcend the artificial specialisation imposed by disciplinary boundaries.

In trying to work out a way forward it is tempting to dodge the theoretical difficulties involved by saying that we only need good empirical studies of the reality of reorganisation. But this both overstates the value of empirical work (Mills, 1970, pp.222–6) and also begs the fundamental prior question of *what* research should be undertaken (Myrdal, 1957, p.160). Moreover, the contemporary reorganisation of British local government is still in its infancy and so the ultimate and crucial implications of that reorganisation will not have developed sufficiently for direct observation at this stage. At the present time, empirical work is not in itself the answer. The major task which lies before anyone who wishes to understand reorganisation is to set down a broad perspective on it that can then be discussed, and can be developed to guide future research studies. This is the second concern of my study. What does it involve?

I should not, and indeed cannot, proceed on the basis of being a freelance intellectual anarchist wilfully pursuing what I see as my very own line of vital questioning. I might thereby be vulnerable to an unthinking reliance upon the dominant mode of thought caught up within the particular tradition of scholarship of which I was a part. Or, if I avoided this danger, then I might fail to recognise that I am intellectually affected by my social background and by the particular reference group to which I look for political approval, so ignoring the fact that 'my' view of the world is shaped by a whole variety of historical and social forces and is likely to embody a crude perspective on reorganisation that is only acceptable to certain sections of society (Connolly, 1967, p.144). I have already pointed to the limitations of the British tradition of scholarship on reorganisation and so have perhaps avoided a facet of the first danger. Moreover, I am mindful that my background and ideology have shaped my reaction to the established literature and my broad view of local politics and reorganisation. Having said that, I obviously think that my attempt to build on a view from below does justice to the facts, and I also think that it provides the basis for a better — more realistic — understanding of reorganisation than that which we get from the established literature, because I am less unthinkingly caught up in a particular tradition of debate and in an unquestioned belief in the moral integrity of liberal democracy.

Let me begin by moving off cautiously, setting down the two main ingredients of my approach, before I go on to identify work from outside the study of British local government which I think can help advance our understanding of it.

First we have to recognise that we can really only understand anything by setting it within a context which gives it some sort of meaning and significance. If we are to avoid the danger of abstracted empiricism, then no matter what we are studying we have to situate it within a wider societal context; we have to see how it fits into the historical trend of our times; and we have to assess its significance for the different groups and interests in society (Mills, 1967, p.572). The necessity for this cannot be doubted when we are faced with something of such massive significance as local government, which

> spends some £13 thousand million a year on its work. It services
> a capital debt of some £25 thousand million. Nearly three million
> people are now employed in the service of local authorities. These
> authorities are also among the biggest landlords and landowners in
> the country. Together they comprise one of the biggest enterprises
> in the land. By any standards their operations are of major public
> importance.   (Committee of Inquiry into Local Government
>   Finance, 1976, pp.13–14)

Reorganisation must have some effect on all of this.

Second, and more specifically, I reject that apolitical presumption entrenched in the reformist literature which sees governmental reform as bringing the benefit of efficiency, effectiveness, and democracy to all at the same time, as it harms absolutely no one. The reformist orientation has been dominant for so long that it does not admit the possibility of overtly political questions about reorganisation that centre on its inevitable implications for the control of governmental power and public policy to the advantage of some groups over others. But it is impossible to accept an analysis which assumes the general existence (or at least the *local* possibility) of societal consensus, since this analysis is at odds with the reality of basic division and conflict. The need for reorganisation is never a given, and it is never self-evidently necessary. There is unlikely to be agreement around any assessment of what is wrong with established structures or what proposals should be put forward to effect change. Some will be dissatisfied with the established system and will want change (and for their own particular reasons), just as others may disagree and oppose it, and even more will have no real idea of what is going on and why. 'No society adopts fundamental change because its dominant groups have suddenly acquired virtue or become horrified at waste' (Altshuler, 1970, p.191). We should not rule out the possibility that reorganisation may be an overt strategy designed to place the control of government in particular hands — a strategy that is seen as necessary and possible by certain groups at particular points in time when they feel that they are not winning, and *cannot* win, within the established rules of the governmental game. Short-term political victories can get converted into longer-term strategic gains if they can become institutionalised in new constitutions, structures and processes of government. The governmental power of various groups is partly a result of the rules that have been made to govern, as 'some publics have been able to shape political institutions and practices . . . This is . . . a matter . . . of the institutional framework of politics, and the very rules of the political game itself, being systematically biased in favour of certain interests rather than others' (Newton, 1976, p.236).

The reorganisation of local government is something that is so central to the political world of organised power for particular advantage, that it must have implications for the continuing societal struggle to control government. This should not be regarded as controversial. After all, we can easily accept that electoral rules have crucial implications for the access of interests to governmental power, and I am only suggesting that we go on to recognise that *all* facets of governmental organisation can be seen as having such implications. At the most obvious level we can see the political significance of the qualifications for the franchise (Rae, 1971), and the political significance of qualifications for elected office. For example, under the 1835 Municipal Corporations Act a candidate for election to the borough council had to be on the burgess roll and satisfy a further (high) property qualification. These clearly limited the section of society from which councillors could be drawn, and the implications of these rules were reinforced by the fact that council service was unpaid and meetings occurred during normal working hours. More specifically, the Audit (Local Authorities) Act, 1927, disqualified any person surcharged for more than £500 for five years from membership of any local authority. 'The Labour Party saw that the main purpose was to exclude the Socialist members from the local authorities in East London' (Keith-Lucas, 1952, p.179). Baldly expressed, 'governmental arrangements are not neutral. We do not organise in a vacuum . . . Organisational arrangements tend to give some interests, some perspectives, more effective access to those with decision making authority' (Seidman, 1975, p.14). Governments are organisations; organisations are rules; rules carry within themselves implications for who can gain effective access to power within the organisation; and whosoever is in the best position to win power is more easily able to affect organisational policies to their own group's perceived advantage.

In my view, therefore, a political perspective on reorganisation has to recognise that new boundaries, new structures, and new processes *all* have implications for the access of different interests to local government, and therefore for the likely direction of public policy. Moreover, to give any such perspective on reorganisation meaning and significance we have to situate it in time and look at it within the wider context of political struggle and conflict.

Although I have been critical of the orthodox literature advocating and discussing reorganisation, at the most simple level my perspective does little more than lay bare and build on the overtly political anxieties of the reformers themselves. One anxiety is of long-standing importance and the reorganisation proposals that are grounded on it embody an overt recognition of the implications of the rules of the governmental game for access to local government. Orthodox opinion has long attested to the decline in councillor 'calibre' and there has also been considerable anxiety as to the 'calibre' of the permanent officials. It is tempting to dismiss the whole confused debate on this matter (Rees, 1968, p.133). Calibre cannot really be measured (Sharpe, 1962, p.204), and 'the antiquity of the complaints suggests that there may have been no decline at all' (Jones, 1969, p.152). Both these points are true, but they are irrelevant to the impact which this concern has had on the course of reorganisation. Advocates of reorganisation *think* they can measure calibre and 'in the plea for a better calibre of councillor there frequently may be detected an assumption that businessmen and professionals would make a better job of it than housewives, small shopkeepers and trade union officials' (Cox, 1976, p.103; see also Hennock, 1973, pp.323, 341; A West Midland Study Group, 1956, p.287; Sharpe, 1962, p.208). In hard terms, anxiety about councillor calibre embraces an appreciation of two trends with respect to the changing class composition of local councils, as 'the "gentlemen" are being crowded out and the working men are coming in' (Howe, 1907, p.35). First, there is a sense of regret that social leaders and businessmen now assume less of a role on local councils than was once the case in the golden age of local government. Second, it is regretted that young business executives and professionals have not stepped into this breach. It is as the working class have moved into local government, aided and abetted by the rise of the Labour Party, that so many councillors have been judged as of 'illiterate speech and low social standing' (Hasluck, 1936, p.48) and as of inadequate and declining calibre.

There has been a grudging recognition of the limits of social engineering in this matter, but those concerned with the health of local government have not been prepared to take this trend of decline lying down. In a highly class conscious way they quickly latched on to the fact that reorganising local government could alter the class composition of councils, so ensuring a renewed supply of high calibre councillors and officials. In Chapter 4, I will show that at least part of the case for reorganising local government boundaries and creating larger local authorities has been grounded in an appreciation that this could have the effect of increasing the likelihood that large urban local authorities would have councils composed of businessmen and professionals. For example, the Royal Commission on Local Government in Greater London (1960, p.63) considered that 'there does seem to be some relationship between the size and scope of the authority and the capacity of the councillors and officials attracted . . . a certain minimum size and scope of authority seems to be needed to attract councillors and officers of the right calibre'. More fundamentally, these sorts of proposals have also been based on a realistic appreciation of the developing social geography of cities, and on the implications of the growth of the suburbs for the control of local government if established boundaries were to have been left unchanged. In Chapter 8, I will show that when advocates of reorganisation have sought to solve the management problem then they have shown a similar concern to restructure so as to make it easier for businessmen to control local government. The Working Group on Local Authority Management Structures (1972, p.30) has not been alone in taking the view that 'some potential members, particularly professional and businessmen, are . . . deterred from putting themselves forward for election because of the amount of time traditionally occupied by Council affairs', and neither has it been alone in the hope 'that streamlining the structure and management processes will result in more of these potential candidates being willing to play an active part in local government'.

So, although I am adopting a perspective which recognises that reorganisation has implications for class access to local government, it is abundantly clear that advocates of reorganisation must actually agree with the relevance of this since they have been frank in their concern to increase calibre through their reorganisation proposals. It is amazing that no one has ever chosen to pick up their lead in order to explore the implications of reorganisation for the control and direction of local government, or to ask *why* certain people should be so acutely worried about the calibre of councillors and officials at certain moments.

In order to go further with this sort of perspective, we need to look for help from a literature wider than that which tends to be referred to within the closed British debate. The fashionable thing would be to introduce Marxist inspired literature. I will be considering some of this work in my concluding Chapter 9, but not at this stage. It would not convince most students of reorganisation of the value of the perspective I am seeking to develop, and although I am mindful of the limitations of empirical research I am equally mindful of the dangers of an over-emphasis upon abstract theory. We can best move ahead on the basis of comparative work on local politics.[10] My focus is on America, and I am particularly interested in the literature on the reorganisation of their own system of local government. I am in good and relevant company in my eagerness to look at this, because advocates of reorganisation in Britain and America have been very attentive to developments across the Atlantic and have often tried to copy facets of each other's practice. Not surprisingly, therefore, a tremendous similarity exists with respect to the whole language of discourse about local government, its problems and prospects. In both countries there has been a lot of writing about the need for efficiency and the virtues of local self-government, and advocates of reorganisation have long been concerned with the calibre of their elected representatives and with the implications of this for services and expenditure. Moreover, in both countries there has been anxiety about the inefficiency caused by the presence of too many too small authorities, and fragmentation in the overall system and within individual local authorities has been pointed to as harmful and as a problem needing solution.

10 There is now an increased interest in comparative work in the field of local politics as witnessed in the journals, *Comparative Local Government, Comparative Urban Research*, and the important *International Journal of Urban and Regional Research*; see also, Ashford, 1975, 1975A; Newton, 1969, 1975; Alford, 1967; Miller, 1970; Walton and Masotti, 1976; Kesselman, 1970; Kantor, 1974; Savitch and Adler, 1974.

Much of the American literature on local government and reorganisation has been riddled with the same faults that have bedevilled our own writing. Many American political scientists have adopted a reformist orientation. They have assumed the same social engineering role as their colleagues here and have seen it as their proper task to prescribe remedies for the ills of city government (Sayre and Polsby, 1965; Long, 1967). Adrian (1961, p.148) reminds us that

> academic municipal reformers of some years back drew their programmes from the goals of a segment of the business community that wanted to apply 'business principles' to local government. They did not seek to expand the horizons of knowledge by empirical examination of the assumptions of business leaders. Similarly much metropology since 1945 has dealt with the efforts to propagandize on behalf of efficiency and economy goals. In neither period of urban history . . . has the problem of local democracy been the central focus of participating academics.

Where the American literature was not openly prescriptive, then, like our own, it often simply presented 'facts that have been gathered with little regard for the construction of general theories, and at the same time it is beset with theories that have been advanced without ever being checked against available empirical data' (Herson, 1957, p.330). 'Very few of the studies have involved substantial amounts of fieldwork' (Daland, 1957, p.506). The situation has been one in which orthodoxies have dominated the field and Richards (1954, p.274) at least was keenly aware that 'students and practitioners of local government tend to become victims of their traditions, to be dominated by their habit patterns. They become blinded by their own "truths" and their own environs.' If this was the sole stuff of the American literature then there would be little point in paying it any attention. But this is not the full story. The parallels with respect to our own debate do end, and it is precisely because of this that we should be particularly interested in that body of American literature which is situated outside the reformist mould. What literature do I have in mind and why is it relevant to us?

First, there has been the growth of urban political science committed to empirical description and explanation. This has involved the 'questioning [of] established doctrine' in a way that has really only just begun over here (Sayre and Polsby, 1965, p.125). In effect, political scientists have followed Richards' advice and spent 'some of their time testing the validity of currently accepted conclusions' (1954, p.274). Fresh factual air has blown apart the same stale old orthodoxies that still tend to dominate discussion over here.

Second, and more important, there is another tradition of scholarship which is self-consciously located outside, and directed against, the ideological confines of the reformist orientation. This tradition provides us with a critical and political perspective on both the reformist tradition and reorganisation. It is this literature which has convinced me of the value of the understanding I am seeking to develop. I am especially mindful of the treatment of municipal reform in the Progressive Era by those historians who are part of the New Urban History and I will be setting down their work in Chapter 8. But work has also been undertaken on the political implications of larger, metropolitan-wide, units of government. The message of this research (set down in Appendix 1) also leads us into an awareness of the effect which the boundaries of local government have for the class who will be in the best position to control government and public policy to their advantage.

As I see it, this American literature and experience contains lessons for an understanding of the reorganisation of British local government. It raises questions of relevance to practically *any* reorganisation, and although their relevance is only demonstrated with respect to the American situation we can nevertheless put them, and the perspective which they embody, on to our own research agenda knowing that they would never get there if we persisted in staying within the orthodox context of British debate. We are bound to find that answers to the questions will be hard to come by, and they may be very different from those revealed in American practice, but simply to raise them is to introduce the clear possibility of a different sort of analysis which cannot help but throw shafts of light deep into unexplored corners of our own reorganisation experience.

1 We are forced to consider the limits of our own reformist perspective on reorganisation. In the American context hard research into a similar batch of orthodoxies has now made it abundantly clear that this sort of perspective only serves to misrepresent the essentials and the effects of reorganisation.

3 This literature buttresses the political perspective I am seeking to develop.

3 We must recognise that there are massive problems lying in

the way of implementing the reorganisation proposals especially in so far as they involve the concern to create a corporate approach to solve the management problem.

4 Finally, the very richness of the critical historical accounts of the reorganisation of American city government at the turn of this century clearly derives from the fact that the whole movement for change has been looked at in the round and in the context of the political, social and economic life of the cities of which it was an inextricable part. In other words, we can truly *understand* just what that reorganisation was about because students have developed a political perspective. They have asked hard and basic questions of the reality of the movement, and they have situated it all in a context which gives their more specific focus meaning and significance in a way which has never been seen as necessary in the analyses of British reorganisation. In my concluding chapter, I will be paying more attention to the context which gives meaning to my own understanding of British reorganisation. I will also be identifying the persistent and orthodox anxiety about the direction and scale of local government expenditure and the more recent anxiety about the credibility and legitimacy of the system of local government itself: the anxiety about declining councillor calibre does not stand alone.

This book is in two parts. Part One deals with the boundary problem and the concern to create larger units of local government. Part Two deals with the management problem and the concern to introduce the corporate approach. The first two chapters of each part set down and challenge the orthodoxies that are central to the established debate. The last chapter of each part focuses on the concern about the calibre of councillors and officers and on the implications of reorganisation for the control of local government. Chapter 7 considers the problem of implementing the corporate approach, and Chapter 9 takes up the themes sketched out above.

Part One

The Boundary Problem

. . . the reiteration of stock arguments for or against extensions of
boundaries in general, such as, 'the larger areas mean more efficient
administration', or 'a smaller area is more conducive to keen interest'
. . . — I felt I could have reeled it all off mechanically if I had just
been told on which side I was to plead. As to the evidence it was all
of the nature of personal opinions, obviously *ex parte* opinions:
no attempt was made to prove the truth or the falsehood of all this
assertion, and counter-assertion.
(Beatrice Webb, 1948, pp.164—5, diary entry 31 January 1900 con-
    cerning an enquiry into the extension of the Borough of Torquay)

Some social scientists . . . see metropolitan government as a neutral
instrument . . . Yet metropolitan government does not seem to be a
neutral structure. Larger governmental units necessarily cut down
the numerical representation of minorities.   (Marshall, 1972, p.25)

In 1885 Chamberlain (p.235) considered that 'in the large towns
no serious fault can be found with the working of the system [of
local government]', and the President of the Local Government
Board echoed this assessment when he told the House of Commons
in 1893 that 'no man can point to a single instance in which our
municipal system has broken down'. Once the 'century of reform'
finally closed (Hammond, 1935, p.37), it fell to a Moravian
professor of constitutional law at the University of Vienna to
write a definitive assessment of the impact of the 'revolution
in the form of local government' (Clarke, 1939, p.108). Dr Josef
Redlich (1903, vol.2, p.408, vol.1, pp.215—16, 278) pointed to
'the marvellous increase in the efficiency of local government and
the equally marvellous growth in its functions', and he heaped
praise on the flourishing system of democratic local government,
noting how 'the gradual substitution of a democratic for a privi-
ledged franchise has not done away with the governing classes . . .
democracy was not found to have deprived the upper classes of
political leadership'.

Since this happy late Victorian golden age of democracy,

efficiency, autonomy from central control and high calibre councillors, most commentators have seen local government as on a steady downhill slide. Just what should be done has depended on how the system has been described, explained, and assessed. What, then, are the orthodoxies on these matters that are relevant to the boundary problem and its solution?

Most commentators have *described* the system as democratic, inefficient, subject to massive and increasing central control, and dominated by councillors (and officers) of declining calibre.

If a naive student of local government were to follow this up and ask an orthodox master of the subject to *explain* this, then he would be provided with the conventional explanatory wisdom which, stripped of any subtlety, could be set down as follows.

The system is democratic because local authorities are subject to popular election. Moreover, the system is more democratic than the central government because the units of government are small and based on communities, so ensuring a closeness to the people and a special intimacy and responsiveness.

The system has become increasingly inefficient because it is out of step with the modern age. There are too many, too small, authorities. These can neither reap the economies of scale which business practice has shown to be so important, nor secure the services of men of calibre as officers or councillors.

The massive extent of central control is partly explained by the rise of a national public opinion and the demand for minimum, or even uniform, standards of service across the country. More important, however, is the increasing financial dependence of local authorities upon the central exchequer. With the central government paying the piper is it so surprising that it calls the tune?

The issue of declining calibre is more tricky and complex. Part of the blame lies at the door of social and economic changes. Even so, men of calibre are deterred from becoming councillors and officers because they lack the opportunity to take truly important decisions in a situation where many local authorities are small and where the whole system is dominated by the central government. Party politics, the time-consuming way local authorities conduct their business, and the established boundaries of local authorities also deter good men from standing for council. A career in the local government service is unattractive because the scope for official action is invariably restricted by meddlesome councillors.

What has been the orthodox *assessment* of the established system? Only the democratic quality of it has been applauded. Inefficiency, too much central control, and declining calibre have all been seen as problems that need to be eliminated through 'reform'. In part at least, all these assessments derive from the entrenched commitment to an autonomous and democratic local self-government operating in the context of a consensual deferential community such as was seen as existing in the golden age. Central control is regarded as a problem precisely because it is seen as a twentieth-century intrusion into the world of local democracy. Inefficiency is deplored, partly at least, because it may lead to even more central control. The Labour Government's White Paper on the *Reform of Local Government in England* (1970, paras. 10, 97) shared the view of the Royal Commission on Local Government in England that

> unless local government is organised to meet the needs of the future, and in particular is organised in units large enough to match the technical and administrative requirements of the services which it administers, its powers must diminish, and with it the power of local democracy . . . Radical change is overdue. And only if such change occurs, and local government is organised in strong units with power to take major decisions, will present trends toward centralisation be reversed, and local democracy secure its place as a major part of our democratic system.[1]

Solving all these problems has never been seen as presenting a major difficulty, as entrenched within the British tradition of debate, there are certain simple *rules of reform* which have long served as the basis on which to adjust the local government machine. One rule relates directly to the issue of democracy and efficiency and can be expressed simply: 'Large is efficient whereas small is democratic.' Fairly obviously, it is also part of this orthodoxy to assert that small is inefficient whereas large is undemocratic, and there is the view that it is not really possible to attain both democracy and efficiency within the one local government system. Given the assessment of the system as inefficient and the concern

---

1 For similar views see Royal Commission on Local Government in Greater London, 1960, paras. 227, 707; Money, 1973, p.319. Some commentators had grown so impatient with the system's alleged inefficiency that they were ready to bolt the British tradition of a commitment to democratic local self-government in order to throw in their lot with the efficiency that was seen to follow from increased centralisation and control (Griffith, 1969, p.866; Hartley, 1971, p.451).

to ward off even more central control, there has been the consistent and untiring advocacy of the need for larger local authorities. But, at the same time, there has been a certain sneaking anxiety about the implications of all this for the democracy of the system. Another rule of reform relates to the issue of central control and local autonomy and derives from the orthodox explanation for the extent of central control. If you wish to decrease central control, and so increase the extent of local autonomy, then you should provide new sources of local revenue, so reducing local dependence upon the central exchequer. Solving the calibre problem has always been seen as rather more difficult but there is an orthodox package of proposals and some of these will need to be considered in this part of the book precisely because they centre on the manipulation of the boundaries of local government.

So, there are four boxes of orthodoxies that have a bearing on the boundary problem: democracy, efficiency; central control; and calibre. Each box is made up of four main compartments: descriptions; explanations; assessments and a statement of the problems; and rules of reform to eliminate them. It would be impossible to deal with all this, and so it is important to decide what are the key orthodoxies that should be set down and subjected to critical consideration. The choice tends to be made for us as commissions and committees looking into the problems of local government have generally been advised to have regard to the need to secure 'effective and convenient local government'[2] – to have regard, that is, to efficiency and democracy.

In Chapter 2, I will set down the widely shared and long-established statements that relate to democracy in local government. In Chapter 3 I will set down the orthodoxies that relate to the issue of efficiency in local government. In both these chapters I will also be concerned to advance a critique against the orthodox positions.

In Chapter 4, I will go on to consider the anxiety about declining councillor calibre. I will not be so concerned to offer a critical

2 These two objectives focus on the provision of services, and on local democracy. They also look back to John Stuart Mill's (1861, pp.193, 195) ideas on the two 'criteria of the goodness of government' as a 'set of organised arrangements for public business' where efficiency and limited participation were the order of the day, and as a 'great influence acting on the human mind' where participation was needed 'to increase the sum of good qualities in the governed, collectively and individually'. The idea that the attainment of democracy and efficiency are in conflict goes back at least to Mill.

(and essentially negative) consideration of the orthodoxies caught up in the anxiety. I want to be more positive and I intend to build my political perspective on reorganisation on this anxiety. I will be concerned to deal with the meaning of calibre; with the hard intentions of the advocates of reorganisation who are concerned to increase it; and with the actual implications of larger local authorities for councillor calibre, party control of local government, and hence for the probable developments with respect to the scope of local government itself.[3]

3 You will see from this outline of the three chapters comprising my discussion of 'The Boundary Problem' that I will not be dealing any more with the orthodoxies pertaining to central control. These are not of such pressing importance as are those pertaining to democracy, efficiency, and calibre, and space precludes their being treated more fully than was the case in Dearlove (1973, ch. 1).

2

Democracy in Local Government

> It is clearly important to ascertain whether local government is in
> a special sense democratic.　　　　　　　　　　(Political and Economic
> 　　　　　　　　　　　　　　　　　　　　　　　　　Planning, 1947, p.4)

This chapter will set down the orthodoxies which revolve around
the description and explanation of the democracy of British local
government. I will go on to advance a critique by suggesting that
none of them do justice to the reality of local government and
politics, and that those interested in reorganisation have been
guilty of misrepresenting and exaggerating the democratic quality
of local government.

However, before I do this, it is important to first emphasise
both the traditional commitment to democratic local self-
government, and the lines of justification that are conventionally
used to defend such a commitment. I say this for a number of
reasons. First, commitment has encouraged a situation in which
local political reality has been defined, and even explained, in
terms of prescriptive theory and the liberal justifications for
democratic local self-government.[1] This commitment has also
been at the root of selective attention to the nineteenth-century
history of reorganisation. In effect, twentieth-century orthodoxy
has involved 'systematically underestimating the utilitarian
reforms' and minimising the extent of central control in that
period (Wickwar, 1970, p.53; see also Thornhill, 1971, p.1).
In this way a mythical golden past is created which can then be
used as a stick to beat what are seen as the evils of contemporary
practice to be eliminated through reform. Second, commitment
has been the mainspring of the conventional assessment of the

---

1 Sharpe (1970, p.159) has recognised this, but he has actually sought to work the
　other way around to 'evolve a consistent theoretical justification for local government
　that claims to bear some resemblance to actual practice'. See also Smith (1969,
　pp.346—7).

problems of the established system. Third, and of critical importance, commitment has taken the edge off, and set unconscious limits on, the nature of empirical enquiry into local politics. Selective research has been the order of the day, with problems and shortcomings of democracy *within* local authorities going unnoticed, unstudied, or misinterpreted.

1. The Commitment to Democratic Local Self-Government

It would be no mark of scholarly research to identify writers and reformers who have written forcefully and lovingly of their commitment to democratic local self-government.[2] The commitment lies beyond the pen and conscious thought of individuals. 'Local self-government is now part of the English constitution, the English notion of what proper government ought to be ... Local government is not secondary but primary; it is axiomatic . . . [There] is this ethical commitment to an extremely vague notion of local self-government' (MacKenzie, 1961, pp.5–7). Boaden (1970, p.175) reminds us that 'the inarticulate major premise' underlying most thinking on British local government is that 'autonomous local government is necessary'; Richards (1968, p.46) is aware that 'there is a strong tradition that local communities should be able to decide how to deal with their own problems'; and so it is hardly surprising that 'one of the primary values which have infused the debate about the need for reorganisation is that of local autonomy' (Bristow, 1972, p.143).

2. The Justification for Democratic Local Self-Government

The entrenchment of this particular commitment has resulted in the general view that 'the case . . . for a strong system of local government is clear almost beyond the needs of discussion' (Laski, 1950, p.411). In consequence, 'there is no normative theory from which we can deduce what local government ought to be', and we are just left with the bald 'traditionalist defence, that "it exists"

2 But see, for example, Royal Commission on Local Government in England, 1969, vol.1, pp.11, 30; Committee on the Management of Local Government, 1967, vol.1, p.68; Robson, 1961, p.61; 1966, p.150; Royal Commission on Local Government in Greater London, 1960, p.270; Self, 1962, pp.159–60; Mill, 1861, pp.347–8; Harris, 1939, p.395; Finer, 1945, p.viii.

or "it works"' (MacKenzie, 1961, p.5; Sharpe, 1965, p.4; see also Sancton, 1976; Hill, 1974, p.16; Wilson, 1948, p.1; Sharpe, 1970; Money, 1973; Meghen, 1964).

Although it is true that 'the arguments get a little threadbare when it comes to the . . . question of why we have local government' (Sharpe, 1965, p.1), there is nevertheless 'the traditional orthodox theory of territorial democracy . . . that strange bundle of doctrines and attitudes which support (justify is probably a better word) the presence of local or territorial governments in democratic political systems' (Bulpitt, 1972, p.282).[3] This package of orthodox themes emphasises the importance and value of public participation[4] as an end in itself for the individual's self-development; for the well-being and stability of the state and the established order; and as of instrumental importance in the context of local politics as enabling individuals to have the regular and organised opportunity of bending public policy to the popular will. I will be considering this last argument in the rest of this chapter because it lies at the core of the orthodox description and explanation of the democracy of local government.

3. The Democracy of Local Government: Traditional Orthodoxy

Consider the following statements: they all give expression to the essentials of the traditional orthodoxy.

In 1960 the Royal Commission on Local Government in Greater London (p.59) asserted that 'local government is with us an instance of democracy at work, and no amount of potential administrative efficiency can make up for the loss of active participation in the work by capable, public-spirited people, elected by, responsible to, and in touch with those who elected them'. The Committee on the Management of Local Government (1967, vol.1, p.91) considered that 'the importance of local government lies in the involvement in local public affairs not only of those

---

3 It is no longer part of the British tradition to defend local government *not* based on principles of representation (Whalen, 1960A; Langrod, 1953; Panter-Brick, 1953, 1954; Moulin, 1954; but see Greenleaf, 1975) and neither is much of a case made for local administrative bodies to serve as agents of the central government (but see Hartley, 1971).

4 There is however a 'justification or value of local government . . . as an efficient agent for providing services' (Sharpe, 1970, p.166; see also MacKenzie, 1961, p.14; Warren, 1957, p.5; Maddick, 1963, p.107; Wickwar, 1970, pp.60ff). Nowadays, given the orthodoxy that local government is inefficient, this is not much aired.

who are elected, but also, indirectly, of the community at large who elect them and to whom they are ultimately accountable'.

In the 1890s Beatrice and Sidney Webb went to America. Beatrice (1898, p.117) did not care for their system of city government and she was moved to write admiringly of what she saw as the essentials of the British system where 'there is no divided responsibility in the . . . local governments of Great Britain. There is a chain of responsibilities. The civil service is responsible and therefore dependent on the representatives, and the representative is dependent on the elector.' At the turn of the century Redlich (1903, vol.1, pp.215–16) suggested that 'the grand principle of representative democracy has been fully applied to local government'. He went on to argue that

> as with the national Parliament so with the local councils. They are
> elected by the people in the locality. They work under the censor-
> ship of local opinion. These little Parliaments of the county, the
> town, and the village, like the great Parliament of the nation, employ
> paid officers to execute their commands . . . England has created
> for herself 'self-government' in the true sense of the word . . . the
> right of the people to legislate, to deliberate, and to administer
> through councils or Parliaments elected on the basis of popular
> suffrage, and with a civil service of municipal and imperial officials
> entirely subordinated to the popular will in law and in fact.

In 1947, Jennings (p.17) pointed out that under our 'historic system of local self-government local authorities . . . consist of persons responsible to the local electorate, or of persons appointed by other persons who are responsible to the local electorate. Within the limits laid down by Parliament and of central control, they adopt a policy which accords, as they think, with the views of the local electorate'. In similar vein, but in 1971, Spencer (pp.172–4) argued that the 'basic model of accountability' in local government is made up of links in a chain, and 'each link from the electorate of the community . . . through the council, to the provision of public services may be expressed both in terms of appointment in one direction and of a corresponding account-ability in the other'.

What do all these statements have in common? First, they describe the British system of local government as democratic, and they see the local electorate, the councillors, and the officers, as the key participants. Second, they provide a theory to explain the relationships between these participants and the process of local policy-making. In this Electoral Chain of Command Theory, policy demands flow from electors to councillors (through the agency of regular elections) and then on from councillors to officers (through a key convention of representative government, which assigns officials to the role of passive administration). Responsibility or accountability flows back down the line. The result is that votes inserted at one end become popular public policies at the other.

From this sort of perspective on local government a number of things are seen as of particular importance with respect to the democracy of the British system.

First, informed and extensive public participation is of quite crucial importance and 'no system of local government can be complete which does not secure the whole-hearted support of each individual citizen' (Clarke, 1939, p.36).

Second, councillors should be in close touch with the public, as 'the councillors are merely the representatives of the citizens, elected by them to carry out their desires' (Suthers, 1905, p.10). Boyden (1961, p.13) considers that 'councillors usually know their electors and the feelings in their wards much better than the critics think', and Laski (1950, p.413) claims that the whole system of democratic local self-government cannot help but bring 'the mass of citizens into intimate contact with the persons responsible for decisions'. Councillors are generally seen as possessed of 'local knowledge' where they 'are in touch with the circumstances, feelings and needs of their areas' (Chester, 1951, p.342).[5] The Committee of Inquiry into Local Government Finance (1976, p.53) noted how 'it is often claimed that local government enhances accountability because it brings those who are responsible for decisions close to their electors', and a recent textbook on local government has blandly asserted that the system 'obtains a sensitivity which is peculiar to it. Whenever a controversial matter requires decision, a council will test the local climate of opinion before taking action and will have in mind the consequences of taking an unpopular line' (Redcliffe-Maud and Wood, 1974, p.21). Orthodoxy asserts that the councillor '*must* give constant and close attention to the affairs of his ward' as 'very real control does . . . exist' in the hands of the citizens and 'the opportunity for exercising it is at the periodical elections' (Snell, 1935,

5 See also Finer, 1943, p.55; Dell, 1960; Finer, 1950; Maddick, 1963; A West Midland Study Group, 1956; Royal Commission on Local Government in England, 1969, vol.1, pp.10–11.

pp.67—74; see also Dell, 1960, pp.334—5). The *Written Evidence of the Ministry of Housing and Local Government* to the Royal Commission on Local Government in England (1969, p.53) argued that

> a democratically elected body has a special incentive to take account of the varying needs of the particular parts of its area and to gauge the strength of local feelings when decisions about new developments and changes have to be taken . . . Local government provides a means for the ordinary citizen to take part in public affairs at local level: as electors people have an opportunity through their vote to exercise a decisive influence on the general direction of local affairs.

Hill (1970, pp.44, 48) recognises that 'local elections are not a perfect measure of opinion' but even so, 'councillors must always consider the power which local voters wield. They owe their position to the popular will' and if they are out of accord with it then 'the electoral process should remove them just as the parliamentary election removes an unpopular government' (Chester, 1951, p.342; see also Shelley, 1939, pp.182—3; Town Planning Institute, 1968, pp.343—4). In this situation 'mistaken policy or flagrant maladministration can be corrected at the polls . . . The nemesis of local maladministration is swift and direct' (Finer, 1950, pp.85—91). Lord Redcliffe-Maud and Bruce Wood (1974, pp.73—4) have argued that 'it remains possible to argue that local councils are *automatically* responsive to local demands and needs . . . Indeed if this were not the case, there would be less reason to have local government or spend energies in trying to make it work.'

Third, 'the control of the expert by the amateur representing his fellow citizen is the key to the whole of our system of government. It is probably what people have at the back of their minds when they use the words "democracy" or "democratic"' (Royal Commission on Local Government in Greater London, 1960, p.62). Redlich (1903, vol.1, pp.334, 350) considered that 'the English municipal code . . . placed the paid officers and servants of the borough under the town council and its committees regarding them simply as the executive instruments of a local autonomy . . . The officials are the purely executive organ.' Atlee and Robson (1925, p.34) would not disagree since they argued that 'it is the elected members of the Authority . . . who determine the policy and issue the orders of the Authority. But in the local council . . . it is the Civil Service that carries out the day-to-day administration, advises the Council and its Committees, and is, in the last resort, obedient to any decision the Council may choose to make.' An enquiry by the Ministry of Housing and Local Government (1965, p.66) vindicated the actions of the Bognor Regis council when it dismissed its town clerk. It regarded the clerk as 'the employee of his council . . . [and] he should leave them to come to their own decision. It is the duty of the councillors to formulate the policy for the local authority as they are directly answerable for their actions to the ratepayers at the polls.' Almost by definition orthodox statements are regarded as obvious and so are not seen as warranting any special attention. By and large, orthodoxy is content to assert that 'the members of the council take the decisions as to policy, and the officers report on the questions requiring decision and see that the decisions are carried out' (Jennings, 1947, p.119; see also Warren, 1950, p.14; 1952, p.182; 1961, p.101; Cole, 1956, pp.115–16; Marshall, 1960, p.23; Reynolds, 1971, pp.11–12).

Local government is not just described as democratic. It is part of traditional orthodoxy to describe it as *especially* democratic, since it enjoys 'a democratic primacy over national government' (Sharpe, 1970, p.160). Not only is local government 'by its nature in closer touch than Parliament or Ministers can be with local conditions, local needs [and] local opinions', but the 'local government officer has less influence than a civil servant' (Royal Commission on Local Government in England, 1969, vol.1, p.11; Sharpe, 1965, p.6; see also Warren, 1957, p.10). *Local* democracy is seen as especially vital because of a clutch of ancient orthodoxies which suggest that democracy truly flowers in communities and in small areas.

Plato calculated the optimal number of citizens as 5,040, and Aristotle thought even this number too large. 'Until quite recently – around the end of the eighteenth century – there was little dissent among political philosphers from the view that a democracy or a republic had to be small' (Dahl and Tufte, 1974, p.4). By the middle of the nineteenth century, however, doctrines were thoroughly adapted to the nation state, but the older, classical, conception has lived on to enjoy a treasured place in the literature on local government the world over. The International Union of Local Authorities (1953, p.5) undertook a survey of twenty countries. In practically every case the experts agreed that 'the strength of the small municipality' lay in the control of the officers by those elected by the people, and in the 'greater public spirit of the local population (smaller distance between governors and governed)'.

The home of representative government was hardly likely to be immune from an easy acceptance of these sorts of arguments and the literature on British local government is stuffed through and through with the conviction that small size is the automatic guarantee of healthy democracy. The established system of local government may have contained too many too small local authorities to be truly efficient, but this was all to the good so far as the health of local democracy was concerned. The Local Government Commission for Wales (1963, p.70) pointed out that 'if convenience were the only factor to be considered all local government would be exercised over very small areas', and the Royal Commission on Local Government in Greater London (1960, p.194) was aware of the danger of 'remoteness' and saw 'substantial advantages in having as many services as possible concentrated in the town hall, where they are administered by officers responsible to councillors representing a population of reasonable size'. Who can doubt all this, or dare to question it: it is all just so much common-sense. Finer (1950, p.85) reckoned that the 'first great advantage' of local government lay in the 'local knowledge' which it possessed as 'the local area and population is small enough for the officials as well as the councillors to know it intimately'. In similar vein, Morris (1960, p.103) argued that 'in the smaller authority . . . practically every ratepayer knows at least one or two councillors or officials personally. As a result the whole atmosphere of local administration is more intimate.' Garner (1960, pp.232–3) has written glowingly of democracy in small authorities:

> Relations between the public and the council should be good in the case of the smaller authority. There is little excuse for any sense of remoteness from 'they' who govern among members of the public when the council meeting place is probably no more than a mile from any part of the borough and the mayor and his council can be seen going robed to church on special occasions two or three times a year. Members of the council will probably be known personally to many ratepayers, and the chief officers will be familiar figures who play their part in the life of the town by their membership of the Rotary Club or other local organisations. Everything the council do — or propose to do — will be the subject of public comment and discussion.

Not surprisingly, Garner considers that 'by the close links between the council and the public that usually exist in the small town, it is possible to achieve a sense of true democracy akin to that which governed the City States of Ancient Greece'.[6]

Traditional orthodoxy regards the small area as the natural basis of consensual communities where the 'sense of solidarity among neighbours' provides a 'tie', so ensuring the development of 'civic spirit and civic understanding' where local government is possessed of 'a sense of common purpose' (Webb and Webb, 1920, pp.213—14; Gibbon, 1931, p.107).[7] The Royal Commission on Local Government in England (1969, vol.1, p.60) recognised this since they 'were impressed by the extent to which the idea of community, although extremely difficult to define, figures in most of the discussion about the desirable pre-requisites of a good local government system'.

The arguments and assertions of the last few pages hang together to form a facet of the traditional liberal theory of the state. Whalen (1960, p.7) sets down the essentials of this:

> Political life in small, purposive, individualistic, yet essentially harmonious, communities is considered to supply those conditions most conducive to *real* democracy. If the mass electorate in an elongated political and social system abdicates its responsibilities because public issues have grown too complex, in local politics, so the argument runs, life is simple; public affairs are non-technical and straightforward; the lag between a decision and its consequences is short; the control of officials is more perfectly attainable in face-to-face relationships; and citizens are the more easily able to pay their rightful parts as thoughtful discussants and participants. Here the assumptions of political individualism receive their fullest application: it is demonstrated that political conditions in the local community permit rational action, to which is added the ethical imperative that men should so act, and the conclusion is frequently drawn that men in fact do so act.

Bulpitt (1972, p.283) reminds us that 'the full advantage of this happy state of affairs can only be reaped if the remote and bureaucratic central authorities leave the governments of the local communities enough freedom to get on with their job'. Central control is objected to precisely because 'local authorities are elected by

6 For similar sorts of views, see Everest, 1925; Royal Commission on Local Government in England, 1969, vol.2, p.81; Robson, 1954, p.154; *Local Government: Functions of County Councils and County District Councils in England and Wales*, 1957; Hobhouse, 1911; Mackintosh, 1968, p.36; Fordham, 1911; Money, 1973, p.324.

7 See also, Baker and Young, 1971; Scottish Development Department, 1974; Hampton, 1970; Local Government Commission for England, 1961, p.79; Jessup, 1949, p.85; *Local Government in England*, 1971, p.6; Robson, 1972, p.30.

the people of the area not to carry out as agents of the central government the policy of that government, but to carry out the policy which meets with the approval of the electors of the area' (Jennings, 1947, p.187). The implication is clear: cut down on central control and you increase the viability of a real local democracy functioning in crisp accord with the Electoral Chain of Command Theory.

Central control is not the only blot that is seen on the local democratic copy book. Aldermen have long been disliked because they tended to 'make the council less sensitive to a change in local opinion than a wholly elected body might be' (Maud and Finer, 1960, p.90; see also Hart, 1968, pp.92–3). Similarly, orthodoxy has asserted that *ad hoc* authorities are bad because they are 'not politically responsible' (Robson, 1972, p.77). More fundamentally, this whole conception of local democracy has allowed no room for political conflict and no room, therefore, for political parties.

It is at this point in the argument that we must turn to the evolving orthodoxies with respect to the democratic quality of local government. Orthodoxy has not stood still, and the British tradition embraces a certain variety.

4. The Democracy of Local Government: The Evolving Orthodoxy

(i) *Political Parties*

In the 1950s we were advised that 'there has been little formal study of the workings of party in local government' (Brennan, Cooney and Pollins, 1954, p.76); in the 1960s we were told that 'we know very little about the activities of political parties in local government' (Bulpitt, 1963, p.11); and then again in the 1970s it was noted that 'the role of the party groups in the actual running of the council [has] . . . been almost as little studied as their relations with the outside parties' (Buxton, 1973, p.85). The Royal Commission on Local Government in Greater London (1960, p.65) did 'not conceive it as any part of our duty to have regard to considerations of party politics', and the Committee on the Management of Local Government (1967, vol.1, p.112) brashly stated that 'we have made no study of the work of party groups'.

So party politics in local government has rarely been the subject of serious study. More than this, there has been a resistance to noting the *real* part which they play. The commitment to the liberal theory of the state has caused this: political parties were not noticed and were not studied because they *should* not have been there. When their existence could no longer be ignored then it was often claimed that their involvement was recent and caused by the Labour Party (Committee on the Management of Local Government, 1967, vol.1, p.111; Warren, 1952; MacColl, 1949). This is nonsense. 'It is clear that party involvement in local government predates the rise of the Labour Party' (Young, 1975, p.29) and has been of long-standing importance.[8] The initial reaction of academic writers to the intrusive involvement of party in local government was to condemn it. In this vein the Committee on the Management of Local Government (1967, vol.1, p.111) 'argued that local authorities are not concerned with "principles" because these are thought out by the government of the day . . . It is commonly said that much that local authorities do has no political content; this is true.' Jessup (1949, p.193) saw little place for parties in local government because it was 'concerned chiefly with administration' and called for 'the devising or common sense solutions to concrete problems'.[9] Moreover, orthodoxy has had it that party politics, because it involves 'the sacrifice of independent judgement', has a bad 'effect on the calibre of council personnel' (Warren, 1952, p.187; see also, Hasluck, 1936, p.35; Keith-Lucas, 1961, p.8).

An 'independent system' may be preferred (Hasluck, 1936, p.34), but at the same time there has been a grudging recognition that parties *are* involved and that there is no going back to some sort of mythical pre-party golden age. Just as democratic theories had to be adjusted to legitimise representative government in the nation state, so it has become necessary for those whose first concern has been to applaud the democracy of local government

8 Fraser, 1976; Hennock, 1973; Muir, 1907; Hanham, 1959; Newton, 1968; Brand, 1974, pp.133–4; Bulpitt, 1967, p.5. In a similar vein it is sometimes claimed that although parties have long been involved in *elections* they have only recently been involved in the *day-to-day* work of a local authority (see Hasluck, 1936, pp.32–3; Harris, 1939A, p.42; MacColl, 1949). Again, I know of no work which seriously sustains the accuracy of this position.

9 See also, Warren, 1952; Gibbon, 1937, p.18; Robson, 1972, p.85; Hasluck, 1936, p.35. The opposition to party politics in local government has a partisan and re-actionary flavour to it. It embodies an attack on the Labour Party and desire to shift back to a consensual polity in which leadership is confined to the upper classes. We should not forget that conservative partisanship was discreet yet highly potent (Young, 1975, p.31; Grant, 1971, 1972).

to adjust theory and explanation to the fact of party. Parties had come to be seen as 'indispensable' at the national level (Bassett, 1935, p.29); could they be judged to have a part to play in enhancing democracy at the local level?[10]

Parties in local government have gradually come in from the cold. At first, they were not noticed; then they were condemned; then there was 'total disagreement as to the effect of the party system, some holding it to be disastrous, others holding it to be the only basis for effective government' (Simon, 1928, p.200); now many are prepared to praise their involvement since they are seen as the 'indispensable element in the conversion of local councils into responsible governments' (Dunsire, 1956, p.87).

Parties in local government are said to 'arouse electoral interest' and make for 'coherent administration' and 'an integrated policy for the locality' (Warren, 1952, p.191; Morrison, 1931, p.75). Fundamentally, however, party involvement is defended and justified because 'it renders responsibility for the general level of council achievement visible to the public, facilitates judgement at the polls, and through the ups and downs of party fortunes at successive elections, brings shifts in public feeling forcibly to the council's notice' (Warren, 1952, p.191). Buxton (1973, p.96) has suggested that 'the claim can be made for the importance of party politics as a means of enabling the electorate to pass a realistic judgement on the performance of their representatives', and even the Prime Minister's Committee on Local Government Rules of Conduct (1974, vol.1, p.7) was prepared to put forward a guarded defence of party as 'if sensibly operated [it] can make for vigour, coherence and responsiveness'. Richards (1975, p.116) would not disagree since he considered that the 'party representing the dominant stream of opinion becomes responsible for the conduct of public affairs for a limited time and may be displaced from power at a subsequent election if it displeases the voters'. Margaret Cole (1956, p.174) and Herbert Morrison (1931), on the basis of their knowledge of the workings of party government in the London County Council, have both been concerned to describe and explain the role of party and justify its involvement as con-

---

10 In fact there are those who recognise that if practice were to conform to the pre-party idea embodied in the Electoral Chain of Command Theory then it would be very difficult to see *how* responsibility could be *organised* (Dunsire, 1956; Buxton, 1973, p.91).

tributing to the democratic quality of local government.[11] An academic study of Wolverhampton reached the conclusion that 'the parties have enabled individuals to devise a programme of policies and to implement it, and they have presented these programmes to the public in a dramatic and comprehensible way, enabling the public to judge a team of men and measures; thus the accountability of government to the electorate has been strengthened' (Jones, 1969, pp.348—9).

In a word, orthodoxy with respect to the description and explanation of the democracy of local government has evolved. The Electoral Chain of Command Theory lingers on, but another theory has been advanced to make better sense of local politics. The theoretical state of local government studies is such that no one says as much, but even so it is clear that party involvement is applauded because it is seen as in broad conformity with the essentials of the model of Responsible Party Government.[12] The trouble is that this position has usually been taken in the absence of any decent enquiry into the part which political parties *actually* play in local government. Reasoning is back to front. Local government has long been seen as democratic; political parties are now involved; and so the reality of party practice must contribute to that democracy. Commitment first, theory second; and facts last, or not at all. This is the essential stuff of so much of local government studies.

We need research into the part which political parties actually play in local politics. The model of Responsible Party Government provides a checklist of questions to be directed at the facts of the situation in any particular authority. Recent urban political science suggests that practice is more likely than not to be out of accord with this prescriptive theory. Certainly the situation in Kensington and Chelsea does not conform to the essentials of the model (Dearlove, 1973); 'the basic model of accountability is weak' in Aberton (Spencer, 1971, p.197); two American studies of party involvement in London government raise questions as to the descriptive and explanatory utility of the model (Glass-

11 See also, Gibbon, 1937; Cole, 1947, p.245; Laski, 1935, p.85; MacColl, 1949, p.75; Clarke, 1939, p.15; Hornsby, 1957; Robson, 1937. Orthodoxy also suggests that party politics weakens the influence of the officials on Council policy (Richards, 1968, p.99; Cole, 1956, pp.115—16).
12 For an outline of the essentials of this theory, see Ranney, 1962; American Political Science Association, Committee on Political Parties, 1950; Dearlove, 1973, ch. 2.

berg, 1973 and Kantor, 1974; see also Butterworth, 1966); and the situation in both Birmingham and Sheffield cannot really be squared with this theory (Newton, 1976; Hampton, 1970).[13] Baldly expressed, it is usually found that parties do not behave as they should according to this particular theory of local democracy. Traditional orthodoxy may have evolved but it still cannot be regarded as providing an adequate description and explanation of local politics — at least in so far as party politics is concerned.

(ii) *Public Participation*

It is not just party practice which is at odds with the traditional democratic ideal and with the orthodox description and explanation of local politics. Nowhere is there a bigger gap between ideal and reality than with respect to the public and their involvement with local government. It will be instructive to see just how those committed to the democracy of local government have coped with facts which appear to cast a body blow to an essential aspect of their description. Orthodoxy evolved to domesticate the fact of party politics, so let us see if the facts about low levels of public participation and high levels of public ignorance have been twisted into conformity with some new model of local democracy.

'That few people vote in local elections even when they have the opportunity to do so, and that many people are ignorant of the most elementary facts about their local governments, are points which can hardly be disputed' (Royal Commission on Local Government in England, 1969, Research Study 1, p.18). Electoral participation is low and declining,[14] and those who do vote are more likely to do so on the basis of their assessment of the government's performance nationally than on the basis of purely local

13 See also, Griffith, 1963; Wiseman, 1963, 1963A, 1967; Bulpitt, 1963, 1967. For a useful summary, see Gyford, 1976, ch. 3.

14 'Mean voting for the entire local government system has fallen from 50.2% in 1949 to 42.1% in 1967' (Ashford, 1973, p.6). See also Fletcher, 1967; Harris, 1939A, p.263; Political and Economic Planning, 1948, pp.163—4; Royal Commission on Local Government in England, 1969, Research Study 9; Redcliffe-Maud and Wood, 1974, p.61; Newton, 1976, pp.21—4. For a discussion of the impact of different variables on turnout see: Bochel and Denver, 1971, 1972; Morris and Newton, 1971; Newton, 1972, 1972A; Denver and Hands, 1972; Pimlott, 1972, 1973; Brown, 1958; Fletcher, 1969; Birch, 1950; Birch and Campbell, 1950; Sharpe, 1960; Brennan, Cooney and Pollins, 1954; Political and Economic Planning, 1948, 1955; Davies and Newton, 1974.

issues or events.[15] Survey after survey highlights general public ignorance about local government and its services.[16] It would be tedious to cite chapter and verse on all this. Even orthodox masters of local government have long since ceased to see the reality of public participation and interest in terms of the ideals set down by Mill, Bryce, or de Tocqueville. The facts just could not be ignored. Theorists of local government had only two options. They could abandon orthodox theories as the basis of their conceptualisation of local politics, or they could try and bend the facts into conformity with democratic theory. The entrenched commitment to the essential democracy of local self-government favoured the second option and the full implications of the facts about the public and local government have been neatly sidestepped. Bizarre and defensive ideas have been developed which have 'explained' and interpreted these facts in such a way that they have posed only a minimal disruption to the democratic conceptualisation of local government. Orthodoxy and tradition have continued to dominate. What, then, are these ideas, and how cogent are they?

First, the fact of low polls is by-passed with the suggestion that non-voting is not a good measure of apathy or a lack of interest. In a marvellous Newspeak, non-participation gets defined as participation; interest is seen as more widespread than electoral participation would suggest;[17] and low turnout is seen as reflecting well on the knowledge and grasp which the local citizens have of the true dynamics of local government. Research undertaken for the Royal Commission on Local Government in England (Research Study 2, 1969, p.38) pointed out that 'a man may refrain from voting not because of apathy but because he is displeased with the performance of his party, but is not ready to transfer his allegiance. His non-voting is in fact a sort of participation.' Maud and Finer (1960, p.81) have suggested that 'it may be, not that we are apathetic about local affairs but that we are

---

15 Budge, Brand, Margolis, and Smith, 1972, pp.112, 107; Royal Commission on Local Government in England, 1969, Research Study 1; NALGO Reconstruction Committee, 1945; Newton, 1976; Spencer, 1971; Fletcher, 1967; Butler and Stokes, 1969, p.39; Rees, 1968; Grundy, 1950; Hill, 1970; Sharpe, 1962A; Richards, 1968; Bealey, Blondel and McCann, 1965; Buxton, 1973, pp.91–2.

16 Committee on the Management of Local Government, 1967, vol.3; Royal Commission on Local Government in England, 1969, Research Study 9; Committee of Inquiry into Local Government Finance, 1976, p.9. See also Budge, 1965; Bealey and Bartholomew, 1962; Birch, 1959, ch. 6; Smith, 1969, p.340.

17 See, for example, Bonnor, 1954.

more interested than most countries in our national elections'. Redlich (1903, vol.1, p.274) considered that there was extensive 'genuine interest' in local government but this did not follow through to voting as 'the burgesses do not believe in the distinction between Liberal and Conservative candidates for their council . . . They know that the laws must be carried out whichever party is in power.' In a similar vein, Griffith (1963, p.16) considers that 'the Briton is politically conscious' and so a low poll 'may reflect the intelligence rather than the ignorance of the local electorate: it may be that the local electorate believes that he will get much the same quality of local service at much the same cost whoever is in local power'.[18] Funnily enough this line of explanation which suggests that the public does not participate because it is knowledgeable is flatly contradicted by those who assert that the public does not participate because it is ignorant.[19] Hard evidence is never presented to support either of these claims.

A second response does not by-pass the low polls but frontally attacks them, suggesting that they are not *really* low as much non-voting is 'involuntary'. Sharpe (1962A, p.74) considers that many are 'prevented from voting by circumstances beyond their control'. An earlier survey of a ward in an urban district in the North of England suggested that 'the official poll of 56.5% does not reveal an apathy of 43.5%' as a number of the non-voters 'had good excuses for not voting' and so 'at the worst, there exists real indifference among 23.2% of the electorate'. Even so this was not good enough for Grundy (1950, pp.97–9) who thought that 'the apathy of the elector who will not put himself out a little to vote before going out for the day has to be disturbed'.[20] These ideas quite clearly minimise the fact of non-voting and they have been developed because of an attachment to a tradition which has seen voting as of importance. What can we make of them? If you choose to believe that there is a regular coincidence between local elections and people being sick or leaving the area all day (whereas there is not this coincidence at a general election!) then you will be satisfied with this explanation. If not, then you will need to look elsewhere.

18 See also Mackintosh, 1968, p.11; Banwell, 1963, p.336; Dell, 1960.
19 Harris, 1939A, p.264; Consultative Committee on Publicity for Local Government, 1947, p.3; Redcliffe-Maud and Wood, 1974, p.61; Jessup, 1949, p.126; Political and Economic Planning, 1947, p.12.
20 See also Committee on the Management of Local Government, 1967, vol.3, pp.82–3; Political and Economic Planning, 1947, p.7.

A third, and more dominant response has been to interpret non-voting and the comparative absence of public participation as indicative of 'satisfaction' with local government and public policy. In an article in *A Century of Municipal Progress* (the title of which says all!), Lord Snell (1935, p.78) writes that

> local authorities in England usually function so quietly and smoothly that little is heard of them outside the council chambers. Their work is taken for granted by the general public, and when the periodical elections take place, only a comparatively small proportion of the electors trouble to record their votes. This widespread apathy is in great part due to the general excellence of local government administration, and to the probity and devotion to the public good of the great and honourable body of men and women whose labours have won for the local government service of their country the admiration of the world.

More recently Hill (1970, pp.68—9, 53—4) has similarly suggested that 'a lack of positive involvement may be contentment rather than disillusioned apathy' reflecting 'the smooth working of an accepted system . . . [and] a real, if largely unexpressed, respect for government's achievements'. Richards (1975, p.168) agrees:

> The picture of indifference is not surprising. Life is short and the potential range of human endeavour and interest is vast. It is not unreasonable to feel that there are other and better things to do than to concern oneself with the problem of local government. Apathy can be a measure of contentment. If people are satisfied with social conditions why should they bother to change them?[21]

Evidence is rarely assembled to support this line of argument, which needs research.[22] Even so, there are snippets of information which do not sit comfortably within this interpretation. In Newcastle-Under-Lyme '24% of all respondents were dissatisfied with their council's services' (Bealey, Blondel and McCann, 1965, p.245). The survey of electors carried out for the Committee on the Management of Local Government (1967, vol.3, p.62) found that only 'just over a quarter of our informants thought their local council was very well run'. A survey undertaken for *The Times* (6 August 1973) found 65% of respondents agreeing that 'too many decisions are influenced by business interests of councillors involved', and 41% agreeing that 'many [councillors] get a dishonest financial advantage from being on the council'. More important than the evidence of sample surveys is the political

---

21 See also, Jones, 1969A, p.19; Hill, 1973, p.32.
22 Robson (1972, p.89) is absolutely right: 'What has not been sufficiently studied is the reasons which cause apathy towards city government.'

reality of interest group involvement in local politics, and I will be considering the implications of this shortly. The theory of satisfaction is unsatisfactory. It 'cannot be taken very seriously as it suggests that the perfect democracy would be one where no electors bothered to vote at all' (Mackintosh, 1968, p.11). Moreover, it contains a silly liberal presumption of political rationality whereby both participation *and* non-participation are seen as reflecting a keen assessment of what needs to be done to secure individual advantage at the hands of government. The line of argument which centres on the satisfaction and contentment of non-participants can easily lead to activity being condemned and inactivity and apathy being applauded.[23] More fundamentally it can lead in to a redefinition of the essential ingredients of democracy. The critique of participation and the defence of apathy have, to a considerable extent, emerged as a result of a commitment to a participatory tradition of democracy. But, defending the tradition in the face of facts that are clearly at odds with it has led to the paradox of the tradition itself being stripped of its essentials as the struggle to accommodate troublesome facts has led to their actually being praised. It is this sort of reasoning which led to the Committee on the Management of Local Government (1967, vol.1, p.94) arguing that 'local authorities have democratic procedures in excess of what the majority of the people need or want from local government as it now exists'.

So far I have set down three bundles of orthodoxies which have all minimised the facts on public participation and knowledge about local government. This does not exhaust the orthodox response. A fourth response does not so much minimise the facts as explain them by seeing them as caused by factors *outside* the local situation. Central control has always been orthodoxy's major guilty party, and it is no surprise that it is blamed with respect to the 'problem' of the public and local government. 'In our view', said a West Midland Study Group (1956, pp.5–6), 'the main drawbacks of centralisation are the loss of interest of the electorate in local affairs, a consequent decline in the enthusiasm of members . . . ; and the unwillingness of men and women of calibre to come forward as local government candidates.' Their prescription for improvement was obvious: 'if the relationship between central and local government is adjusted so that the sense

23 Political and Economic Planning, 1955, p.51; 1947, p.7; Sharpe, 1960, p.170; Morris-Jones, 1954; Martin, 1960.

of responsibility returns to the latter local government may recover from its sickness'. In effect, the orthodox argument suggests that 'local authorities have become so weakened as to be unable to arouse any interest in their work amongst the vast body of the citizens of the locality' (Hookham, 1948, p.245).[24] No evidence is advanced to support this explanation. If central control is not blamed then the 'high level of ignorance and confusion that has been shown to exist among the general public with regard to local authority services may . . . be due to the complexity of the local authority system itself' (Committee on the Management of Local Government, 1967, vol.3, p.14).[25] Both the Royal Commission on Local Government in England (1969, vol.1, pp.28–9) and the Royal Commission on Local Government in Greater London (1960, p.180) argued that 'defects' and 'complications' in the overall structure of local government caused the 'fatalism', 'ignorance' and 'indifference' which the public displayed to their local authorities. 'In short, what is needed is a clarification of the local government system . . . We believe that the public would then become more aware of local government and more interested in it.' Again, no evidence is advanced to support this explanation. Moreover, it is open to question and challenge. 'The London Government reforms . . . made little impact on the voting behaviour of the electorate' (Royal Commission on Local Government in England, 1969, Research Study 2, p.50), and Rees (1968, pp.137–8) 'is doubtful if change would make much difference'.[26] From one point of view it does not much matter whether these explanations are right or wrong. Either way they are functional for the survival of the orthodox master's belief in the essential democracy of the British system of democratic local self-government. In effect, they are content to say that there is nothing wrong with the democracy *within* local authorities that could not be put right if local authorities were given more autonomy and the system was made simpler.

Given this stance, it is not surprising that efforts to increase and enhance popular participation in local government are conspicuous by their absence, weakness or naivity. One study, after

24 See also, Jessup, 1949, p.121; Laski, 1935, p.107; Harris, 1939A, p.277; Howe, 1907; Committee on the Management of Local Government, 1967, vol.1, p.91.
25 See also NALGO Reconstruction Committee, 1945, p.4; Local Government Commission for England, 1961, p.19.
26 Redcliffe-Maud and Wood, 1974, p.61; Royal Commission on Local Government in England, 1969, Research Study 9, p.8.

pointing to the 'popular ignorance of local government', had a crisp little section headed 'The remedy — public relations' (NALGO Reconstruction Committee, 1945, p.5).[27] If the problem of public participation is minimised is it so surprising that reforms to 'solve' the problem are minimal? The Royal Commission on Local Government in England (1969, vol.1, p.64) was content to sit out the problem looking to the 'hopeful' sign that 'on the fairly safe assumption that more people will reach a higher level of education in the future, we may expect that interest in local government will steadily increase rather than fall off'.

(iii) *Interest Groups*

Orthodox descriptions of local politics have tended to treat the public as an undifferentiated mass. They are regarded simply as electors. Not surprisingly, therefore, Birch (1959, p.165) could argue that 'the influence of pressure groups . . . on the local level appear[s] never to have been studied'. A decade later Sharpe (1967, p.1) noted how 'we have no systematic treatise on . . . local pressure groups', and in 1976 Newton (p.31) still considered that 'relatively little empirical work has been done on them'. This is the familiar stuff of local government studies. Explanatory theories dependent on a commitment to a certain kind of local democracy leave no room for facts out of accord with those theories. At one time political parties were not noticed. More recently this has been the fate with respect to local interest groups. Orthodoxy evolved to take account of party involvement in local government. Moreover, the theory utilised to explain their role was one first developed to make sense of the practice of central government. The fact that theory at the level of the central government has further evolved to take into account the fact of pressure groups (McKenzie, 1958; Finer, 1956; Beer, 1965) surely suggests that we may find local explanatory orthodoxy again evolving to legitimise the involvement of interest groups as contributing to a still more vital local democracy.[28] The Greater

27 See also Bayliss, 1958; Boyden, 1961; Committee on the Management of Local Government, 1967, vol.1, pp.120–31.

28 Just as with the study of political parties in local government, we now hear the claim that the involvement of interest groups in local politics is of only recent importance (Hill, 1970; Richards, 1968; Sharpe, 1967; Donnison, 1973; Civic Trust, 1976; Holman, 1972). But there is no real evidence of an age when interest groups were not involved in local politics (see, for example, Chaloner, 1950; Moorhouse, Wilson and Chamberlain, 1972; and especially Fraser, 1976, part 4).

London Group from the London School of Economics is aware of the facts about low polls and it considers that 'local democracy ought to provide a means whereby the citizen can make his views felt and have his interests safeguarded'. The group went on to argue that 'voting is only one possible means, and it is not necessarily the most effective means for the second half of the twentieth century . . . democratic local government should not be thought of simply in terms of voting figures; attention should be concentrated more on other ways in which participation of citizens can be secured and, in particular, group participation' (Royal Commission on Local Government in England, 1969, Research Study 1, pp.19, 22). 'Sometimes we are too depressed about local politics', soothes Professor Crick (1970, p.xvii), but the depression is unnecessary and arises 'largely because we perceive it too narrowly. Only a minority of the electorate may vote . . . ; but voting is only the most formal kind of participation.' He argues that we need to have regard to membership of voluntary organisations 'as a criterion of some degree of participation . . . [as] these group affiliations may well be the future building blocks of a heightened local democracy'. Richards (1968, p.154) agrees that the growing vitality of 'vigorous local groups' is a 'peculiarly valuable element in maintaining a spirit of local democracy', and Hill (1970, p.44) reminds us that 'the individual makes his views and demands known through a variety of channels and elections may be regarded as merely an ultimate sanction'.

It is still early days, but democratic orthodoxy appears to show signs of evolving yet again as students begin to assess the role of interest groups as enhancing of local democracy. 'Pluralism has become the orthodox theory of American city politics, and to a lesser extent of politics in British cities also' (Newton, 1976; Cousins, 1973, 1974, 1977). There is the idea that the interest group world is one of reasonably perfect competition, where the rules of the game ensure fair play and the equal access of all to the favourable decision of those in government. How adequate is this assessment of interest groups in local politics? There is enough material around to suggest that the evolving orthodoxy is quite sharply contradicted by the reality of group influence in local politics. Against the orthodox ideology of liberal democracy we can set down examples of local authorities being active in resisting, obstructing, and excluding the public and their groups from any effective involvement in the shaping of policies that will affect them. 'A great deal of lip service is paid to the need to involve the people more closely with the activities of local authorities, and publicly apathy is ritualistically deplored at civic functions, but if a tenants' association or a parents' association takes a critical interest in local politics then the council moves quickly into a defensive position' (Hampton, 1969, p.158; see also Rees, 1968, p.137). Councillors may want public participation, but they only welcome it if it is supportive of them and their policies (Tilley, 1975, p.90).[29]

We do, however, get no nearer to the reality of group involvement with local government if we simply trade in the tired ideology of representative democracy, with its promise of responsiveness to all, for the hard rhetoric which talks only of resistance and obstruction. Both views contain elements of truth. The simple fact we can take to *any* local situation is the reasonable expectation that groups will be enjoying differential access to the ear and action of government. Some will meet with a favourable response and, at the same time, others will find their demands resisted. The research to be undertaken in any local authority is clear enough. It is important to identify and explain the basis of the council's response: what are their rules of access, and what are the implications of these rules for the stability of public policy?

In my study of Kensington and Chelsea I dealt with this question (Dearlove, 1973, ch. 8). The council response to groups revolved around councillor assessment of groups, demands and communication styles. Groups were seen as helpful or unhelpful; demands as acceptable or unacceptable; and methods of group communication as proper or improper. Patterns of assessment went together. Helpful groups raised demands that were acceptable because they were consonant with the policies which the councillors felt the council should be pursuing and they went through the proper channels. By way of contrast the unhelpful groups were involved in unacceptable demands which they were forced to push through improper channels. These were the two usual patterns. But there were two tendencies which served to limit the possibility of change and responsiveness being introduced into council policy by way of interest group activity. First, it was

29 The ideology of liberal democracy with its traditional stress on the electoral channel of influence and control can actually *encourage* those elected by the public to insulate themselves from interest group demands. Hostility and obstruction can come to be legitimised as democratic!

highly *likely* that the unhelpful groups would change the nature of their activity and demands so that they ceased to pose any substantial challenge to the councillors' conception of the proper scope of public policy. Second, it was highly *unlikely* that the helpful groups would change the pattern of their activity and there were good reasons why they were reluctant to take up unacceptable demands and forge alliances with unhelpful groups. Demands for change or innovation in council policy came from groups that were regarded as unhelpful, but these groups could only survive at the cost of their dropping these demands and ceasing to pose any substantial challenge to the continuance of established council policy.

Other studies lend support to these ideas. Cousins' study of the relationships between interest groups and councillors in three South London boroughs noted that 'councillors were adamant in maintaining that demonstrations were a very bad means of influencing the council', and he noted how 'groups receiving council help . . . showed a disinclination to indulge in the use of contentious techniques of influence' (1976, pp.71–3). Of course, some groups that 'lacked the close links with the council . . . did frequently make use of the more overt techniques of influence . . . These deliberately belligerent attitudes only tended to reinforce the distrust of the groups by councillors and officials.'[30] Newton's (1976, pp.46, 86–8, 62) comprehensive study of politics in Birmingham provides perhaps the most important evidence we have on interest group involvement in local politics. He found that the 'established' groups enjoyed 'easy access to decision-makers' and were able to 'press for the maintenance of the status quo' in a 'relatively quiet and unnoticed way'. On the other hand, the 'poorly established' groups may find it difficult to contact decision makers and so have to resort to 'pressure group campaigns' which only serve to underline just how 'powerless' they are in the local political system. Just as in Kensington and Chelsea, the groups which challenge the existing order 'either . . . become more moderate to gain acceptance with decision-makers, or else they preserve their policy but remain relatively powerless'. It is hardly surprising that Newton concludes that 'propositions from pluralist theory' fare 'poorly against the empirical evidence'. Studies of

30 See also Bealey, Blondel, and McCann, 1965, pp.380–1; Tilley, 1975, pp.90–1; Donnison, 1973; Miller, 1970, p.42; Hill, 1974, p.142; CIS, 1973, p.60; Ambrose and Colenutt, 1975, p.150; O'Malley, 1977; Newton and Morris, 1975.

interest groups in local politics do not just document the extent to which some groups lack any influence, since it is also pointed out how the local authorities *themselves* are able actually to influence these groups, so controlling them and manipulating them to authoritative advantage. Liberal theory can quite literally be stood on its head! Many groups have to run a 'long drawn out political obstacle race' before the local authority moves in to 'take over and control by incorporation' (Sills, 1976, pp.120, 124). Local authorities possess a variety of devices, strategies, and tactics which enable them to defend their established policies; their right to govern unchecked; and the legitimacy of their resistance to dissenting residents and activists. Examples abound of local authorities changing the political activity of groups in order to better secure the status quo and protect the position of the established groups and the interests which lie behind them.[31]

Although it is important to recognise and explain differential group access and the control of some groups by local authorities, it is also important to be aware of the dog that did not bark in order to note those sections of the population which are left outside the world of organisation and action. Although it is clear that the interest group 'heavenly chorus sings with a strong upper class accent' (Schattschneider, 1960, p.35),[32] so that there is 'relative inactivity where one might expect people to be more bellicose in their demands' (Hill, 1970, p.70), no points can be made solely on the basis of identifying which sections are in or out of the local group world. This is because there is no one-to-one relationship between participation and political power as so often tends to be assumed by writers of a pluralistic persuasion. Public pressure group activity may be a sign of political weakness (Saunders, 1975, p.38; Newton, 1976, p.88; Green, 1974). Equally, the inactivity of a particular section of the local population may occur precisely *because* that interest is built into the very heart of the council itself. Clearly this latter sort of inactivity may reasonably be interpreted as indicative of satisfaction, but we should not forget that inactivity on the part of those whose

31 See, for example, Jacobs, 1975; Dearlove, 1973, 1974; Davies, 1972; Saunders, 1975; Clark and Hopkins, 1969; Burn, 1972; Parkin, 1974; Mason, 1977; Dennis, 1970, 1972; Pahl, 1970, pp.88—9; Chapeltown News, 1975; Brier and Dowse, 1966; Kimber and Richardson, 1977; Leonard, 1975.

32 See Civic Trust, 1976; Gregory, 1967; Barr, 1968; Coates and Silburn, 1970; Newton, 1976; Committee on the Management of Local Government, 1967, vol.3.

interest is not built into government may be 'an unthinking and routine response to an ongoing situation of exclusion and deprivation' which is seen as hateful but as hopelessly beyond the possibility of political change through their own organisation (Saunders, 1975, p.39). Just how you choose to interpret the significance of action or inaction depends on the social theory which you bring to the local situation.

The points I have been making in my discussion of interest groups in local politics suggest work for the future. In the context of my limited concern in this chapter two points need to be stressed. First, interest groups are clearly of importance at the local level and must not be ignored: no description and explanation of local politics which excludes them from consideration can be considered as adequate to the facts of the situation. But, second, it is no good seeing interest groups as the latest saviours of local democracy. We must spike the possibility of the evolving orthodoxy coming to dominate our thinking about the part which interest groups play in local politics, and the best way to avoid this is if interest and organisation are studied in the round from a self-consciously theoretical perspective.

5. Orthodoxy Explored

Rees (1968, p.119), after citing the Herbert Commission's view that local government is a 'living thing, an organism . . . which seeks to give outward form to the inward unity of a living community', goes on to note that 'the reality clearly falls some way short of the ideal'.[33] More generally, Whalen (1960, p.7) considers that 'the result of much sociological research . . . indicates that much liberal mythology concerning local political processes ought to be discounted'.

In this section I am concerned to lend substance to statements of this kind and so continue to add to the points of critique which I started to assemble in the last section. Local government has been seen as democratic because it provided for extensive public participation; ensured that councillors were close to the public; and enabled councillors to make policy and control the officers.

---

33 For a similar point see Buxton, 1973, p.277. For an explanation of the reality of
the claim that local government serves as a training ground for national office, see
Smith, 1969; Keith-Lucas, 1955; MacKenzie, 1951, 1954; Butler, 1953; Mellors,
1974.

I have already pointed out that the reality of public participation is at odds with the democratic ideal and I did not have much time for those orthodox theories which minimised this state of affairs. I now want to deal with the relationship between councillors and the public, and councillors and officers. Is there a gap between the orthodox ideal and the broad reality of the situation?

(i) *Councillors and the Public*

According to traditional orthodoxy the fact of local elections forces councillors to stay in touch with their public. The trouble is that local elections do not work as they should as the result usually hinges on the public's assessment of national politics.[34] Defenders of local representative government have bounced back in the face of this disturbing evidence to suggest that elections 'work' if those subject to them *think* they work. It is another example of an elegant little theory which seeks to minimise the pressing reality of local politics, but the evidence suggests that most councillors are perfectly well aware that they do not stand or fall on the strength of their record in office.[35] We should not make too much of this: 'election is only one part of representation. It becomes full representation only if the elected person speaks with the authentic accents of those who elected him . . . he should share their values; that is, be in touch with their realities' (Bevan, 1952, pp.14–15). In this regard I think that the composition of local councils is of quite crucial importance. A survey carried out for the Committee on the Management of Local Government (1967, vol.2, pp.8, 53) showed that 'councillors are much older on average than the general population. Relatively only a small proportion are women . . . The largest group of councillors are the employers and managers of smaller businesses. 20% of all councillors fall into this category. This is 3 times as big as the proportion of this group in the population.' By way of stark contrast skilled manual workers and unskilled workers were dramatically under-

---

34 However, both Hampton, 1970, ch. 10 and Painter, 1969 point to situations when local factors *were* of importance in the local election result.
35 The theory finds its fullest expression in Kingdon, 1967. See also Gregory, 1969; Spencer, 1971; Kantor, 1974, p.18; Dearlove, 1973, p.42; Newton, 1976, pp.17–21; Buxton, 1973, pp.42–3; Committee on the Management of Local Government, 1967, vol.2, pp.216, 230.

represented.[36] Even so, we shall see in later chapters that this fact of working class representation has constituted a key facet of the particular problem of local government that reorganisation has been designed to solve. For the moment, however, we must assess the significance of the petty bourgeois nature of council composition for the likely relationship between councillors and the public, not just because a sample of electors interviewed for the Committee did 'tend to want councillors to be people like themselves' (vol.3, p.92), but because of the evidence which suggests that people tend to interact with others who are of similar social and economic standing. Moreover, we also know that differing ideas as to the direction and scope of public policy are not randomly scattered throughout the population at large but relate to class position. In other words, the unrepresentative composition of local councils does not make for close contact between councillors and the public, and even suggests that we may expect to find something of an ideological gulf between them. The survey of councillors carried out for the Committee on the Management of Local Government (1967, vol.2, pp.8, 11, 235, 218) pointed out that 'half of all councillors spend less than five hours per month on electors' problems' and 'many councillors do not have a large number of direct personal contacts with electors'. Not surprisingly, the survey pointed to 'major discrepancies between the views of electors and councillors' and noted that 'such a hiatus can only result from a major failure in communication between the two sides of the democratic process in local government'. In line with my point about the likelihood of an ideological gulf between councillors and the public, the survey found that 'in general, electors are more likely than councillors to feel that more council activity is needed'. Unfortunately, further 'empirical work is sparse [on the] links between citizens and the political elite' (Newton, 1976, p.165). Even so, the Maud Committee's point that 'time spent with electors declines as income rises' (1967, vol.2, p.111) has been confirmed by a number of more limited studies[37] which clearly show that working class councillors and

36 The survey relates to the system that was swept away by the 1972 reorganisation 'but there is no reason to suppose that the new is fundamentally different' (Stanyer, 1976, p.108) — indeed Chapter 4 will show that composition now could be even more unrepresentative.
37 Dearlove, 1973; Hampton, 1970; Newton, 1976; Connelly, 1970. See also Rees and Smith, 1964, pp.46–9; Political and Economic Planning, 1947, p.10. Other studies which have a bearing on the relationship between councillors and the public would

Labour councillors have greater contact with electors. This reinforces my suggestion that the unrepresentative character of councils *does* have an adverse effect on councillor-constituent contact. According to the ideology of local democracy, 'the member's information function is a two way process; he is the channel whereby local feeling and knowledge are communicated to the authority, and whereby knowledge of the authorities' actions and of the reasons for them passes back to the locality' (Jessup, 1949, p.103). However, work carried out for the Committee on the Management of Local Government (1967, vol.5, p.27) pointed out that 'very little indication was found that members play a significant role in supplying information about the council and its policies to the public in their locality'.[38] The gap between ideal and reality so far as councillors and the public are concerned seems to know no bounds, so let me now turn to consider the relationship between the councillors and the officers. Is the 'sacred formula' which talks of policy-making controlling councillors and administering official servants anything more than a 'legal fiction'? (Buxton, 1973, p.27; Davies, 1972, p.89.)

(ii) *Councillors and Officers*

Collins, Hinings, and Walsh (1976, p.1) have recognised that the persistent 'use of a formalistic democratic model . . . is . . . responsible in part for the paucity of academic work on the position of the officer in policy-making'. Orthodoxy has inhibited research and so 'one of the major actors in the decision making process is noticeable primarily for his absence from the studies of local politics' (Rhodes, 1975, p.43).[39] As usual, therefore, orthodoxy is unsupported by any solid research evidence and so has to be regarded as offering a highly suspect description.

Nowadays it is seen as a mark of hard, realistic and relevant scholarship to retreat into a critical cynicism asserting that councillors are mere rubber stamps and that all power lies with the officers.[40] Clearly officers are of more significance now than they were in the nineteenth century (Hennock, 1973, p.335; Cox,

---

have to include Higgins and Richardson, 1971; Kohn, 1976; Budge, Brand, Margolis, and Smith, 1972, esp. pp.111–12; 201, 254.

38 See, for example, Jacobs, 1975; Bennington, 1973.

39 For similar assessments see Stanyer, 1976, p.116; Kohn, 1976, p.128; Lewis, 1975, p.66; Gyford, 1976, p.43.

40 See, for example, Heclo, 1969; Reid and Richmond, 1974.

1976, p.50), but the very plausibility of the 'dictatorship of the official thesis' should not lead to our ignoring the fact that 'it has very little empirical evidence to support it' (Newton, 1976, p.148). Indeed, there are a number of empirical studies[41] which paint a picture at odds with the traditional orthodoxy, without, at the same time, slipping into the simple and tart vulgarity which talks only of official domination. We need more research on this, but a few things are already clear. First, the policy-administration dichotomy is a quite inadequate way to describe the working of public bodies and the division of labour between elected and official participants. Second, the issue is not whether officials have power, but to what *extent* they have power. Third, it is not possible to generalise over time, place and issue as to the relationship between councillors and officers. If you are interested in this sort of political whodunnit then it is important to try and specify the variables which will have a bearing on the impact of the different participants.[42] Finally, and the only point of real importance in the context of my limited concern to explore orthodoxy, it is surely beyond dispute that 'the model that officers are simply responsible for policy implementation, while councillors are responsible for policy formulation is totally useless' (Kohn, 1976, p.153).[43]

8. Concluding Remarks

This has been a long chapter but my concern has been a simple one. I have sought to accomplish two things. First, I have sought to sustain my view that orthodoxy has seen the established system of local government as democratic — as especially democratic —

41 See, for example, Elkin, 1974, esp. pp.117—18; Dennis, 1972; Muchnick, 1970; Birley, 1970; Kogan and van der Eyken, 1973; Peschek and Brand, 1966; Saran, 1973; Lee, 1963; Batley, O'Brien and Parris, 1970.

42 Newton (1976, p.160) and Richards (1975, p.130) suggest that the rise of party politics has strengthened the position of councillors. Saran (1973, p.253) and Cox (1976, p.101) suggest that Conservative controlled councils allow more scope to the officers than do Labour controlled councils. In addition it is often suggested that officers have more sway in a situation where local authorities meet infrequently, and Bealey, Blondel and McCann (1965, p.268) limply assert that 'the more expertise needed for policy decisions the more likely are the officials to affect the outcome'.

43 In the light of this we can probably expect theory to develop to both minimise and legitimise the power of officials as in conformity with some special kind of democracy. Hill (1974, p.99) talks of 'democratic administration' and notes how 'today, it is argued, the main way in which officials can be held responsible is through the non-legal, conventional operation of professional standards'.

and so has explained the policy-making behaviour of local authorities through a reliance on liberal democratic theories. Second, I have attempted to challenge the credibility and adequacy of these orthodoxies as at odds with the reality of local politics.

In effect, traditional orthodoxy with respect to the democracy of local government offers us some sort of perfect competition model of local politics. The vote is political money, and if the consumer spends it wisely in elections then he can purchase a package of public policies to his, and society's, advantage, because the possibility of any clash between individual self-interest and wider societal interest is seen as non-existent in this model of happy harmony. I made it clear that the British tradition of discourse about democracy in local government has not continued to be this simple, because we are not presented with just the one bundle of orthodoxies, but with a variety. Traditional orthodoxy has evolved. First, students of local government have kept pace with the 'new' facts of party and pressure group. Second, new orthodoxies have been developed to minimise the significance of those facts so obviously bruising to the conception of local government as the home of a special democracy. The commitment to autonomous and democratic local self-government has been the constant rock behind all these developments, and there has been a mutually supportive relationship between commitment, poor research, and the continuing concern to describe and explain local government as democratic.

There are massive problems with respect to the adequacy of all the orthodoxies. The traditional orthodoxy has always lacked cogency and been unrealistic; party practice is unlikely to conform to the model of Responsible Party Government; local elections do not work as they should; the reality of interest group involvement is at odds with any simple model of a rejigged local democracy; the facts about public participation and knowledge do disturb the democratic conception of local government and should not be minimised; there are good grounds for supposing that the relationship between councillors and the public is not a close one; and the orthodox view of the relationship between councillors and officials is at best simplistic and at worst wrong.

If aspects of local politics have been misinterpreted because of the commitment to democratic local self-government, then it is also true that aspects of local politics are *still* ignored and unstudied because they do not fit into the simple models of local democracy. Wishful thinking about the lack of conflict within local 'communities' inhibited the perception of party involvement in local government and it still inhibits a recognition that political ideology is inextricably and unavoidably caught up in local politics and policy-making. Orthodox students of local politics have paid scant attention to the internal organisation of local authorities, or rather when they have thought about this then they have seen it simply in terms of the *formal* organisation of committees and the orthodox relationship between councillors and officials. This is not enough, as I will show in Chapter 6. More fundamentally, 'little thought is given to local government's relationship with the overall political system which it inhabits' (Bulpitt, 1972, p.281). Students of local *government* may now have sought to understand it within the wider context of local *politics*, but there is still this tendency to look at local politics as somehow self-contained, and subject only to the unwarranted intrusions of central control. There is a failure to recognise the limits of locally based studies of local politics, and there is no conception of the necessity of situating local government *and* politics within the wider context of its political and economic setting. I will be returning to this in my concluding chapter.

Democratic orthodoxy presents the ideology of representative and responsible government as the essential local politics. This ideology is important precisely because it is *not* an adequate description and explanation. It serves to mystify, and even conceal, the more fundamental reality of governmental power as it focuses on *process* and so ignores what governments actually *do* and who they *benefit*. In doing this the ideology helps to secure public legitimacy for a system of rule when such support could be very much more problematic if a keen appreciation of governmental action were crisply revealed and widely disseminated. At best, students of local government have innocently made the mistake of regarding the liberal ideology as an adequate language of description and explanation. The cruel paradox of local government reorganisation is that notwithstanding the fact that 'nowhere in the world is a more lofty degree of homage paid to the local government ideal . . . nowhere else is this local government ideal treated with more underlying ambivalence if not hypocrisy' (Smallwood, 1965, p.128). It is the traditional commitment to democratic local self-government which has partly *led* to a reform thrust which has been primarily concerned to increase efficiency.

The concern to extend local democracy has always been but a 'minor theme' (Editorial, 1969, p.411) in *spite of*, but at the same time *because of*, the commitment to local democracy entrenched within the British tradition. Commitment has narrowed vision and a keen perception of the problems of democracy *within* local authorities, and has encouraged an unself-conscious reliance upon prescriptive theory and justification as description and explanation. The system has always been *seen* as essentially democratic, and so reorganisation could centre on increasing efficiency — the more so since the sheer scale of local government services has tended to mean that local government is increasingly being seen as primarily 'a local service agency' (Wickwar, 1970, pp.60ff).

Given the entrenchment of orthodoxies which pictured local government as democratic but inefficient, it was not surprising that the Royal Commission on Local Government in England was only required to have regard to the need 'to *sustain* a viable system of local democracy', and so could pursue the major task of increasing efficiency. Let us now, therefore, consider some of the orthodoxies which relate to the issue of efficiency and local government.

3

Efficiency and Local Government

Although size alone, however measured, cannot be the sole deter-
minant of efficiency, it has become increasingly apparent that for
all the main county functions . . . modern conditions require large
administrative units.   (*Local Government in Wales*, 1967, p.3)

Be efficient! There is in modern man a deeply-rooted belief that
objectives should be obtained at the least cost. Who can quarrel
with that?   (Wildavsky, 1973, p.142)

Students of public administration have argued long and correctly
that 'efficiency' or 'management' can rarely be 'improved' without
some effect on the substantive goals of the organisation.
                                               (Wilson, 1968, p.193)

Practically every academic textbook and virutally all official
reports on local government contain diagnoses of the ills of the
pre-1972 system. There has been constant and general agreement
as to the 'problems', 'defects' or 'weaknesses':

1 The boundaries of most authorities were seen as out of date
   so that local government areas no longer corresponded to the
   pattern of life and work in England.
2 The fragmentation of England into counties and county
   boroughs was said to make for hostility, and entrenched a
   division between town and country which made proper planning
   and transportation policies impossible.
3 In a similar way the division of responsibility and the system
   of shared functions and delegation between the counties and
   the county districts was also seen as leading to conflict and
   delay.
4 Orthodoxy has long asserted that there was too much central
   control so that local authorities were robbed of their rightful
   autonomy.
5 There was increasing anxiety as to the relationship between
   local authorities and the public.

6 The whole system was seen as too complex and inflexible. In particular, too many authorities, whether county, county borough or county district councils, were seen as too small in terms of area, population and resources to be efficient in the discharge of their mounting responsibilities.

Clearly not all these problems have been seen as of equally pressing importance. Local government has traditionally been judged according to its efficiency and democracy, and I made it clear in the last chapter that the democracy, or convenience, of the established system has never been in question.[1] 'Perhaps the most frequently voiced criticism', and 'the main failing of the pre-1972 system . . . was that many of the . . . units were too small' for efficiency. Moreover, in considering what changes were needed, orthodoxy has asserted that 'to correct these structural and other defects there is one fundamental question. What size of authority, or range of size, in terms of population and of area, is needed for the democratic and efficient provision of particular services and for local self-government as a whole?' (Royal Commission on Local Government in England, 1969, vol.1, pp.28, 3; Richards, 1973, p.39). Even in 1911, Harris (p.11) could note how 'the question of what is a suitable area for the provision of the various services is one which in this country . . . is *constantly to the fore*'.

There are a number of orthodoxies pertaining to this issue of efficiency in local government.

1 The established system of local government as it existed before the Local Government Act 1972 was described as inefficient.
2 This inefficiency was explained by pointing out that the overall structure of many small local authorities had failed to adjust to modern needs and changed circumstances. The existence of so many small authorities meant that men of calibre, economies of scale and the benefits of specialisation, all lay way beyond the capture of established practice at the same time as they were all seen as essential if efficiency were to be increased.
3 Inefficiency within the system was assessed as a particularly acute problem demanding reform attention — the more so

1 Maybe the relationship between local authorities and the public was 'not satisfactory', but the Royal Commission on Local Government in England (1969, vol.1, p.28) articulated the consensus on this when it felt sure that 'the public's attitude to local government is largely due to the defects in the structure' and to the weight of central control.

because things were seen as satisfactory with respect to local democracy.

4 The fact that the inefficiency of the system had been explained by pointing to the smallness of many of the local authorities meant that orthodoxy saw a key association existing between size and efficiency. Reformers have, therefore, been able to operate on the basis of a rule of reform which suggests that efficiency will be increased if the size of local authorities is increased.

5 Because small is to democracy as large is to efficiency, democracy and efficiency have been seen as in conflict.[2]

6 This being the case, the pursuit of efficiency through the creation of larger local authorities has been seen as introducing an 'undemocratic' element into any new system which just did not exist in the old system made up of small democratic (but inefficient) authorities. In order to minimise and counter these problems, 'optional extras' (Rees, 1971, p.92) have been grafted onto the new system of larger authorities, and more thoughtful sections of orthodox opinion have redefined the essentials of local democracy so that prescriptive theory is twisted into conformity with the new practice and the desirability of public participation is denied.

1.   Efficiency Lost: The Problem of Small Authorities

In the nineteenth century, before the reorganisation of local government had run its course, few people had a good word to say for the efficiency of the old system. 'Confusion of areas' was seen as the problem, and 'in the interests of good government it was absolutely necessary to remedy some of these evils, for in many places the existing conditions were fatal to administrative efficiency' (Redlich, 1903, vol.1, p.192).[3] When the President of the

---

2 I will not be discussing this position, but you will find it set down in the following: Astor, Simon and Burgess, n.d; Lipman, 1949, p.444; Crossman, cited in Wood, 1976, p.38; Robson, 1945, p.285; Birch, 1959, p.156; Local Government Commission for England, 1961, para. 56; Local Government Boundary Commission, 1947, para. 25; *Local Government in England*, 1971, para. 13; Griffith, 1966A, p.140; Sharp, 1962, p.385; MacColl, 1951, pp.21–9; Ward, 1968; Maddick, 1963; Rees, 1968.

3 For similar assessments, see Wright and Hobhouse, 1884; Chamberlain, 1885, esp. p.235.

Local Government Board introduced the Local Government (England and Wales) Bill in 1893 he told the House that 'our local government system has been extravagant in the time which is occupied in its administration, extravagant in the men needed to administer its affairs, and extravagant in the cost of that administration'. Once that Bill was passed, Redlich (1903, vol.2, p.408) felt able to point to 'the marvellous increase in the efficiency of local government' and Lowell (1908, vol.2, p.196) could argue that 'municipal administration in England today is throughout efficient, solid and businesslike'. Notwithstanding these favourable assessments, for most of this century most academics and official committees have considered that 'local government was not capable of providing an efficient service' (Buxton, 1973, p.57).[4] Why have they taken this view? What had gone wrong?

There has long been the view that 'the effectiveness of the system cannot be divorced from the social changes at work today' (Gowan, 1957, p.11). People continue to agree with the observation made by Wright and Hobhouse in 1884 (p.vi) that 'the increase in population and in the requirements of the time has outgrown the capacity of local machinery created for more limited objects'. As Richards (1975, p.33) put it some ninety years later: 'the structure as it stood in 1972 had been created in a different age for the needs of a different age, when the duties of local authorities were far more limited and before the internal combustion engine had revolutionised the means of transport . . . the local government map failed to adjust to the movements and growth of population'.[5] This sort of view is made up of three ingredients. First, we are offered a potted history of social and economic change in twentieth-century Britain.[6] Second, we are told of the enlarged responsibilities of local government and 'as the services run by local authorities have increased in number and

---

4 There are, of course, exceptions to this view. The Royal Commission on London Government (1923, p.69) rejected the LCC's scheme because it had 'regard to the unquestioned efficiency of administration in the highly organised districts outside the county'; and Hasluck (1936, pp.323–4) felt that 'taking the system over the country as a whole, there is no local government service that is marked by scandalous inefficiency'.

5 For similar views, see Conservative Research Department, 1971, p.89; Green, 1959, pp.15–20.

6 The Royal Commission on Local Government in England (1969, vol.1, p.11) pointed to 'revolutionary changes in our society', and *The Times* (9 April 1948) noted how 'the petrol engine, the telephone, vast shifts of industry and population have transformed the human map of England'.

importance, [so] the problem of securing a high level of modern efficiency has also increased' (Jackson, 1963, p.207). Third, in the face of these two changes the overall structure of local government has remained unchanged in its essentials. In other words things have not so much gone wrong with local government;[7] it is seen as more the case that local government has just failed to adapt to 'new problems' and 'new duties' (*Local Government in England and Wales During the Period of Reconstruction*, 1945, p.3). In effect, a stable governmental structure has been described as inefficient in the face of social and economic change. Governmental authority has remained 'fragmented' while the growing conurbations enjoy an economic and social integration. 'Lilliputian organisations' were seen as no longer up to the task of managing the technical means of satisfying the everyday needs of those who lived in the great cities (Green, 1959, p.17).

This inefficiency has been *explained* by pointing out that 'there are too many local authorities, the majority of which are too small . . . too many authorities lack the population and rate revenue necessary to provide essential services' (Labour Party, 1942, pp.5—6).[8] There is nothing new in this line of explanation. The Poor Law Report of 1834, when it considered the 'means by which . . . workhouses can be provided', pointed out that 'the first difficulty arises from the small population of a large proportion of the parishes . . . Even the parishes which are somewhat more populous . . . in the few cases in which they possess an efficient management, obtain it at a disproportionate expense' (Checkland and Checkland, 1974, p.425). In 1903 H. G. Wells (pp.402—3) urged the Fabian Society to 'condemn' the existing local authorities as they were inadequate to the task of efficient service provision and 'the general reason' for this was that 'their areas of activity . . . [were] impossibly small'. In similar vein the Medical Officer of the Local Government Board in his annual report for the year 1904—5 argued that 'if a district be so small . . . the result

---

7 Although Brodrick (1875, p.27) considered the nineteenth-century reorganisation to have been based on 'unscientific legislation', and Robson (1954, p.264) considered that even then it offered only a 'piecemeal solution to the particular problems'.

8 See also, Sharpe, 1965, p.11; Sharp, 1962; Redcliffe-Maud and Wood, 1974, pp. 24—31; Robson, 1966, pp.125—7; 1954, p.113; Royal Commission on Local Government in England, 1969, vol.1, pp.28, 2; Local Government Commission for Wales, 1963, esp. pp.69ff; *Local Government in Wales*, 1967, p.23; Royal Commission on the Police, 1962, pp.85, 145; *Local Government in England*, 1971, para. 6; *Local Government: Areas and Status of Local Authorities in England and Wales*, 1956; NALGO Reconstruction Committee, 1945.

of subdivision is clearly decrease in efficiency of administration' (cited in McGrath, 1925, p.300). The Committee of Enquiry into the Anti-Tuberculosis Service in Wales was of the 'opinion that many authorities owing to their small population . . . are quite incapable of carrying out their public health duties properly' (Ministry of Health, 1939, para. 388).[9]

No one can doubt the entrenchment of an orthodoxy which asserts that small authorities are inefficient. Moreover, if you wish to push behind this bald statement in order to ask why this should be seen as so, then you can tease out an orthodox package of themes which serve to fill it out. First, small authorities are seen as unable to secure the services of councillors or officers of high calibre. In 1966, Griffith (p.542) argued that 'the smaller authorities have greater staffing difficulties'; in 1939 the Committee of Enquiry into the Anti-Tuberculosis Service in Wales pointed out that 'small authorities of necessity cannot obtain the services of the best type of official' (Ministry of Health, 1939, para. 397); and in 1911 Hobhouse (p.403) wrote of the 'tendency of the smaller local bodies to appoint inefficient officers'. On the councillor side, Sharp (1962, p.383) considered that 'part of the trouble in getting enough good people to serve arises, I believe, from the fact that the areas and status of local authorities are often today too cramped or too small'; and in 1911 Fordham (p.406) made a similar sort of point when he argued that in the parish 'there is neither business important and interesting enough to attract capable people'.[10] Second (and I will be returning to this point in my next section), small authorities are seen as unable to secure the benefits that are alleged to derive from economies of scale. Third, and related to this, small authorities cannot secure the benefits of specialisation and division of labour whereby competent specialists are employed for particular tasks, as 'it is difficult to justify the employment of the range of necessary specialists unless the case load is large' (Griffith, 1966, p.543).

How adequate is this orthodox description, explanation, and assessment of the inefficiency of the pre-1972 system of local

9 See also Royal Commission on Local Government, 1925, 1928, 1929, esp. part I. Evidence submitted to the Commission convinced the members that there were serious weaknesses in the provision of efficient sanitation in the smaller authorities. See also, Heath, 1925, esp. p.319.
10 See also Poulanzas, 1960, p.281.

government? 'There is little, if any, evidence of any weight to indicate that county districts generally, and small districts in particular, fail in the provision of necessary services' (Morris, 1960, pp.96–7). In common with most committees and academics the Local Government Commission for Wales (1963, pp.106, 70, 78) 'made no attempt to prove inefficiency on the part of any particular county'; it 'simply' started from the 'proposition that there is a minimum size in terms of population and resources below which the full range of county functions cannot be carried out'. The truth of the matter is that 'the effects of local authority size was a relatively neglected subject before the Royal Commission on Local Government in England sponsored research into it', and we shall soon see that this research did nothing to support the orthodoxy about the relationship between size and efficiency (Davies, 1969, p.225).[11] Simply expressed, all the orthodoxies pertaining to the issue of the inefficiency of the established system of local government have been left unquestioned even though they have been unsupported by any solid evidence.

2. Efficiency Regained: The Promise of Large Authorities

The orthodoxy which explained the inefficiency of the established system by pointing to the weakness of the small authorities carries within itself a number of ideas. First, there is the idea that the 'provision of services and the size of areas are interdependent' (Jackson, 1965, p.289);[12] second there is the idea that within the established system 'functions . . . bear little or no relation to area' (Finer, 1950, p.93); and third, all this leads smoothly into a rule of reform which points to 'the need for larger areas' in order to increase efficiency (Robson, 1954, p.124). Pick up any book which touches on the boundary problem and you will be told that 'the arguments in favour of larger local authorities are many, various, and strong' (Griffith, 1966, p.543). 'Again and again we meet the proposition that there is a minimum size for which it is reasonable to have a separate local authority service' (Jackson, 1965, p.326). In a word, the 'prevailing official and academic view' subscribed to what Rees (1969, pp.423, 421) has called the

11 Lomax, 1943, 1952; Baker, 1910; Brown *et al.*, 1953; James, 1966, are among the few studies that explored the relationship between size and efficiency before research was undertaken by the Redcliffe-Maud Commission.
12 See also Local Government Commission for Wales, 1963, p.66.

'doctrine of the minimum size for an efficient authority'. Certainly the Royal Commission on Local Government in England was appointed by a Minister who 'had no doubt that an impartial body would support his contention that larger units were needed' (Morton, 1970, p.17), and the Commission itself in considering 'proposals for a new structure started from the basis that most existing units are too small for the provision of the main services' (1969, vol.1, p.42).

By the time the Redcliffe-Maud Commission latched on to this rule of reform it was well-established. But in 1834 it was something of a novelty, as 'in the minds of many, management on a large scale, and large establishments, are associated with large expenses'. The authors of the Poor Law Report had no time for this view. They had no doubt that 'in the small parish the expense per head of the persons entitled to relief is generally the greatest', and they advocated the union of parishes for the purpose of providing indoor relief in order to secure a 'great gain in efficiency' and 'considerable economy' (Checkland and Checkland, 1974, pp.423—44). However, because the commissioners were giving expression to a new idea they buttressed it with some evidence[13] in a way which has not since been seen as necessary, as constant repetition has given the rule the status of obvious common-sense. By 1947 the Local Government Boundary Commission (para. 19) could effortlessly assert that 'the practical advantages of large scale organisation *need no emphasis*'. In a similar way, the Local Government Commission for Wales (1963, p.70) regarded the 'advantages of economies of scale' in larger authorities as 'obvious'; Self (1962, p.16) could criticise the Herbert Commission's proposals for London Government because they did not 'realise all the *admitted* advantages of large scale organisation'; and numerous writers on local government could unthinkingly point out that 'for various reasons bigger authorities were *demanded*' (Sharp, 1969, p.49; see also Sharpe, 1965, p.29; Robson, 1972, p.74; Maddick, 1963, pp.115ff; Richards, 1973, p.34). In effect, local authorities *had* to be 'substantially enlarged in size and rationalised in shape. This may be a hard pill to swallow, but what other alternative exists?' (Robson, 1948, p.355). Sensible advocates of

13 The Report noted how 'Mr. Mott states that if 500 persons cost £10 per head or £5,000; 1,000 persons would cost only £9 per head, or £9,000. He also states that there would be no more difficulty in managing 5 or 6 combined workhouses than 5 or 6 separate wards or rooms in one house' (Checkland and Checkland, 1974, p.438).

reorganisation had no choice: the 'pressure of . . . [the] tendency towards uniformity and specialisation *compels* the central government itself, whenever it reorganises a public service in order to increase its efficiency, to design large areas of administration' (Hadfield and MacColl, 1948, p.142; West Midland Group, 1948, p.59). Practically no one has stood outside a broad acceptance of the idea that larger local authorities were the key to increased efficiency. A research appendix from the Royal Commission on Local Government in England (1969, vol.3, Appendix 9, p.197) rather confirms the point. It aimed to 'summarise the findings of reports on local government services where they relate to the size of unit necessary for effective execution of the service', and it found that 'the general drift of the recommendations of most reports has been towards larger units of administration'.[14]

The case for larger authorities may not have been buttressed by facts and *evidence* from the world of local government, but this does not mean that *arguments* have not been advanced to sustain the case. Fundamentally, however, orthodox masters have done little more than push the parallels between business and local government. They steal the ideas of classical economists theorising about the firm. In 1925 Heath (p.319) pointed out that 'the commercial world has satisfied itself of the advantages, financial and otherwise, of the combination and absorption of smaller interests into the larger whole' and he saw 'no reason why such benefits should not . . . be applied to local government'. Robson (1954, p.125) argued that 'just as the technique of industrial and commercial administration now requires far larger units of authority than formerly, so does the technique of efficient municipal administration now demand more extensive units of local government'. This broad argument breaks down into the dual claim that with an increase in size come both economies of scale, and the related advantages of specialisation and division of labour.

The Local Government Boundary Commission argued that 'a single large unit should be able to achieve economies in terms of manpower and money more easily than several smaller ones' (1947, para. 24), and the *Written Evidence of the Ministry of Housing and Local Government* to the Royal Commission on Local Government in England (1969, pp.38, 51) pointed out that 'small-scale operations in refuse disposal are uneconomic and

14 For a similar point, see Jackson, 1965, p.311.

inconvenient in various ways' and, more generally, they argued that 'a small authority is less likely to possess modern plant, equipment or specialist appliances . . . [has] less room for new developments in services . . . [and] little margin for unexpected contingencies'. Even an economist was prepared to argue that 'economic criteria . . . call for larger areas' as he considered that economies of scale 'certainly exist in the provision of the main engineering services' and 'economies may result from the greater efficiency of larger local authority administrations' (Hughes, 1967, pp.134, 127).[15] In other words, in addition to technical economies he also considered that larger authorities might benefit from managerial economies. Naturally enough, the Royal Commission on Local Government in England (1969, vol.2, p.60) went along with this line of argument since it was 'taken for granted . . . that economies of scale would be found to play a large part'.

Hadfield and MacColl (1948, p.141) remind us that 'it was a famous proposition of Adam Smith that the division of labour is limited by the extent of the market', and they went on to argue that 'it is true of local government', pointing out that 'the more specialised the services to be provided, the larger the area they need to cover, if enough people are to use them'. The Royal Commission on Local Government in England (1969, vol.1, p.59) did not doubt the wisdom of Adam Smith, since they also considered it 'clear that larger authorities offer advantages of specialisation in staff and institutions', and some while earlier the Commission's Director of Intelligence, L. J. Sharpe (1965, p.29), pointed out that 'larger populations . . . mean that large enough case loads will exist to warrant the provision of those specialised institutions and staff which make it possible for services to be provided to modern standards'.

Talk about the *economic* advantages of increased size does not exhaust the orthodox case for larger local authorities since it has long been claimed that larger authorities will be better placed to attract councillors and officers of calibre. This is a crucially important political plank in the orthodox case. The Royal Commission on Local Government in Greater London (1960, p.63) considered that 'a certain minimum size and scope of authority seems to be needed to attract councillors and officers of the

15 See also Robson, 1961; Local Government Commission for Wales, 1963; International Union of Local Authorities, 1953; Checkland and Checkland, 1974; Finer, 1950, p.94.

right calibre'. In 1967, the government of the day pointed out that 'the large authority is better able than the small to provide the conditions of service, the career structure and the scope for the exercise of specialised professional skills which are needed to attract and retain sufficient good quality staff' (*Local Government in Wales*, p.3). The Royal Commission's Director of Intelligence considered that 'larger authorities will be better placed to attract expert staff' (Sharpe, 1965, p.29); and the *Written Evidence of the Ministry of Housing and Local Government* to the Commission pointed to 'the ability of larger authorities to attract better qualified professional officers' and 'chief officers of a higher calibre' (p.50). It was hardly surprising that the Commission itself (1969, vol.1, p.69) accepted this argument, noting that 'only an authority serving a population of some 250,000 will have at its disposal the range and calibre of staff . . . necessary for effective provision of [education, housing and the personal services]'.[16] The Minister of Housing and Local Government highlighted the consensus on all this when he told the House on the occasion of the Second Reading of the Local Government Bill in December 1957 'that *everyone agrees* that some small boroughs and some small districts cannot survive as they are . . . for they really are too weak, and in particular, they may not be able to attract and pay good enough staff'.

How cogent are these arguments?

3. Orthodoxy Explored

In 1966, James (p.470) concluded that 'an authority of about 60,000 to 70,000 population' was best able to provide 'the most intimate and personalised social services'. On the basis of a larger sample of authorities, but using the same indicators, Davies (1969, p.244) claimed that 'the larger welfare authorities appear to perform better'. Griffith (1966A, p.143) was absolutely right: there was 'the need for research . . . [as] until we know more, especially about the relation between area and function, . . . we can only guess . . . what is the "right" size'.

When the Royal Commission on Local Government in England

---

16 For similar views, see also Local Government Boundary Commission, 1947; Sharp, 1962; Mackintosh, 1968; Astor, Simon and Burgess, n.d.; Local Government Commission for Wales, 1963, pp.75–6; Local Government Commission for England, 1964, p.8; Ministry of Housing and Local Government Circular, 35/62.

came to consider their 'fundamental question' — the relationship between the size of a local authority and its performance — they had at their disposal three studies undertaken by outside bodies, two studies made by government departments, and a study made by their own research staff. In addition two of the Greater London Group's functional studies of local authorities in South East England had a bearing on these questions.[17] The Royal Commission (1969, vol.1, p.58) correctly noted that

> the overriding impression which emerges from the three studies
> by outside bodies and from our own study of staffing is that size
> cannot statistically be proved to have a very important effect on
> performance. There were a few scattered instances where economies
> of scale seemed to be operating . . . But, in general, size did not seem
> to have a greater bearing on performance than some environmental
> characteristics of local authorities.

More than this, some of the findings of Research Study 3, on *Economies of Scale in Local Government Services* (p.6), 'refute not only the prevalent view that economies of scale would be achieved by increasing the present size of . . . local authorities, but also provide some evidence that *dis*economies of scale operate with an increase in population size'. In addition, Myra Woolf, in an unpublished paper on 'The effects of population size on local authority services', admitted that she started her work within the orthodoxy feeling that 'the extent and quality of the . . . services provided by local authorities were related to the size of the authority and that certain authorities were limited in their ability to provide services because of their size'. But her research evidence only served to *dis*prove the orthodoxy and she was forced to come to the 'general conclusion that population size, on its own, accounted for only a small proportion of the difference between local authorities' provision of services' (Research Study 5, p.1). There was no joy for the Royal Commission in these findings, and the other studies did nothing to substantiate the orthodox rule of reform. The Commissioners (1969, vol.1, pp.50, 38, 19) were forced to recognise that in the Greater London Group's study of *Local Government in South East England* 'scale appeared to have little measurable relationship with performance except in fairly limited fields'; in the Department of Education and Science's *Enquiry into Efficiency of Local Education Authorities* 'there

---

17 Royal Commission on Local Government in England, Research Study 3, 4, 5; vol.3, Research Appendix 11, 12, 10; Research Study 1, 2.

was no straightforward correlation of efficiency with size'; and the Home Office assessment of the performance of authorities responsible for the children's service revealed 'as with the survey of education authorities by the D.E.S., [that] there was no straightforward correlation of size with efficiency'.

Part of the case for larger authorities was based on the argument that with an increase in size would come an automatic increase in the calibre of councillors and officers. I will consider the issue of councillor calibre in the next chapter, but what is the evidence on the issue of official calibre? The Royal Commission on Local Government in Greater London (1960, p.72) noted that 'reliable comparisons are hard to get', but research undertaken for the Royal Commission on Local Government in England aimed to get to grips with the orthodoxy. The researchers recognised that 'large authorities are often said to be better staffed than small' and they recognised that the 'proposition that authorities of large population can cope better with . . . [the] shortage [of professional staff in local government] forms a significant part of the argument of some witnesses who call for the creation of substantially larger units'. But they concluded that 'the results of the exercise do *not* show population size as affecting staffing. It has not appeared to be the case that large authorities are better able than small to attract and retain good quality staff' (1969, vol.3, Appendix 10, pp.211, 222). This should not have been regarded as surprising since some years earlier the Committee on the Staffing of Local Government (1967, p.72) had come to the 'conclusion that on the figures available to us there was *no* clear indication that small authorities (in terms of their population) experienced generally a more intense difficulty in recruiting staff than the larger authorities'. Orthodoxy explored was orthodoxy condemned. The whole argument is over simple and over general.[18]

We can surely conclude that 'the objective research published by the Commission failed to establish that size has an important effect on performance' (Rees, 1971, p.21). The argument that large local authorities are more efficient is more than merely

18 The following studies all have a bearing on the issue of size and performance. Davies, Barton and McMillan, 1972; Davies, Barton, McMillan and Williamson, 1971; Davies and Barton, 1974; Hughes, 1967; Cumming, 1971; Nicholson and Topham, 1972; Richardson, 1973, p.85. None of them are prepared to go along with the simplistic orthodoxy.

'unproved' (Stewart, 1971, p.1064), as 'the one thing these researches have put beyond doubt is that no positive correlation whatever between population size and performance can be statistically established, even in the present local government system' (Royal Commission on Local Government in England, 1969, vol.2, p.62). In the face of all this the Commission 'came to the only possible conclusion — namely, that neither research nor submitted evidence had proved that any particular size of authority was best for any function' (Morton, 1970, p.59).

Here was a Commission which had grounded its whole approach in the orthodoxies of local government. They operated under 'the influence of economic fashion about the relationship between size and efficiency' (Self, 1971, p.191), and Morton (1970, p.77) gained the distinct 'impression that the majority had already made up their minds about [the minimum] population' necessary for efficiency long before any evidence disproved the conventional wisdom. The Commissioners had sat on the orthodox reform mat only to have it pulled rudely from beneath them by their own research staff. What could they do?

There were only two options. They could accept the evidence of the research studies, cast the orthodox rule of reform to the wind, operate outside the framework and assumptions of the conventional wisdom, and devise some alternative formula to guide the course of their reorganising endeavours. Alternatively, they could stand by the orthodoxy, in which case they would need to discredit the research studies and find some alternative base from which to legitimise their approach to reorganisation. It was a fight between fact and preconceived commitment and 'knowledge'. There was no contest: the widely shared and long-established rule of reform was seen as right, and the facts were wrong — or at least that is what the Commissioners were forced to try and argue. They had little difficulty in disposing of the research studies. These were 'the prisoners of the existing structure . . . they could not tell us how a new pattern of authorities might perform', and, anyway, it was seen as very difficult to find a satisfactory measure of performance in the provision of services. Fair enough, but the Local Government Operational Research Unit wanted to use a model that would overcome these difficulties and 'the Royal Commission refused to allow the Unit to proceed with the analysis which would have avoided the[se] criticisms' (Stanyer, 1973, p.138). Moreover, if the Commissioners were prepared to recognise that the old orthodoxy lacked cogency in the context of the established system, how could they then go on to argue that it would hold good in a reorganised system as the new authorities would somehow be in 'a better position'? (vol.1, p.58). The Commission's need to bolster their sagging orthodoxy led to their looking favourably at two studies by central government departments which they regarded as 'particularly helpful since they enabled us to supplement what were essentially statistical exercises with the subjective impressions of those who have direct, disinterested knowledge of the quality of local authority performance in two major services'. Needless to say, 'both showed that size was related to performance' (1969, vol.1, p.59). In addition to this 'evidence', the Commission considered that 'the movement of opinion in favour of large authorities is impressive' (vol.1, p.33), and 'despite the inconclusiveness of the objective research, the Commission took advantage of the general atmosphere which surrounded its work' (Redcliffe-Maud and Wood, 1974, p.35). The trouble is that the 'evidence from the Ministries rarely reflected lengthy rational analysis' (Wood, 1976, p.56), and the two central government studies were hardly an adequate 'efficiency test' (Beloff, 1971, p.xiii). They were 'pseudo-scientific' and 'put forward by possibly the least disinterested bodies in the whole discussion, two departments of a service which, well in advance of the studies, was already convinced of the superiority of large authorities' (Rees, 1971, pp.25, 21; see also Stanyer, 1973, p.139). Moreover, to make a case for larger authorities on the strength of the 'movement of opinion' or the 'general atmosphere' is merely to defend and justify an orthodoxy by citing as proof the existence of the orthodoxy itself! 'The fact must be faced that no objective basis exists on which to attribute any material significance to population size as a factor in any way influencing the performance of existing major authorities' (Royal Commission on Local Government in England, 1969, vol.2, p.63).

4. Orthodoxy Explored — Continued

So far I have assembled evidence critical of the orthodox rule of reform which associates large local authorities with efficiency. I think we can take our critique further than this. First, it is reasonable to suggest that the very expectation — or hypothesis — that there would be such an association so that we could somehow arrive at an optimum size of local authority has been based on a quite mistaken belief about the parallels between government and business. Second, those who have made a case for larger local authorities on the strength of their knowledge of economic arguments have revealed a quite inadequate appreciation of the economic literature on the theory of the firm. Third, and more fundamentally, we have to pay critical attention to the objective of efficiency itself. Let me deal with each of these points in turn.

When we think of economies of scale in industry then we probably think of the production of manufactured goods being concentrated in a large factory where there is a heavy reliance on the use of specialised machinery. But the services provided by local government cannot be produced in one large plant and then distributed to the local populace in a fleet of lorries. By their very nature most of the services provided by a local authority require geographic proximity of service units to recipients and this prevents the establishment of huge primary schools, fire stations, police stations, or libraries. Moreover, local government services tend to be labour intensive, with wages and salaries often accounting for more than two-thirds of current costs. In other words, many of the services provided by local authorities are produced under constant cost conditions where cheaper, large machine inputs just *cannot* be substituted for labour as more output is produced. You simply cannot double the output of a school teacher by increasing the size of the school! Even if it is admitted that the scope for 'technical' economies in local government is limited, it is still part of orthodoxy to suggest that larger authorities provide scope for 'managerial' economies, because we now have one director of education instead of two, one education office instead of two, and so on (Hasluck, 1936, p.351). In theory this may be so. In practice the picture may well be different. Salary levels are inextricably bound up with the population of an authority (Sherman, 1974),[19] and there has been the political necessity of absorbing staff from the old system into the new, and both these factors have served to limit the possibility of these economies being reaped in the real world. The Committee of Inquiry into

---

19 On a different tack, Hirsch (1970, p.274) points out that 'a concentration of manpower can increase the bargaining power of labor and this, in turn, increases costs', and Ingham (1970) explores the implications of size for industrial relations.

Local Government Finance (1976, p.28) has recognised that 'a reorganisation of the scale undertaken in England and Wales in 1974 . . . was bound in the short run to give rise to considerable expense'. Nowadays it is becoming rather fashionable to bolt orthodoxy and point to the existence of inefficiency and managerial diseconomies in the new system. This may well be the case, but Richardson (1973, p.90) is right: 'the plausible arguments in favour of managerial scale economies can be matched with equally plausible, but untested, arguments on the other side . . . This is an area where opinions have developed much further than the supporting facts' and we could do with some decent research on the subject.[20]

Many private firms have competitors, and they all have definite — and measurable — criteria of success which provide them with an incentive to be as efficient (producing at minimum cost) as the circumstances permit. Local authorities are not in this position. They are area monopolists; they are not attempting to, and neither could they, maximise profits; and they lack unambiguous indicators of standards of performance. Some of the goods produced by local authorities are 'public goods' where each individual's consumption leads to no subtractions from any other individual's consumption. In this sort of situation pricing is next to impossible. Since an efficient allocation of resources occurs when price equals marginal cost it is clear that the production of non-priced goods at an efficient level can really only occur by chance (Brown, 1974, ch. 8). Moreover, if you are serious about trying to estimate cost functions then you have to hold constant the quality of the product. This problem can, in principle, be coped with when we are dealing with the products of private manufacture,[21] but it is impossible to hold constant, or measure, the differences in quality when we are dealing with the services provided by local authorities (Thompson, 1965, p.267; Hirsch, 1970, p.164).[22] It is this difficulty of getting adequate measures of local authority *output* and productivity that has placed a premium on the simple measure-

20 See also Spann, 1962.
21 On the methods *and* problems of measuring economies of scale in private industry see Pratten, Dean and Silbertson, 1965; Shepherd, 1967—8; Chenery, 1949; Haldi and Whitcomb, 1967; Committee of Inquiry on Small Firms, 1971.
22 This problem is recognised within the British debate — at least by some people — but its full *implications* are not always recognised. See Wood, 1976, p.57; Royal Commission on Local Government in England, 1969, vol.2, p.61; Research Study 4, esp. p.12.

ment of crude *inputs*, which has, in turn, served to put the smaller local authorities into a vicious 'Catch 22' situation where they just cannot win: 'to spend more per head on a service than the national average means that you are uneconomically small; to spend less means you cannot afford a full service' (Rees, 1971, p.54). Problems of measurement do not stop here.[23] For single-product plants the economies of scale are the potential reductions in average unit costs of production associated with higher levels of production capacity. For multi-product plants scale is a multi-dimensional concept and may be changed not only by altering the overall capacity but also in other ways. Local government is· a provider of many services and so dealing with the issue of economies of scale is a very tricky exercise. In a very limited way this is recognised within the orthodox literature. Robson (1931, pp.140, 130) notes that the 'determination of areas for land drainage proceeds on entirely different principles from that relating to public libraries', and in consequence, 'there is no division of the country which will suit all municipal functions'. This means that advocates of reorganisation, who are obsessed with the goal of efficiency and the means of size, are faced with a problem: 'should the requirement of the service needing the largest unit dictate the size of new authorities at the cost of possibly creating unnecessarily large authorities for other services?' (Wood, 1976, p.58).[24] We should realise that this is not a problem, since if we cannot even arrive at an optimum size of authority for a *single* service it makes little sense to pursue this line of thought further in order to try and work out the one best size of authority for everything.[25] On occasions advocates of larger local authorities are themselves inclined to admit that variables other than those of size just might be of relevance to the issue of standards and efficiency,[26] but

23 There is also the problem of taking *private* costs into account as well. For example, services are concentrated into one central location in a large new local authority in the hope that economies of scale will reduce public costs, but if this pushes up private costs of travel and delay how then should we judge the efficiency and cost effectiveness of the new scheme?

24 See Webb and Webb, 1920, and Cole, 1921, ch. 17 for one ingenious solution to this problem.

25 The issue of efficient service provision has tended to rather dominate the British debate, and so it is less well-recognised that what may be a good size of authority to perform some given set of public services may not cover an appropriate area to finance them (see Thompson, 1965, pp. 286–7; Richardson, 1973, p.85).

26 See, for example, Robson, 1972, p.123; Royal Commission on Local Government in England, 1969, Research Study 7, p.196; Davies, Barton, McMillan and Williamson, 1971, p.22.

they have not been inclined to follow this up in a rigorous and systematic way.

Baldly, and more crisply expressed, all these varied points should make it clear that 'the conditions which help private industry to benefit from scale economies . . . do not appear to exist when local urban governments grow or consolidate' (Hirsch, 1967, p.38).[27] It is not really surprising that there has been little evidence to support the orthodoxy about size and efficiency in local government. It is surely more surprising that students of local government were prepared to assume that there even could be.

The rule of reform which associates large size with efficiency and talks about economies of scale is grounded in a very superficial appreciation of the neo-classical theory of the firm. Economists are increasingly aware of the limitations of this theory. As early as 1933, Florence (p.118, see also 1969) was arguing that 'as industry is conducted by fewer and larger organisations questions of political science become more important relatively to questions of economics . . . [as] more and more of the transactions of industry are carried on inside the organisation without exchange for a price'. Many critics of the neo-classical theory are proposing an integration of organisation theory with the theory of the firm. As firms have got bigger, economists have been forced to drop their heroic simplifying assumption of the single entrepreneur to involve themselves in organisational literature because 'virtually all the interesting bureaucratic behaviour observed to exist in large government bureaucracies finds its counterpart in large non-government bureaucracies as well' (Williamson, 1967, p.134). The behavioural approach to the theory of the firm[28] is still in its infancy, but its intrusion into economic analysis will encourage a shift away from any simple equation between size and efficiency and will force economists to involve themselves in dealing with the problems of innovation, adaptation, and decision-making in an *organisational* setting. It is ironic that as we in government have looked to the simple theory of the firm for inspiration in re-organising local government, so economists have admitted to the limitations of that theory and have looked to us for help in

27 See also Johnson, 1963; Cuckney, 1974.
28 See especially Cyert and March, 1963; McGuire, 1964.

providing them with a more adequate way to make sense of the behaviour of firms.[29]

This chapter has been a bit like Hamlet without the Prince. It has revolved around the arguments of those who have been concerned to increase 'efficiency' in local government, but at no point have I made it clear just what they have meant by this term. This has not simply been a thoughtless omission on my part, but rather reflects the absence of any such overt concern within the traditional discourse. Even so, I have rather gone along with it all, and assumed that everyone *knew* what efficiency meant and regarded it as a self-evidently good thing. In taking this position it has been inevitable that my critique has been situated *within* the confines of the British tradition. Although I have sought to question whether the orthodox *means* of larger local authorities will actually attain the efficiency *goal*, I have left the goal itself unexplored. Let me now make good this omission.

'Strictly speaking, efficiency is a purely abstract and colourless term. It relates simply to the ratio of results achieved to the means used' ('Efficiency', 1948, p.439). Efficiency is about choosing the best (lowest cost) means to attain a given end. In this sense it is an inadequate political objective. Or rather, it only makes *sense* if we are prepared to take politics away and assume that the ends of public activity are given, beyond question, or agreed by all. These assumptions are indeed entrenched within the British tradition of debate about local government. Pessimistic talk about the pressing weight of central control leads smoothly, and inevitably, into the view that local authorities are merely the passive agents of the central government. Similarly, optimistic talk about local democracy leaves no room for local politics, as local authorities become passive servants of the local electorate where there is a presumption of a consensus on the ends of public policy which leaves the local council with the same limited task of implementation and administration. If you accept the central control thesis, or the notion of a conflict-free local democracy, then you can honestly go along with a reorganisation objective which assumes away the problem of the politics of local authority action. However, I see both these theses as wrong. The ends of local govern-

29 If we are interested in economic theory then oligopoly theory may be of *more* importance than competitive theory concerned with cost minimisation and optimum size. (See Bish and Warren, 1972; Thompson, 1965, p.268; Williams, 1966.)

ment activity are *not* strictly given by the central government. There is the problem of *what* services to provide and for *whom* in a situation where the ideal of a consensual community is a romantic dream.

Having said this, precisely because efficiency is an inadequate political objective, it is highly relevant politically. It is of political significance that *the* problem of local government has continually been defined as one of inefficiency and that the goal of reorganisation has been to increase it. A social theory is caught up in this which contains policy implications embodying the interests of a particular section of society at the time as bland talk about efficiency rather conceals the fact.

The concern to increase efficiency would seem to be a neutral political objective — the honest desire to get more out of what we have got; the effort to rather better. But in reality such an objective also assumes away (by ignoring) other more substantial problems. Those whose first concern is with governmental inefficiency tend to focus their critical attention on the faults of government alone. Moreover, debate becomes restricted to questions of technique so that a concern with the more fundamental issues of access and representation is suppressed and defined as perversely political. The trouble is that efficiency is a luxurious political objective which comes from, and embodies, the interests of those who first seek to restrain the cost of government before moving on to restrict the scope of government activity itself. It is surely only those who benefit totally from the private sector alone who have less need of public services, and so in calling for increased governmental efficiency they can hope to reduce their own financial contribution to the state. More than this, the concern to attain efficiency easily pushes into, and is usually the public face of, a highly political effort actually to prune government of 'unnecessary' services. A little detective work among the books on the problems of local government quickly makes it abundantly clear that the desire to increase efficiency is perhaps better expressed in terms of the concern to cut public spending and the scope of government.

The goal of efficiency is the natural political objective of those classes which, in seeking to minimise both conflict and politics, also seek to minimise government. It is also an objective which relates to the issue of councillor calibre, and I will be dealing with this in my next chapter.

4

Councillor Calibre and the Boundary Problem

> For a variety of reasons those who by virtue of their education,
> leisure, business training, or strong personality would, and should,
> be the most valuable members of the public service, stood aside in
> greater numbers and declined to serve.
>> (The Mayor of Exeter in a speech to the Congress of the Royal
>> Sanitary Institution, 1913, cited in Newton, 1968, p.xviii)

> The migration of the upper class from central to outlying areas
> created a geographical distance between its residential communities
> and its economic institutions. To protect the latter required involve-
> ment . . . in the larger city government.   (Hays, 1964, p.161)

The concern to increase efficiency in local government is related
to the concern to raise councillor calibre. In this chapter I want to
deal with the anxiety about councillor calibre in the context of
the anxiety about 'outdated' boundaries, since these are related
each to the other.

It has been geographers and planners who have been particularly
concerned to argue that local government boundaries were 'artificial, antiquated relics of the past' because they 'rarely kept up
with' the shifts in population and with the new facts of social
geography (Green, 1959, p.219; Perry, 1975, p.44; see also
Freeman, 1959, 1968). Cities were in flood (Self, 1961). Old and
established administrative boundaries were 'obliterated' (Cullingworth, 1967, p.268). Planning was seen as impossible. The Royal
Commission on Local Government in England (1969, vol.1,
pp.25—6) gave crisp expression to these ideas when it argued that
'local government areas no longer correspond to the pattern of
life and work in England. Population has long since over-run
many of the old boundaries . . . The failure to recognise [the
interdependence of town and country] is the most fatal defect of
the present structure.'
Dame Evelyn Sharp, Permanent Secretary to the Ministry of

Housing and Local Government, told the 1960 Annual Conference of the Association of Municipal Corporations:

> I do not think that enough really able people are interested today in taking part in local government. I do not think that enough people from business, from industry, from agriculture and the professions are going into it . . . Most people engaged or interested in local government agree . . . that the calibre of local government is not equal all round to its responsibilities.

Anxiety about councillor calibre has been long standing. 'During the 1850s . . . the personnel of town councils repeatedly attracted critical comment. It seemed to many observers that there had been a change for the worse since 1835' (Hennock, 1973, p.312). Certainly John Stuart Mill (1861, p.351) regarded 'the low calibre of the men by whom they are almost always carried on [as] . . . the greatest imperfection of popular local institutions'. In 1902 Ostrogorski (vol.1, p.49) noted a 'decline in the intellectual, and to some extent, moral standards of the personnel of the town councils', and Lowell (1908, vol.2, p.199) agreed, as he had 'no doubt that the average standing of the councillors has gone down'. In the 1960s this concern again bubbled to the surface. The Committee on the Management of Local Government was appointed to 'consider in the light of modern conditions how local government might best continue to attract and retain people (both elected representatives and principal officers) of the calibre necessary to ensure its maximum effectiveness', and much of the evidence to the Royal Commissions on Local Government in England and Scotland considered 'it is a view widely held that the standards of elected representatives is not as high as it might or should be'[1] and that something should be done to improve matters.

In my opening chapter it was made clear that the anxiety about calibre reflects, in hard terms, a particular assessment of changes in the class composition of local councils. Although those who hold to this position are usually guilty of grossly misrepresenting both the current extent of working class representation and the demise of the businessman-councillor,[2] it is still important for us

---

1 Memorandum of the Council of the Scottish Chamber of Commerce to the Royal Commission on Local Government in Scotland, 1969, *Written Evidence* 9, p.6. See also Keith-Lucas, 1961.
2 Research undertaken for the Committee on the Management of Local Government (1967, vol.2, p.289) made it quite clear that 'it is not the case that those with professional or managerial experience do not take up council work. 19% of all councillors are either professional workers or employers and managers in large businesses. This is

to gain an appreciation of the changes in local political leadership precisely because there has been the attempt to arrest and reverse these changes through boundary reorganisation.

1. Calibre Lost: Described

Generalising across the field of local politics is dangerous. Even so, we can detect two major shifts in council composition in the past century and a half.

In Cheshire 'county government by country gentlemen . . . was transformed between 1840 and 1880 . . . by the introduction of businessmen and industrialists into the county magistracy . . . The landed gentry were displaced from their monopoly of local politics by new social leaders . . . who had made their wealth out of the expansion of urban industry.' By the end of the Second World War, however, 'the county society of social leaders was replaced by a community of public persons . . . and the county council . . . gradually became a body of elected representatives . . . each of whom was dependent for his position not on his social standing but on his experience in public service' (Lee, 1963, pp.4–5, 79, 212–13). In Hampshire councillors of the 'squire' type were still being elected in 1955 (Hornsby, 1957, pp.93–4). But in Nottinghamshire the landed gentry 'have virtually disappeared' (Long, 1964, pp.418–20); in South Devon, although 'leadership in local affairs until the Great Depression (1874–1912) was largely in the hands of the squirearchy who had the traditional assistance of the clergy . . . in the last 75 years both these elements have tended to disappear' (Mitchell, 1951, p.394); and in Kent, too, Keith-Lucas (1977, pp.78–9) has pointed to the 'process by which the old county families who ruled before 1914 were superseded by the new business executives and commercial councillors'.

Change was not confined to the government of the countryside and the counties. Changes of a similar, but more far-reaching, kind were at work in the towns. Even in traditional market towns such as Exeter,

> if a detailed comparison were to be made between the circumstances of each member of the council in 1837 and on the eve of the first

nearly three times the proportion of such groups in the general population.' On the middle class position of many councillors see Sharpe, 1962, 1962A; Hampton, 1970, p.189; Morris and Newton, 1970; *The Economist*, 30 January 1960.

> world war it would be found that the former did in fact represent
> a much higher proportion of the wealth and social status of the
> city . . . There was no longer in 1914 that close link between the
> council and county society and politics.[3]   (Newton, 1968, p.317)

Before 1866,

> Glossop was governed by . . . a combination of the mill owners with
> the landowner and his agents . . . The borough of council elected
> in December 1866 was a 'cottonocracy'. Twelve mill owners and a
> manager were elected amongst 18 councillors . . . In 1919 . . . the
> old families were soon to die out or drift away . . . The shopkeepers,
> artisans, civil servants and schoolmasters . . . inherited the responsi-
> bilities of local political leadership.   (Birch, 1959, pp.23—31)

'Until the early nineteenth century Leeds was dominated economically, socially and politically by . . . [an] oligarchy of
merchants . . . closely connected with the local landed gentry . . .
Between 1806 and 1835 the merchant oligarchy of Leeds came
under both economic and political pressure . . . continuity was
broken and the oldest families dislodged from their position of
pre-eminence.' Hennock (1973, pp.179—96, 225—6) goes on to
point out that up to this time 'the occupational structure of the
council had changed little': the really striking change was in the
party complexion and religious composition.[4] However, by the
1850s 'this was no longer so'. There was a 'decline in the number
of substantial men' — a 'decline in the representation of the social
and economic elite' — and a rise in the representation of retailers:
'really small businessmen . . . In terms of business ability and of
local standing the council had reached a nadir by the second half
of the 1880's.' Powell (1958, p.145) continues the story up until
1953: 'the most marked changes in the social structure of the
council have been the decline in the membership of . . . the
businessmen, manufacturers, and shopkeepers, and the increase
in employee representation'.

Fraser (1976, pp.14, 281—3) is probably right to remind us that
for the most part the politics of official city life in the middle
decades of the nineteenth century were not 'dominated by a class
struggle between bourgeoisie and proletariat' but by a 'contest
for power within the upper middle class itself and between the

---

3 In Bristol after the Second World War those of independent means and landowners
  were no longer on the council and there was something of a split between 'political
  and civic leadership' (Political and Economic Planning, 1947, p.15). See also Clements,
  1969.
4 Fraser, 1976, p.118 makes this same point more generally across Victorian city
  politics.

urban elite and the landed gentry'.[5] Even so, he recognises that 'a coherent working class' emerged after 1880 which gave 'birth to a parallel political proletarian movement in the creation of the Labour Party' so that the 'half century beyond 1880 witnessed a fundamental change in the political process . . . [and] the very organisation of politics in late Victorian England inevitably weakened the hold of an urban elite which had for half a century dominated town politics'. We must pay particular attention, not so much to the earlier shift from a traditional elite of landed and commercial wealth to a rising class of capitalists, but to this more recent change in which 'businessmen have withdrawn to some extent from local politics' (Morris and Newton, 1970, p.111) to be replaced by representatives from the working class. In addition to the studies I have already cited, this change is also noted with respect to other local authorities. 'In the [Wolverhampton] council of 1888–9 the largest single occupational group was the manufacturers comprising 38% of the Council . . . The Council of 1962–3 bore little occupational resemblance to that of 1888–9. The manufacturers had fallen to 7% and no longer represented the leading industries of the locality' (Jones, 1969, p.106). In Newcastle-Under-Lyme 'the manufacturers, after a period of service, left . . . at about the time of the First World War' and by that time 'the "lower-middle class" had come to power' (Bealey, Blondel and McCann, 1965, pp.54, 28). In Bath, businessmen formed almost half of the council in 1938 but by 1962 they made up barely one-fifth of the total council (Green, 1968). In both Croydon and Birmingham the demise of the businessman-councillor has been less dramatic. In Croydon, council membership was 'dominated by private business' in the 1950s and 1960s (Saunders, 1978, p.7; 1975A, ch. 4). In Birmingham, businessmen comprised 41% of the council in 1862 and 33% in 1902, but by 1920 their numbers had swollen to embrace 55% of the council, and even by 1966 they still accounted for 35% of council membership (Hennock, 1973, p.34; Morris and Newton, 1970, p.113).[6] I will return to deal with the case of Birmingham

5 See also Rubinstein, 1977, and Therborn, 1977. But see Foster (1974) for a rich account of exactly this sort of struggle in nineteenth-century Oldham.

6 In Sheffield, 61% of the councillors and aldermen who held office in the years 1843–93 were manufacturers in the staple trades, professional men or brewers. In the council of 1967–8 41% of the councillors were employers, professionals or farmers and there had been a 'gradual decline in the proportion of Conservative councillors coming from business' (Pollard, 1959, p.120; Hampton, 1970, pp. 188–90).

later in this chapter. The opposite side of the coin to these developments, particularly in the large industrial cities, involves the
entry of working class representatives standing mainly in the name
of the Labour Party. Banbury is clearly not the only place where
'traditional leadership . . . from the higher occupational status
groups' is being 'challenged by the leaders of the non-traditional
workers through the trade-union and Labour movements' (Stacey,
1960, pp.36—7).

2. Calibre Lost: Explained

In order to explain these changes we need a certain sensitivity to
the economic and social history of Britain and must pay particular
attention to the implications of the Industrial Revolution for
social and political relations.

England was not an urban nation in 1700. Over three-quarters
of the population of between five and six million lived in the
countryside and most of the people earned their living by work on
the land. Power was grounded in land ownership and social
relations in the inequalities which it imposed. In the rural community the nature of work and the pattern of settlement encouraged face-to-face relationships of custom and habit. These
cemented vertical ties on the basis of an identity with ruling class
values without any need for overt organisation as a binding force
between landlords and tenants. Exploitation was both tempered
and sustained by deference from below and paternalism from
above (Williams, 1955). This resulted in a pattern of 'natural'
politics in which those of economic power (and their ideological
allies) enjoyed traditional authority restrained only by an ordered
distribution of rights and benefits which served to hold the
delicate balance in check.

Towns were small and widely distributed with most only
assuming a local trading function.[7] Even the more substantial
'manufacturing towns were as much service centres for a partially
industrial hinterland as sites of industry themselves' (Chalklin,
1974, p.7). Industry was rural rather than urban and the population
was closely connected with agriculture. The extraction of coal and
the smelting of iron demanded a certain concentration of labour

---

7 In 1700 London had a population of half a million, but the second largest city was
  Norwich and that had a population of only 30,000.

but the process was usually under the control of the owners of land and the workers themselves were close to the soil. Wool provided the material for an activity second only to agriculture in the number of people it employed and the volume of trade it supported. For the most part this trade, like many others, was carried on under the domestic system of production. Gradually, however, the independent craft worker and the small farmer working on his own materials came to lose their independence as merchants intervened, first to ease the problem of marketing, and then to supply materials and orders, thus reducing them to an employee paid on a piecework basis. This system was 'plagued by problems of irregularity of production, loss of materials in transit and through embezzlement, slowness of manufacture, lack of uniformity and uncertainty of the quality of the product', and limited by its inability to change the basic processes of production (Braverman, 1974, p.63). However, this 'early capitalist production involved immediate face-to-face contact between employer and employed' (Foster, 1974, p.25) and, as Ashton (1948, p.51) reminds us, 'relations between employers and workers are generally best when they are direct' as the possibility of labour organisation is inhibited. Overall, 'feudal society existed as a precarious balance between the advanced and the primitive' (Foster, 1974, p.15). Agricultural productivity was near stagnant. Market demand from small farmers and labourers was limited in the extreme, and although the feudal surplus was the basis of a demand for specialised products that was serviced by merchants operating out of the larger regional centres, it was never•on a scale sufficient to make for sustained investment.

'Some time in the 1780s, and for the first time in human history, the shackles were taken off the productive power of human societies' (Hobsbawm, 1973, p.43). Britain was the pioneer in industrialisation, and it has been customary to term this take-off into self-sustained growth, the Industrial Revolution. The eighteenth-century increase in population, the enclosures, and the improvements in agricultural productivity, shook people off the land and created a labour reserve that could be redeployed away from agricultural production. 'At the same time there was taking place a rapid increase of capital' (Ashton, 1948, p.7), and a number of technological advances were available. The growth of empire provided a colonial surplus and Britain succeeded in gaining a competitive edge over her continental rivals that enabled her to capture the growing world market. One thing fed on another to contribute to an upward spiral of change and growth.

No one should exaggerate the extent or pace of the changes, especially in so far as social relations and local political leadership were concerned. When we think of industrialisation then we tend to think of mass employment in large factories, but 'in 1830 "industry" and "factory" in anything like the modern sense still meant almost exclusively the cotton areas of the United Kingdom', and 'observers in the 1830s and 1840s were still exclaiming at the novelty of the "factory system"' (Hobsbawm, 1973, p.53; Thompson, 1968, p.208). A rapidly emerging class of capitalists may have recognised that effective control of production without centralisation of employment was very difficult as the gathering of workers under a single roof was a basic precondition for proper management and labour discipline. But the problem was that labour had no strong desire to submit to the rigours of the factory system and for many businesses early industrial technology hardly demanded large-scale production. Attempts to obtain adult labour for factory work often proved futile, and even in 1841 it was estimated that 60% of the workers in cotton factories were under twenty years of age. The domestic system of production continued for a long while and meshed neatly into the emerging factory system. For example, in cotton, the firm of Horrocks had 700 spinners working in factories at Preston in 1830 but an army of outworkers numbering over 6,000 who carried on their trade in isolation at home and in largely rural surroundings. Despite the survival of the old ways and the resistance to the new, agricultural employment which had absorbed 35% of the population in 1811 was absorbing only 22% in 1841, and by 1851 the distribution of the population had changed in favour of the townsman. By 1835 not far short of a quarter of a million people were employed in the weaving and spinning factories of the cotton industry; by 1851 some 1.7 million people were employed in the mechanised industries including coal; and in 1867 it was calculated that the male, adult, urban working class numbered nearly three millions (Hobson, 1926, p.385; Hammond and Hammond, 1966, p.188; Chambers, 1968, p.15; Cole, 1955, pp.55—7).

The destruction of the peasant village and the destruction of custom in industry as a result of the related expansion of an existing capitalist economy to an altogether new size meant that 'when every caution has been made, the outstanding fact of the period between 1790 and 1830 is the formation of "the working class"' (Thompson, 1968, p.212). They were faced with three possibilities: 'they could strive to become bourgeois; they could allow themselves to be ground down, or they could rebel' (Hobsbawm, 1973, p.245). There were increasing obstacles to the first course of action[8] at the same time as the possibility of their own organisation was opening up, since they were working and living alongside each other in virtual isolation from direct relationships with those above them. The centralisation of employment may have made for labour discipline and management control, but it was also the very basis of working class organisation opposed to the logic of the system itself. From 1760 onwards, the coalfields, the ports, and the textile villages were often the scenes of spontaneous uprising, but by the end of the eighteenth century trade unionism was beginning to appear as a movement, and 'for the first twenty years of the nineteenth century industrial strife was endemic' (Marshall, 1973, p.145). The Industrial Revolution placed quite new strains on the social and political system, and on the established patterns of social control and political leadership. The vertical ties built into the face-to-face rural community were weakening as personal contact between rich and poor, employer and worker, became more problematic. From the one side, 'the new type of industrial employer did not automatically accept the welfare of his employees as a personal obligation' (Simey, 1951, p.24), and from the other, the growth in working class 'self-respect and political consciousness . . . dispelled some forms of superstition and of deference and made certain kinds of oppression no longer tolerable' (Thompson, 1968, p.464). Overt organisation among economic equals together with the politics of class was taking over from the customary ties binding unequals to the politics of community. Labour was free to be conscious of its lack of freedom, and it was forced to confront the new problems of slump and unemployment which, in posing a challenge to labour, also challenged the credibility of the system and those who were at its helm.

Of course, the effect of economic change on working class

---

8 For example, in 1845 it was estimated that the fixed capital of a well-appointed English cotton mill worked out to be about two years' wages of an operative, but by 1890 it was estimated that the plant employed amounted to about five years' wages for every man, woman or child employed (Hobson, 1926, p.117).

organisation and hence on social structure and political relations was variable and the immediate social effect of the Industrial Revolution was to make cities not more, but less, alike (Cornford, 1963, p.62). The old type of social structure did not suddenly break up; it did not break up everywhere; and the precise timing of its essential breakdown in any one locality was dependent on a variety of circumstances.

Obviously, an upheaval in the politics of deference and in established patterns of local political leadership was very much less apparent in rural society.[9] But in the more industrialised areas of the country the establishment of the politics of class seems to have depended not just on the scale and extent of factory enterprise, but on patterns of ownership and management as well.

Cobden pointed out that

> in Birmingham where a manufacturer employs his three or four hands and sometimes but an apprentice or two, there is much more cordial and united feeling among the two classes. In fact the social steps connecting one class with another are so gradual that instead of the great gulf which separates masters and workmen in Stockport or Manchester it is difficult to know where the line which divides the two is to be found.   (cited in Fraser, 1976, p.20)

(See also Engels, 1892, pp.235—6.) Briggs (1952, p.297; 1950, p.71) has put this to the test, for he sought to 'examine more closely social relationships and political leadership in Birmingham, Manchester, and Leeds, and their effect upon the politics of reform' in the period 1830—2. He found that the social structure of Birmingham, grounded as it was on small workshops, small masters, and social mobility, 'made for middle class co-operation with the working classes' in a way that was not possible in the other two cities which were dominated by the factory system and by cleavage social separation, and open class antagonisms. Victorian London was 'a city virtually without a factory proletariat'. It was a city in which small-scale production was carried on in the small workshop or the home 'and the relative absence of the factory meant that the social character of London's industrial population was highly individual' (Jones, 1971, pp.337, 31). 'London was never a trade union stronghold' (Thompson, 1967, p.39). Mid-nineteenth-century Oldham stood in stark contrast to this, for in

9 In South Devon in the 1950s there was a 'very small number of skilled and manual workers prepared to stand for election, due almost entirely to the problem of traditional legitimacy . . . ; despite the legal right there is no belief in a social right to stand for election' (Mitchell, 1951, p.398).

that cotton town twelve thousand worker families sold their labour to seventy capitalist families. Until patterns of class collaboration set in in the 1840s, social relations were characterised by antagonism and conflict. Indeed 'within only a decade of building their first factories Oldham's employers had been forced to put on army uniforms and use their sabres' (Foster, 1974, p.34).

The location of ownership and the related conduct of management was also a factor that had a crucial bearing on the breakdown of traditional patterns of social relations and control. For example, in South West Wales,

> even as late as 1923 most of the collieries were one-company or one-family concerns, but in the space of a very few years the organisation of the industry was altered. This meant the immediate breaking up of the old-fashioned paternal pattern and its replacement by an impersonal and alien organisation. The previously fairly harmonious relations between miners and owners came to an end and henceforth miners had to deal with a manager whose power was limited. Older miners who remembered the change suggested to us that, among other things, it meant that difficulties could now quite reasonably be 'blamed on the boss' . . . These changes are clearly likely to have had an effect on the attitude of local politically minded workers . . . The class conflict seemed more obvious, especially as the employer was no longer a local man and could therefore be more easily denounced.

It was at this point that the 'organised working class began to take over control of local affairs . . . [although] in some cases it was not until the late 1930s and even the 1940s, that some of the local councils had a labour majority' (Brennan, Cooney, and Pollins, 1954A, pp.149—54). The implications of local ownership have been brought out by Birch (1959, pp.34, 20—2) in the case of Glossop, where in the nineteenth century 'the real rulers of the town were the industrialists' who owned the cotton mills, lived in the locality, and enjoyed a 'paternal relationship to the town . . . The workers themselves seem for the most part to have accepted the leadership of their employers . . . Their relations with their employers seem to have been exceptionally good . . . Antagonisms in Glossop were not between classes but between rival religious groups, representing complete vertical sections through the class structure.'

Notwithstanding the importance of factory size and ownership, the making of manufactured goods for a mass market did not just make the English working class: it made them *politically*. It was only a matter of time before they would demand a change in the rules of the political game to enable them to gain access to, and control over, positions of governmental power at both the national and the local level (Therborn, 1977). Equally, it was only a matter of time before such changes would be granted in the hope of ensuring the political incorporation of that class (Moorhouse, 1973).

The statutes affecting the local government franchise are to be numbered in scores, but almost until the end of Queen Victoria's reign no person was entitled to vote 'unless he made some direct contribution to the funds which the local authority administered' (Keith-Lucas, 1952, p.221). In the years after 1835 rating authorities did not usually trouble to rate the smaller houses, and if they did then they usually resorted to compounding — levying a rate on the owner who then recouped it from his tenants who (because they did not pay in law) did not have the vote. The Municipal Franchise Act of 1869 qualified these compounding occupiers for the franchise and greatly increased the municipal electorate.[10]

> Many people expected that it would result in a sudden increase in
> expenditure, particularly in sanitary improvements in the towns,
> where the poor lived in such deplorable conditions . . . [In fact]
> there was little such demand on the part of the newly enfranchised
> labourers. Their failure to take advantage of their new powers in
> this way may be attributed to three main causes: their ignorance;
> their fear of their landlords in an age when voting was not secret . . . ;
> and the survival of high property qualifications for councillors
> which prevented labourers themselves standing for election to the
> councils.   (Keith-Lucas, 1952, p.225)

It was not until 1882 that the property qualification was abolished. Even then, 'would-be working men town councillors found themselves hampered in that most of the council committee meetings were held in the morning and afternoon' (Chaloner, 1950, 166). In addition, the principle of the unpaid council representative helped to ensure a continued '"distortion" of the membership of authorities', as was recognised by the Interdepartmental Committee on Expenses for Members of Local Authorities as late as 1947 (p.23), when it was 'persuaded that at the present time there are

---

10 The increase should not be exaggerated. In 1871 the municipal electorate was not
more than 19% of the population in Birmingham, Maidstone, Ipswich, or Leeds
(Hennock, 1973, p.12).

suitable and keen persons who cannot without hardship become members of local authorities'.[11]

Nineteenth-century observers may have been anxious as to the implications of electoral reform for the calibre of councillors and the extent of local taxation, but these other obstacles to working class representation helped to hold back any 'decline'. In 1903, Redlich (vol.1, p.278) pointed out that

> when the franchise was extended lower and lower down the social scale, until it practically embraced the whole community, and gave the working classes a potential control over municipal as well as Parliamentary elections, democracy was not found to have deprived the upper classes of political leadership . . . [I]t is difficult . . . to point to a single important case (West Ham excepted) in which municipal administration is controlled by representatives who are themselves working men.

When local working class representation did eventually occur it was common to explain it by pointing to the 'indifference to local government among the highest classes' (Brodrick, 1875, p.71) who were said to be 'deterred' from involvement by 'the nauseating incidents of an electoral campaign' (Ostrogorski, 1902, vol.1, p.490) and by the fact that a seat on the local council was no longer a highly valued prize. The truth of the matter is that these explanations fail to recognise the most fundamental development of late-nineteenth-century politics; that 'with the extension of the suffrage class was becoming the most important single factor in deciding political allegiance' (Cornford, 1963, p.37; see also, Rubinstein, 1977, p.124). The working class through the Labour Party did much to 'push businessmen off the council' (Morris and Newton, 1970, p.122). In Crewe the first Labour town councillor took his seat in 1902, and in Wolverhampton 'the growth of labour representation on the council is due largely to the extension of the franchise in 1918' (Jones, 1969, p.58). In London in the 1880s and 1890s labour emerged 'as a new political force, supported by an extended trade unionism, and capable of winning elections for either liberals or socialists'. In the 1919 local elections Labour secured control of half the Metropolitan Borough Councils, and by 1934 had captured the London County Council (Thompson, 1967, pp.110, 286). In Leeds in 1902 'the representation of the working class had still been of insignificant proportions and

---

11 On the implications of unpaid work for council composition, see Laski, 1950, p.416; Webb and Webb, 1920, p.212.

channelled through the Liberal Party [but] by 1912 one council
member in ten was a manual worker or trade union official . . .
and . . . they belonged with one exception to the Labour Party'
(Hennock, 1973, p.270). The history of most large urban local
authorities in the period 1880—1920 would be a history of 'the
"gentlemen" . . . being crowded out and the working men . . .
coming in' (Howe, 1907, p.35), aided and abetted by the rise of
the Labour Party.

3. City Growth and Residential Segregation

So far my explanation for changes in council composition has
tended to dwell on the implications of economic change. This is
not enough. An inextricable aspect of these changes was the
increase in population and its redistribution within the country.
The centralisation of employment inevitably meant a changed
pattern of settlement. It meant rural depopulation and a drift to
the rising centres of manufacture; it meant urbanisation; and it
meant city growth. Cities were both creating, and being created
by, the new class society: they were 'the instrument of bourgeois
power and the potential instrument of the proletariat' (Harris,
1974, p.353). In 1801 the population of England and Wales was
nine millions and 17% lived in towns of over twenty thousand. A
hundred years later the population stood at 32½ millions and over
50% of the population were town dwellers. The rate of city
growth was staggering, but (and more important) patterns of
settlement were changing *within* the built up areas. It is these
changes that are of particular significance for the boundary
problem. They are at the heart of the concern about local government areas no longer corresponding to the pattern of life and work
in England, and they have aggravated — and are seen to have
aggravated — the problem of declining councillor calibre.

Pre-industrial cities tended to be small and 'class organisation of
city space was not so obvious as it is in urban areas today' (Vance,
1971, p.106). Medieval borough society was characterised by the
outward tide of the gentry, but the practice of the gentry settling
in the towns was growing in the sixteenth century (Platt, 1976,
p.189). In so far as social segregation existed then there tended to
be a wealthy and exclusive central core — a mercantile quarter —
that was ringed by the populous suburbs which served as 'reception

centres for the urban poor' (Langton, 1975; Sjoberg, 1960; Dyos, 1961, p.36). In the industrial city of the early nineteenth century, patterns of settlement were fluid. 'Workplaces and residential areas tended to be intermingled' (Hall *et al.*, 1973, vol.1, p.75; see also Rathbone, 1905, p.56). Both people *and* jobs were tending to centralise. The social controls built into the face-to-face relationships between employers and employees were reinforced in the residential patterns where there was an absence of any geographical gulf between rich and poor. This situation was not to last as the conditions that made for the informal influence of property and social status through personal knowledge and contact were being eroded in the cities.

In Leicester, 'as early as the 1780s . . . there had been a trend for the homes and workplaces of business and professional people to become separated' (Pritchard, 1976, p.43). The sheer pace of city growth led to overcrowding and to a deterioration in urban conditions as was revealed in the housing and sanitary inquiries of the 1840s. Even the rich and the powerful were unable to maintain conditions in the centre of the city where they had traditionally lived and they deserted them for new dwellings on the edge of town. 'Eighteenth century London had been a tangled mixture. Fashionable squares and aristocratic town houses jostled up against overcrowded slum tenements, sharing the same epidemics, the same polluted water and insanitary drainage' (Thompson, 1967, p.7). Nineteenth-century London was a very different place.

> The social distance between rich and poor expressed itself in ever sharper geographical segregation of the city. Merchants and employers no longer lived above their places of work . . . The beginnings of the middle class migration to the new suburbs had been recorded in the middle of the eighteenth century. But . . . it was insignificant beside the massive and unprecedented growth of the suburbs in the last two thirds of the nineteenth century.
>
> (Jones, 1971, pp.13, 159)

In Liverpool 'those who could afford to do so, moved from the neighbourhood of such squalor . . . As fast as homes elsewhere could be built for them, the merchant aristocracy withdrew from the river side' (Simey, 1951, p.11). Of sixty-six Sheffield attorneys in 1841, forty-one lived in the country, and ten of the remaining twenty-five were newcomers to the town (Thompson, 1968, p.355). Only 10% of the people listed in the 'court' section of the 1870 Leicester directory lived in parts of the city built before

1800; a third lived in high quality suburban housing; and a quarter lived right outside the built-up area with half of these living beyond the inner ring of suburban settlements in truly rural areas of the county (Pritchard, 1976, p.45). In Manchester 'the influx of industry made the centre of the city a less attractive place in which to live. By 1830 the leading citizens were moving out to the suburbs and converting their erstwhile residences into warehouses' (Marshall, 1973, p.34). This process of residential segregation may have been carried further in London than elsewhere since 'by 1861 it was practically complete' (Jones, 1971, p.247), but the more general history of nineteenth-century city growth is a history of expanding suburbs for the middle and upper classes and growing overcrowding for the working class in central city slums.

Even in the early nineteenth century the rapid increase in the size of towns 'amazed and alarmed politicians and administrators . . . [who] were afraid of large masses of people over whom they could at best administer a distant control' (Briggs, 1950, p.67). The situation could only get worse. As class divisions were reinforced by geographical divisions there were sown the seeds of a process of social disintegration. The growing isolation of the poor was 'a theme which ran like a crimson thread through so many Victorian social commentaries' (Dyos, 1961, p.25; see, for example, Masterman, 1910, esp. ch. 3). Life in the town no longer resembled that in a rural community. It may just have been possible for employers to retain elements of the old face-to-face social relations in their expanding factories, but this was becoming increasingly problematic at the same time as such relationships were no longer being sustained by the emerging pattern of residential settlement. The cement of deference, paternalism, order, custom, habit, and tradition no longer held social classes together in large cities. Engels (1892, pp.161—2) reminds us that 'the great cities are the birthplaces of labour movements'. Without 'manufacture on a grand scale *and* in great cities' it was possible for the employer under 'old conditions' to secure against revolt by 'bestowing a trifle of patronising friendliness'. Cities had a 'forcing influence upon the popular intelligence'; they broke the 'sentimental bond' between employer and employee and so 'destroyed the last remnant of the patriarchal relation between working men and employers'.

The significance of new settlement patterns was well recognised by those in control of society. New techniques were needed to bind class to class in a fierce commitment to the emerging economic order. Charity was one of the 'efforts of the rich to bridge the gulf between themselves and their fellow citizens' (Simey, 1951, p.18; Jones, 1971, pp.241–61; Engels, 1892, pp.314–15); settlements were another (Barnett, 1921, esp. p.153); religion was not without its significance; and we should not forget the development of policing. In the context of my concern, however, we must recognise that the extension of the franchise and the democratisation of local government were also regarded as of importance for the process of societal re-integration. The President of the Local Government Board told the House when he introduced the Local Government (England and Wales) Bill in 1893 that he believed that the institutions of local democracy 'are not only good for the purposes for which they are devised but are good for the state' since they would serve to educate and socialise the public into an acceptance of the established configuration of power.[12]

The problem was, however, that local government was being democratised at a time when the classes were pulling apart socially *and* geographically, and when there was an increasing problem of control and cohesion. This was bound to have quite profound implications for the control of local government. In fact in 1900, 'Exeter, still a small city, was yet becoming too large for the old social influences to be effective. The growth in the size of the city, *which coincided with a change in the composition of the council* was remarked on, and often lamented by contemporaries' (Newton, 1968, p.313, my italics). This problem was much more acute in the *centres* of the major built-up areas. The central city was the home of the working class, and although it was the centre of business activity and employment it was no longer the place in which the gentry and employers chose to live. Those who continued to hold property in the central area were entitled to vote and to stand for election even if they no longer lived there. But this was hardly enough to retain governmental control in business hands, since the growing middle class were *also* moving out, but (unlike the businessman) they left no property behind and so were

---

12 See also Brodrick, 1875, pp.94–5. For a more recent statement see Warren, 1957, p.12.

denied the right to vote in his support.[13] Put in the orthodox language, local government areas did not correspond to the pattern of life and work in England, and there was the problem of declining councillor calibre.

4. Residential Segregation, Outdated Boundaries, and Councillor Calibre

Nowadays we are all aware of these broad patterns of residential settlement in cities.[14] Advocates of larger local authorities have gone further and looked at these patterns in relation to the established boundaries of local authorities, recognising that, taken together, they have implications for the class control of local government in the central cities.

In the late 1850s serious concern first began to be expressed about 'the alleged deterioration of local administration in the East End and other poor areas. The exodus of the wealthy from the East End had left the vestries and local boards in the hands of small property owners, contractors, and tradesmen' (Jones, 1971, pp.247–8). Certainly Brodrick (1875, pp.71–80) felt able to point to 'districts in the Metropolis where petty tradespeople predominate in the local constituencies and absolutely rule the vestries unchecked by any resident gentry'. He deplored the 'indifference to local government among the highest classes', noting how 'the merchant princes of the city, and the richest capitalists in the manufacturing towns . . . find a far more complete justification in the colossal questions of trade and in the management of country estates far removed from their place of business'. In a similar way, Lady Chorley (1950, p.139) has described how the well-to-do businessmen moved out of Manchester to the exclusive suburb of Alderley Edge so depriving the city of many vigorous and capable leaders who had been active in the political life of the city. 'The city became the place they worked in by day and abandoned in the evening as quickly as might be . . . The city was no longer the centre of their cultural lives and . . . they tended to withdraw their services from the city council.' Robson (1972, pp.122, 89–90) has bemoaned 'the difficulty of finding men and women of high mental and moral calibre who are willing to serve

---

13 For a recognition of the implications of this movement for the control of local government in core cities, see Sharpe, 1966, p.149.
14 For more recent research see, Hall *et al.*, 1973, and Rex and Moore, 1967.

on the city council', and he had no doubt that

> the most important factor in our view is the inadequacy of the
> local government institutions in metropolitan areas. Nowhere do the
> local authorities correspond to the social, economic and political
> realities of the area . . . If a proper system of metropolitan govern-
> ment were introduced, the Alderley Edges would become part of
> the Greater Manchesters to which they belong, and the 'moving
> out' process would not necessarily produce such unfortunate results.

E. D. Simon would have agreed with this since he was keenly alive
to the implications of middle class suburban growth for the control
of local government in Manchester, noting how

> our most successful citizens quite naturally go out to live in beautiful
> surroundings in Cheshire, and so, as regards their homes, are lost to
> the city. I suggest that we ought to follow the example of Birming-
> ham which recently extended its area. We should in this way keep
> our best businessmen who have many of the qualities most needed
> in public life as full citizens.   (cited in Hennock, 1973, p.323)

(See also, Simon, 1938, pp.399–405.) In fact the creation of
Greater Birmingham in 1911 did *not* lead to an increase in the
percentage of big businessmen on the city council, but the 'inclusion of areas with a social structure different from that of the
central area and with their own established patterns of local
politics and representation naturally produced a city council
that was not merely the old one writ large'. Hennock (1973,
pp.39–51) points to two changes. First, 'the percentage of small
businessmen rose . . . [and] this change was entirely the consequence of boundary extension. In the old wards the proportion
had remained the same; in the new wards it was as high as 25.5%.'
Second, the extension had the effect of watering down the rising
representation of the working class on the council. Figures for
1892 and 1912 show the presence of working men to have risen
by no more than 0.6%, but this 'is an occasion where the boundary
extension masks the real change that occurred. In the area of the
pre 1911 city the percentage was 10.8 which shows a much more
substantial rise.' Notwithstanding rising working class representation, businessmen have continued to make up a large proportion
of the Birmingham council, and this has to be partly explained by
the fact that the city 'is unique in that it has preserved an exclusively high class residential area in the very heart of the city and
it is not at all surprising that many businessmen on the council
live in this area' (Morris and Newton, 1970, p.121).

Official committees concerned with the boundary problem have
been keenly alive to the implications of 'outdated boundaries'

for councillor calibre. The Local Government Commission for England in their report on the West Midlands Special Review Area (1961, p.19) pointed out that

> the county boroughs, representing the main urban centres are losing population to the peripheral areas . . . As a result, the county boroughs, as well as other authorities in the heart of the conurbation are beginning to lose variety in the social and economic make-up of their populations. This is bad for the vigour of local government and reduces the supply of voluntary leadership of all kinds. It means that the larger authorities have difficulty in finding councillors of sufficient calibre to make the best use of the authority's potentialities, while first-class people who have moved to the outer areas either take no interest in local government or find themselves, as members of the smaller authorities, with too little scope for their abilities.

The Commission were also well aware that the calibre of councillors had implications for council policy since they pointed out that the 'Black Country . . . is notably poor in the amenities of civilised living', and they explained this by saying that 'many of the people most likely to be interested in such things have no say in their provision, because as electors they are cut off by meaningless administrative boundaries from the main civic centres in which such provision should be made'. In a later report on the York and North Midlands General Review Area (1964A, para. 16—26), the Commission recognised that those who moved out from the major urban centres were 'the younger families' and 'the more prosperous sections of the community'. In the Commission's view,

> there must be something wrong in a process which gradually sorts out the more prosperous and younger families into one local government camp and leaves the less prosperous and older in the other camp. As long as this goes on local government is helping to build up rather than diminish social distinctions, or rather it reinforces them by its own divisions, and takes away the opportunity for different sorts of people to talk together and share a responsibility for services to the community.

Contemporary business groups[15] and their spokesmen have echoed all these sentiments. After a quick reference to the inadequate 'standard' or 'calibre' of local authority representatives

15 All references in the following section, unless otherwise stated, are taken from the *Written Evidence of Commercial, Industrial and Political Organisations* to the Royal Commission on Local Government in England (1969). See also Committee of Inquiry into Local Government Finance (1976), Appendix 4; and Royal Commission on Local Government in Scotland, 1969, *Written Evidence* 9.

they warm to their theme and point out that 'local councils only attract members from a limited section of the community and lack sufficient representation from industry and the professions' (CBI, p.71). The British Iron and Steel Federation went so far as to advise the Redcliffe-Maud Commission that 'industry and commerce have no voice in local affairs' (p.38). Sherman (1970, pp.4, 6) talks of a situation in which industry enjoys local 'taxation without representation' as its

> representation has been whittled down. First, came the post-war abolition of the business vote which allowed the business ratepayer a voice in how his rates were to be spent. Now, the latest Representation of the People Act denies citizens the right to serve as councillors in authorities where they work and bring prosperity. The result is to preclude most of the men who own and manage industry from any direct say in administration and expenditure of authorities where it is situated.

In effect, 'the lack of balance in council composition' is a specific commentary on a situation in which '*big* business above all is conspicuous by its absence . . . [as] managers, executives, directors — except in small family firms — are a rarity in the Council chamber' (Freeman, 1976, p.27). Aims of Industry's evidence to the Royal Commission on Local Government in England was alive to the boundary problem aggravating this state of affairs:

> Given the present pattern of local authority boundaries and social structure in England, industry's directors and executives rarely live in local authorities where industry is situated, and are even more rarely represented on these authorities. As a general rule, the large and medium county and municipal boroughs, London Boroughs and urban district councils where industry is sited and the few county councils of predominantly industrial counties tend to be controlled by the Labour Party. Conversely, where industrial management is represented — or has the opportunity of being represented — in local government, it is usually in residential areas, mainly county districts (or London Boroughs) with little or no industry. The result is that industry goes without adequate representation locally.
>
> (p.6)

The party political implications of outdated boundaries have not escaped the attention of politicians. When Richard Crossman was Minister of Housing and Local Government he had to decide the fate of the proposals for local government boundaries being made to him by the Local Government Commissions. He reported in his diary:

> I soon discovered that as a Labour politician these are for me not merely decisions about the boundaries of local authorities but decisions

which will influence the boundaries of constituencies . . . every
time . . . I alter a county borough boundary I may affect the fate
of the M.P. sitting for this borough . . . Politically all I have to do
is prevent 30 or 40 Labour seats going to the Tories.

The general problem which Crossman faced was simple: 'how I can
best adjudicate to avoid bringing Conservative suburbs into Labour
cities like Leicester and Nottingham and so undermining safe
Labour Parliamentary seats' and giving a built in majority to the
Conservatives on the new local councils. Naturally enough, Crossman did not broadcast the fact that when taking boundary
decisions he took 'the greatest care to see that politically they
were acceptable to the Labour group[s] on the town council[s]
and to the Labour member[s]' (Crossman, 1975, pp.64–5, 132;
175–6, 160, 240, 312). Party political concerns were also caught
up in the reorganisation of London Government.

> The Labour Party enjoyed a virtual monopoly over central London
> politics . . . The Conservatives, on the other hand, possessed their
> greatest strength outside London County . . . When these two facts
> are lumped together, it stands to reason that the Labour Party would
> be inclined to take a very dim view of any metropolitan reorgan-
> isation plan that threatened to amalgamate the suburban forces of
> Conservatism with its very reliable central stronghold of socialism
> . . . The London Labour Party was flatly opposed to any reform
> that would lead to the abolition of its local political prize, the LCC,
> and dilute its central area strength in a sea of Conservative suburban
> votes.   (Smallwood, 1965, pp.95–103)

Henry Brooke had been leader of the Conservative opposition on
the LCC and as Minister of Housing and Local Government 'he
was anxious to see the Herbert Commission's proposals adopted
primarily for the political advantage that he saw in them of putting
an end to Labour's control of London' (Rhodes, 1970, p.108).
    Simply expressed, the fact of residential segregation means that
local authority boundaries have implications both for councillor
calibre and for party control, and hence for the very direction and
scope of local government itself.

5. Calibre Regained

The situation in which the rules of the political game give one man
one vote place a limit on the extent to which councillor calibre
can be increased. Not surprisingly, therefore, there has long been
hostility to elections, especially if political parties are involved
(Hasluck, 1936, p.35; Hennock, 1973, p.13; Warren, 1952, p.187;

Keith-Lucas, 1961, p.8). More modestly, however, the National
Chamber of Trade argued that

> consideration should be given to the question of the franchise in
> local government elections . . . Local business has a most important
> place in every local community and we are of the opinion that the
> fact is to be deplored that in many cases, because shops or other
> premises are occupied by limited companies, the 'High Street' has
> no vote. This is probably a . . . contributory factor to the poverty
> of quality of many local councils . . . Provision should be made for
> the directors of a limited company . . . to vote in local elections.
> (p.145)[16]

The qualifications, or rules, for election on to a local authority
are also of significance. The Committee on the Management of
Local Government (1967, vol.1, p.120) recommended 'an additional alternative qualification for election to a local authority,
namely that the person should have had a principal place of work
within the area of the authority during the whole of the twelve
months preceding the election'.[17] Changes of this kind have been
specifically designed to increase councillor calibre, but they have
been seen as inadequate in the face of the 'problem', and business
groups have often urged more direct representation of their
interest. Aims of Industry felt that 'given the present politicisation
of local government, the only way to end industry's isolation from
local decision-making and administration would be to introduce
an element of bi-cameralism' (p.7). The Confederation of British
Industry suggested that provision should be made for the 'inclusion
of co-opted, or nominated representatives, from industry';[18] and
the Association of British Chambers of Commerce thought that
'the Royal Commission should give some very definite lead which
would cause local authorities to accept, as a matter of course,
consultation with their local chamber of commerce or other
representative body, and to co-opt nominees of such bodies to
their committees far more frequently than they do at present'
(pp.70, 22). Proposals have been put forward to reorganise the
structures and processes of decision within local authorities and
these will be considered in Chapter 8. But here it is important for
us to recognise that business groups have been part of that tide of

---

16 Unless otherwise stated all page references are from Royal Commission on Local
   Government in England, 1969, *Written Evidence of Commercial, Industrial and
   Political Organisations.*
17 See also Manchester Chamber of Commerce, p.138.
18 See also Green, 1959, p.249.

opinion which has pointed to the advantage of larger local authorities securing the services of better calibre councillors.

The strategy of manipulating the boundaries of local authorities to increase councillor calibre is made up of two strands. First, an increase in size is seen as leading to an increase in the scope and responsibility of local government which will make the position of councillor more attractive to businessmen. Hennock (1973, p.322) has recognised that 'the view that to attract good men to the council was to increase the scope of its work was indeed a central belief of the Birmingham School. By 1890 the emphasis which had originated in Birmingham had become something like orthodoxy.' Nearer to the present time, Sharp (1962, p.383) has pointed out that 'the areas and status of local authorities are often today too cramped or too small to enable a satisfactory job to be done'.[19] The second aspect of the strategy is grounded in a realistic appreciation of patterns of settlement in the major built-up areas and recognises that the middle classes who live in the suburbs are disenfranchised from formal and direct participation in the politics of the economically important central city.

It was hardly surprising that as soon as the proposals of the Redcliffe-Maud commission were published all party headquarters 'immediately' engaged in the exercise of weighing up the 'chance of taking political control of . . . [the] proposed new authorities', and the Conservative's Local Government Act of 1972 naturally 'treated Conservative strongholds favourably' (Wood, 1976, pp.55, 113), so that it was dubbed by *New Society* (18 February 1971, p.259) as 'a pure political carve up, devoid of all justification in terms of social geography or of good planning'.

Steed (1969, pp.951–2) considered that if 'Maud is implemented by 1974, most authorities involved in mergers will be Conservative-inclined if not Conservative controlled'. *The Economist* (24 March 1973, p.17) calculated that the new metropolitan counties would all go Labour in the 1973 election, as was indeed the case. However, although Labour was, for example, the beneficiary from the creation of Greater Manchester, Clark (1973, p.130) makes the

19 For similar views, see also Eversley, 1974, pp.250–2; Royal Commission on London Government, 1923, p.18; Royal Commission on Local Government in Greater London, 1960, p.63; Fordham, 1911, p.406; Bunce, 1882; Brodrick, 1875; Royal Commission on the Distribution of the Industrial Population, 1940, p.182; Clarke, 1939, p.181; Wells, 1903, p.407; Royal Commission on Local Government in England, 1969, *Written Evidence of the Ministry of Housing and Local Government*, p.73.

point that 'in one respect both parties benefit . . . [as] far more of Greater Manchester at both district and county level can look forward to changes of control between the parties which is surely a good thing for healthy local democracy'. On a more general basis Steed (1969, p.952) agreed, as he also recognised that 'by creating areas which are rather more functionally united, but socially heterogenous, the Maud structure will mean that there are fewer councils in England which are politically and socially unbalanced'. Put in more political language they are saying that larger local authorities embracing city and suburb reduce the unfettered control which working class voters and Labour dominated councils can have over the affairs of the central city, as they are now in less of a position to enjoy a monopoly of power and a continuity of rule. Moreover, their point that *both* parties benefit is perhaps better expressed by saying that the credibility of the *system* as a whole is strengthened as the practice of local party government is dragged more into line with its legitimising competitive ideal.

Notwithstanding these assessments, we desperately need fuller research on the party political implications of larger local authorities,[20] and given the spatial dimension of the problem and its connection with social geography, this is clearly a field of research which could be best covered by political geographers. So far 'local elections have received relatively little attention . . . and practically no survey work has been undertaken by electoral geographers in the United Kingdom' (Busteed, 1975, p.54). Useful examples of this mode of research are however available,[21] and it is to be hoped that some of the best of it could be replicated with respect to the local British situation precisely because it links facts of social geography to party control of government and thence on to the implications of all this for the way in which policy issues are decided.

In addition we also need research on the implications of the larger local authorities for the class composition of the new

20 Jones' (1969, p.59) study of boundary extensions in Wolverhampton in 1926 and 1932 does, however, point to the party political implications of such change. See also Dyos, 1961, p.24.
21 See, for example, Prescott, 1972; Rowley, 1971; Cox, 1968, 1973; and especially Kasperson, 1965, 1969. For studies of geography and voting which are of particular significance to late-nineteenth-century British cities, see Thompson, 1967, appendix A; Pelling, 1967; Cornford, 1963; Fraser, 1976, p.217. See also Shepherd, Westaway and Lee, 1974, esp. p.106.

councils. Gyford (1976, pp.26—7) points out that

> the experience of local government reorganisation in Greater London
> in the 1960s may be something of a guide to what happens when
> local authorities are recast into larger units. Thus the councillors
> elected to the new London Borough of Camden in 1964 contained
> a higher proportion of owner-occupiers, professional men, and those
> with some further education, than did the membership of the
> smaller outgoing Metropolitan Borough Councils. This would suggest,
> albeit tentatively, that the introduction of larger authorities may
> lead to increasing representation on the council of the professional
> middle class and skilled working class at the expense of other groups
> in the community.[22]

Maybe we should not make too much of this, but Morris and
Newton's (1970, p.122) 'data also suggest a relationship between
city size and the involvement of businessmen in decision making
. . . It is not surprising that larger cities tend to attract to their
decision-making body businessmen of greater wealth and status
than smaller cities.' Hill (1974, p.213) had no doubt that the new
'metropolitan counties are likely to attract younger, better educated, more middle class members more interested in policy,
"management" and the long-term issues. Working class representation at this level will be reduced . . . Outside the metropolitan
areas similar middle class trends may be expected due to the
problem of travel, day time meetings and committee time.'
Jennings' (1975, p.22) study of the changes in council composition
that took place with reorganisation in three shire counties in
England paints a picture very much in accord with the hopes and
expectations of those concerned about declining councillor
calibre:

> the membership of these county councils changed dramatically at
> the 1973 . . . elections . . . Not only did the age range change but the
> type of people coming onto these three local governments also
> changed. Many new councillors can be described much as the chief
> executive in the rural county noted, 'middle class, young executives
> and small businessmen, much more interested in local government
> and much more management oriented'.

6. Concluding Remarks

The concern about declining councillor calibre embodies a bitter
lament that a variety of changes have conspired to result in a

---

22 See Wistrich, 1972, pp.68ff; Rhodes, 1972, pp.470—1; Cockburn, 1977, p.6.

situation in which there is now a less close and direct relationship between economic power, social status, and the political control of local government than was once the case in the Victorian age when local government enjoyed the leadership of businessmen and local notables. Business groups consider that in some places 'decline' has reached such a pitch that local political power has become almost totally divorced from economic power and may even be working against its interest. Moreover, the fact that declining calibre is seen as inextricably linked to the extension of the franchise and the rise of the Labour Party helps to give real political meaning and substance to the anti-party politics sentiment and highlights the entrenchment of anti-democratic thought within the British tradition. In effect, the concern to increase calibre embodies a concern to recapture the social relations, style of politics, and class of leadership, that existed before the franchise was extended and before the working class rose to some sort of position of local political power through the Labour Party. At best there is a romantic desire to recapture some idealised form of conflict-free deferential democracy (Rees and Smith, 1964, p.113); at worst an overt intent to reset local governmental power once again directly on top of economic power.

Larger units of local government are about more than the simple pursuit of efficiency and economy, and they should not be criticised on the strength of a simple logic which sees their size as a threat to local democracy. They must be understood in the context of a struggle to control public power. They must be assessed in terms of their implications for who can control that power and to whose advantage, and attention should also centre on the implications of any change for the legitimacy and support of that rule.

Appendix 1
Metropolitan Reorganisation in America

In America, as in Britain, 'the consolidation of metropolitan area governments is widely advocated on the premise that it will reduce per capita expenditures on local government services' (Hirsch, 1959, p.232). Similarly, American advocates of larger areas have operated on the 'presumption . . . that the case for larger political structures is obvious and overpowering' and so, in consequence, 'what is usually absent is any quantification of the purported economies foregone and/or the public quality presumably sacrificed by retaining fragmented local government' (Thompson, 1965, p.257). American economists have now done a massive amount of work on cost functions in local public services, and Richardson (1972, p.197) has concluded that 'generally . . . there are no significant scale economies in public services'. Dahl (1967, p.966) is more cautious: he is prepared to recognise that there are a 'few items on which increasing size does lead to decreasing unit costs', but he goes on to note that these 'are too small a proportion of total . . . outlays to lead to significant economies; and even these reductions are probably offset by rising costs for other services'. Hirsch (1959, pp.232, 241) suggests that 'economic efficiency may be highest in medium sized communities of 50,000 to 100,000 inhabitants'. More important, he recognises that although the case for metropolitan government can be based on arguments other than those which centre on efficiency and economy, 'nevertheless it seems fair to say that in the past the economy argument has been used more frequently and forcefully than any of the others'. He goes on: 'Could it have been used in error?'

From a rather different tack, in America, as in Britain, there has long been the idea that the structures of local government, although adequate for the 'simpler needs of earlier times', are no longer in this position because they have failed to keep pace with social and economic change (Committee for Economic Development, 1966, p.8). In particular, it is usually pointed out that although the metropolitan area is a 'social, economic, and sometimes physical unit . . . Politically . . . it is not a unit, for the city and its suburbs are usually organised as separate political entities' (Studenski, 1930, p.7; Jones, 1942). The existence of many small local authorities was seen as making for weakness and 'inefficiency' (Fesler, 1949, p.133). Larger units of government were needed in order to overcome the 'fragmentation' of governmental authority (Anderson, 1945, pp.45–6; Campbell and Sacks, 1964). As a recent textbook on metropolitan politics has put it:

> prior to the sixties metropolitan experts . . . agreed almost unani-
> mously that the decentralised political system was the basic cause
> of many urban inadequacies and a critical hindrance to the solution
> of all the problems associated with growth and change. The metro-
> polis, argued the metropolitan reformers, was a socioeconomic com-
> munity lacking an inclusive set of political institutions . . . The
> inadequacy of the structure of government, then, was *the* metro-
> politan problem.   (Danielson, 1971, pp.247–8, italics in original)

Just as in Britain, 'the problem was simple: too many governments. The solution was equally simple: metropolitan government' (Herman, 1963, p.16).

The trouble with all this is that 'most research on metropolitan area government has been reform-oriented, and undertaken to solve problems rather than to study government per se. This framework has tended to place major emphasis upon what government should be rather than upon what exists and how it works' (Warren, 1966, p.35). An eager academic preparedness to operate within the confines of this perspective has inhibited the provision of a political understanding of the government and political economy of metropolitan areas, and has rendered irrelevant the concern to develop a critical and political perspective on the struggle to overcome fragmentation through metropolitan-wide government. The limitations of this reformist orientation are now well-recognised in America. A literature has developed which has not only explored the support and opposition for the reorganisation of metropolitan government, but has also sought to assess the political intent behind it, and the likely winners and losers from its successful introduction.

In Chapter 8, I will discuss the leading role played by business groups in promoting the reorganisation of city government around the turn of this century. In the context of my present concern, it is significant that

> most of the early writings on metropolitan government were the product of men who shortly before had been primarily concerned with efforts to reform city government ... Many people who had been seeking to reduce the costs of city government by introducing business practices and scientific management principles a few years earlier now saw simplified and integrated metropolitan government as a vehicle for obtaining additional economy and efficiency in administration.   (Warren, 1966, pp.5–6, 8)

Once municipal 'reform' was effected it was natural that business-men would move on to see the logic of larger units of local govern-ment. After all, as the vice president of the Pennsylvania Railroad pointed out in 1929, 'this is an era of consolidation in business in which the larger the scale of operations the greater the economy. If business prospers through consolidation it seems reasonable to suppose that a city would do likewise' (cited in Jones, 1942, p.xxii). Small wonder, then, that 'much of the impetus for metro-politan reorganisation has come from the top business leadership of the area acting through either the central city chamber of commerce or more exclusive organisations' (Bollens and Schmandt, 1970, p.377; see also, Greer, 1963; Adrian, 1961; Banfield and Grodzins, 1958). In contrast to this pattern of support there has been 'lower-class resistance to metropolitan reform' (Flinn, 1970, p.149; see also Watson and Romani, 1961), and 'a majority of blacks typically opposes metropolitan reorganisation proposals' (Marshall, 1972, p.15; see also Greer, 1963, p.28; Hawkins, 1966).

Once you remember that many metropolitan areas display a particular kind of residential segregation, and a particular pattern with respect to the location of economic enterprise, then it is not too difficult to account for this pattern of support and opposition. You need scarcely have made a special study of American cities to be aware that many of them are increasingly made up of a poor black residential core, which is surrounded by a more affluent white suburban ring. Moreover, although the central city has been losing jobs (especially in the large-scale manufacturing plants), 'virtually all the headquarters of America's one hundred largest industrial corporations are in the large cities. The central business districts of these cities have continued to grow' (Katznelson and Kesselman, 1975, p.405). The conjunction of these facts suggests two things. First, the control of central city governments is likely to be in black hands and rest upon the electoral support of the poorer sections of those who live in the metropolitan area. Second, and precisely because this situation involves a 'decline' in councillor calibre and the erosion of direct business control of local government, it is likely to be looked on with disfavour by those who have a financial stake in the continued viability of the central business districts.

As central cities have approached black majority status, black mayors, congressmen, officials and commissioners are being elected in large numbers. In 1976 black mayors presided over ninety-six cities and within a decade it is estimated that black administrations will head the majority of the country's ten largest cities (Hill, 1976, p.41). Black power in city hall was a necessary prerequisite to changing budget priorities, and political struggle has produced important gains in many central cities. But for all this, such control may be more a matter of form than of substance (Friesma, 1969), because the fiscal crisis of the central cities — 'the inability of their local governments to provide enough resources to cover the required public facilities because of the increasing gap between the fiscal resources and the public needs and demands' (Castells, 1976, p.3) — damps down the possibility of black demands being fully translated into appropriate public policies. Moreover, if city governments do redirect and increase social expenditures and lay the bill for them at the doorstep of corporate institutions then they may only fuel their exodus from the city. The blacks in central cities are in a 'Catch 22' political situation. If they are in a situation when they can win control of city government then they are operating within an area which will not give them sufficient resources and finance to enable them to satisfy the demands of their voters (Harvey, 1973, p.93; Castells, 1977, p.391). If, on the other hand, the area of government is extended to cover the suburbs so as to increase the finances available for public services, then the support base of that government will be very much less grounded on the poor: there will be little possibility of black control, or of services being provided to match central city need. 'Black leaders have not been hesitant in expressing their dissatisfaction with reformed governments', and Marshall (1972, pp.18—24) considers that 'the possibility that metropolitan government actually will benefit minorities seems extremely remote', as although some services may be upgraded it 'will not deal with the services minorities care most about, namely the social services'. Piven and Cloward (1967) think that metropolitan reorganisation will be harmful to the interests and political power of minorities, and they consider it is being advocated more intensely as part of a Federal strategy to deny political power to minorities in the central city and thus appeal to white suburban voters, who (in Altshuler's view (1970, p.51)) are becoming more favourable to metropolitan government as black political power grows. More modestly, Erie, Kirlin and Rabinovitz (1972, p.28) are of the opinion that at best 'reform schemes tend to guarantee that black influence remains unchanged', but they too note that 'in the long run' the access of minorities may be 'diluted'. Perhaps it is not surprising, therefore, that 'some of the support for larger units of urban government reflects illiberal motives. Larger units tend to dilute the newly active strength of blacks and other low income minorities who are clustered together' (Fantini, Gittell, and Magat, 1970, p.230; see also Steiner, 1966, pp.10–11).

> One element of the business community, the downtown interests, has a . . . personal stake in metropolitan reorganisation. Concerned with the economic position of the central business district, many merchants and property owners feel that area-wide governmental change may in some way aid the center by giving it greater prominence in a reconstituted polity.(Bollens and Schmandt, 1970, p.378)

Under the established system, the deterioration of municipal services and the social environment threatened the very existence of the central business districts which corporate capital had a very specific interest in maintaining. There was not only the economic imperative of maintaining the value of public infrastructure and private construction in central cities, but the value of central city properties was the bedrock on which municipal loans were based. As Markusen (1976, p.61) reminds us, 'despite the scare of the 1960's, it is clear that corporations are not going to leave the major American central cities because their need for elaborate administrative, financial and control functions ties them to the agglomeration of facilities downtown'.

It may be comparatively easy to analyse the stance and interest of inner city minority groups and central city businessmen, but the ambivalent position of suburban residents complicates any simple analysis which talks only of a capitalist class in support of metropolitan reorganisation faced by a black working class and lumpenproletariat in opposition. Not only is there differentiation along class, ethnic, and racial lines *within* the suburbs, but the promise of a suburban existence for both white *and* blue collar workers encourages individualised aspirations outside the workplace which become centred on the issue of residential location. This attenuates the rigours of class conflict and consciousness, and those who have struggled to grasp the gains of suburban existence have also been able to insulate their public sector amenities from urban claims and their ability to pay from urban fiscal demands. They are unlikely to be willing to lose their political autonomy even though it threatens the continued viability of the central business district. Markusen (1976, p.62) in fact suggests that 'we may see a struggle in the future between suburban subclasses militant in their desire to preserve their local public sector autonomy and large capitalist interests pushing for planned, rationalized metropolitan wide government'.

Part Two

The Management Problem

No suggestion for reform is more common than 'what we need is more coordination'.   (Pressman and Wildavsky, 1973, p.133)

Corporate planning ... has become a phrase to which it is increasingly difficult to give real meaning.   (Greenwood, Hinings, Ranson and Walsh, 1976, p.18)

... new forms [of city government in America] facilitated the inflow of the commercial and upper class elements into the centres of municipal power at the price of ethnic and lower class representation ... The nation had finally tailored the urban political organisation to the most powerful economic forces in the city.
(Holli, 1969, pp.179–81)

An approach to local government which centred on such grand concerns as democracy, efficiency and central control, hardly had time to notice matters so mundane as the actual working of particular local authorities. Local government was either pure administration, or a self-regulating democracy, and from these perspectives the management of local government could easily be assumed away as an irrelevant, taken-for-granted blur.

However, thinking on the boundary problem, and the struggle to increase efficiency, leant heavily on a simple appreciation of the early literature on the theory of the firm. Since that literature also pointed to managerial *dis*economies and the problem of co-ordination in large firms[1] it was likely to be the case that students of local government would confront the problem of management once larger local authorities were created. There was indeed the widespread view that 'if larger areas are to be contemplated in order to provide for more efficient administration of some services than is at present possible within the local government field, the

---

1 Robinson, 1931, p.44; Cairncross, 1960, p.136; Jones, 1933, p.127; Pratten, Dean and Silbertson, 1965. For a critique of some of this literature see Beckman, 1960.

emphasis on management must necessarily grow' (Hart, 1965, p.7).[2]

In fact, this simple account of the 'rise of the management movement' (Tudor and Stanyer, 1970, p.3) fails to recognise the long-standing, continuous, and consistent criticism which has been directed against 'traditional administration'. In Chapter 5 I will set down what I see as the essentials of the orthodox — the widely shared and long-established, rarely questioned, and ill-researched — stance to the problem of 'traditional administration' and its reform. In Chapter 6 I will explore the adequacy of the orthodox description and assessment of traditional administration, and the adequacy of the orthodox approach to building up a package of proposals for new structures and processes of management geared to the implementation of a 'corporate' approach in local government.

Anyone who seeks to go beyond this limited sort of critique is not faced with an easy task. There is not much critical comment around, and such comment as does exist rarely raises fundamental questions. Naturally enough, the bulk of the literature on reorganisation has been generated by the practical advocates of change who are reluctant, and even unable, to look dispassionately upon it. Moreover, their disciplinary frame of reference is rarely conducive to any concern to situate management developments within their wider political and economic context.[3] On the other hand, outsiders to the reorganisation movement — such as myself — find it hard to get to grips with reorganisation and change. So, we are confronted with yet another 'Catch 22' situation so far as criticism of reorganisation is concerned: 'few participants in reform can remain objective about it, and even fewer non-participants can know what really transpired' (Caiden, 1970, p.192; see also Mosher, 1965, p.130).

In my honest attempt to come to terms with management

2 See also Royal Commission on Local Government in England, 1969, vol.1, pp.123—4; Ripley, 1970, p.21; Long, 1975; Stanyer, 1970, pp.15—16; Bennett, 1972, p.452; Stewart, 1971A, p.919; LAMSAC, 1972, p.36; Long and Norton, 1972, p.124.
3 We should not forget that 'the management explosion in local government has provided a profitable new source of business for management consultants' (Knowles, 1971, p.230) and this has helped to restrict critique to 'practical' matters which tend to centre on rather limited sorts of questions: should the minority party be on the policy committee? should the council be divided into back-benchers and front-benchers? should the chief executive officer have legal training? and should he have his own department? what should be the size of committees and the basis on which functions are divided amongst them? and so on.

reorganisation I have read many pieces of work which sought to lay bare the essentials of what should be done. The more I read, the more confused I became.[4] The whole thing kept slipping through my fingers. Just as I struggled to a critical appreciation of the planning, programming, budgeting system (PPBS), it was being dropped by erstwhile advocates of its introduction into British local government as they sniffed the strong winds of attack blowing over from America. I found it impossible to keep up with the rapid changes in reorganisation fashion. In the space of well under a decade we have witnessed the rise (and sometimes the fall!) of PPBS, performance budgeting, output budgeting, management by objectives, corporate management, corporate planning, inter-corporate planning, resource planning, community planning, social planning, long-range planning, connective planning, policy analysis, network analysis, area management, and many more such things, not to mention the longer-standing advocacy of such management techniques and services as O and M (organisation and methods), work study, operational research, and cost-benefit analysis. It was proving impossible to gain a firm grasp on the strange new fruits that were held out as promising the very salvation of local government and its services.

I was caught between two rather different assessments of 'corporateness'. On the one hand, I frequently could not understand what it was that local authorities should be doing if they wished to curry favour with the advocates of change. To say that 'corporate planning involves drawing together of professional and other skills to attack problems facing local government' (Eddison, 1973, p.9) tells us nothing, and yet general statements of this kind abound in the literature.[5] On the other hand, when I could seem to grasp what was being urged on local authorities then I was presented with a package of promises that seemed to be quite beyond the critique of any reasonable man: they seemed to offer everything you could possibly desire to see snugly fitted into the body politic. Who could seriously 'quarrel with an approach' (Rose, 1969, p.52) which promised innovation, co-ordination, rational decision-making and problem-solving, all grounded in a sensitivity to the needs of the whole community? Immerse yourself

4 Some Americans were refreshingly confused about PPBS (planning, programming, budgeting system). See Mosher, 1967; Bickner, 1971.
5 See for example Lucking, Greenwood and Howard, 1974, p.135; and Hill, 1973, p.2, for particularly vacuous 'definitions' of corporate planning.

in the literature on reorganisation and you will find yourself bewildered and confused, or disarmed and sucked into the warm embrace of the orthodox package. If you do hold firm to some churlish concern to remain critical, then you will probably wish to retain a low profile, as you take risks if you come out with any sort of criticism. First, you risk revealing your ignorance of something you have never quite understood and you can stand accused of criticising some outdated system and of 'misunderstanding' what reorganisation is really all about. Second, if you are critical of new structures and processes then you can stand accused as some Luddite defender of the status quo who prefers the fragmentation and incrementalism said to typify traditional administration. Third, if you protest that you do not seek to defend the status quo then your critique must be constructive and situated within the reformist tradition as it is seen 'as incumbent on anyone who raises a note of caution about policy planning to make some statement as to how the problem of achieving the best possible allocation of resources can be tackled' (James, 1973, p.155).

Gradually I learnt to stop worrying about my lack of ability to really understand the corporate approach. I came to realise that it was actually *impossible* to get to sure grips with it. A slippery lack of precision was the one thing that was of its *essence*. Vagueness was important in that it gave it a kind of featherbed resilience and a marked invulnerability to criticism. It was also a major selling point in its favour since no one could stand out against something he could not quite understand when it was so convincingly presented as promising everything. In recognising this, I also came to realise that I was barking up the wrong tree in even wanting to criticise the package of proposals and promises that were the corporate approach in *abstract*. Advocates of the internal reorganisation of local authorities have been concerned to remake the style and process of local policy-making and so they must be judged accordingly. Caiden (1970, p.159) reminds us that 'to take reformers at their word is unscientific, certainly distorting. They should be judged by their deeds alone.' Neither understanding nor critique can be based on the promises of the corporate package but must centre on its actual *implementation* and on the reality of its *practice* with concern focusing on its inevitable implications for power and policies.[6]

6 Advocates of any systems approach are usually concerned to maintain a crisp dis-

In Chapter 7 I will highlight the problem of implementing a system which seeks to make governmental decision-making more co-ordinated, rational, and innovatory, and will also do my best to report on the changes that have occurred. In Chapter 8 I will suggest that particular attention should centre on the implications of the new structures and processes for the thorny issue of councillor calibre. At this stage, the comparative novelty of the attempts to introduce the corporate approach into local government inhibits the possibility of our providing substantial or definitive studies of its practice. I do not see this as a 'body blow to . . . premature critics' (Eddison, 1973, p.80), but it does mean that we should pay particular attention to the development of lines of enquiry and questioning that can then be taken up by students who are concerned to pursue detailed studies of corporate practice in particular local authorities. It is in this spirit that you should read these chapters.

tinction between theory and practice and 'when faced with work done in . . . [the] field their stock defense is that the theory is fine but that the particular applications might have been poor or the practitioners unqualified' (Hoos, 1972, p.11). My point is that this distinction is irrelevant and *spurious* in a situation where theory is so vague that it can only be seriously explored in the specific context of its practice.

5

From Traditional Administration to Corporate Management

> ... the traditional departmental attitude within much of local
> government must give way to a wider-ranging corporate outlook.
> (Working Group on Local Authority
> Management Structures, 1972, p.6)

The notion of 'traditional administration' is not of my invention, and in Chapter 6 I will actually suggest that there is little sense in it. But in the context of this chapter, where I am presenting the case for the internal reorganisation of local authorities, it must be made absolutely clear that I am not seeking to erect a straw man, but am dealing with a notion that lies at the very heart of that body of literature which points to the need for total reorganisation. Stewart (1970, p.3) and Knowles (1971, p.15) both refer to the 'traditional pattern' of management and organisation; the influential Working Group on Local Authority Management Structures (1972, p.4) advocated reforms which 'challenged [a] ... number of traditional practices'; and K. E. Rose (1970, p.204), one of the earliest advocates of PPBS in British local government, has written critically of 'the traditional organisation of a local authority'.[1]

My concern, then, is to set down what I see as the orthodox description and assessment of traditional administration, together with the reorganisation proposals that have been put forward to change it. Fairly obviously I will inevitably be painting with a broad brush as there are differences of emphasis within the texts I am discussing. Having said that, I do not see myself as providing a mere caricature of the debate since there is revealed a widely shared and long-established view as to what is traditional administration, what is wrong with it, and what should be put in its place.

1 For a similar recognition of something called 'traditional administration', see also
Greenwood, Smith and Stewart, 1971; Greenwood, Hinings, Ranson and Walsh,
1976, p.91; IMTA, 1970; Lucking, Greenwood and Howard, 1974; LAMSAC, 1972;
Cartwright, 1975; Hart, 1965; MacColl, 1951.

1. Traditional Administration Described

A complete descriptive account of orthodoxy must set down the answers to five questions. First, who are the personnel involved? Second, what are the structures within which the personnel decide and interact? Third, and crucially, how is the policy-making process characterised? Fourth, what is the 'style' of policy-making? Fifth, what is the view of the overall role of local government — what part is it seen as playing in the life of the local community?

(i) *Personnel*

'The two vital elements in local administration are formed by the elected members of local authorities on the one hand, and the paid officers employed by the authorities on the other' (Hart, 1968, p.120). 'The two elements of elected members and permanent officers form the traditional pattern of local government' (Hart, 1965, p.5).

(ii) *Structures*

For every administrative area there is a council elected by universal suffrage and all power is vested in it. 'Where the council consists of a small number of members it would be quite possible for the full council to come together regularly to discuss every item of business. But where a council consists of a large number of people this would be quite impossible' (Tillett, 1949, p.46; see also Jha, 1957, p.7; Maud, 1932, p.94). Moreover, the 'close supervision over the actual work of local administration means that the business to be performed by the elected members of local authorities is too great in amount adequately to be performed at council meetings' (Hart, 1968, p.128). In a word, 'most councils have insufficient time and too much business to decide everything in council' (Harris, 1966, p.37; see also Hasluck, 1936, p.185). To ease the burden on councillors and to divide up the work of the council, 'partly to tradition, and partly to legislation, there has grown up within nearly every council a number of committees' (Larkin, 1932, p.66). Perhaps more than anything else, the committee system is seen as the essential defining element of traditional administration: it is 'fundamental to local government' (Jewell, 1975, p.27) and 'the characteristic method of working'

(Benemy, 1960, p.175). 'It is often said, with truth, that the real work of the council is done in committee' (Morrell and Watson, 1928, p.37; Simon, 1926, p.2; Cole, 1956, p.32), for there is general agreement that committees are 'the real workshops of local government' (Warren, 1950, p.15; Finer, 1945, p.220; Gyford, 1976, p.49). The committee system is regarded as 'an essentially English invention' (Harris, 1939A, p.60; Gibbon, 1928, p.205); and in Hart's view, 'the committee system is the characteristic mark of local government, just as the Cabinet system is typical of the Central Government' (1968, p.128). Wheare (1955, p.163) provides the classic statement of the orthodox position: 'local administration in Britain is administration by committees'.

Departments are to committees as officers are to councillors. The 'orthodox system' is one of 'separate departments' (MacColl, 1951, p.15), and traditional administration is characterized by a 'departmental style of management' (Lucking, Greenwood, and Howard, 1974, p.131; see also Drain, 1966, p.79) which lacks any real 'hierarchic structure' (Hart, 1965, p.6).

So, 'the traditional pattern . . . is dominated by the committee system, through which council members carry out their work, and by the departmental structure, through which the permanent officers perform their executive tasks' (Knowles, 1971, p.15). As new functions have been heaped upon local authorities so new committees have sprung up according to 'the principle of "one function, one committee"' (Ripley, 1970, p.25; Stanyer, 1967, p.24). Because 'each committee likes to have its own officer' (Marshall, 1965, p.17) so committee growth has been matched by the growth of new departments. The Treasury O and M Division in their investigation into the departmental structure at Coventry made the point that 'the outstanding feature of the Corporation's organisation structure, and indeed that of local authorities generally . . . is the large number of virtually self-contained departments each responsible through its controlling committee to the council' (Policy Advisory Committee, 1954, p.80; see also McKinsey and Co., 1971, p.1-1).

(iii) *The Policy-Making Process*

In Chapter 2 I set down the orthodox Electoral Chain of Command Theory. The theory has a crisp simplicity and coherence to it, but — quite rightly — it does not satisfy the hard-nosed advocates of management reorganisation.

'In theory policy making is the work of the council', but in practice 'the full council rarely initiates anything', and its proceedings have 'become more and more formal and ritualistic' (Maddick and Pritchard, 1958, p.149; Knowles, 1971, p.18; Working Group on Local Authority Management Structures, 1972, p.20). 'The real decisions are in general made elsewhere' (Committee on the Management of Local Government, 1967, vol.5, p.390).

In a survey undertaken for the Committee on the Management of Local Government (1967, vol.5, p.194), 'a large number of the clerks . . . stressed that . . . policy ideas . . . often originate in the individual service committees'. In contrast, Friend and Jessop (1969, pp.56—7) considered that the various 'limitations to the effectiveness of the committee as a decision-making body meant that the reality of the decision-making process tended to become largely concentrated within the departmental offices'. Regardless of the truth of these two positions, there is a higher consensus around the idea that policy-making centres on particular services. 'The practice is that each service or function of the authority is administered by a committee working through a corresponding principal officer heading a department. Service or function, committee, principal officer and department tend to be interlocked and self-contained' (Committee on the Management of Local Government, 1967, vol.1, p.28). Given this sort of picture, 'if a general theme can be distinguished, it is that under present arrangements, policy seems more likely to be initiated with the needs of individual services in mind than in relation to the council's activities as a whole' (vol.5, p.197).

'The traditional and conventional "flow of business"' is summed up by Knowles (1971, pp.15—18): 'Each matter . . . is ordinarily routed by way of a departmental head to the appropriate committee for consideration and report to the council sitting in full assembly and then back to the departmental head for any necessary executive action.' In similar vein, Friend and Jessop (1969, p.48)[2] provide a diagram to summarise 'the formal sequence of steps in the decision-making process in Coventry' which they see

2 Unlike most writers on traditional administration, Friend and Jessop do go on to qualify this picture since they recognise that political parties assume a crucial role in the reality of the policy-making process.

as 'similar to that in any other all-purpose authority in the United Kingdom'.

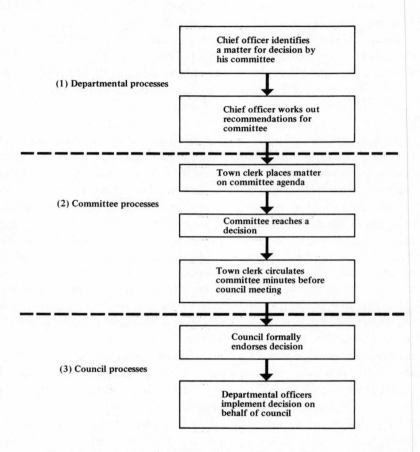

The formal process of decision. From Friend and Jessop, 1969, p.48, fig. 10

So far my presentation of the orthodox view of the policy process has rather glossed over the relationship between councillors and officers, and I have not dealt with the particular, and problematic, part which the officers are seen as playing in the process. Students of traditional administration tend to display something of an ambivalence with respect to the role of the officers within that system. On the one hand they are prepared to recognise that in practice officers have long enjoyed varying degrees of delegation, and this would suggest that they are suspicious of the adequacy of the established orthodoxy which assigns officers to administration alone.[3] But on the other hand, they are unanimous in their view that the scope of official responsibility is far too restricted within the traditional system and this would surely suggest that they are tending to see the orthodox account as an adequate representation of the situation of the officials, albeit one that should be changed through reorganisation.

(iv) *The Policy-Making 'Style'*

It is really only recently that students of traditional administration have been explicitly concerned to characterise what might be called the overall style of policy-making, and Professor J. D. Stewart from the Institute of Local Government Studies is the most important and articulate figure to give form and expression to this. He has noted how departments are 'structured around the requirements of the day-to-day operations of the services for which they are responsible' (1970, p.19) and how

> the traditional management style of local government is geared to the assumption that existing activities have to be carried on and that the only choice the local authority faces is whether the activities should grow. The assumption that existing activities should continue to be carried on and in the manner in which they have been traditionally carried on underlines the prevalent management style (1970A, p.9)

(See also, 1971B, 1973, 1974.) Stewart is by no means alone in his description of the traditional style. Beatrice and Sidney Webb (1932, p.196) noted how local authorities muddled through 'by the methods of trial and error', and more recently, Ward (1970, p.1) has pointed out how 'local government has controlled its affairs by making short-term projections of the expenditure required to deal with current difficulties and tasks' and has been geared simply to 'solving problems as they appear'. Headrick (1962, p.160) has noted how 'by and large the work of the council drifts along the same path from year to year unless for some reason the central government steps in to alter it. This is the pattern of English local government.' P.A. Management Consultants (1969, pp.5—7), in the report of their investigation into the

---

3 For example, research for the Committee on the Management of Local Government (1967, vol.5, pp.196—7) pointed out that the reality of the relationship between councillors and officers often presents 'a very different picture from that suggested by the facile generalisation that members are responsible for policy and officers for its execution'.

organisation of the London Borough of Brent, put the orthodox position tersely:

> The London Borough of Brent in common with many local authorities exhibits rather negative management. Not much goes wrong, but there is a lack of something; an absence of drive, of enthusiasm which characterises the best commercial organisations . . . The tendency for negative management to be more prominent than creativity . . . in turn leads to a strong tendency to maintain the status quo and an inertia which resists change and new ideas.[4]

In a word, we are supposedly facing the 'traditional, amateur, muddling through attitude of local authorities' (Cartwright, 1975, p.269). 'Local government is unimaginative in its approach to problem solving, preferring old familiar policies to the radical solutions which the situation demands' (Hill, 1973, p.2).

(v) *The Role of Local Government*

Traditional administration is seen as revolving around particular services, and local authorities are often seen as geared to 'the local administration of a policy laid down in broad lines by the central government' (MacColl, 1951, p.10). Both these factors are said to encourage a situation in which local authorities conceive of their role in very narrow terms as limited to the provision of separate services which are seen in isolation each from the other and from the problems and needs in the local community. Armstrong (1973, p.105) has pointed out how 'local government tended to be seen as a process of administering a collection of services imposed or permitted by statute, and having little or no connection with each other except that they were largely financed from a common source'. Indeed, there is the view that local authorities are just engaged in 'managing a bundle of separate independent services' because they have 'traditionally been considered as local agencies responsible for a collection of essentially separate services defined by statute and drawn together within the same organisation for administrative and political convenience. Their role in short, was prescribed and restricted' (Redcliffe-Maud, 1967, p.350; Greenwood, Smith and Stewart, 1971, p.5).

---

4 See also Ripley, 1970, p.105; Knowles, 1971, p.39; Lucking, Greenwood, and Howard, 1974, p.144; Cranston, 1969, p.67; Eddison, 1973, p.22; Hallows, 1974.

2. Traditional Administration Assessed

I would be guilty of exaggeration if I were to suggest that everyone who has written on the subject of traditional administration has always assessed the system as deficient and in need of urgent and fundamental reform.[5] Having said that, praise has never been predominant. What, then, has been seen as wrong with the system? Put more fully, what are the aspects *within* traditional administration that are regarded with disfavour by its critics, and what are defined as the characteristics of good government that they regret do *not* exist within the system?

(i) *The Existence of Fragmentation and the Absence of Co-ordination*

'Fragmentation' is the word most frequently used to capture what is seen as essential to, and wrong with, traditional administration.[6] Critics also point to the conflict and competition which they see as bedevilling relations within the typical authority. Indeed, 'one of the chief organisational problems affecting local authorities is the excessively competitive behaviour existing between departments [and] between members and officers' (Gill, 1973, p.40). Friend and Jessop (1969, p.66) were mindful of the 'rifts created by the fundamental distinction between the salaried professional and the elected layman', and the Working Group on Local Authority Management Structures (1972, p.5) pointed to the 'friction and competition' between councillors and officers who were 'too often suspicious and critical of each other's role'.[7]

Committees, departments, and technically trained professional officers have usually been seen as the major cause of this sorry state of affairs.

Hardly anyone has had a good word to say for the committee system. The Committee on the Management of Local Government

---

5 See the general assessments of Roberts, 1929, p.25, and Morris, 1960, p.46; the enthusiasm for the system of administration in the LCC by Haward, 1932, p.56, and Loomis, 1939, p.365; and the suggestion that administration is much better in small or medium sized authorities in Headrick, 1962, pp.158—60, 208, and Garner, 1960.

6 See, for example, Ripley, 1970, p.15; Knowles, 1971, p.27; Stanyer, 1967, p.25; Policy Advisory Committee, 1954, p.81; Chester, 1954, p.17; Sharp, 1962; Webb and Webb, 1932, p.194; McKinsey and Co., 1971, pp.1-8, 2-7; Committee on Local Authority and Allied Personal Social Services, 1968, p.23.

7 See also Davies, 1972, p.39; Grierson, 1928, p.218.

(1967, vol.1, p.35) was of the opinion that 'the virtues of committees are, at present, outweighed by the failures and inadequacies of the committee system', and the Working Group on Local Authority Management Structures (1972, p.4) talked cryptically of the 'misuse of the committee system'. There is nothing at all novel about this sort of critique. In their diary entry for 1899, Beatrice and Sidney Webb (1932, p.196) wrote of the 'confusion' of Manchester city government, a confusion 'worse confounded [as] each committee considers itself like an independent company and reports as little as it dare to the Town Council'. Down the years critics have bemoaned the independence, or 'autonomy', of committees,[8] and have pointed to the dangerous disease of 'committee-itis' or 'committee-mindedness' (Policy Advisory Committee, 1954, p.81; Ripley, 1970, p.22). In Wheare's (1955, p.155) words, 'this is perhaps the commonest besetting sin of committees in local government'. Moreover, 'present committees are not on the whole formed on a scientific basis as regards size, division, and grouping of functions, and powers' (Page, 1936, p.28; see also Maud, 1932, p.95), and traditional administration was seen as possessed of too many committees and subcommittees, most of which were seen as too large.[9] Besides contributing to the problem of fragmentation, committees were seen as 'inimical to proper financial control' (Committee on the Management of Local Government, 1967, vol.1, p.35) and were said to have a disastrous effect on the calibre of both councillors and officers.

Committees were never seen as the only cause of fragmentation. Departmentalism has been seen as the 'complementary phenomenon' of committee mindedness. Ripley (1970, pp. 22, 19) reminds us that

> this phenomenon has been described as the besetting sin of local administration and involves far more than simply the tendency of departments to proliferate; it is a mental condition, a philosophy. 'Departmentalism' implies an administrative situation whereby the multitude of departments think of themselves as self-contained

8 See, for example, Larkin, 1932, p.66; Etherton, 1924, p.393; Morrell and Watson, 1928, p.25; Rudd, 1933, p.212; Harris, 1939A, p.75; LAMSAC, 1972, p.5; Headrick, 1962, p.25; Raine, 1928.

9 In 1939, Birmingham had 32 committees, and 118 subcommittees (Harris, 1939A, p.61). In 1967 at least one county borough in England and Wales could boast 35 committees whereas another had 160 subcommittees (Committee on the Management of Local Government, 1967, vol.5, pp.539–40).

bodies, justifying their actions in their own professional terms and strongly insulated from those influences representing the purpose of the organisation as a whole.

It is argued that the 'disadvantage of the officer system of management arises almost directly from the committee system' ('The Basildon Experiment', 1966, p.216), but the problem has been still further worsened by the fact of professionalism. Just about everyone who has written on traditional administration attests to the fact of 'excessive departmentalism' and the evils of 'professionalism'.[10]

Within the context of the established discourse on traditional administration, talk about the problem of fragmentation is also talk about the problem of co-ordination. 'Since committees have in general so much freedom of action, arrangements for co-ordination are of considerable importance if the authority is to act effectively as a unit' (Maddick and Pritchard, 1958, p.148). How, then, was 'the whole problem of municipal co-ordination' seen as solved within the traditional system? (Stanyer, 1967, p.24.)

'In theory, co-ordination of all local authority services could be effectively achieved throughout the whole council which has a collective responsibility for all of them' — after all, 'it is the council . . . which is supposed to see that the work of committees is co-ordinated' (Committee on Local Authority and Allied Personal Social Services, 1968, p.28; Maud, 1932, p.124; see also Tee, 1927, p.444; Laski, 1935, p.98). In practice, however, most students consider that council 'control is without serious practical worth', since 'councils are, as a rule, unfitted for the proper performance of this duty' (Finer, 1945, p.232; Page, 1936, p.272; see also Harris, 1939A, p.75; Gibbon, 1931, 1932).[11] The mayor, or the chairman of the council, 'can do little in the way of supervising the work' (Simon, 1926, p.190; Webb and Webb, 1932,

10 See, for example, Committee on the Management of Local Government, 1967, vol.1, pp.18, 28; Cranston, 1969, p.67; Policy Advisory Committee, 1954, p.81; James, 1973, p.149; Smith, 1944, p.37; Roberts, 1929, p.250; MacColl, 1951, p.11; Knowles, 1971, p.28; LAMSAC, 1972, p.6; McKinsey and Co., 1971, p.19. But for a different perspective on committees, departments, and professionals, see Redlich, 1903, vol.1, pp.307–11; Tillett, 1949, p.46; Gibbon and Bell, 1939, p.662; Hilary, 1929; Millington, 1928; Board, 1925; Picken, 1934; Keith, 1928; Royal Commission on Local Government, 1929, pp.130ff.
11 But see Hart, 1968, pp.133–4, Warren, 1950, pp.15–16, and Grierson, 1928, p.217, for a different view of the role of the council.

p.195), and although some writers[12] point to the co-ordinating effect of the standing orders and the terms of reference of committees, most attention has centred on aspects of the committee system and the role of the town clerk.

Committees have been seen as contributing to co-ordination in three ways. First, the fact that councillors may belong to several committees 'should perhaps in theory tend to produce more mutually consistent policy-making by the committees' (Committee on the Management of Local Government, 1967, vol.5, p.204; see also, Grierson, 1928, p.217). Second, 'co-ordination is sometimes carried out by means of joint committees or sub-committees' (Harris, 1939A, p.74).[13] Finally, and of more recognised importance, there is the system of horizontal committees — 'committees created specifically, or specifically used, to achieve a degree of co-ordination among, and supervision over, the service committees' (Committee on the Management of Local Government, 1967, vol.1, p.25). Hasluck (1936, p.192) was of the opinion that 'in the great majority of councils there is one committee that stands out as dominant, co-ordinating the work of all the other committees, and to a certain extent controlling their activities'. In the LCC Roberts (1954, p.264) tells us that the Finance, Establishments, and General Purposes committees between them served 'to co-ordinate the work of all the committees'. Any account of the co-ordinating role played by the horizontal committees inevitably tends to centre upon the particular contribution made by the Finance Committee. Indeed, Finer (1945, p.235) came to the conclusion that 'organised co-ordination, in so far as it exists, now operates with varying efficiency . . . through the Finance Committee'.[14] Whatever co-ordinating role the Finance Committee does or does not play, it is quite clear that a body of opinion considers that it is an inappropriate vehicle for this function.[15] More generally, Ripley (1970, pp.231ff) is critical of the co-ordinating value of horizontal committees, and the Policy

---

12 See, for example, Page, 1936, p.37; Knowles, 1971, p.23; F. C. Minshull, 1929, p.302.
13 See also Ripley, 1970, p.25; Page, 1936, p.182.
14 On the importance of the Finance Committee in Stockport, see Booz-Allen and Hamilton, 1971, p.12.
15 See, for example, Finer, 1945; Ripley, 1970, ch. 4; Page, 1936, p.351; Committee on the Management of Local Government, 1967, vol.5, pp.192, 207; Gibbon, 1931.

Advisory Committee in Coventry (1954, p.82) felt that 'these horizontal committees have not always been entirely successful'.

Officers have been seen as having a part to play in the co-ordination of traditional administration. Grierson (1928, p.219) has pointed out that 'an official, while keen on the work of his department, has sufficient common-sense to recognise that he is not independent of his brother officials, and is not averse to consult with them where the need for such consultation arises'. Some writers have pointed to the importance of 'meetings of chief officers' or a 'chief officials' monthly luncheon club',[16] while others have seen the treasurer as playing a particularly vital role in co-ordination.[17] However, the overwhelming emphasis in the literature centres on the role of the clerk. In the nineteenth century the clerk may have been just a lawyer and a record keeper (Headrick, 1962, pp.23–5), but by 1929 the increase in local responsibilities led the Royal Commission on Local Government (p.136) to consider it 'imperative that one officer of the council should be in a position to survey the various activities of the Authority, and to secure that they are properly focused and co-ordinated with reasonable uniformity and continuity'. They saw the clerk as best capable of assuming this role and so 'by a gradual and almost unconscious process, town and county clerks began to feel responsibility for the initiative in . . . co-ordination' (Finer, 1945, p.241). The situation has evolved to one where 'the town clerk is traditionally expected to assume the role of co-ordination at officer level', as it has become a 'text book convention to regard the clerk . . . as the first among equals in his relationship with the other principal officers' (Harris, 1966, p.38; Committee on the Management of Local Government, 1967, vol.1, p.28).[18] Notwithstanding these developments, the co-ordinating role of the clerk is generally seen as 'limited' (McKinsey and Co., 1971, p.1-4), and Ripley (1970, p.41) sums up the consensus when he noted how 'neither his formal authority, his abilities, nor often his inclinations are adequate to the task demanded . . . The broad answers to the question what clerks could do and what they actually do in improving and helping to unify the administration

16 See, for example, Society of Clerks of Urban District Councils, 1951, pp.54–6; F. C. Minshull, 1929, p.302.
17 See, for example, Roberts, 1951; Ripley, 1970, p.55; 'Municipal Management', 1949.
18 See also Policy Advisory Committee, 1954, p.85; Wheare, 1955, p.198.

of local authorities are "not very much" and "rather less".[19]

Given this sort of account of the arrangements for co-ordination within traditional administration, it should not surprise us that critics have seen co-ordination as effectively absent from the system.[20] To be more precise, although traditional administration was seen as having developed to embrace the low level co-ordination of administrative arrangements and policy implementation, the more fundamental co-ordination of policy formulation and resource management was still seen as absent from the system. Quite simply, orthodoxy asserts that 'there is no systematic attempt . . . to conceive and co-ordinate policy as a whole'; the 'consistent overall policy, the integrated programme for borough or city improvement is not there'; and so 'in many authorities, at least, the problems of co-ordination have not been adequately solved' (Committee on the Management of Local Government, 1967, vol.5, pp.214, 202; Headrick, 1962, p.160). In a word, 'the problem of ensuring co-operation between council committees is perhaps the most important problem in local government' (Wheare, 1955, p.198).[21]

(ii) *The Existence of Incrementalism and the Absence of Innovation*

In the first part of this chapter, I made it clear that 'the conventional approach to management in local authorities in this country . . . has been described as the most malignant disease of government, that of "creeping incrementalism"' (Cossey, 1971, p.5). Local government is regarded as 'generally non-innovative in its management style' and yet there is the perception of a 'need for innovation' (Cox, 1976, p.113; Stewart, 1970, p.21). Flexibility, imagination, long-term planning, explicit policy-making and the systematic monitoring and review of implemented policies, are all seen as aspects of good government that are missing from traditional administration.[22]

19 See also, Committee on the Management of Local Government, 1967, vol.5, p.232; Headrick, 1962, pp.151, 183; Webb and Webb, 1932, p.195; Simon, 1926, p.196; Hart, 1965, p.6.
20 But see Hart, 1968; Maddick and Pritchard, 1958, pp.154—5; Warren, 1950.
21 See also Harris, 1939A, p.300; Rogers, 1968, p.5; Gibbon, 1931, p.102; MacColl, 1951, pp.12—18; Rudd, 1933; 'Municpal Management', 1949; Hill, 1973; Page, 1936, esp. p.18; Ripley, 1970, p.9; Simon, 1926, pp.189—90; Committee on the Management of Local Government, 1967, vol.1, p.26; Finer, 1945, p.232.
22 See, for example, Harris, 1939A, p.300; Page, 1936; Stewart, 1971B, p.38; LAMSAC,

(iii) *Concluding Remarks: Changing the Role of Local Government*

At the very core of the orthodox unease with all the facets that make up what have been seen as the essentials of traditional administration there lies a rejection of the narrow, administrative role of local government as quite inappropriate to the needs and changed circumstances of the twentieth century.

Local government is seen as big business.[23] The increasing range of responsibilities heaped upon local government, the recognition that services impinge upon one another, and that problems in the local areas are inter-related,[24] gives rather more solid meaning to the anxiety which refers to the existence of fragmentation and the need for co-ordination. Similarly, the fact that local government is seen as operating in a period of increasingly rapid flux and change explains the criticism of incrementalism and the anxiety about the absence of innovation.[25] We are told that the situation has become one in which local authorities should no longer be content with the mere administration of separate services, but should instead turn to the more positive task of managing the overall policy of the authority. As the Working Group on Local Authority Management Structures (1972, p.6) put it, 'local government is not, in our view, limited to the narrow provision of a series of services to the local community . . . It has within its purview the overall economic, cultural, and physical well-being of that community.' In this sort of situation, 'the task of the local authority . . . must be defined in terms of general management — the management of the activities of the authority as a whole in relation to problems which are best seen as inter-related problems within a common environment' (Stewart, 1971B, p.vii).[26]

It is easy to see how critics of traditional administration can go on from their rejection of the 'traditional' role of local government to make a case for wholesale reorganisation. They point to a variety

1972, p.5; Working Group on Local Authority Management Structures, 1972, p.xiv.
23 Harris, 1966, p.37; Ministry of Health, 1924, p.62; Smith, 1965.
24 Finer, 1945, pp.240, 232; Marshall, 1965, p.11; Working Group on Local Authority Management Structures, 1972, p.6; McKinsey and Co., 1971, p.1-1; Etherton, 1924, p.389; Royal Commission on Local Government, 1929, p.118; Burke, 1971.
25 On the problem of actually attaining innovation and co-ordination, see Chapter 7.
26 Within traditional administration councillors 'for the most part . . . perform their management task inadequately if indeed . . . they can be said to perform the management task at all' (Burke, 1971, p.4; Knowles, 1971, p.62).

of changes that have affected local government but they all agree that 'the system of local government administration has its roots in [the] nineteenth century' and that 'the management structures of many local authorities remain those which emerged from the development of local government in the nineteenth century' (Committee on the Management of Local Government, 1967, vol.1, p.35; Working Group on Local Authority Management Structures, 1972, p.4). In effect, they are maintaining that a twentieth-century management role geared to new circumstances and the necessity of co-ordination and innovation cannot be adequately performed within the restricted context of the established nineteenth-century structures and practices. There is a broad consensus around the idea that local government has 'outgrown its organisation' (Webb and Webb, 1932, p.195).

> Machinery which in the old times was sufficient for its limited purpose has become obsolete and new obligations on local authorities demand new methods and new measures . . . The time . . . has come, indeed if it has not already passed, when the problems of local government have attained such dimensions that attention must be directed to the consideration of judicious arrangements in the conduct of local government. (Etherton, 1924, p.389)

The Royal Commission on Local Government in England (1969, vol.1, p.123) noted that the 'system' of traditional administration 'stems from the days when local affairs were so circumscribed that committees of laymen could transact government business in much the same way as that of voluntary organisations', and it went on to note 'that in present day conditions the traditional committee system and departmental approach need . . . radical modification'.[27]

3. Traditional Administration Reformed

The Committee on the Management of Local Government is at something of a turning point between an older and a more recent interest in the internal reorganisation of local authorities. In keeping with the older tradition, the Committee (1967, vol.1, p.48) sets down a new 'organisation . . . [which] provides a framework for effective management', but in anticipation of things to come the Committee recognises that 'this is not enough. The

---

27 See also Grierson, 1928; Marshall, 1965; Finer, 1945; Committee on the Management of Local Government, 1967, vol.1, esp. p.ix; Whyte, 1928; Hart, 1965, p.7.

organisation will not be fully effective unless the *processes* of management are understood and applied.'

(i) *New Structures for Local Government*

Historically, eliminating the bad features of traditional administration and attaining a better system has involved changing the structural basis of local government. Critics have looked outside the experience of British local government and they have seen (a) the system of cabinet government, (b) the organisation of foreign local government, and (c) the organisation of private enterprise, as models for change. Let us look briefly at each of these in turn.

(a) 'The adaptation of the cabinet system to the work of large councils has been discussed on many occasions' (Chester, 1968, p.288). This is hardly surprising, given the entrenchment of a view which suggests that 'the main task of the cabinet is to co-ordinate the work of the various departments and committees and thus ensure that the activity of the government has a certain coherence' (Mackintosh, 1968A, p.413; see also Moodie, 1971, p.88; Bailey, 1959, pp.175–6; Machinery of Government Committee, 1918, p.5). Those critics of traditional administration who admire the cabinet system are suggesting that local authorities should set up some sort of political executive.[28] The core of the Maud Committee's proposals was their suggestion that each council should appoint a Management Board of five to nine members who would 'lead and co-ordinate the work of the authority'. Richards (1973, p.150) had absolutely no doubt that the general effect of their proposals 'would have been to transform each local government unit into a minor model of our system of national government. The Council was Parliament, or perhaps the House of Commons [and] the Management Board was the Cabinet.'[29]

(b) In American local government there is the 'strong mayor' and the council–manager system; in Holland there is the figure of the burgomaster upon whom 'falls the work of political co-

28 See, for example, Marshall, 1965, p.18; Griffith, 1966A; Finer, 1945, esp. pp.221–2; Royal Commission on Local Government in England, 1969, vol.1, p.126; Burke, 1971, p.9; Cossey, 1971, p.34; Smith, 1965.

29 See also Redcliffe-Maud, 1967, pp.350–1. The Maud Committee may have seen cabinet government as some kind of model for local government, but their hatred of party politics led to their drawing back. Their advocacy of minority party representation on the Management Board (later echoed in the Bains Report) really made an unrealistic nonsense of the role which they wanted it to play.

ordination within the local authority'; and 'Swedish local government conforms to the *normal* European pattern of a separate executive organ for advising the council and executing its decisions' (Committee on the Management of Local Government, 1967, vol.4, pp.127, 60, my italics). Stanyer (1970, pp.63—4) was of the opinion that 'if there is one central point in the [Maud] Committee's reasoning, it is that by comparison with other countries there is an absence of unity in the work of a local authority in Britain'. It was hardly surprising that the Committee itself considered that 'foreign experience has clearly a great deal to teach us' (1967, vol.1, p.18).[30]

(c) Gibbon (1931, p.101) has said:

> Now, the work of the local authority, just as a business concern, is often far the largest in the area; and if it were an ordinary business concern there would be a directorate or a management whose job it would be to plan and generally to supervise . . . Would there not be some advantage if there were a committee of carefully selected members of the council, with the particular duty of formulating, so far as that was necessary, long-term programmes for the decision of the council, and still more . . . of seeing that such programmes are prepared by the various committees and of co-ordinating the plan?[31]

It has all been seen as so very simple. Local government is a big business; local government should, therefore, be organised like a business; and local government should be managed by businessmen — by men of calibre who will provide 'vigorous leadership' and 'think about the big things' (Headrick, 1962, p.160; Simon, 1926, p.190). Advocates of reorganisation have consistently shown themselves to be sensitive to more than just the practice and organisation of private enterprise. They have also had intuitive appreciation of a particular tradition of writing on the 'one best way' of organising business management, and I will be discussing the implications of this in my next chapter.

All the sad observations about the state of traditional administration really boil down to a lament that there is an absence of a neatly planned and ordered system based on the principles of

---

30 Finer (1945, pp.253, 243) was alive to the fact that students and practitioners of British local government were attentive to the development of the council—manager form of government in America precisely because 'English conditions were pointing towards a similar institution'. For favourable comments on foreign local government see MacColl, 1951; Page, 1936; Harris, 1939A; Chester, 1968.
31 See also Simon, 1926, p.191; 1932, pp.279—83; New Towns Committee, 1946, p.56; Webb and Webb, 1932, p.195; National Board for Prices and Incomes, 1967, p.23.

scientific management (Page, 1936; Maud, 1932; Jones, 1973); an absence of a decent hierarchic system of control (Committee on the Management of Local Government, 1967, vol.1, p.28; Hart, 1965, p.6); and above all an absence of strong leadership and management whether in the hands of one man or a small group (Harris, 1939A; Webb and Webb, 1932, p.195; Simon, 1932, p.282). Advocates of reorganisation have admired cabinet government, foreign local government, and business management, precisely because they held out the promise of order, hierarchy and leadership, control and co-ordination, and integration based upon simple principles and clean-cut structures.

Let me be more precise as to the particular reorganisation proposals that are part of this tradition. At the core of the proposals on the councillor side is the advocacy of some sort of small central committee to assume responsibility for the control and co-ordination of policy and the overall discharge of the executive and governing function. The case for forming some kind of central group of members is seen as 'unanswerable' (Friend and Jessop, 1969, p.252). An inevitable part of this proposal is the concern to reduce the powers and responsibilities of the separate service committees. This was pushed furthest by the Committee on the Management of Local Government (1967, vol.1, p.43) which considered that committees 'should not be directing or controlling bodies nor should they be concerned with routine administration', but should be 'deliberative and representative bodies' having no direct access to the council but making 'recommendations to the Management Board'. Some critics of traditional administration took exception to the Maud Committee proposals for a Management Board, but there has been a consensus around the proposal to decrease the number of committees and sub-committees, and their overall size. In addition, it is the established view that the committee cycle should be lengthened and that functions should somehow be allocated on a scientific basis centring on 'programmes'. There has been a long-standing concern both to minimise the demands made on members' time, and to concentrate their attention on major matters of policy alone. Indeed, part of the justification for the proposals I have just set down hinges upon their having just this effect. But, in addition, advocates of reorganisation have continually sought to effect a crisper division of labour between councillors and officers based upon the distinction between matters of policy and matters of administration.[32]

On the official side, attention has traditionally centred on the figure of the town clerk who is now much more likely to be called the chief executive officer or even the manager, in keeping with the view that he should be 'recognised as head of the authority's paid service, and have authority over other principal officers so far as this is necessary for the efficient management and execution of the authority's functions' (Committee on the Management of Local Government, 1967, vol.1, p.47). The consensus is such that it is seen as 'difficult to dispute the case for appointing one senior officer to act as overall co-ordinator reporting to the central group of members' (Friend and Jessop, 1969, p.253). To overcome the fragmentation caused by departmentalism and professionalism, local authorities have been urged to create a management team made up of some of the principal officers, and there has been the consistent advocacy of increased recognition being given to administrators and management training at the expense of professionals, technicians and technical training. There has always been a touching faith in the qualities of university graduates, and there has been a general concern with qualifications, recruitment, and training. Needless to say, the number of departments should be reduced, but (in keeping with the sensitivity to the principles of scientific management) local authorities are also urged to have 'regard to the span of control which can be effectively exerted by any head of a department' (Committee on the Management of Local Government, 1967, vol.1, p.58). 'Finally, you have got to trust your officials', and there must be 'more delegation to officers' (Banwell, 1963, p.339). Indeed, in the fictitious authority of 'Newbound',

> it is only to be expected that the elected leaders of the council will wish to give their departmental heads as wide a range of discretion as possible in the running of their departments, so as to free both officers and members from the frustrations of 'committee-itis', which many of them will remember as one of the most inhibiting characteristics of the traditional system of local government.
> (Friend and Jessop, 1969, p.260)

32 See, for example, Local Government Manpower Committee, 1951, p.5; Committee on the Management of Local Government, 1967, vol.1, p.x; Rogers, 1968, p.5.

(ii) *New Processes for Local Government*

Since the mid 1960s advocates of reorganisation have seen structural change alone as inadequate to solve the problem of traditional administration. The Royal Commission on Local Government in England (1969, vol.1, p.123) argued that 'improved co-ordination of largely independent committees and departments will not be enough. Arrangements to ensure a corporate, as opposed to a departmental, view must be an integral part of an authority's organisation, not merely an additional layer on top of an existing system.' Officially, this newer emphasis finds its fullest expression in the 1972 report of the Working Group on Local Authority Management Structures, but a concern to deal with the recent advocacy of internal reorganisation cannot rest content with a study of these official reports alone because academics and management consultants have been involved. In effect, there is an attempt to break away from 'a preoccupation in administration . . . with the structure of an organisation' in order that 'attention is paid to the much more difficult task of the processes that lie behind whatever structure is adopted'. Co-ordination may have been the 'fashionable word in administration a few years ago' but it has come to be recognised as 'compromise too late' (Eddison, 1974, p.12). What is it that progressive authorities should be doing?

In the early 1970s Professor J. D. Stewart was making a case for 'local authority policy planning' which he saw as rather like cost-benefit analysis and meeting 'the need for an authority to consider its activities as a whole in relation to the problems of the area it controls' (1971B, pp.ix, xiii, 132). To this end, local authorities needed to develop 'an action plan as a means of giving expression to the process of policy planning' (1970, p.6), but later he noted that local authorities were pursuing rather different ways of building policy planning with some using programme budgeting, while others relied on structure planning, position statements, or environmental analysis (1972, p.v). By 1974 Stewart had dropped the use of the term 'policy planning' in favour of the term 'corporate planning'. Nowadays the term 'corporate' has come to assume the centre stage in the movement for management change in local government. Knowing this does not contribute much to our understanding. We need to see what is meant by the corporate approach, and we must try and see how

local authorities are advised to go about the process of corporate
planning and management.

The Working Group on Local Authority Management Structures
(1972, pp.83, 49) argued that 'it is of the essence of the corporate
approach to management which we are advocating that there should
be a realistic attempt to plan ahead on an authority wide basis,
to formulate objectives, evaluate alternative methods of achieving
those objectives, and measure the effectiveness of ultimate performance against those objectives'. Local authorities should
recognise 'that there are few if any major decisions which can be
made in isolation . . . [and] corporate management requires that
the implications for the authority as a whole should be considered
and discussed before decisions are taken'. A variety of definitions
of the corporate approach exist within the literature, but the
authoritative definition of corporate planning is provided by Greenwood and Stewart (1974, p.2): 'the word "corporate", represents
an attempt to secure unity of purpose in the affairs of the local
authority. The second element, which corresponds to the word
"planning", emphasises the adjustment of activities to changing
needs and problems.' Now, 'corporate planning and structure
planning cannot be regarded as separate exercises' since they are
'two processes [that] must be closely related' (Stewart, 1971C,
p.132; see also Stewart and Eddison, 1971). In addition, Glendinning and Bullock (1973) argue that corporate planning is also
related to management by objectives, and the chief executive at
Sheffield makes the point that 'management by objectives works
up from the bottom to meet planning, programming, budgeting
coming down from the top' (cited in Cossey, 1971, p.32).

It is difficult not to be confused by the plethora of terms that
are now part of a burgeoning literature, and one chief executive
has recognised that a 'comprehension gap' exists in local government itself because 'the terminology of corporate planning is not
easy' (Rogers, cited in Cossey, 1971, p.20; see also Amos, 1972,
p.20). Having said this, we can surely avoid the semantic confusion
by suggesting that the general advocacy of something involving
'corporateness' is the basic response to the problem of fragmentation that was seen to exist *within* the practice of individual
local authorities. This may be true, but we are also told that
'corporate planning is not enough . . . The making of strategic
decisions must be considered not merely as a corporate but also
as an inter-organisational process.' 'Practical working guidelines'

are needed to contribute to the success of 'inter-corporate' or 'connective' planning based on 'multi-organisations' where skilled 'community reticulists' develop the 'outwardly connective capacities of governmental bodies' and 'manage inter-agency decision networks' (Friend, Power and Yewlett, 1974; Friend and Jessop, 1969; Friend and Yewlett, 1971). Those[33] who press this case are hoping to eliminate the fragmentation that was seen as existing because of the division of responsibilities *between* local authorities, and although this problem is now receiving increasing attention I will restrict my attention to the less complex matter of corporate planning within a single local authority.

To advise a local authority to engage in corporate planning does not tell it what to do. 'The ideas of corporate planning had to be translated into process and procedures . . . [and] early attempts at translation drew heavily upon the framework offered by PPBS' (Greenwood and Stewart, 1974, p.7). PPBS is seen as 'basically the same approach' as corporate planning, and 'there is one clear management conclusion to be drawn from PPBS. It can only be properly implemented in authorities that accept the concept of corporate management.' In a word, 'implementing PPBS . . . entails promoting and improving the corporate management of an authority as one unit' (K. E. Rose, 1970, pp.203, 209; Butt, 1970, p.48). There has been broad agreement on all this. If PPBS is not regarded as a 'comprehensive system of corporate planning' (LAMSAC, 1972, p.5), then it is at least viewed as a 'framework' (Eddison, 1973, p.35), as an 'expression', or as 'an instrument of corporate planning' (Stewart, 1971C, p.131).[34]

PPBS was developed in America.[35] It was introduced into the Department of Defense in 1961. President Johnson was impressed

---

33 For an early recognition of this problem, see Ministry of Health, 1928, p.xv; Warburg, 1929; Harris, 1939A, p.252; Royal Commission on Local Government, 1929, p.35. More recently Eversley (1973, pp.4—7) has referred to the need to develop 'social planning'; Stewart (1972, pp.65—6; 1972A; 1972B) has pointed to the need for 'community planning'; and the Working Group on Local Authority Management Structures (1972, ch. 8) has talked of the necessity of developing the 'community approach'. All these would seem to be different terms for inter-corporate planning.

34 For similar views, see Greater London Council, 1972, p.22; Stewart, 1971B, ch. 3; Lucking, Greenwood and Howard, 1974, pp.137—8; Greenwood, Smith and Stewart, 1971A, p.91; Burridge, 1974, p.21.

35 To gain a certain appreciation of PPBS in America, see Merewitz and Sosnick, 1971; Wildavsky, 1975; Davis, 1969; Novick, 1973; Lyden and Miller, 1972; Schultze, 1968; Schick, 1966; Anthony, 1965; Gross, 1969; Smithies, 1965. For early work on PPBS see McKinsey, 1922; Novick, 1954; Smithies, 1955; Mosher, 1954.

by the 'brilliant success' of the system, and in 1965 he asked all federal agency heads to introduce the system. State and local governments were not left outside the movement. By the end of the 1960s there was a consensus that America faced an 'urban crisis'. It was recognised, just as in Britain, that 'the machinery of city government has been inadequate and inflexible in the face of . . . new and continuing challenges. Too many city agencies at best functioned in a caretaker capacity, unable and unwilling to deal with change and trying instead to keep going and conserve what was there' (Hawley and Rogers, 1974, pp.11—13). The entrenchment of 'departmental thinking'; the 'fragmentation of approach by separate agencies each working on its own mission'; and 'the severe restriction of financial resources' were all 'complexities that . . . stimulated an increasing number of cities throughout the United States to seek improved staff work and better information for decision-making by implementing PPB systems' which were seen as providing an 'explicit mechanism' for ensuring that 'all options are considered in the development of new municipal programs' (Overly, 1967; Mushkin, 1969). As early as 1968, twenty-eight states and sixty local governments reported that they were taking steps toward the implementation of PPBS, and an additional 155 local governments reported that they were considering implementation.

PPBS has come to sweep the world. Canada, Australia, Belgium, Japan, East Africa, France, Sweden, Norway, and the United Nations itself[36] have all enjoyed flirtations with the system and Britain has not been immune from the temptation. Indeed, when a member of the Employment and Social Services Sub-Committee of the Expenditure Committee asked a witness from the Department of Health and Social Security why his department had adopted the system he was told, 'PPBS has become very fashionable, as the Committee will know'.

In 1964 the Ministry of Defence adopted 'a system similar to the PPB system in the United States Department of Defense' (Memorandum by the Treasury in *First Report from the Select Committee on Procedure*, 1968—9, pp.186—93). 'By 1966 the success of the . . . system in the Ministry of Defence . . . caused the Treasury to consider how far such systems might usefully

36 Johnson, 1973; Davey, 1972; Hansen, 1974; Wildavsky, 1975; Greater London Council, 1972; Novick, 1973.

help the civil departments' and a number of feasibility studies were carried out (Bridgeman, 1973, p.93).[37] In 1969 work started on producing a fully operational system for educational policy-making.[38] Programme budgeting may have been 'developing gradually in Britain' (Hirsch, 1973, p.120), but by 1972 there was no doubt that government and Whitehall were 'investing a cautious but considerable stake in PPBS' (Klein, 1972, p.270).

'Local government in England did not hear about PPBS until late in 1967 and early 1968' (Eddison, 1973, p.80), but things have moved swiftly since then. The Council of the Institute of Municipal Treasurers and Accountants in their 1968—9 Annual Report considered 'that the development of planning, programming, budgeting systems (PPBS) is of the utmost importance both professionally and in relation to changes in the management structure and processes in local and public authority finance'. A Midlands Group of the IMTA agreed with their Council that 'programme budgeting is of such importance that its implications need to be fully explored', and a London conference of the IMTA was told that 'programme budgeting is the name of a technique which seems likely to contribute to several of local government's most difficult management problems' (Cranston, 1969, p.70; IMTA, 1970, p.3). PPBS was seen as 'vital' (Plummer, 1969, p.39), 'inevitable' (Shapero, 1969, p.154), and with 'a lot to contribute if correctly interpreted' (Armstrong, 1969, p.458).

By 1970 programme budgeting was 'arousing increasing interest in local government' (Stewart, 1970, p.12). An IMTA survey revealed that 'most of the larger local authorities tend to be giving programme budgeting serious thought, if not action' (Butt, 1970A, p.293), and, in a 'Preliminary statement', members of the IMTA Programme Budgeting Working Party pointed out that 'programme budgeting is necessary' (IMTA, 1971A, p.7).

'1971 was in some ways the turning point' (Skitt, 1975, p.4). The nature of the debate was changing. The IMTA held a seminar on the theme 'Programme budgeting — some practical problems of implementation' which, as the Director of the Programme Office

37 The first feasibility study was carried out by the Home Office and it led to the development of a PPB structure for the Police (Williams, 1967; Wasserman, 1970). A feasibility study was also undertaken for the Department of Education and Science (1970); and significant work was undertaken with respect to expenditure in support of external policy and in the Ministry of Transport.
38 Brierley, 1973; Pile, 1974.

at the GLC pointed out, 'implies I think . . . that most of us accept as reasonable some at least of the various concepts of programme budgeting (or PPBS) and have now reached the stage where we are ready to do something about it' (IMTA, 1970, p.21). This may have been the year of the 'feasibility study', but by 1972 the O and M Work Study Panel of the Local Authorities Management Services and Computer Committee urged that 'the system should be implemented "across the board"' (LAMSAC, 1972, p.41). In 1973, Armstrong (p.109) felt able to argue that 'programme budgeting has already had more influence in local government than any other approach or technique introduced in the post-war period . . . All the indications are that whatever the specific results from particular experiments may be, local government decision-making is undergoing a radical re-appraisal in the light of the insights provided by the programme budgeting approach.' In the same year, Stewart (1973A, p.14) noted how 'most of the corporate planning system has been based upon or been influenced by planning-programming-budgeting-systems (PPBS)'. What, then, is PPBS?

This is not an easy question to answer, because 'the meaning of PPB has not become standardised; it means different things to different people' (Merewitz and Sosnick, 1971, p.1). We can begin by saying that 'programme budgeting is a form of systems analysis', but this does not help us very much as 'no-one can define what systems analysis is or how it should be practiced' (Wildavsky, 1975, pp.326, 320). More specifically, it is clear that those who are advocating the introduction of PPBS into government are rejecting what they see as the essentials of the established process and style of local policy-making. 'Piecemeal improvements are not enough' (LAMSAC, 1972, p.5), and although '"muddling through" may be adequate when the mud is not more than three feet deep, when the mud is ten feet deep, clearly some other method for getting through is necessary' (Dror in Skitt, 1975, p.vii; see also Schick, 1969, p.141; Tudor, 1970, p.3; Rose, 1969). PPBS is this other method. Stewart (1970A, p.10) makes the point that 'the first contribution of programme budgeting is — to challenge prevalent styles of management — to challenge a tradition based on carrying on'. Fairly obviously, then, programme budgeting 'is not descriptive. It is prescriptive. It is based upon a model of how decisions should be made. It is based on a model decision-maker — and on his requirements in making decisions . . . in determining policy' (Stewart, 1971B, p.28; see also, Schultze, 1968, pp.35, 77). This model of how decisions should be made is usually expressed as a series of steps that should be followed by the decision-maker, and it is these steps which, taken together, constitute PPBS. Numerous statements of just what these steps are exist within the literature,[39] but at the same time advocates of the system are concerned to stress how it is all little more than 'a case for more common-sense at the higher levels of activity in . . . government' (K. E. Rose, 1970, p.210). Rivlin (1971, p.3) makes the point that

> anyone faced with the problem of running a government programme
> . . . would want to take these steps to ensure a good job: 1. Define
> the objectives of the organisation as clearly as possible; 2. find out
> what the money was being spent for and what was being ac-
> complished; 3. define alternative policies for the future and collect
> as much information as possible about what each would cost and
> what it would do; 4. set up a systematic procedure for bringing
> the relevant information together at the time the decisions were to
> be made.

She saw PPBS as 'simply an attempt to institutionalise this common-sense approach' and from this sort of perspective it is the 'spirit' (Gross, 1969, p.116) or the 'philosophy' (Eddison, 1973, p.43) that is regarded as all important.

Recently, contemporary advocates of management reorganisation in local government have sought to distance themselves from the PPB system they were so enthusiastically urging on local authorities in the early 1970s. They would admit that PPBS *was* influential in the early days of the movement for corporate planning, but they would go on to point out that 'the initial influence of such projects only waned as doubts were raised of the relevance of foreign experiments, as awareness grew of the problems encountered in those experiments, as experience in this country deepened, and as further influences (e.g. the impact of structure planning, or developing concepts of social planning) began to bear upon the debate' (Greenwood and Stewart, 1974, pp.7–8). The point that must be stressed is that the differences between PPBS, policy planning, corporate planning, corporate management or any other such system or approach to policy-making are entirely inconsequential. At most they differ in terms of the scale or ambition of the analysis or in terms of the claims

---

39 See, for example, Greater London Council, 1970, p.10; Amos, 1970, pp.5–6; Shapero, 1969; K. E. Rose, 1970; Smithies, 1965; LAMSAC, 1972.

that are made for their effect. In reality they are the labels that are equivalent to Wolsley, Austin, or Morris badges on a Leyland car, and, like those badges, they simply represent the reorganising salesman's attempt to capture the market of students and consultancy contracts through the differentiation of his own particular product from the common basic model. Not only are 'most UK corporate planning systems . . . derived from PPBS', but, just like PPBS, 'corporate planning and management [are seen as] . . . little more than the application of common-sense together with the use of rigorous analytical techniques' (Skitt, 1975, pp.42, 6). No matter *what* particular system you study they *all* embody an attack upon incrementalism; muddling through; satisficing; fragmentation; specialist management; professionalism; vagueness of objectives and the failure to make policies explicit; the limited analysis of alternatives; short-term planning; the absence of monitoring and review of performance, and so on. Moreover, to a greater or lesser degree, they all seek to create some new system free of those faults. They seek to implement, that is, a system of general management which starts with the overt formulation of objectives; moves through the careful evaluation of alternative means to the attainment of those objectives before implementing particular policies; finishing up with a careful review of the effectiveness of the chosen policies in meeting the initial objectives, so re-starting the whole cycle of policy-making.

(iii) *Concluding Remarks: New Processes and New Structures*

The new advocates of reorganisation are well aware that wanting a new system of management and actually getting it are two different things. They bring us back full circle when they advise us that '*structural* conditions must be fulfilled before work can proceed on reforming the *processes* of management in a corporate direction' (Hill, 1973, p.9, italics in original). Corporate planning may be 'concerned with the management process, rather than any particular form of organisation structure. Nevertheless it requires — and indeed can only work through — an organisation structure which will serve and not frustrate this process' (LAMSAC, 1972, pp.33—4). Simply expressed, 'without organisational change policy planning will not be established. Unless local authority policy planning is nurtured and sustained by appropriate organisation, the traditional pattern of management will prevail' (Stewart, 1970, p.19).[40] The basic organisational building blocks for the new processes are the familiar policy committee of councillors (which will 'be the main committee responsible for corporate planning' (Stewart, 1974, p.105)), matched by a management team on the officer side led by a strengthened town clerk who will be transformed into a chief executive officer. Of course there exist many variants with subtle additions to the basic orthodox package, but it is difficult to see proposals for an executive office, for a chief executive officer without a department, for departments without committees (and committees without departments!), or for a performance review subcommittee, as being of importance except at the level of detailed variation.

To a considerable extent, then, we are dealing with familiar old wine that has recently been decanted into strong new misty bottles that are now blessed with modern technocratic labels. Not only are local authorities urged to adopt 'new' structures, the essentials of which have been around in the literature for most of this century, but the whole *approach* to reorganisation is in much the same mould as the earlier tradition. Business organisation and practice is still admired,[41] advocates of reorganisation are more sensitive than ever to writing on the principles of good management, and they have shown themselves to be especially attentive to contemporary movements for governmental reorganisation in America. Even so, we should not minimise the extent to which the emphasis has swung from structure to process, and any assessment of the 'success' of reorganisation should pay particular attention to changes in the process and style of policy-making, since nowadays structure has come to be regarded as but a means to this more fundamental end.

40 For similar views on the need for new structures to support new processes see Amos, 1970, p.8; Cranston, 1969, p.67; Greenwood and Stewart, 1972, p.26; 1973, p.65; Greenwood, Smith, and Stewart, 1971, p.17; Stewart, 1971B, pp.158ff.
41 After all, corporate planning and PPBS were both pioneered in the business world. On corporate planning in business see Baynes, 1973; Fulmer, 1974; Ackoff, 1970; Ansoff, 1965.

6

Orthodoxy Explored

Before we decide the future shape of local authorities should we not know how councils work at present? (MacColl, 1951, p.18)

Now that the survey is completed I realise that I have shifted from seeking dramatic and speedy remedies for administrative failing to recognising the many obstacles in the path of reformers.
(Caiden, 1970, p.xi)

I want to explore the essentials of the last chapter — I want to explore, that is, the *case* that has been made for the internal reorganisation of local authorities in Britain.

1. The Problem with 'Traditional Administration Described'

We are provided with an inadequate characterisation of what is called traditional administration. It would be possible to challenge practically all the assumptions, theories and facts that are part of it. We just do not know enough about how things worked within unreformed local authorities. A bibliography of research studies into the actual practice of local policy-making would be very short indeed.

The description of traditional administration is a funny mixture of things. From that tradition of writing which sees local authorities as agents of the central government there is the stress on the importance of law and the inevitable emphasis upon formal structures and processes: local government is seen as simple administration and so there is 'excessive legalism' and '"what should be" is treated as if it were "what is"' (Stanyer, 1976, pp.21–2). From the rival tradition which sees local authorities as the perfect embodiment of a vital local democracy we are provided with normative theories which are brimful with the optimistic assumptions of liberal democratic theory. The excesses of the

146

Electoral Chain of Command Theory may have been tempered, but 'the normative description of the budget-making process . . . is normally the only available description' (Danziger, 1974, p.306). Much of the orthodox literature has been contributed by those who have been part of the system. From the acid pen of these insiders there is sometimes the cynical recognition of the gap between theory and practice, and there is always the crushing assumption that all is revealed through experience without the need for any research. All these various approaches to description are grounded in a potted history of the development of local government in the nineteenth century, and the whole mixture is piously stirred with the spoon of common-sense.

The essence of any critique of the orthodox description of traditional administration must revolve around two things. First, there is inadequate research into the things that are seen as of importance within the system. Second, aspects of government and politics that have to be regarded as of importance to an adequate understanding are not simply left unresearched but are actually ignored. It is all seen as so simple and so obvious.

'It is . . . a relatively easy system to study because things are pretty well what they purport to be. It is not necessary to keep saying that such and such is the law or the theory or that is what is supposed to happen, whereas the reality is quite different. There are few matters where such divergencies exist' (Jackson, 1965, p.viii).[1] It is seen as necessary to study conventions and informal practices when we are dealing with the central government, 'but in the case of local authorities many of these matters which in the case of the central government are left to be determined by mere conventions are prescribed by the law' (Hart, 1968, p.120). In other words, there is often the view that research into local authority practice is not even needed.[2]

Even though there have been those who have deplored the absence of any serious study into the practice of local government,[3] still the gap persists. Stanyer (1971, p.76; 1967A; 1970, pp.64,58) has long bemoaned the 'complete absence of relevant work' and the 'lack of study of the distinctive characteristics of local authorities', and he has mounted a devastating critique against the

1 But see Simon, 1932, p.278.
2 Poor research is often defended and Richards (1973, p.157) defends the partial research base of the Bains Committee.
3 See Wallas in Simon, 1926, pp.viiff; MacKenzie, 1951, p.349; 1953, p.235.

Report of the Maud Committee, claiming that it rested content with the presentation of the 'popular mythology' and the uncritical appreciation of the evidence from 'insiders'. Steer and Lofts (1970) have made much the same points with respect to the Mallaby Committee, and Davies (1973, p.9) has pointed out that a 'lack of rigorous method can be noted in the research carried out by the Working Group [on Local Authority Management Structures]'. Let me be fair. Researchers working for the Committee on the Management of Local Government (1967, vol.5, p.1) recognised the 'lack of detailed work in this field . . . of the existing administrative structure and management processes of local authorities' and they sought to fill the gap. The trouble is that much of the more recent research into local government is totally inadequate. Because everyone already 'knew' how things worked, what was wrong, and what to do, research had been loaded in favour of simply confirming the orthodoxies. Studies that purport to deal with the 'practice' of local government are nothing of the kind,[4] and books on 'management in local government' usually boil down to a series of questions about the ideal number of committees for an individual local authority (Stanyer, 1971, p.73).

We are provided with a simple description which has got more cavalier as the years have passed. The very notion of 'traditional administration' is itself a massive generalisation. It presupposes a uniformity of practice which is a 'myth' (Stanyer, 1976, p.17), and it ignores the sheer variety and complexity of local political practice. The fact that traditional administration is usually characterised as static and unchanging ignores the evolutionary changes that are continually taking place. We are given little more than a snapshot of the governmental personnel and the formal structures of local government. Movie cameras have rarely been trained on local government and its practices, and orthodox accounts provide a hopeless description of councils in action and a useless explanation of the process of decision-making even within the restricted context of governmental relations.

Descriptions of traditional administration persistently ignore the *informal* aspects of politics and they fail to understand and assess the impact of factors from *outside* the town hall. In the first part of this book I have already noted how anti-party moralising

4 See, for example, Hart, 1968, ch. 5; Drain, 1966.

led writers to ignore and underplay the part which parties actually played in the process of local government. If you choose to focus on formal structures alone then of course you will not see a 'separate executive' and you will not see anything resembling a cabinet to provide for a measure of co-ordination. But if you recognise the pressing reality of party in so many authorities then there is the ingredient for something resembling cabinet government, and there is the extra-legal and informal force to provide for as much co-ordination as exists in the central government. Nowadays, there is a grudging recognition and defence of party in local government, but the part which it actually plays is still not adequately researched and studied. Moreover, even if this particular research gap were plugged there are still other factors that would need to be considered if we are to be provided with adequate descriptions of the real processes of local policy-making. Informal rules for councillor recruitment and behaviour have been shown to have a crucial bearing on the development of council policy, and the importance of councillor ideology and information cannot be ignored (Dearlove, 1973; Newton, 1976). Orthodox descriptions of traditional administration never push beyond a consideration of formal structures and governmental personnel to provide us with decent accounts of other factors *internal* to a local authority. They certainly do not consider the impact which the wider *local political environment* has upon governmental action, and it is never part of their brief to have any regard to the impact of forces from *outside* the boundaries of a local authority except to bemoan the supposed weight of central control.

2. The Problem with 'Traditional Administration Assessed'

We can start this brief section with little confidence in the orthodox assessment and critique of traditional administration. If we are provided with an inadequate description then it is unlikely that the diagnosis of (and the explanation for) the faults that are said to exist within the system are going to be any more adequate to the reality of local politics.

We may share the reformers' gut feeling that local government has been dominated by fragmentation and incrementalism, and we may even agree that local government has persisted in assuming a narrow role when this is no longer appropriate, but where are the studies which actually document the extent of these practices and 'problems'? Let us pass over this startling omission. Let us assume that advocates of reorganisation are broadly right in their assessment of the faults of 'traditional administration', and so move on to ascertain the adequacy of the explanations that are offered as to the causes of fragmentation and incrementalism.

Given the emphasis of description it is not too surprising that blame is laid at the door of formal structure. The faults of the system are seen as caused by committees, departments, and professionals. I am not aware of any studies which bother to show just *how* these things affect council action. In effect 'explanation' is made up of the slogans: 'committee mindedness'; 'excessive departmentalism'; and 'professionalism'. These three bad men have been fingered so often that we can easily come to believe that they actually tell us something of real moment, and we cease to ask *what* they mean, let alone *how* and in what conditions they affect the course of council action.

So far I have argued that we do not really know what is wrong with local administration, and I have further suggested that what is usually assumed to cause the 'problems' has never been demonstrated, or proved, to be to blame. I think we can go further than this. We can surely question whether formal structures and institutions *are* the root cause of any fragmentation and incrementalism. Of course we cannot be sure of this, but we do know that advocates of reorganisation have paid scant regard to the political, informal, and economic factors which impinge upon local government and these may well play a much more vital part in sustaining a fragmented and incremental approach to public policy. More to the point, in my study of politics in Kensington and Chelsea I did actually demonstrate that the council was reluctant to innovate. I noted that this went beyond a simple incremental muddling through as it was more involved in the maintenance of a pattern of established commitments. When I went on to try and explain the entrenchment of this approach to public policy I did not find it necessary to refer to committees, departments and professionals. As I saw it, formal structure could *not* be regarded as the major cause of this style and process of policy-making. My explanation, based upon careful research and self-conscious theorising, centred upon the importance of informal rules for the recruitment and behaviour of councillors; the recognition of councillor selectivity with respect to the perception of the local environment and the use of information; and the part played by councillor ideology.

Nowadays as 'knowledge' of the faults of the system of traditional administration has become more widespread, and as criticism of local government has become the fashionable hallmakr of the 'realistic' and dispassionate observer of the local scene, so the case against traditional administration has become less subtle and qualified and even more bald and savage. Expensively employed management consultants, fresh from business and eager to advocate their own particular brand of the principles of management, have come to their new subject with a ready-made analysis and package of proposals which are strongly coloured by their business experience and lightly tinted by a quick flick through of some of the basic texts on problems of local government.[5] Their reorganising tracts are always prefaced by a very brief section on the 'weaknesses in the present system of administration' or the 'problem of the present organisation' (McKinsey and Co., 1971, ch. 1; P. A. Management Consultants, 1969, ch. 1). Wise books on *Practical Corporate Planning in Local Government* now have crisp forewords by international masters of policy science who tartly attest to the 'relatively primitive nature of existing decision-making systems in many of the pre-reorganisation authorities', all on the strength of a brief talkabout with the orthodox masters of local government and its problems (Dror in Skitt, 1975, p.vii). Where is the research, and what is the evidence?

3. The Problem with the Approach of 'Traditional Administration Reformed'

Orthodoxy only gets worse and worse. 'Traditional Administration Reformed' is built not only upon an inadequate appreciation of what is, but also upon a faulty diagnosis and explanation of the supposed ills of traditional administration. We are dealing with the attempt to get rid of problems that are not properly explored in a system that is not adequately understood! Given the limitations of research and the inadequacy of diagnosis, then it is almost inevitably going to be the case that we are presented with a package of prescriptions for improvement that miss the very target they are aimed at. My concern now is to argue that these

5 For a more general comment along these lines, see Self, 1972, p.13.

problems are further compounded by the approach to reorganisation which is firmly grounded in a particular and limited tradition of organisation theory. Advocates of reorganisation situate themselves within classical organisation theory and they carry and use the principles of administration. Three questions must be answered. First, what is classical organisation theory? Second, how can we tell that local government reformers are part of this tradition? Third, and fundamentally, what is wrong with the tradition?

(i) *Classical Organisation Theory*

We can distinguish two distinct strands of classical organisation theory. First, and deriving from the work of Taylor (1911), there is 'physiological organisation theory'. The relevance of Taylorism is really restricted to the level of the shopfloor as on the basis of time and motion studies it aims to ascertain the 'one best way' of performing a particular routine task. Second, built on the pioneering work of Fayol (1916) and later work by Urwick (1943), there is 'administrative management theory' (March and Simon, 1958, p.22), which is more concerned with the grand organisational problems of departmental division of work and coordination. The work of Taylor and Fayol was complementary. Both operated in the interests of the owners of capital and both applied a scientific method to the problem of personnel and its management. However, Taylor worked on the bottom of the industrial hierarchy, whereas Fayol was concerned to provide advice for top management. It is this second strand of management theory that is of particular interest to me because I consider that advocates of management reorganisation in British local government situate themselves within the restrictive context of its thought and assumptions.

In effect, given the general purpose or objective of an organisation, this particular theory is 'concerned with the dual fundamental of achieving effective and clear subdivision of the management responsibility . . . while maintaining integrated unity in action' (Brech, 1965, p.146). To this end classical theorists have been concerned to discover and set down concise and simple principles which would guide managers in building up a formal structure to secure an effective balance between the division of labour and a unity of control,[6] so enabling them to administer and control the established organisation in a rational way (Mouzelis, 1975, p.88).

The fourteen 'general principles of management' set down by Fayol (1916, ch.4, p.vii) were not based on any systematic research, but were the 'fruit of his 30 years of outstanding practical success'. Indeed, 'with few exceptions, the classical writings have not been based on formal empirical research, but on judgement supported by personal experience and thoughts of the writers' (Massie, 1965, p.387). Urwick (1943, p.117), for example, concluded his study on *The Elements of Administration* with the bold and helpful advice: 'Let reason and common-sense prevail'!

In the pioneering days of 1916, Fayol (pp.15, 19) could argue that there was 'no generally accepted theory of management', although he was clear in his own mind that 'the soundness and good working order of the body corporate depends on a certain number of conditions termed indiscriminately principles, laws, rules'. Over the years, the opinions set down in the steady dribble of books by businessmen began to display such 'a remarkable consensus of agreement' that it was regarded as 'strong evidence that there is a common element in all experience of the conduct of social groups, that a true science of administration is ultimately possible' (Urwick, 1943, pp.117–18). Constant repetition of much the same things succeeded in transforming opinion and anecdote into hard-nosed universal principles that were seen as valid in all management situations.

Once you admit that administration is a science and that management is a technical skill which can easily be acquired by those made conversant with the principles of good management, then you open up the 'possibility of management teaching', as there exists a 'body of professional knowledge without which those who attempt to manage other people appear increasingly amateurish' (Fayol, 1916, p.14; Urwick, 1943, p.7). What, then, are the principles of management that form the core of this science of administration?

The famous POSDCORB[7] is often used as a convenient reminder of many of the principles. One of the most specific relates to the

---

6 'The classical theorist assumes that it is possible to determine in advance all the management tasks and processes necessary for the accomplishment of the organisation's objectives' (Massie, 1965, p.400).

7 Planning, Organising, Staffing, Directing, Coordinating, O, Reporting, Budgeting.

'Span of Control': no superior can supervise directly the work of more than five, or at the most six, subordinates whose work interlocks. The 'Exception Principle' suggests that decisions which recur frequently should be reduced to routine and taken low down in the organisation. Various writers refer to the 'Scalar Principle' and the 'Principle of Co-ordination', and it would be possible to set down many more such principles around which there is a broad level of agreement. Rather than trying to offer a comprehensive list it is more important to note that a preoccupation with leadership, control and disciplined hierarchy is really at 'the heart of the classical organisational structure' (Massie, 1965, p.396). Theorists really are obsessed with the tidy-minded desire to spell out everything in advance of any action: 'if there are gaps in the administrative apparatus, these are often pointers to weaknesses in the organisation or to faults in the running of the undertaking' (Fayol, 1916, p.x). All relationships should be clearly defined and nicely set down on an organisation chart according to the principle of order: 'a place for everyone and everyone in his place' (Fayol, 1916, p.36).

Although it is the case that 'the outlines of such principles have appeared first in industry' (Urwick, 1943, p.9), it is of the essence of this approach to argue that such principles have every bit as much relevance for government. Certainly in America 'a great number of changes in the structure of Federal, State, and Local Governments have been urged or justified in terms of the ideas and concepts of "scientific management"' (Self, 1972, pp.19–20).[8] In Britain, the Machinery of Government Committee (1918) provided a classic example of this rationalist approach to reform, and the more recent Committee of Inquiry into the Civil Service (1968, p.13) was also committed to deducing change from general principles, taking the view that 'one basic guiding principle should . . . govern the future shape of the civil service . . . look at the job first'. What about the approach to the internal reorganisation of local government?

(ii) *Local Government Reorganisation and Classical Organisation Theory*

If advocates of reorganisation do not proudly tell us that they are

---

8 For a similar assessment, see Emmerich, 1950; Seidman, 1975. For an interesting critique of this approach to reorganisation in Israel see Shani, 1976.

keen advocates of the principles of administration, then they leave enough tell-tale droppings for us to follow them back into the lair of this tradition.

In 1929, Larkin and Ralph (p.149) pointed to 'the growing recognition of the fact that public administration is a distinct science', and a year later Bunbury (1930, p.275), mindful of the movement for scientific management in industry, thought it 'worthwhile to consider how far it is possible to apply to administrative work the body of ideas, principles, and discoveries, which, in the industrial sphere, is coming to be known, more conveniently than elegantly, as rationalisation'. By 1936, Page (pp.28, 15, 3) — whose book is now much in vogue in reorganisation circles — was in no doubt as to the relevance of this new work on scientific management. He criticised the failure of local authorities to organise committees on 'a scientific basis', and he noted that 'councils do not as a whole realise the necessity for clarity in their internal organisation, as a preliminary to a co-ordinated — and therefore balanced — development'. For Page, the 'first step' to the goal of co-ordination lay in the creation of 'an internally perfected organisation'. In 1934, the Hadow Committee (Ministry of Health, p.33) argued that local government 'officers should be encouraged to study the principles of public administration', and just after the war, Finer (1945, p.280) was urging his readers of the need for the local civil service to receive strict instruction in 'the principles of administration' as this would serve as 'a means of supplying the incentive to co-ordination in each unit to be co-ordinated'. In 1951, the Local Government Manpower Committee (p.5) wanted the various local authority associations to 'formulate general principles which they could commend to their constituent members as a guide when they were reviewing their organisation and procedure'. More recently, E. B. Mayne, a businessman and a member of the Maud Committee, told a RIPA Conference (1967, pp.8, 17) that 'there are a few simple little rules that apply to the organisation of most group activities'. Mayne's own awareness of these rules enabled him to make a swift critique of local government organisation, and gave him the confidence to assert: 'we know the cure for the ills [and] how to bring health and vitality to local government'. At another RIPA Conference (1973, p.53), the Chairman of the Working Group on Local Authority Management Structures, M. A. Bains, urged his audience to look at his report 'in conjunction with some of the principles of modern management', as he thought it 'would

be generally accepted that there are certain matters which are
fundamental to all types of organisation — whether it be in the
company world, a nationalised industry, or a local authority'.[9]
A Member of the Central Training Council was aware that 'local
government explicitly recognises the need to improve its management performance', and he went on to argue that 'the best way
to serve communities has to be worked out from first principles;
past practice alone can be dangerously misleading' (Humble in
Glendinning and Bullock, 1973, p.vii). Knowles (1971, pp.10–11,
14) would not disagree. He was mindful of Fayol's work, aware of
the 'scientific approach to management', and attentive to the fact
that 'certain guidelines . . . are widely accepted'. In his view,
'good organisation is basically straight-forward, clean cut, streamlined', and that was what local government should have been
aiming for.

Naturally enough it is the numerous management consultants
involved in giving advice on the internal reorganisation of local
authorities who have shown themselves to be the most eager to
situate themselves within the classical framework. For example,
in their report on organisation and staffing in the Borough of
Swindon, the P-E Consulting Group (1970, p.B-2) noted that
'the principles of good organisation should . . . be borne in mind',
and they went on to list eight such principles which 'should be the
aims of an organisation'.[10]

Of course much of the literature that I am criticising has been
contributed by insiders and practical men — by people who not
only reject theory but who, in all probability, have never heard of
classical organisation theory let alone read any of the major works
in the tradition. Consciously or not, they are nevertheless working
within the confines of this approach to reorganisation. The absence
of systematic research; the emphasis upon formal structure; the
desire to sweep the slate clean and build up a neat, simple, and
ordered system in which hierarchy and leadership prevail; the
very concern to picture the before and after of organisational
reform; the consistent cry that we need training in management;
and the belief that the parallels which exist between government
and business are such as to warrant attention being paid to the

9 Davies (1973, p.9) sees the Bains Report as 'primarily based upon "classical" management principles'.
10 See also P.A. Management Consultants, 1969; Southend-on-Sea County Borough
   Council, 1969; Booz-Allen and Hamilton, 1969.

best of business practice, are all features of this literature as much as they are hallmarks of classical organisation theory. More specifically, the persistent concern to keep the number of committees down, and the size of the management team and the Policy Committee small, reflects an intuitive sensitivity to the 'commonsense' of the principle of the Span of Control; the desire to effect a crisp division of labour between councillors and officers entails an attachment to the Principle of Order; and the concern to increase the responsibility of the officers ensuring that 'the exercise of discretion is forced as low in the administrative hierarchy as is feasible' is surely grounded in a regard for the Exception Principle (Ripley, 1970, p.108; see also Working Group on Local Authority Management Structures, 1972, p.38).

I could go on, but I have surely done enough to sustain my claim that the approach to reorganisation in British local government is essentially confined within the assumptions of classical organisation theory. Contemporary technocratic advocates of reorganisation may deny that this is so, but they would face an uphill task if they wished to convince me that the limitations of their work were not partly attributable to their operating within the framework of assumptions typical of those who can be more easily labelled classical organisation theorists.[11]

(iii) *The Problem with Classical Organisation Theory*

The fact that the approach to reorganisation is grounded in classical organisation theory tells us nothing of critical importance. We must go on to ask if it matters that local government reformers are part of this tradition. In other words, we have to be sensitive to the limits of classical organisation theory and to the critique that has been advanced against this tradition of work precisely because it must rub off on, and pose a challenge to, the orthodox approach to the internal reorganisation of local government in this country.

At the core of classical theory are the principles of administration, which, if followed by the busy manager, are seen as inevitably leading to his running an efficient and productive organisation. The most direct challenge to the entire classical

---

11 Both Landau (1969) and Wildavsky (1966) recognise the similarity between scientific management and programme budgeting.

school was first expressed by H. A. Simon in 1947 (1957, p.20):[12]

> It is a fatal defect of the current principles of administration that, like proverbs, they occur in pairs. For almost every principle we can find an equally plausible and acceptable contradictory principle. Although the two principles of the pair will lead to exactly opposite organisational recommendations, there is nothing in the theory to indicate which is the proper one to apply.

The principles are mere truisms. They are little more than platitudes, and the number of them could be increased almost *ad infinitum*. They certainly do not provide any sort of basis for effecting governmental reorganisation. They can only ever serve as a pseudo-scientific seal of approval which varnishes over the prejudices and assumptions built into the mundane.

More fundamentally, classical organisation theory needs to be seen and assessed within the context of the industrial and organisational practice it was designed to shape. The enormous growth in the size of enterprises increased the scope for the division of labour at the same time as it exacerbated the problem of coordination. Even more to the point the aggregation of large numbers of workers in one place increased the possibility of their own organisation in the face of capital, and so intensified the problem of controlling alienated labour. Both strands of classical theory have to be seen as a response to this crisis of control in a situation where what Taylor called 'ordinary' management was not up to the mark. This whole tradition of scholarship 'starts . . . from the capitalist point of view, from the point of view of the management of a refractory workforce in a setting of antagonistic social relations' (Braverman, 1974, p.86).[13] Such theory not only serves to '"dehumanise" the individual' (Pfiffner and Sherwood, 1960, p.109) but students who operate within the framework of its assumptions and values are acting as the simple 'servants of power' (Baritz, 1960). There is no doubt that the most crucial critique of classical organisation theory lies in the necessity of challenging the integrity and morality of theorists in terms of the interests they are serving in the name of science.

Having raised this I shall not pursue it further, partly because it is of more limited relevance in the context of governmental organisation where conflicts take a rather different, and more

---

12 But see Coker, 1922; Hyneman, 1939. See also Fesler, 1957.
13 See also Merkle, 1968.

complex, form than those experienced in the industrial sphere. Even so, at a more modest level, the fact that classical theorists are involved in understanding an organisation from the perspective of top management does inevitably mean that they are operating on the basis of particular assumptions which lead to their providing us with an inadequate and blinkered perspective on organisations (Seidman, 1975, pp.5—6). This inadequacy is still further compounded by the fact that administrative management theorists have abstained from any decent empirical research and observation. As a consequence of all this they have consistently 'minimised the effects of the human factor in organisation', and neglected the psychological and sociological variables of organisational behaviour. 'Such concepts as loyalties, identification, informal organisation, statutes, power, human interaction, influence, and information . . . are not found in the strictly classical approaches' (Massie, 1965, pp.386, 403). Not surprisingly, administrative reformers, being part of this tradition, have persistently failed to take into consideration

> the requirements of motivational and behavioural factors and patterns, the subcultural traits of the work groups, the forces and factors making for resistance to administrative change, and the vital points where actual power is located as against formal authority. These behavioural aspects are no less important than the mechanistic conception of unity of command, span of control, precedents and rules; and unless they are paid due attention it is doubtful if any administrative reform or reorganisation, based largely on the scientific management approach, will effectively and comprehensively improve the operations of government.   (Banerjee, 1963, p.455)

The truth of the matter is that 'the framework of action provided by group ties is of prime administrative importance. If the directives of [informal] groups with which a person identifies himself are antagonistic to administrative goals, the administrative task becomes more difficult' (Grodzins, 1951, p.90; see also, Page, 1946—7). Built into the classical perspective is a reluctance to recognise conflict and note the part which politics play in organisational life. Classical theorists do not simply fail to take such 'human factors' into account because they reject their relevance: 'the idea that organisations should be built around and adjusted to individual idiosyncrasies, rather than that the individuals should be adapted to the requirements of sound principles of organisation, is as foolish as attempting to design an engine to accord with the whimsies of one's maiden aunt rather than with the laws of mechanical science' (Urwick, 1937, p.85). In the field of public administration all this finds expression in the concern to maintain a crisp distinction between policy and administration, and in the particular field of British local government studies we find two influential writers arguing that the study of public administration and research into local government reorganisation 'should be comparative with the field of organisation theory rather than of political science' (Hinings and Greenwood, 1973, p.33).

Classical theorists provide us with an extremely simple, limited and partial view of organisation and organisational behaviour.[14] The emphasis is on formal structure and disciplined organisation. An organisation is seen as task-oriented alone, and in so far as it is recognised as a community (or as more than a means to an end) then this is viewed as an aberration or as something to be specially harnessed to organisational purpose. It is assumed that careful planning and a judicious blend of the carrot and the stick can succeed in effecting co-ordination and ensuring that all behaviour is mechanically brought into line in the service of the organisational objective laid down from on high. In the more specific context of administrative reorganisation this approach 'sets up quite inaccurate models often about what the system is and, always, about what it can be' (Schaffer, 1973, p.99). Administrative reform is conceived as 'primarily a technical problem', and 'the myth persists that we can resolve deep-seated and intractable issues of substance by reorganisation' (Leiserson, 1947, p.68; Seidman, 1975, p.4). We are thrust into the murky waters of what Schaffer (1976, p.33) has called the 'fallacy of neo-institutional therapy': a tendency in administrative behaviour is observed (or imagined!); is described as pathological; is seen as caused by particular institutional arrangements; and so 'the necessary therapy must be a new institution'. The ignorant simplicity and naive confidence of such a crude formula needs no critical comment, but it does bedevil the case for administrative reorganisation in British local government. For example, a research team working for the Royal Commission on Local Government in England (1969, Research Study 7, p.184) was pondering the problem of co-ordination in a large local authority. It took the view that 'these problems can be overcome . . . by establishing formal channels of communication and by developing customs which keep the number of informal channels which are actually manifested well below the theoretical maximum'.

14 March and Simon, 1958, p.33; Massie, 1965, p.405.

The problem with this sort of approach to reorganisation lies in the fact that such theory now represents 'only a quite small part of the total theory relevant to organisational behaviour' (March and Simon, 1958, p.33). 'There are significant intellectual lines that need to be explored as a result of recent scholarship in organisation theory, politics and philosophy' (Elden, 1971, p.36). This work, and the work of the human relations school in particular, focuses on many of the crucial aspects of organisation and behaviour that have been persistently ignored within the classical formulation, just as they have been ignored by reorganising students of local government in Britain. It not only provides a challenge to any simple conception of organisation, but it also raises massive problems as to the feasibility and possibility of actually implementing the dramatic sorts of reorganisation that are proposed by those who choose to situate themselves in the context of this tradition. These problems will be more fully discussed in the next chapter, but for the moment it is enough to note that any organisation is much less malleable and amenable to social engineering from above than classical theorists would have us believe. (On this see Caiden, 1970, esp. ch. 6.) Like it or not, organisations *can* become ends in themselves; goals are complicated, muddled and ill-defined; motivation is a problem that cannot be assumed away; conflict and politics are everyday features of organisational life; and even managers have capacities far below the duties that are thrust on them by classical theorists. It is a dangerous illusion to believe that a crisp and effective division of labour can be co-ordinated around the organisational objective. It is unlikely that there is one objective; the demise of the policy—administration dichotomy shows the impossibility of effecting such a division of labour; and the struggle to attain co-ordination is a dream, as compartmentalism is quite simply 'inescapable' (Schaffer, 1976, p.10).

Any critique of scientific management and classical organisation theory can also slip into a more generalised critique and discussion of the limits of the discipline of public administration itself, especially as it has been practised in Britain.[15] It is no part of my brief to deal with this, but it is interesting to note that the strong orientation to reform within this tradition has involved an absence of decent research and an inadequate conceptualisation of governmental organisation, at the very same time that there has been an

15 For a critical discussion of public administration, see Rhodes, 1976; Ridley, 1972.

intuitive groping towards some sort of principled approach to solving the enduring problem of 'inefficiency'. Indeed, the persistence of the view that government is 'inefficient' has made it a natural target for the salesmen with the bag of principles of administration, and the 'traditional principles have kept more appeal as prescriptions for government than for business' (Self, 1972, p.28).

It is true that there has been a certain sensitivity to the limitations of the 'old style public administration',[16] and although this has not been well-developed in the British context there are nevertheless influential figures who take the view that 'public administration could perhaps develop towards . . . policy science' (Stewart, 1971D, p.42). This newer approach has been more committed to empirical research, but it has adopted an orientation to policy and to those in power which has set severe limits on the nature of enquiry. In the world of local government there are strong pressures for the establishment of closer links between local government and the universities where research is helpful to those in government, and where academics engage in providing modern management training for councillors and officers in order to help them to manage in the face of opposition. I comment on this in Appendix 2.

4. Conclusion

'So often one encounters situations where a lot of helter-skelter activity is generated to solve administrative problems of which there is no real and genuine perception' (Butani, 1966, p.612; see also Harrison, 1952, p.141). This is what has been happening with respect to the internal reorganisation of local authorities in Britain. The approach to reorganisation is based on inadequate theory, and, related to this, it is guided by a deficient understanding of what is, and by a hopeless diagnosis of what is wrong. Practical men, eager to be relevant, have been concerned to describe and criticise quickly before moving on to their task of suggesting changes and making things 'better'. Their failure to engage in any systematic research, and their need for a simple key to improvement, led them towards the principles of admin-

16 This development has progressed especially far in America. See Marini, 1971; Waldo, 1971.

istration. The acceptability of the prescriptions contained in these principles is dependent upon constant repetition by people who are seen as having a reputation for knowledge and wisdom about local government and administrative reorganisation. In the world of British local government all the influential figures and institutions have long been broadly united in their description and assessment of traditional administration and in the package of principled proposals to set things aright. In consequence orthodoxy has enjoyed an immunity from attack which is quite unjustified.

7

Organisational Change and the Problem of Implementation

accepting the concepts and implementing them are two very
different things.   (Taylor, 1972, p.251)

. . . bookcases are full of glossy corporate plans which are incapable
of realisation. (Letter from a personal assistant to the chief executive
and town clerk of a large metropolitan district)

Needless to say, most local councils in general and the London
Borough of Lambeth in particular, fall about as far short of the
ideal corporate scheme as a rowing boat does of a nuclear submarine.
                                        (Cockburn, 1977, pp.10—11)

It is one thing cavalierly to condemn 'traditional administration',
but it is quite another thing to change it. The implementation of
planned organisational change is always a problem and it is likely
to be a particularly acute problem with respect to the package of
proposals that is the focus of this study. This chapter is anchored
around two related concerns. First, I want to outline the changes
that have occurred within local authorities in the last decade or so.
Second, I want to deal with the problem of implementing any
rational-comprehensive approach to local policy-making, be it in
the guise of PPBS, corporate planning, or just plain corporateness.
This latter task will involve my considering the history of similar
attempts at governmental reorganisation that have been made
elsewhere. In addition, I will need to have regard to the related
theories that have been advanced to explain why policy-making
tends to be 'irrational', 'fragmented', and 'incremental'.

1. The Extent of Change

'There are signs of . . . change' (Drain, 1966, p.72). 'Local government decision-making is undergoing a radical reappraisal', and as
'the movement towards corporate planning' picks up so 'local
government is now becoming more corporate minded' with 'an

increasing number of authorities . . . seeking to establish' policy planning or some such new and improved system of policy-making (Armstrong, 1973, p.109; Stewart, 1974, p.9; Lawrence, 1975—6, p.2; Stewart, 1971E, p.968). Statements of this kind are two a penny. They are worthless. They tell us virtually nothing about the extent or the success of particular reorganisation attempts. In hard terms, what has changed; what is new; and to what extent have the orthodox proposals for new structures and new processes in local government actually been put into effect?

We cannot answer these questions with any real precision. We do not have decent information on unreformed local authorities; the fact that corporate planning is a recent innovation means that we cannot expect there to be substantial and detailed studies of reorganised practice; and it is impossible to summarise the new situation briefly and generally because 'variation . . . exists' (Greenwood, Lomer, Hinings, and Ranson, 1975, p.80). It may be the case that there has been no 'slavish adoption of any single new system' so that there is 'no dangerous new orthodoxy', but there are, nevertheless, 'instances of deep similarity' and it is these that I wish to grasp and set down in the first part of this chapter (Ripley, 1970, pp.122—3; Greenwood, Smith and Stewart, 1971A, p.85). Any attempt to document the general state of play with respect to the changes in the internal organisation of local authorities has to rely on the surveys that have been carried out by members of the Institute of Local Government Studies at Birmingham University.

Their first survey[1] looked at management reorganisation in the light of the proposals made by the Maud Committee and dealt with the situation in 1969—70. The Institute was concerned 'to examine the pattern of organisation throughout local authorities: and to examine the extent to which local authorities have moved towards a system of corporate planning for the authority as a whole'. Given the orthodox view that traditional administration suffered from fragmentation because of the excessive structural 'differentiation' associated with the existence of numerous independent committees and departments, the Institute survey was

---

1 Greenwood, Norton, and Stewart, 1969; 1969A; 1969B; 1969C; Greenwood, Stewart, and Smith, 1972; Greenwood, Smith and Stewart, 1971; 1971A; 1972. Unless otherwise stated, all quotations in my presentation of the survey results are drawn from one of these sources, and they will not be cited more specifically. See also Booz-Allen and Hamilton, 1970.

concerned to discover just how far the 'integrative' mechanisms of policy committees, principal officers, and management teams had been introduced into local government, together with three supporting approaches to co-ordination based on interlocking committee memberships, co-ordinating officers, and working parties of officers. Few authorities ignored the report: 'the diagnosis . . . has largely been accepted by local authorities' and most chose to review their internal organisation. What has been the result?

All local authorities rejected the Maud Committee's central proposal for a management board, but there was 'widespread acceptance' of the need for an overall co-ordinating policy committee. 'The vast majority of London Boroughs, the majority of County Boroughs, and nearly half the County Councils have a policy committee. This is a recent development', but they have nevertheless 'become an established feature of English local government . . . [in] the quiet revolution that has overtaken the management structures of many local authorities since 1967'. In addition, although not going as far as the Committee would have liked, 'it is clear that there have been serious reductions in the numbers of committees and subcommittees by authorities', and although moves to reduce the size of committees were rather less successful, size has been held constant and in some places the cycle of meetings was lengthened.[2] This evidence suggests that the effect of these changes has 'led to a great reduction in the number of committee and subcommittee meetings to which members are summoned monthly, and contributed to a lowering of the time consumed in attendance at such meetings'. Several authorities have also removed a 'considerable number of matters of detail from committee agendas' but this has generally fallen 'a long way below the level the Maud Committee contemplates as possible within the present law'.

Maud-type proposals for the officer side of the local government machine were implemented less frequently. 'Few authorities have changed the formal position of the clerk' although 'under the impact of the movement towards corporate planning there have been signs that a wider conception of the role of the principal

---

2 However, there was 'little indication that county authorities are altering the frequency of committee meetings'. In fact, pruning the committee structure has been a long-established practice. In 1929, Edinburgh cut the number of committees to ten (for a while!), and major cuts were made in Blackpool in the late 1950s (Swaffield, 1960).

officer has been gaining acceptance'. A number of local authorities created chief officers' groups, but although 'a management team is found in two-thirds of all county boroughs and London Boroughs' they vary in size and frequency of meetings. Only a 'limited number of authorities . . . have carried out a radical regrouping of departments' and 'many county councils' clearly considered that the proposals to decrease the number of departments 'do not apply to county authorities generally or themselves in particular'. Those members of the Institute who conducted the survey were mindful of the variation which existed in the response of the various local authorities, and their survey revealed the differences regarding the extent to which local authorities had established a policy committee, a principal officer, and a management team. '57% of the London Boroughs, 31% of the county boroughs, and 21% of the county authorities use all approaches. None of the three approaches were in use in one of the London Boroughs, 19% of the county boroughs, and 32% of the county authorities.'

This early survey was solely concerned to note *structural* change. Nothing was done to explore the extent to which local authorities were changing the *process* and style of their policy making in spite of the fact that members of the Institute were in the forefront of this particular movement for change. In fact, the authors drew conclusions which went way beyond the evidence they had collected, since they were of the opinion that the structural forms which were emerging in 1969—70 were 'clear evidence that the majority of local authorities are in the process of drawing together their sum total of activities in an attempt to improve "co-ordination"'. There was the view that 'the movement for organisational change is still strong, and . . . in a considerable number of authorities the purpose of change is probably to secure the advantages of administrative efficiency . . . however . . . in a limited, but significant, proportion of authorities, especially in the London and county boroughs, the purpose of change is to establish a system of corporate planning'.

In the summer of 1973, members of the Institute started work on a second survey.[3] 'The Local Government Act of 1972 provided

---

3 Greenwood, Lomer, Hinings, and Ranson, 1975; Greenwood, Hinings, and Ranson, 1975; Hinings, Greenwood, and Ranson, 1975; Hinings, Ranson, and Greenwood, 1974. Unless otherwise stated all quotations in my presentation of this survey are drawn from one of these four sources, and they are not cited more specifically in my account. See also Lucking, Greenwood, and Howard, 1974.

local government with an opportunity to implement many of the new ideas on management organisation.' The Report of the Working Group on Local Authority Management Structures had been published, and local authorities were under substantial pressure to put into effect the corporate approach.

The survey sought to identify the salient features of the management structures of the new authorities in order to see how they compared with the structures prevalent before reorganisation. On the councillor side 'local authorities are now considerably more streamlined (in terms of numbers of committees) than was previously the case', and 'relatively few sub-committees have been set up'. However, in spite of the orthodox advocacy of small committees, local authorities have not implemented this proposal and many have even been forced to 'reinflate numbers of members per committee in order to give members "something to do"'. The Working Group went beyond simply proposing a reduction in the number and size of committees, since it also had regard as to the *criteria* to be used in dividing up committee responsibilities. Local authorities were advised to adopt the 'programme committee' concept, and although this 'has not been rejected explicitly by local authorities . . . the specific committees set out in the Working Group's Report are not always accepted . . . [and] several traditional committees have survived reorganisation'. The survey also discussed the emergence of area committees and the use of informal working groups of councillors, but it recognised that these were 'still comparatively rare innovations'. It was clear from the earlier survey that the policy committee was an 'established feature' of English local government, and 'reorganisation . . . has brought to a head the pre-reorganisation movement towards the policy committee as the hub of the committee system'. But although the Bains Report stressed the quite crucial importance of monitoring and reviewing established policies and commitments and wanted to see a performance review subcommittee, 'fewer than half' the new authorities have followed this crucial piece of advice. On the official side, the good news for advocates of reorganisation is that 'all but one authority has a chief executive' and 'all authorities have a management team'; but the bad news is that 'traditional departments have, by and large, retained their status' and 'few authorities would appear to have broken from the professional base'. After documenting the extent of these various structural changes, the authors go on to identify the degree to which the various structural characteristics hang together to form organisational patterns and they attempt to explain the similarities and variations they uncover by relying upon 'contingency theory'. The explanatory part of this work need not concern us, and although it is important to be aware that variation exists, the authors feel able to make the general point that there has been 'the widespread acceptance of a number of central concepts and of the corporate approach'.

This survey (like their first one) simply documented the extent to which new formal structures had been introduced into local government. There was again a tendency to assume something of an automatic match between the new formal structures that *have* been introduced and the new processes of rational-comprehensive policy-making which advocates of reorganisation *wanted* to see introduced. For example, Greenwood and Stewart (1973) have assumed that a particular conception as to the role of local government and the style and process of local policy making 'would manifest certain structural features appropriate to it but less appropriate to another'. In an authority with an 'integral' view of its role and geared to corporate planning they would expect to find a chief executive officer, a management team, and policy committee. In saying this they are choosing to see formal structure as a simple *measure* of the reality of the policy process.[4] Given what we know about the relationship between formal structure and organisational behaviour this has to be sharply questioned, because informal structure and non-structural variables have a quite crucial impact on behaviour almost regardless of the state of formal structure. Fortunately, the authors of the second survey seem to have realised this point. They were aware that their questionnaire surveys of structural change were of only 'limited value' because 'they tell us very little of how particular structures are actually *operating*' to change the process and style of policy-making.

In order to fill this gap, work started on a third study[5] of a 'limited number of authorities in order to appreciate the processes of management supported by particular structural arrangements'. This study, based largely on interviews with chief officers in

4 See also Greenwood, Smith and Stewart, 1971A, p.56; 1972. They argue that corporate management is 'expressed' in the officers' management team.
5 Greenwood, Hinings, Ranson, and Walsh, 1976. All quotations that follow are drawn from this source and are not cited more specifically.

twenty-seven authorities, sought to explore 'the process of organisation functioning' and focused particularly on the way policy-
making was managed and on the budgetary process. The findings
with respect to the reality of the policy process in these authorities
are of particular interest to us, given the fact that 'corporate
planning represents an attempt to be explicit about the system
of policy making'[6] where there is 'an attempt to secure unity of
purpose in the affairs of the local authority' by breaking down the
professionally or departmentally based policy-making focus that
was seen as so typical of traditional administration. The authors
'think of the policy-making process in local government as being
organised along a professional-departmental—corporate dimension',
and although they do not deal too much with the actual explicitness of the process they do spend a lot of time identifying
the focal point of policy-making power in order to see whether it
is still rooted in committees, departments, and professionals, or
whether it is now located in the corporate structures of chief
executive, management team, or policy committee.

'There are a number of authorities, particularly counties and to
a lesser extent shire districts' which still adopt the 'traditional . . .
professional-department approach'. These authorities all have the
'primary corporate mechanisms' of chief executives, management
teams, and policy committees, but they simply 'do not operate
in the corporate way that was envisaged by Bains'. The truth of
the matter is that 'there are some local authorities where the
corporate structure exists on paper but it has little or nothing to
do with the actual operation of policy-making'. Even at a more
general level, the 'corporate additions of the chief executive,
management team, corporate groups, and policy committee . . .
[have] to a large extent . . . been overlain onto the ongoing
operating structure of line departments and service committees'.
Advocates of corporate planning may, nevertheless, gain a certain
comfort from the fact that some authorities ('found across all
types') have adopted a 'collaborative approach (a cautious evolutionary approach) to corporate working' where the management
team, the chief executive and the policy committee are all coming
to assume rather more of an interventionist role. In those auth-

6 That is, policy-makers should be explicit in 'deciding long-term objectives; analysing
  alternative courses of action; deciding between alternatives; implementation and
  monitoring' (Greenwood, Hinings, Ranson, and Walsh, 1976, p.17). It hardly needs
  saying that to seek this sort of explicitness embodies the essentials of the common-
  sense of programme budgeting.

orities which are supposedly struggling towards a 'comprehensive corporate approach' (and we are not told just how many are attempting this) then the 'chief executive will have an active role as the policy adviser and director'; the policy committee will be 'directive in its relations with the service committees'; and 'the management team will probably see itself as the officer corollary of the policy committee'.

At a general level, 'the departmental structures, established at the time of reorganisation, have changed little since then', and the 'tension . . . between central departments and service departments . . . has . . . been exacerbated since reorganisation'. New departments that have been created out of a number of other departments have 'often suffered more from cutbacks' and have been the subject of major 'conflicts' and 'antagonisms'. The continuing strength of the established departments and professional groups is revealed in 'the lack of commitment to interdisciplinary working groups in many authorities'; in the 'considerable doubt in many authorities about the value of central corporate planning units'; in the fact that 'very few authorities have central research and intelligence units'; and in the fact that personnel management 'does not tend to play an important part as was envisaged before reorganisation'. For the committed advocate of the corporate approach 'the ideal of the way in which a chief officer should operate is that of a general, positive, policy adviser', and it can give such a person little comfort to know that 'the reality has been different . . . Chief officers have had to spend their time "plugging the gaps"' and this has not simply been the result of reorganisation as 'this tendency is on the increase rather than the decrease'.

'Old' structures and ways of working may survive and pose a challenge to the development and implementation of the corporate approach, but it is quite clear that Greenwood and his associates see the development and growth of corporate planning as related to the particular roles assumed by the chief executive, the management team, and the policy committee. Let us see what they have to say about the situation with respect to these roles and structures.

In the smaller shire districts the chief executive will be little more than *primus inter pares*. In the shire county and in the large shire district he will assume the role of 'administrative co-ordinator'. It is really only in the metropolitan authority that the chief executive is anything like 'the policy-maker and director'

defining his responsibility as 'being one of shaping and implementing a policy of corporate management and planning'.
The management team has been a problematic innovation. Few
authorities have followed the orthodox advice and created a small
team because of the 'social problems of resentment, suspicion,
and communication' where certain officers are excluded. Where
a team has tried to develop a sense of 'collective responsibility'
this has 'frequently evoked considerable hostility on the part of
members'. Simply expressed,

> it is not clear that the management team has been one of the
> successes since reorganisation: unity at a personal level has not
> necessarily permeated the authority and subsequently led to
> integrated departmental work relations between the disparate
> departments; agendas have been cluttered with too much detail;
> and consensus management has too often obliterated a necessary
> diversity of opinion.

On the councillor side, although there are some authorities where
the policy committee assumes a 'co-ordinating role', and there are
others where it assumes a corporate and 'interventionist' role,
the 'largest group of local authorities' has a policy committee
which assumes a 'commenting' role where 'the locus of policy-
making is still within the service committee'. Although the authors
continually stress the extent to which the financial situation is
driving local authorities towards an explicit approach to policy-
making, they nevertheless recognise that this may engender
'rumblings and even revolts' from 'backbenchers' which will
clearly limit the political feasibility of such developments.

2. The Problem of Implementation

Can incrementalism and fragmentation be abolished and replaced
by an innovatory and co-ordinated approach to policy-making
which looks at problems and policies in the round on an authority-
wide basis? Put more concisely, can the corporate approach be
implemented in the real world of British local government?

In order to answer this question we need to adopt two complementary approaches. First, we cannot avoid exploring the detailed
reality of public policy-making in different local authorities in
order to see how far it matches up to the corporate ideal. I am
painfully aware of the particular need for good close studies of
those authorities which are held out as being at the very forefront
of the movement for corporate planning. Having said this, we must

not pretend that work of this kind alone[7] will ever provide a definitive answer to our question, as such an approach enables advocates of the new system to claim that full implementation is just around the corner where the problem will be solved given time, good will and changing attitudes. Second, therefore, this kind of work must be buttressed and informed by a particular sensitivity to theory. In my view, we have a lot to learn from the history of, and the literature on, other attempts at governmental reorganisation that have similarly sought to banish incrementalism and fragmentation on the basis of the same sort of rationalist, or principled, approach to change. The best of this literature is of particular interest precisely because it does more than simply *describe* the gap between principled proposals and actual change; it *explains* it as well. In doing so it also explains the reality of public policy-making and why it will always tend to fall a long way short of any co-ordinated or innovatory ideal. Moreover, explanation locks into more powerful theoretical work on policy-making and organisational behaviour. All of this anticipates a literature which I feel must surely develop here as soon as research is conducted into the practice of reorganised local government. It contains lessons for us all, and it poses questions and suggests theories of crushing relevance.

We can make a good start by reading some of the basic texts discussing the sense and fate of the proposals for fundamental change in the structure of the British central government. The principled approach of the 1918 Haldane Committee on the Machinery of Government ignored the crucial fact of party politics, and although 'for a generation of administrative scholars [it] assumed the status almost of holy writ' (MacKenzie, 1950, p.57), 'it has had no actual influence at all' (Schaffer, 1973, p.67; Chester and Willson, 1968, p.294). More specifically, Daalder (1964, p.264) has noted how three themes have recurred with great

---

7 At a general level, and in advance of specific research, we must heed the wealth of evidence in the third INLOGOV study; we can note the problem of effecting fundamental change in a situation where the personnel in government may be those who were responsible for (and perhaps committed to) the 'old' system; we must be sensitive to the implications of party allegiance for management reform (Hampton, 1972); we should be alive to the 'traditional backlash' led by educational administrators (Williams, 1976; Rowan, 1977; Fiske, 1975; see also Michael Harrison's 1976 presidential address to the Society of Education Officers); and we cannot ignore the quite overt moves to dismantle key facets of Bains-type proposals be they in Birmingham, the West Midlands, or Exeter.

frequency in the twentieth-century debate on the reorganisation of cabinet government: '(a) there should be a fundamental redistribution of tasks among departments; (b) a small non-departmental cabinet . . . should be established; and (c) cabinet membership should be restricted.' In three painstaking chapters Daalder takes these proposals apart. His general point is that those who demanded 'basic changes in the machinery of government . . . had little influence on actual developments' (p.311). The proposals for wholesale reorganisation 'were often blocked by resistance from ministers . . . [and] high civil servants also resist basic changes' (p.272). Major attacks from outside only succeeded in provoking defensive reactions. It is perhaps worth paying a little more attention to the proposal for a small policy cabinet, designed to discuss and co-ordinate general policy on the basis of the long view and unfettered by the burden of departmental politics, because it has so much in common with the proposals put forward by those who want to see corporate planning and a small policy committee in local government. A small cabinet of this kind sounds fine in theory, but in practice experiments with them were short-lived because they met with the strong antagonism of the politicians and departments excluded. Chester (1950, p.55) doubts 'whether it would ever be a workable system' precisely because 'it is unlikely that such a small cabinet would accord for long with political realities'. In short, the push for an objective policy for government by a small far-sighted cabinet 'was powerless and unreal in the actual world of personal and group conflict' (Daalder, 1964, p.295).

All these tidy-minded scientific proposals for change have sprung from a technocratic apolitical mentality which embodies an intellectual protest against the messy realities of political and bureaucratic life, but because they have been politically naive they have inevitably lacked political feasibility. 'There is no simple or single formula by whose application all the problems of administrative arrangement can be solved', and Chester and Willson (1968, pp.390, 413) go on to note that it is now 'beyond dispute that the adaptation of the organisation of government must be continuous and cannot be divorced from the normal administrative process'. More pointedly still, MacKenzie (1950, p.82) has argued how 'the great changes in administration have come about through causes partly fortuitous, partly political, but on the whole outside the range of administrative planning'.

So the experience of reorganisation at the level of the central government suggests that the actual implementation of drastic change is unlikely, and although changes do occur they are not 'planned' but are 'usually made *ad hoc* to meet particular circumstances' where the impulse is political and personal rather than purely organisational in character (MacKenzie and Grove, 1957, p.218). Moreover, it is clear that definite political passions lie at the root of the demands for supposedly rational and neutral change in structure and process,[8] and planned change often produced effects that are seen as undesirable and the opposite of those intended.[9]

In America, the principled approach to the reorganisation of the federal government[10] has also been denounced (Meriam and Schmeckebier, 1939). Even so it continues to stage periodic comebacks, but these are unimplementable because 'two basic factors producing "bad" management — clientele and congressional demands — cannot be eliminated' (Fox, 1973, p.405).[11] Over thirty years ago, Leiserson (1947, p.79) was telling us of the 'political limitations on executive reorganisation', noting how 'the alliance . . . between group interests . . . , legislative committees or subcommittees, and operating bureaus or agencies preferring the administrative status quo constitutes the most effective stumbling block to executive reorganisation'. American experience also highlights the point that organisational arrangements (and therefore reorganisation proposals) are not neutral but contain within themselves powerful implications for the distribution of power within government; for the access of interested parties from outside of government; and therefore for public policy itself. Polenberg (1966, p.192) has noted how the Brownlow Committee 'hoped to remove the administrative obstacles that hindered Roosevelt's efforts to implement the New Deal', and Fox (1973) has pointed out how the proposals of Nixon's Advisory Council on Executive Reorganisation would squeeze out poor, under-privileged and less powerful groups from any impact on the process

8 For example, key members of the Haldane Committee hoped that a number of political and social reforms could be realised with the aid of new bureaucratic machinery (Daalder, 1964, p.313; MacKenzie, 1950, pp.57–8).

9 For example, the Fulton Committee was concerned to increase managerial accountability in the civil service, but Jaques (1972) considers that the implementation of their proposals only served to blur, rather than clarify, managerial organisation and accountability.

10 See especially the reports of the Brownlow Committee and the Hoover Commission.

11 See also del Giudice and Warren, 1971; Mosher, 1967A; Mansfield, 1969.

of government. Not only have principled proposals been shown to be dysfunctional for the very objectives they were designed to attain,[12] but some writers go further in their assessment of the implications of American experience, recognising that 'there is no organisational solution for the dilemmas of interdepartmental co-ordination' and that 'the ideal of a neatly symmetrical frictionless organisation structure is a dangerous illusion' (Mansfield, 1969, p.342; Seidman, 1975, p.14).[13]

It is surely right that we pay particular attention to the history of PPBS in America, since early attempts to implement corporate planning in British local government were explicitly based on that system, and even today I have made it clear that corporateness has to be regarded as in the same rational-comprehensive stable as PPBS itself.

One year before President Johnson announced that he was issuing an order instructing all agencies of the Federal Government to introduce PPBS, Wildavsky (1964) was advising those who chose to heed his message that the whole enterprise was doomed to failure. Other commentators held their fire[14] but by 1970, Botner (p.423) could report that 'the Bureau of the Budget and the agencies are still struggling to comply with the order more than four years after its issuance'. In June 1971, the United States Government abandoned its compulsory version of PPBS and 'quietly officialised what has for some time been a reality — the demise of PPBS as a formal system' (Botner, 1972, p.254). In America, 'PPBS failed . . . [and] it died of multiple causes any of which was sufficient' (Schick, 1973, pp.147—8). Some go further to claim that it 'failed to achieve any improvements in the executive budgetary process' at all (Hoos, 1972, p.74).

As promise turned into practice, and rhetoric into reality, so a literature sharply critical of PPBS, and of *any* rational-comprehensive approach to policy-making, began to establish itself.

In the early days writers pointed to the 'brilliant success' of the system at the Department of Defense, but more mature reflection led writers to conclude not only that defense was a

12 See, for example, Landau, 1969; Fox, 1973; Frank, 1963—4.
13 On the problems of implementing planned change in the government of other countries, see Argyriades, 1965; Shani, 1976; Liebenow, 1957. More generally, see Caiden, 1973, 1970.
14 Miller (1968, p.467) thought it was 'too early to predict the eventual outcome of the PPB effort'. See also Churchman and Schainblatt, 1969; Millward, 1968.

bad and misleading model for the rest of the federal government (Mosher, 1969, p.160; Wildavsky, 1975, pp.354–5), but that the Department of Defense was itself 'guilty of so much misman-agement' that it 'stands out, not as exemplar, but as a horrible example of management practices' (Hoos, 1972, p.60; Moynihan, 1970, p.92). Writers have recognised that interests, values, policies, and politics are caught up in PPBS, and Wildavsky (1964, pp.132–3) has tersely noted how 'we cannot speak of "better budgeting" without considering who benefits and who loses'.[15] We should surely not forget that 'organised business groups championed PPB mainly for its promise to limit government expenditures' (Merewitz and Sosnick, 1971, p.9). Fundamentally, PPBS sets down a series of steps that should be followed by the rational policy-maker. Each of these steps to rational and compre-hensive policy-making has been subjected to a blow-by-blow critique which leaves the whole enterprise in intellectual shreds.[16] The big questions are not amenable to analysis. There are problems in identifying needs, defining objectives, and selecting priorities in the real world of political conflict where values clash and where there is no agreement on what the objectives of government actually are, let alone what they should be. Even if we did have specific goals that were agreed on, the knowledge of effective means to achieve them is overwhelmingly inadequate and can serve as no base for a rigorous analysis. There are massive problems of comparing, evaluating and choosing between alternative packages of policy options: a politically informed guess is the best that we can hope for. The literature critical of cost-benefit analysis is huge. The limitations of quantification are increasingly recognised, at the same time as the difficulty of taking into account qualitative considerations is glaringly apparent. Finally, a scientifically crisp measurement of output and a com-parative evaluation of the effectiveness and success of particular policies is an impossibly difficult task which can only be coped with if you add such a huge dose of *ceteris paribus* that it solves the problem of analysis at the expense of its relevance to the real world of complexity, conflict, and uncertainty.

We are provided with two complementary lines of explanation

---

15 See also Fenno, 1968; Hoos, 1972; Wildavsky, 1966, p.305; Seidman, 1970.
16 See especially Merewitz and Sosnick, 1971. I will not be developing this line of critique further because it is well-developed in the literature and its relevance to the British situation has already been suggested by Bennington (1975).

for the failure of PPBS. First, and focusing essentially on the individual decision-maker, it is Wildavsky's (1975, pp.354, 364, 359) 'own view . . . that PPBS fails because it cannot meet a necessary condition for its success — the human knowledge required for performing the operations it stipulates'. A rational-comprehensive approach to policy-making increases the burden of calculation on the participants to decision 'far beyond anyone's capacities'. If you do try to get round the individual's cognitive limits by effecting a division of labour within an organisation then you are inevitably presented with the very problem of co-ordination and control that the system was itself supposed to solve. Second, and focusing more on the political and organisational context of decision, PPBS faces enormous political difficulties. It meets with resistance from politicians who have been socialised into a commitment to the pattern of established policies which they helped to build up and who are happy with their 'established patterns of searching for information' (Jernberg, 1969, p.738). In addition, because established policies 'attract a vocal constituency of beneficiaries' or clients, any attempt to reduce, eliminate, or even question them, inevitably brings forth 'loud cries of anguish' (Gorham, 1968, p.237). The likelihood of personal and organisational resistance is exacerbated by the fact that any rational-comprehensive approach opens up conflict which established bargaining routines have controlled, suppressed, and made more manageable (Schick, 1973; Botner, 1970).

Like it or not, decision-makers 'take short cuts', and they 'deal with their overwhelming burdens by adopting aids to calculation. By far the most important aid to calculation is the incremental method' (Wildavsky, 1964, p.147; Davis, Dempster, and Wildavsky, 1966, p.529). This sort of literature on the failure of PPBS not only provides us with a critique of a particular kind of *prescriptive* theory, but also provides us with a *description* of the established mode of incremental decision-making which is itself *explained* by pointing to the cognitive limits of individual decision-makers and the hard organisational world of *realpolitik*. It is precisely this emphasis on incrementalism which leads us into a wider literature designed to more fully describe, explain, and make sense of established patterns and processes of public policy-making. Lindblom (1959, pp.80, 84) has argued that 'public administrators and policy analysts in general do largely limit their analyses to incremental or marginal differences in policies that are chosen to differ only incrementally', and they do so because any more comprehensive approach is 'impossible' since 'it assumes intellectual capacities and sources of information that men simply do not possess'. Following his work[17] a number of writers[18] have attested to the incremental nature of the budgetary process in particular and policy-making in general, pointing to the sheer impossibility of the rational approach.

The work on incrementalism has not lacked its critics. It is seen as serving as 'an ideological reinforcement of the pro-inertia and anti-innovation forces prevalent in all human organisations' (Dror, 1964, p.155; Etzioni, 1967); and it is seen as 'depressingly weak as an explanatory theory' because it 'overpromises and underdelivers in terms of descriptive precision and explanatory usefulness' (Greenwood, Hinings and Ranson, 1977, p.26; Bailey and O'Connor, 1975, p.60; see also Danziger, 1974, 1976). All this is perfectly true, but few people dispute that the approach describes the behaviour of most decision-makers most of the time, and few people challenge the point about the cognitive limits of decision-makers inhibiting the possibility of truly rational and comprehensive policy making.

Anyway, the pattern of incremental change and bounded rationality is also explained by more rigorous theory which focuses not so much on the cognitive limits of individuals as on 'organisational process' and structure.[19] It is precisely this line of explanation which enriches the hints about the world of *realpolitik* contained in the literature explaining the failure of PPBS. The organisational process approach is founded on the notion that organisational behaviour can be understood by means of reiterative procedures through which conflict is channelled off, uncertainty is minimised, and simple searches for information and alternatives are carried out. The student who chooses to operate within the assumptions of this body of theory would look at the organisation making decisions and study the search strategy; the primary information sources; the standard operating procedures; the order of attending to problems; and the criteria for determining an acceptable decision. Baldly expressed he would have the job of

17 Dahl and Lindblom, 1953; Braybrooke and Lindblom, 1963; Lindblom, 1958, 1965.
18 Wildavsky, 1964; Fenno, 1966; Barber, 1966; Crecine, 1969; Sharkansky, 1968.
19 Cyert and March, 1963; Crecine, 1969; Allison, 1969, 1971; Danziger, 1974.

teasing out the decision routines which are built up to cope with recurring problems.

Let us move back to consider policy-making in British local government, and let us deal with the possibility of implementing the corporate approach. If programme budgeting failed in America because it demanded more of the human intellect than could be given, then the same must surely be true of corporate planning. The very brevity and simplicity of this explanation may not satisfy those who prefer a more complex explanation which is grounded less in a terse statement about the limited capacity of individuals and more in a recognition of the policy implications of the essential features of organisational life. Let me, therefore, highlight the relevance of the organisational process approach for our understanding of the policy process in British local government.

In my study of Kensington and Chelsea (Dearlove, 1973) I was concerned to explain the pattern of public policy by getting to grips with the informal routines and rules which were established and entrenched in the life of the council and which enabled councillors to cope with recurring policy situations with a minimum of fuss and effort. Rhodes (1973), in a review of my study, correctly argued that:

> in almost every respect Dearlove's research reveals obstacles to the successful implementation of corporate planning. To caricature the situation somewhat, the local authority ignores demands from the environment, selectively searches for information consonant with existing policies, evolves rules to minimise the presentation of disruptive alternatives, and is overwhelmingly concerned with maintaining existing policies rather than with the reviewing analysing and changing [of] policy. There could not be a sharper contrast between the aims of the reformers and the political reality of local government.

The implications of my findings cannot be lightly dismissed by the advocates of change. It may be claimed that my case was 'not typical', and this is true because no case ever is, but to take this line is to miss the whole point. What must be borne in mind is the fact that my explanation for the making and maintenance of public policy in Kensington and Chelsea centres on facets of organisational life which *must* be seen as of importance in *any* local authority. In all cases, the search behaviour of councillors; their information sources; and the way in which they choose to relate and respond to interested groups in the locality or outside, must *all* be considered if we want to account for the likely development of public policy. So, too, we cannot ignore the informal rules which recruit people to particular positions and then restrain and shape their behaviour so as to suit organisational purpose, and we must take into account the ideology of those charged with managing the scope of government. Of course, the actual *patterns* of search, rules, and ideologies will be peculiar to each authority, but given what we know from social psychology, we can surely expect the usual pattern of search to be selective, so reinforcing established commitments and entrenched ideology and inhibiting the likelihood of innovation. I suspect, too, that research will reveal that in most authorities positions of power are usually assigned on the basis of seniority, at the same time as new recruits to the council will be expected to assume a quiet, learning, apprenticeship, and both these rules will usually restrain potential policy disturbance and encourage the maintenance of established policies.

The orthodox case for reorganisation diagnoses the ills of 'traditional administration' as lying in the formal structures of committees and departments. The prescription for improvement is essentially grounded in the creation of a chief executive, a management team, and a policy committee — formal structures and positions which will somehow transform the policy process, turning fragmentation into co-ordination and incrementalism into innovation. The sad truth is that these changes do not even recognise, let alone confront or counter, either the facts about the cognitive limits of individual decision-makers or the essential facets of organisational life which I have just set down and suggested are highly pertinent to the nature of policy-making in any situation. These omissions are important because it is these factors (every bit as much as the formal structures of committees and departments) which account for the form, style, and process of policy-making. The trouble is that they are much less amenable to planned change, even though they are quite capable of wrecking just about every stage of the rational comprehensive approach to policy-making currently trading under the name of 'corporateness'.

3. Concluding Remarks

First, there are good grounds for suggesting that it will not be possible to implement the corporate approach. Incrementalism, or even policy maintenance, is likely to characterise the policy process of most local authorities most of the time.[20] Innovation will usually only get the odd look in at moments of crisis, be they locally inspired or the result of pressures from the central government responding to the logic of economic 'necessity'. Fragmentation is inescapable. It certainly cannot be solved or willed away to be replaced by co-ordination[21] simply by reducing the numbers of committees and departments and beefing up the power of central services. Defective machinery may *contribute* to the difficulties of co-ordination, but it is seldom, if ever, at the *root* of the problem. The range and complexity of services; the sheer volume of work they entail; and the absence of basic agreement are the problems. It is pure self-deception to suppose that these obstacles can be overcome by redistributing the same range of problems among fewer departments. For example, in early 1971, new Social Service Departments came into being, but 'no sooner had Seebohm's cause of integrated social services triumphed than committees and directors were faced with the job of how to divide them all up again, in allocating them to various divisions and branches of the new so-called integrated departments' (Rowbottom, Hey and Bliss, 1974, p.58). In this case, the problem of co-ordination was not solved, it was merely relocated. Wildavsky (1973, p.142) is right: 'co-ordination is one of the golden words of our time. I cannot offhand think of any way in which the word is used that implies disapproval'. Advocates of corporate planning use the word a lot. They seldom bother to analyse the term or say what they mean by it unless they talk vaguely about the differences between the co-ordination of policy formulation, policy implementation, resource management, or administrative arrangements. They tell local authorities to co-ordinate their policies so they do not work at cross-purposes, but local authorities already know that: telling them to co-ordinate does not tell them *what* to do or *how* to do it. The simple truth

20 In another context, detailed work on the 1974 reorganisation of the National Health Service has highlighted how 'a radical as distinct from an incremental approach to the use of existing resources is highly unlikely', and this in spite of the fact that 'few administrative changes can have been planned in such detail, or with so much explicit consideration of the precise arrangements needed to secure desired improvements in policy-making' (Brown, Griffin, and Haywood, 1975; Brown, 1976).

21 For a sharp recognition of the sloppiness contained in the slogan 'what we need is more co-ordination', see Pressman and Wildavsky, 1973; Caiden and Wildavsky, 1974.

is that 'the quest for co-ordination is in many respects the twentieth century equivalent of the medieval search for the philosopher's stone' (Seidman, 1975, p.190). If anyone wants a concrete demonstration of the sad truth of that statement then they should read Ely Devons' (1950) account of how the Ministry of Aircraft Production just could not get round 'the problem of co-ordination' when they attempted to plan aircraft production in the Second World War.

Second, new 'corporate' structures *are* being introduced into local authorities. In so far as they succeed in biting into the established distribution of power within an authority then it is quite clear that they emphasise leadership and hierarchy and centralise and concentrate power into the hands of a small group of leading councillors and officers.[22] In the wider literature of organisational sociology, this concern to create a tight, conflict-free, centrally directed, corporate, hierarchical organisation, in which professional judgement is played down, is usually seen as the very antithesis of the organisational form most conducive to genuine innovation and responsiveness.[23] This being the case it is worth exploring whether the practice of the new structures is actually dysfunctional for the innovative and responsive policy process that they were designed to attain.

Third, a sensitivity to other attempts at governmental reorganisation highlights the extent to which no restructuring of government is ever neutral in its implications for who has power and how that power will be used in the development of a particular pattern of public policies. Particular attention should be paid to the policy implications of corporate management.[24] In so far as corporate structures are beginning to gain a powerful hold of the policy process in local authorities, then this is happening precisely because of the imposed necessity for financial stringency. The 'situation is forcing new approaches and methods of working on local authorities . . . as the crunch of inflation has provided local government generally . . . with a strong urge to develop more detailed and explicit systems of policy analysis'. In effect, 'the

22 I say this notwithstanding talk about the need for some kind of 'matrix organisation' (Greenwood and Stewart, 1972).
23 See, for example, Thompson, 1965–6, p.6; Wilson, 1966; Mohr, 1969; Schiff, 1966; Guetzkow, 1965; Burns and Stalker, 1961, esp. pp.85–6, 89, 121–2.
24 Schaffer's (1976, p.32) 'general rule' that behind all fundamental administrative reorganisations there 'lies the steady advance of specific salary awards' provides some sort of simple starting point to this enquiry.

situation of economic cutbacks is forcing local authorities to move to a more interventionist policy committee' (Greenwood, Hinings, Ranson, and Walsh, 1976, pp.5, 88, 197). I will be returning to this in my concluding chapter.

Even if we cannot implement the full rigours of the corporate approach, surely we can make things better? Such a statement only raises the question of better for whom with respect to what and at whose cost. In the next chapter I hope to be able to make a start on dealing with these questions, since they are at the core of any political perspective on the reorganisation of British local government.

8

Councillor and Official Calibre and the Management Problem

to consider in the light of modern conditions how local government might best continue to attract and retain people (both elected
representatives and principal officers) of the calibre necessary to
ensure its maximum effectiveness.

> (Terms of Reference of the Committee on the Management
> of Local Government, 1967, vol.1, p.iii)

[Local authorities] *must* improve their present working methods,
especially the committee system, if they are to get people of the
right calibre for local government in the future.

> (Lord Redcliffe-Maud, 1967, pp.351—2, italics in original)

1. Britain in the Mid Twentieth Century

In my opening chapter I touched on the thorny issue of councillor
calibre. I noted how orthodox opinion had attested to a decline
which advocates of reorganisation were keen to reverse. In Chapter
4 I explored this concern more fully since part of the case for
larger local authorities was based on their having the effect of
increasing councillor calibre. It has long been recognised that this
strategy alone would not do the trick, and a second bite at the
calibre cherry has involved the advocacy of the internal reorganisation of local authorities. Why has orthodox opinion seen this
as facilitating business and professional access to local governmental power? Put another way, what was it about the 'traditional
administration' of local affairs that was seen as inhibiting the
possibility of business control of local government?

In the golden age of local government there was not only 'an
educated and leisured aristocracy with no axes to grind' (Jessup,
1949, p.112), but businessmen were entrenched in the lives of
their localities and had both the time and the inclination to devote
to local government service. Times have changed. Not only have
the upper middle classes migrated to the residential suburbs,

but 'the circumstances of the present day no longer allow the coming forward into public life of men and women able to give so much of their time to voluntary service represented by membership of a local authority' (Swaffield, 1960, p.131). Much more to the point,

> the economic pressures on commerce and industry now make it very difficult for the directors and senior executives of companies to find time for local government work [and so] the standard of the elected representative has declined in recent years . . . because the conduct of a successful business *and* active participation in local affairs take up more time than they did 50 years ago.
> (Association of British Chambers of Commerce, *Written Evidence of Commercial, Industrial and Political Organisations* to the Royal Commission on Local Government in England, 1969,p.18)

The Committee on the Management of Local Government (1967, vol.1, pp.141, 144) noted that 'lack of time is the main reason for not wanting to become a member . . . given by employers, managers, professionals, and farmers', and it saw the 'time factor . . . as the most serious deterrent to service and a major reason for members declining to stand again for election'. A survey of economic and social notables in Bristol showed that 'the reason most frequently given . . . for not becoming local councillors is that council membership levies too heavy a toll upon time, which respondents cannot afford to give' (Clements, 1969, p.54). The Working Group on Local Authority Management Structures (1972, p.30) similarly attested to the fact that 'some potential members, particularly professional and businessmen, are . . . deterred from putting themselves forward for election because of the amount of time traditionally occupied by council affairs'.[1]

Of course, it has never just been seen as a matter of time. 'Elections frequently proved an obstacle to the recruitment of the leading citizens of the borough', and under 'party elections', in particular, 'a number of good men are permanently kept out of local administration' (Hennock, 1973, p.13; Hasluck, 1936, p.35). The Committee on the Management of Local Government (1967, vol.1, p.115) itself considered that 'party politics do deter some people from standing for election'.[2] In addition, 'men who have

---

1 See also, Sharp, 1962, pp.383–4; Birch, 1959, p.148; Etherton, 1924; Chester, 1954A; 'The Basildon Experiment', 1966; Banwell, 1963, p.342; Keith, 1928; and especially, Grierson, 1928, pp.213–14.
2 It is interesting that research undertaken for the Committee on the Management of Local Government (1967, vol.5, p.20) discovered that 'manual workers, in particular,

run their own businesses successfully often find themselves hampered by rules of administrative procedure and are baffled by the difficulties of persuading a committee to agree with them' (MacColl, 1951, p.9). 'Traditional administration' was not seen as businesslike enough to make local government service attractive to businessmen, and this was bad because 'local government should not be a hobby for those whose jobs are routine, dull, or unpleasant' but should be 'an attraction to those whose time is valuable' (Committee on the Management of Local Government, 1967, vol.1, pp.144—5).

At the core of much of this sort of analysis there has been an open attack upon the committee system. 'Of the costliness and indecision of such a system one hardly needs to speak. But the effects on members and officers are equally significant' (Marshall, 1965, p.17). Simon (1932, p.280) reminds us that 'the great fault of committees, which seems to be widespread, is the tendency to do detailed administration themselves instead of leaving it to the official'.[3] The Committee on the Management of Local Government (1967, vol.1, p.10) believed 'the participation of the members in so much detail . . . to be the root cause of local government's administrative troubles'. It is the established view that this has bad effects on both councillor *and* official calibre. On the councillor side it is precisely this involvement in detail which is so time consuming. It also takes away energy from a crisp and substantial involvement in matters of policy,[4] and men used to making large decisions in business and professional life are not going to be attracted to serve in a system of government which concentrates their minds on the trivia to the detriment of any substantial concern with broad matters of policy. On the officer side 'the official feels that he is interfered with and not allowed to get on with his job, and more particularly, not allowed to carry the responsibility of which he is capable. You will never get the best out of your officials if you treat them this way, nor will you get the best people to come to work for you'

find entry almost entirely through the political parties'. This clearly serves to highlight the anti-working class sentiment caught up in the opposition to party politics.

3 See also, Page, 1936, p.14; MacColl, 1951, p.11; Redcliffe-Maud, 1967, p.352; Rogers, 1968, p.5; Jones, 1968; Harris, 1966; Working Group on Local Authority Management Structures, 1972, pp.4, 16; Gibbon, 1928.

4 'The habit of spending considerable time in the discussion of trivialities grows to the detriment of the broader view required when large questions of policy are to be considered' (Hilary, 1929, p.381).

(Banwell, 1963, p.338; see also Committee on the Management of Local Government, 1967, vol.1, p.27).

Given this sort of diagnosis, simple logic enables us to suggest what the orthodox prescription for internal reorganisation will be. Men of calibre will be wooed back onto local councils if the time demands of elective office are reduced and if local government is made more businesslike. After all, local government is increasingly seen as a business and so if you centralise and concentrate power into the hands of the 'best members' (Simon, 1926, p.191) then this will enable them to play a role akin to the board of directors of a private company. The Committee on the Management of Local Government (1967, vol.1, p.63) felt confident that their proposed 'changes in functions and responsibilities of members and of officers, and in the internal organisation, will . . . help to attract candidates for service as members of local authorities, as there will be less demand on their time, and their work will be both more constructive and interesting'. At a RIPA Conference (1967, p.17) E. B. Mayne, a businessman member of the Maud Committee, talked of the importance of restructuring local government so as to increase its appeal to 'men in positions of responsibility'. His message for local government was bold and clear: 'organise your management for effectiveness; make councillors' and officers' jobs worthwhile; and the right people will come forward — though perhaps after a sticky period'. In a word, it has consistently been argued that what is needed is a 'streamlining of the internal organisation of the council, including a reduction in the number and work of committees' (Swaffield, 1960, p.131).[5]

We have to ask a number of questions of this orthodox analysis and prescription. First, are businessmen and professionals deterred from serving on local councils because of the time demands of the position and the unbusinesslike conduct of local affairs, and are they deterred from a career in the local government service because they feel they would not enjoy sufficient responsibilities to tax them? The last chapter was anchored around the recognition that it is one thing to advocate change and quite another thing to implement it, and so we must surely ask, second, if proposals

5 See also, Clements, 1969, p.16; Chester, 1954, p.14; Bulpitt, 1967, p.96; Working Group on Local Authority Management Structures, 1972, p.30.

for change have been implemented so as to reduce the time demands on councillors, and to give some of them more power. Third, and even more to the point, if these proposals have been implemented, have they had their intended effect? Unfortunately we just do not have adequate information to answer any of these questions satisfactorily. They should be the subject of future research, but even so, let me deal very tentatively with each of them in turn.

First, Clements (1969, p.139)[6] does not think that lack of available time is a 'satisfactory explanation, bearing in mind the large amount of time and energy [the social and economic notables in Bristol] chose to devote to other activities which appear to be comparable in many respects'. Even so, we should not pretend that advocates of internal reorganisation present us with a simple explanation. The time factor and the argument about unbusinesslike procedures are only a *part* of the orthodoxy diagnosis of the problem, and streamlining local administration is only a part of a whole package of proposals which have been designed to attract men of calibre back into local government. In other words, we must avoid creating a straw man merely because we want to knock him down. But second, 'the evidence suggests that a number of authorities have achieved significant savings in the amount of time involved at committee meetings' (Greenwood, Norton, and Stewart, 1969B, p.27).[7] Moreover, the introduction of the policy committee into local government has perhaps concentrated formal power and so given a few leading councillors rather more influence than they might otherwise have had and so made them more like a board of directors. Similarly, it is probably reasonable to conclude that officials in general, and certain officials in particular, are now in a position when they enjoy rather more scope for action than was once the case.[8] Third, finally and crucially, has the partial implementation of reforms that were designed to increase calibre succeeded? Notwithstanding the survey work undertaken for the Committee of Inquiry into the System of Remuneration of Members of Local Authorities (1977, vol.2),

6 See also, Committee on the Management of Local Government, 1967, vol.2, p.104.
7 The Committee of Inquiry into the System of Remuneration of Members of Local Authorities found that 'it is clear that councillors are now spending more time on their council activities than in 1964' (1977, vol.2, p.16).
8 For the situation in Cheshire after reorganisation, see Lee, Wood, Solomon and Walters, 1974, p.97; for the situation in Lambeth, see Cockburn, 1977, pp.35–6.

the short and honest answer is that we do not know, even though there is evidence which suggests that the orthodox package of streamlining measures is particularly attractive to young, well-educated, non-manual councillors, at the time as it is less attractive to working class Labour councillors.[9] Success is not, however, guaranteed, and orthodox advocates of reorganisation have grudgingly recognised that 'it is to be expected that there will be opposition to such changes from some existing members' (Working Group on Local Authority Management Structures, 1972, p.30). In other words, Redcliffe-Maud may have a 'grudge against working class people in local government' and he may have been consistent in 'trying to shape local government to attract . . . [and] encourage middle class elements to be involved more and more in local government' (Jones, 1969A, pp.15, 12), but all advocates of reorganisation have been sensitive to the limits of their own social engineering in these matters.

In an important article, Stanyer (1971) has pursued this problem more rigorously. He recognises that the concern to alter the composition of councils is the 'dominant' approach to management reorganisation,[10] but he has questioned whether it is at all possible to operate this 'systematic selection approach' in a situation where we are dealing with popularly elected representatives. His analysis seems cogent, but I want to suggest that the concern to alter the class composition (and therefore the public policy) of local authorities has to be treated seriously. The particular problems of attaining the ideal council and putting increased powers in the hands of the permanent officials should certainly not lead to our dismissing from consideration the class implications of the reorganised structures and processes that are currently being introduced into local government in the name of co-ordination and innovation.

In my view, the importance of all this is revealed if we look at the introduction and implications of the council—manager form of government in America. Not only is a consideration of this case of interest in its own right, but it also beautifully illustrates the relationship between reorganisation and class access to governmental power. In both countries advocates of reorganisation have been concerned about the calibre of elected representatives, the

---

9 See Hampton, 1972; Clements, 1969, p.139; Boaden, 1971, pp.113ff; Royal Commission on Local Government in England, 1969, *Written Evidence of Commercial, Industrial and Political Organisations*, pp.18, 138—9.
10 See also Self, 1971; Young, 1972, 1973.

nature of public services, and the scale of local public expenditure. In both countries these 'problems' have been seen as related each to the other and to the established structure of local government, and structural reorganisation has been seen as providing a 'solution'. Some literature on the American case has adopted an overtly political perspective. This clearly reveals that the business classes were actually *successful* in winning back positions of power within reorganised government when they could no longer hang on, while continuing to play within the established rules of the un-reorganised governmental game. I think we can begin to learn a lot about the reorganisation of British local government from a consideration of this case.

2.   America at the Turn of the Century

(i) *The Orthodox Account of Municipal Reform*

In 1888 Bryce (vol.1, p.608) wrote that 'there is no denying that the government of cities is the one conspicuous failure of the United States'. The municipal tradition was 'rotten' — 'the worst in Christendom' — and in the three decades following the close of the Civil War it entered the 'dark ages' (Webb, 1898, p.42; White, 1890; Munro, 1926, p.431). 'In 1888 . . . city governments were burdened with debt and sodden with corruption and inefficiency' (Reed, 1934, p.115). Things were especially bad in the large cities where the newly arrived immigrants provided a natural core of support for the bosses and machines which had driven all the good citizens out of public life.

The 'tendency' of municipal government may have been 'down-ward', but 'when they reach the lowest depths of degradation, the citizens rise in their might and defeat their persecutors and plunderers' (Conkling, 1894, p.218). This is exactly what happened. Democracy had to 'fight for its life in the cities' but fight it did, for public opinion could take no more (Wilcox, 1897, p.238). At first the movement was weak, for the story of 'the battle for municipal reform' is one of a 'slow awakening of public interest'. However, after 'sporadic outbursts against extravagance, graft, and entrenched corruption' there was a civic awakening and by 1890 the country embarked in its 'great era of reform . . . toward better government' (Patton, 1940). The citizens rose up in a great moral crusade and although they were guided by the emerging science of municipal government and by 'better elements', this was fundamentally a people's movement.

Over the years the movement met with no real opposition. The National Municipal League (the key organ of reform endeavour) represented 'the consensus of thinking people as to what local government should be', and it was 'unchallenged . . . by any but the characters who comprise its target' (Stewart, 1950, p.100; Childs, 1954, p.133). The period between 1895 and 1925 witnessed 'an almost unbelievable improvement all along the line' (Munro, 1926, pp.431—2). These were the years of 'formidable progress', and by the latter date city government was 'much more honest, efficient, and democratic than it was a generation ago' (Reed, 1934, p.330; Anderson, 1925, p.648). In 1888 Bryce may have seen city government as a 'conspicuous failure', but in 1911 he informed the City Club of New York that the 'forms of government are far better over the country . . . than they used to be', and in his study of *Modern Democracies* (1921, vol.2, pp.138—40) he referred specifically to the remarkable growth of the council—manager plan. This form of government was to become the institutional embodiment of reform endeavour. It was non-existent in 1911 and yet by 1920 it was established in 157 cities in the United States and Canada. The plan rapidly secured the support of contemporary political scientists because it was 'the most perfect expression which the American people have yet evolved of the need for combining efficient administration with adequate popular control' (White, 1927, p.295). It was no wonder that it swept the land and 'in little more than half a century it has become the most popular form of local government in the United States' (National Municipal League, 1974, p.3).

Dark ages there have been, but they were followed by a new dawn in which democracy triumphed, and honest, efficient government was back in the hands of the people.

(ii) *The New Urban History*

The above version of governmental reorganisation can be teased out of any number of accounts by contemporary observers and reformers. It is also the picture we get if we look to many academics. Social scientists grew up with, were caught up in, and benefited from their association with the movement. They served as its 'informal brain trust' (Hofstadter, 1955, p.154). They had a 'sharp sense of mission' and 'they saw it as the proper task of political scientists to prescribe the required remedies' for the recognised ills of city government (Sayre and Polsby, 1965, p.115). Not surprisingly, textbooks on municipal government were sympathetic to the movement because they were *part* of it. They took the descriptions of participants at their face value. On the basis of these early accounts orthodoxies about city government and its reorganisation were quickly established, and have endured to shape and restrain later, less involved, perspectives on the period (Wiebe, 1962, pp.206—7).

The trouble is that such accounts are of very limited value. They present the public face of reform. They deal only in its slogans and its ideology which they present as its practice, so failing to recognise that the ideology masks the reality at the time as it serves particular interests. They also ignore the more private anxieties of reformers as to the fundamental realities which they sought to attack and attain. We must challenge the orthodox accounts. We can do so because we can tease out these private anxieties, and we can develop an alternative analysis on the basis of the rediscovery of the city by the 'new urban history' (Thernstrom and Sennett, 1969; Ebner, 1973). Critical research has pushed behind the soft ideological underbelly of reform to questions about its harder reality, and answers to these have served to give us a new understanding of the past. Three questions are of crucial importance. First, who were the reformers, and what were the forces behind change? Second, what exactly were reformers attacking? Third, what were the objectives of reform — and to this end, what were the structural innovations introduced into government; how far have they endured; and what effect have they had?[11]

(a) *Who were the reformers?*

Reformers and their academic sympathisers have presented the movement as 'the people', 'the public', or 'the nation as a whole' engaged in a 'popular crusade' (Dewitt, 1915; Filler, 1961). These views can be given short shrift for want of hard supporting

11 In my account I have sought to build on the crucial insights provided by S. P. Hays, and since his 1964 article is in a journal which is not widely available over here, it can be read in Gordon, 1973; Kennedy, 1971; or Callow, 1969.

evidence, and given the necessity of situating any movement in the bed of societal division. Instead we have to turn our attention to two rather different accounts.

The longest established academic view sees municipal reform as a solidly middle class movement. Hofstadter (1955, pp.137, 135) argues that the 'old-family, college-educated class' turned to reform and progressivism because they were being by-passed by the new businessmen of wealth and were 'victims of an upheaval in status' that left them powerless and alienated on the sidelines of civic life.[12]

More recently, this view has come under attack from those who argue that 'available evidence indicates that the source of support for reform in municipal government did not come from the lower or middle classes, but from the upper class. The leading business groups in each city and professional groups closely allied with them, initiated and dominated municipal movements' (Hays, 1964, p.159).[13] In Baltimore the reformers were 'an upper class of status and property' (Crooks, 1968, p.196); in Chicago it was the businessmen and professionals who spearheaded the drive for governmental reform and city planning (McCarthy, 1970); in Philadelphia the bulk of the members of the 1880 Citizens Reform Committee were well-known Republican merchants and professional men (Allinson, 1887); and in Cincinnati businessmen and professionals were again in the forefront (Taft, 1933). White (1927, pp.ix—x) noted how 'the opposition to bad government usually comes to a head in the local chamber of commerce' and 'with variation in emphasis, this story is repeated from one end of the country to another'. Stone, Price and Stone's (1940, p.25) massive study of the council—manager form of government in fifty cities pointed out that 'civic clubs and business organisations were active in promoting the city manager plan in an overwhelming majority of cities that adopted it'.[14]

There was often little distinction between the old patricians

---

12 For similar views, see also Faulkner, 1959, p.26; Mowry, 1951, pp.86—104; Chandler, 1951—4.
13 This view should not be regarded as either surprising or controversial since reformers admitted as much to each other. The President of the National Municipal League told the 1899 Conference for Good City Government that 'we are not cranks gathered together for argument of a fad; we are businessmen and professional men' (cited in Stewart, 1950, p.168). See also Bliss, 1897, p.907.
14 See also Weinstein, 1962; Phillips, 1935; East, 1965, p.80; Gordon, 1973, p.99; Lowi, 1964; Hayes, 1972, p.189; Kolko, 1967; Schiesl, 1972.

and the new business elites (Frisch, 1969) and there is no dispute that the reform impulse did not spring from the working class[15] since it invariably met with the overt opposition of immigrants, trade unions, and socialists. Immigrants 'did not want government to be a business' as they were mindful that 'efficiency too often expressed itself in an inhuman disregard for the individual' (Handlin, 1973, p.197). The Socialist Party (an active force in municipal politics in the years 1910 to 1919) opposed the spread of the council—manager plan precisely because its members were aware that the structures and processes that were part of it erected barriers to their own access to governmental power (Price, 1941; Rightor, 1919, pp.209—16; Hays, 1964; Weinstein, 1962).

(b) *What were the reformers attacking?*

One thing is clear, that the emphasis on the corruption of the boss and the machine is not the whole story. We have to understand the changing balance of political power in the cities and the implications of this for those who, through reform, were concerned to reverse things. In addition, the reformers knew that government was the mirror reflecting and giving form to social and economic relations and it was the development of these that was at the very gut of their concern.

'The inferior standing and character of persons elected to large American city councils has been a frequent subject of remark' (Fairlie, 1904; White, 1890, p.358). Bugbee (1887, p.31) considered that there had been 'a marked deterioration in the character of the governing body elected by the people' of Boston since 1854, and more generally, Munro (1913, p.183) asserted that around the 1840s and 1850s 'the councils seem to have everywhere declined in the calibre of their membership'. Talk about declining calibre is familiar to our own ears, and so it should not surprise us that the term was riddled with very similar class connotations in America.

'The change in the character of the governing class . . . [involved] the transfer of the legislative and administrative branches of government from the rich to the poor . . . [so that] the work of legislation has been largely given over to the sons of poor men . . . [and] the rich are being gradually and relentlessly excluded

15 But see Buenker, 1973; Hutchmacher, 1962.

as a rule from public office' (Godkin, 1898, pp.180–95). To
some extent the 'best men' withdrew from the local government
to devote their time to 'the acquisative endeavours of a quick
spreading industrial-commercial expansion' and they felt able to
do this precisely because there was less 'upward pressure' from the
'poorer or under-privileged masses' than was experienced in most
European cities (Bryce, 1888, vol.2, p.67; Stewart, 1950, p.2;
Parkman, 1878, p.14; Levermore, 1886, p.59). Even so, it is also
clear that the patricians and the entrepreneurs were 'beginning
to be shouldered off the stage' (Glaab and Brown, 1967, p.171).
The nineteenth century witnessed a trend of change with respect
to the class composition of many local councils. Public office
slipped from the patricians and the old governing families, to the
entrepreneurs and the new men of wealth, until finally settling
into the hands of the proletariat created by the entrepreneurs
(Dahl, 1961; Lowi, 1964; Fox, 1919; Bradley and Zald, 1965;
Thernstrom, 1964; Frisch, 1969; Greenstein, 1964). Governmental power was wrenched from its economic base, and office
holders were often propertyless. For example, in Boston, in the
period from 1822 to 1875, 85 to 95% of the council were owners
of property, and in 1875 the total assessed value of property owned
by council members was in excess of $2,300,000. By 1895, how-
ever, less than 30% of council members were property owners and
the value of their property had fallen to $372,000 (Fairlie, 1904,
p.242).

In this sort of situation the issue was not just about who should
control government; it was more about who should *benefit* from
government as the change in class composition carried within
itself important implications for the likely direction of public
policy. Nathan Matthews (1895, pp.174–5, 181) reminds us that
'the difficulty here is not corruption, but expenditure . . . The real
difficulty to contend with is the demand of individuals, interests,
classes, [and] sections . . . for extravagant expenditure.' There was
the 'difficulty of practising economy in the face of the fact that
a large portion of the people do not want economy . . . [because
those] who do not pay anything directly to the support of government are in an immense and constantly increasing majority'.
It was a battle of 'the voting many versus the taxpaying few'
(Wilder, 1891),[16] and it was 'the . . . uncontrollable increase in

16 See also Parkman, 1878, p.20; Kasson, 1883, p.220; Wilcox, 1904, p.213.

the cost of government that finally jostled the public into an attitude of hostility' to the established mode of city government.[17] For the businessmen the injury of heavy taxation was compounded by the insult of poor and limited public services that did absolutely nothing to make the city an efficient partner with its business (Gilbert, 1919).

Of course these changes in the control and direction of city government were not unrelated to developments within the economy, and those who were worried about the state of city government knew it. Urban America was developing hand-in-hand with industrialisation, and the burgeoning industrial cities were fed by native white rural migrants and by immigrants from foreign shores. 'According to a study made in 1890 seven eighths of the families held but one eighth of the wealth, while one per cent of the people owned more than the remaining ninety-nine' (Faulkner, 1931, p.21). 'Deference disappeared, except in the slave states' (White, 1883, p.256). 'There were evidences of the development of class consciousness, and a tightening of the lines of battle in the conflict between capital and Labour' (Faulkner, 1931, p.3) as 'side by side with [the] . . . concentration of capital has gone the combination of labor in the same vast industries' (Turner, 1920, p.245). In the period from 1897 to 1911, trade union membership increased five-fold. Adna Weber (1899, p.427) was absolutely right; 'the chasm created by the industrial system yawns widest in the cities'. First, 'the more congested the population the lower becomes the ratio of home-owning families' who have a stake in stability and low public expenditure (Munro, 1913, p.48; Goodnow, 1910, pp.33ff). Second, residential segregation and the factory system separated classes, and in place of the social solidarity and control of the face-to-face community there were built up walls of impersonality and estranged fear and resentment. Third, patterns of class cleavage were overlain by ethnic and religious division. All-in-all the situation was one in which the 'better elements' feared the 'dangerous classes' (Brace, 1872) and the constant threat of crime, riots (Headley, 1873), revolts, strikes,[18] and radicalism. At the widest level, this problem

17 See also Rightor, 1919, p.179, and Conkling, 1894, p.20, for a description of the financial impulse for reform in Dayton and Philadelphia.
18 During the strikes of the 1870s city officials were often friendly to workingmen and they refused to use police to protect strike-breakers (Gutman, 1959). This is a clear example of the policy implications of the split between business and local government being injurious to the business interest.

of class conflict was a problem of social control where there was a need to reintegrate the social order so as to reproduce the relations of production on an expanded scale. At the more limited level of local politics the problem manifested itself in terms of a struggle to control city government. What did businessmen do about their loss of direct control?

Many humans are like ostriches and some writers of the period chose to minimise and misread the situation. They grumbled that 'the people of means in all great cities have . . . shamefully neglected their political duties' (Roosevelt, 1885, p.825) and they blamed the problem of bad city government on the 'apathy and shortsightedness' of the upper classes. Many more writers chose to blame the poor and propertyless immigrants: 'in 9 cases out of 10 . . . the degeneracy of our political condition . . . is ascribed to the great influx of ignorant foreigners which has been going on for the last 30 years' (Godkin, 1898, pp.13–14).

More thoughtful commentators knew that explanations which centred on individuals and their personal morality were wide of the mark. These people were alive to the new patterns of cleavage and conflict, but they also recognised that it was the predominant weak mayor–council form of government that was more *immediately* to blame for the loss of business control of government, because it was *structured* in such a way that 'businessmen . . . were being denied easy access to the formal machinery of government' (Schiesl, 1972, p.215). This form of government was derived from English practice, but as soon as universal suffrage was established, working men demanded a change in the formal rules of the local government game. The mass of frequently elected officials; the fragmentation and separation of powers; the checks and balances; and the crucial ward-based electoral system all made it very much easier for working class citizens to gain direct and formal access to city government (Hugins, 1960).

Denied direct access to local government by the legitimate front entrance of election, businessmen were 'often forced to accept other procedures through which they could exercise . . . power . . . the political machine . . . provided the best avenue to economic advancement and public recognition for businessmen in urban society' (Schiesl, 1972, p.215). They had to use the shabby back door and rely on corruption. 'The organisation of our municipal government has been such as to encourage inefficiency and cor-

Mayor — Council form

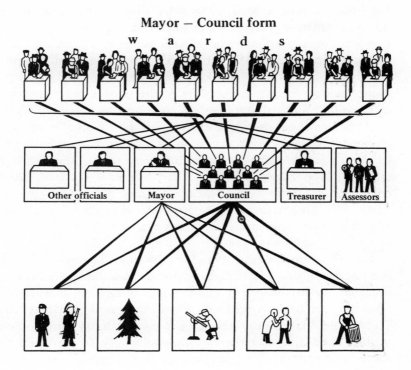

Mayor—council form of government. From Childs, 1952, p.132

ruption', and 'nothing could have been better adapted to the growth of the machine and the solidarity of its power than the constitution of our city government' (MacGregor, 1911, p.14; Allinson, 1887, p.61). It was a neat system. The boss and the machine provided informal leadership 'filling the gap' in the formal structure (Childs, 1914, p.12), and business established a working relationship with the machine. This boss—business relationship is, however, only half of the machine equation. The boss wanted money and business needed contracts and favours of city government, but the boss was in no position to deliver these goods unless he had control of city government. In an age of universal suffrage this meant mobilising a majority of the electors. The machine could do this without too much trouble. It could 'buy' the votes of the immigrant poor with jobs, petty favours, patronage, and on the basis of cut-price pride in ethnic solidarity. 'The machine politician could be viewed as a broker who in return for financial assistance from wealthy elites promoted their policy interests when in office, while passing along a certain portion of the gain to a particularistic electorate from whom he "rented" his authority' (Scott, 1969, p.1155). The machines did more than give business political power, since they also served as an instrument 'to control the discontents of the period and channel them into "safe" political activities' (Katznelson and Kesselman, 1975, p.416). Providing immigrants with petty favours increased the legitimacy of an informal system as the whole emphasis on particular short run gains for individuals occurred at the cost of basic change for a class. In effect, the machine fostered interclass collaboration and face-to-face relationships across the social battlelines, and so held back the open violence of class conflict and did much to ensure the relative stability of urban America in potentially turbulent times.[19]

For all these apparent benefits, the boss—business relationship was never entirely satisfactory to the business community. It involved sharing power; it was a compromise; and it was always a poor second best to more direct, formal, and legitimate access. The whole relationship lacked firm predictability, and sometimes business could lose control of the boss only to find him take a more independent line and truckle to his immigrant supporters with dangerous talk of public policies to *their* advantage. Moreover, as business increased in scale there was a heightened recognition of the way city government could directly help business development through the extensive provision of an infrastructure of efficient city services and basic utilities. Simply, there was a need for a more stable and dependable route to governmental power that was more amenable to the interests of big capital and less expensive.[20]

Slowly, but surely, business began to turn its back on the boss and the machine. They came to embrace reform and attack what had been the informal instrument of their own political power.

19 The National Advisory Council on Civil Disorders (1967, pp.6–7) was in no doubt that the decline of the machines contributed to the black riots of the 1960s. Thomas and Blanshard (1932, p.290) recognised that the New York Tammany machine 'exerts only a moderate commission for keeping the masses quiet, and confirming landlords, bankers, public utility owners, and the whole House of Have in their favored position'.

20 'Gunton's Magazine, the unofficial organ of business in the nineties, complained in 1901 that businessmen were heartily sick of contributing to machine politics and would welcome a thorough purging of the whole machinery of government' (Nye, 1959, pp.26–7).

What was at issue was the 'question of the government of great cities under universal suffrage' (Godkin, 1898, p.122). As Wilcox (1904, pp.11—12) put it: 'the industrial world is divided into two hostile camps . . . and as complete political democracy would open the way for the absolute victory of one industrial party by means of the machinery of government, it becomes a matter of some importance to organised capital to hinder the political organisation of the people along democratic lines'.

(c) *What were the objectives of reformers, and how did they seek to attain them?*

At the widest level the businessman-reformer would have liked to put an end to class conflict, but there were limits as to what could be done given their reluctance to interfere with the inexorable logic of capital concentration that was working to their advantage. Within the more immediate context of local politics there was a concern to relocate *and* redirect governmental power. In addition they would also need to legitimise any new system for those who would be excluded from any serious impact upon it, and to this end it was clearly necessary to mystify the essential nature of reform in an ideology which talked of increasing efficiency and giving power back to the people. Although it would not be easy both to relocate and redirect power, *and* to legitimise these endeavours, for reformers the problem was never one of objectives: the problem was *how* to attain them in a democratic system based on universal suffrage.

'"In Connecticut", said the *National Advocate* of New York, "they disarmed the poorer classes by taking them into the body politic"' (Williamson, 1960, p.190). Universal suffrage may have been a useful device to 'manage the unenlightened class' (Julian, 1878, p.75), but it was always seen as problematic in 'the peculiar conditions of urban life' where class cleavage went deep (Goodnow, 1910, p.139). Moreover, the problem of democracy in the cities was compounded by the 'unfortunate' fact that 'universal suffrage occurred simultaneously with the great tide of emigration which followed the Irish famine' (Godkin, 1898, p.133; Goodnow, 1897, p.178). Giving native-born workers the vote was one thing, but newly arrived immigrants were seen as quite another matter since they had not been socialised into the American way of life. They posed a threat to stability. They might even want to push government into areas that custom had decreed were taboo.

Around the time that these anti-democratic beliefs were in vogue, there was also a growing belief that city government was best regarded as a business to be run like any other corporation (Munro, 1926, p.404; Sparks, 1916, esp. p.xi; Elliot, cited in MacGregor, 1911, p.17). There were two aspects to this. First, as John H. Patterson put it 'a city is a great business enterprise' and it should be 'directed . . . by men who are skilled in business management' (cited in Rightor, 1919, p.2).[21] Second, those who saw the city as a business were also 'generally driven to support a limitation of the suffrage' to the propertied class, and this was one of the commonest 'remedies for the evils of city government' (Matthews, 1895, pp.179, 176). In order to get the 'better class' power it was seen as important to 'offer them an opportunity, by a fair system of representation, to achieve a certain degree of success' (Sterne, 1877, p.646; see also Kasson, 1883; White, 1890; Conkling, 1894, p.189; Shaw, 1907, pp.66ff; Hall, 1906, pp.176ff; Goodnow, 1910, pp.139ff; Wilcox, 1904, pp.244–50).

So the first major 'reform' solution to the problem of bad city government centred upon an attack on the principle of universal suffrage. Those who advocated this measure displayed a keen, if crude, sensitivity to the relationship between rules and access, but although some cities enacted stiffer registration requirements to pare down the vote of the great unwashed, reformers were painfully aware of 'the practical hopelessness of any movement towards a substantial limitation of the suffrage' (Wilcox, 1904, p.263; see also Devlin, 1896, p.27). Disenfranchisement was nice in theory, but it was 'impracticable' (Matthews, 1895, p.176). The problem of how to solve the 'problem' of city government remained.

For a while there were 'bewildered and searching attempts at reform', where the remedies suggested displayed a 'hopeless diversity' and were 'often misguided and ineffectual' (Patton, 1940, p.7; Woodruff, 1903, p.48).

At one time reformers sought to restrict the powers and functions of city governments by increasing the powers of the states whose governments were less amenable to the impact of immigrant

21 John H. Patterson was the President of the National Cash Register Company and an active promoter of the council-manager form of government. Patterson also added that those skilled in 'social science' could assume the control of government since he was mindful of the ideology of most social scientists of the period, especially those who specialised in the science of municipal government.

demands from the cities. This limited the 'damage' which city governments might do, but it did little to make government a useful and effective partner to business enterprise.

More significantly, the early belief that 'good city government was dependent not so much on good forms as upon good men' led to an inevitable stress upon 'turning the rascals out' while leaving the established rules of government unchanged (Stewart, 1950, p.156; Conkling, 1894, p.47). Such an approach was doomed to failure. The men in office were not easy to dislodge; businessmen were reluctant to give the time that was needed to govern within the established system; and when 'goo-goo' ('good government') candidates did come forward they rarely proved to be good campaigners and (more important still) they had no large and loyal base of public support. If reform candidates did get into office 'they seldom survived for a second term' (Schiesl, 1972, p.iv), and even if they did 'the difficulty which was insurmountable lay in the constitution of councils' (Allinson, 1887, p.64). Reformers 'were intolerably handicapped by the existing *system* of municipal government' (Stone, Price and Stone, 1940, p.4; Crooks, 1968, pp.86—99). Munro (1913, pp.377—9) recognised that to try and turn the rascals out involved approaching things from the 'wrong angle . . . Complacently accepting the stupefying formulas of local government which they found in full sway' was based on the quite false belief that 'the existing machinery of government was not seriously defective'. Municipal ills 'lay beyond the mere personnel of city government . . . [and] efforts inspired by the belief that individuals and not institutions were at fault naturally led to sterility in results' and accounted for the limited accomplishments of early reformers. In MacGregor's opinion (1911, p.106), 'the failure of our municipal government in the past has been more largely due to the system than to the men who have administered it'.[22]

Rewriting the rules of the franchise may not have been feasible, but reform opinion was nevertheless thrust back against the necessity of considering the implications of formal rules for access to governmental power. There was no way they were going to get 'good men' and 'good government' in through the front door without new rules to help. Reformers had to find institutional remedies that would be politically acceptable while still attaining

22 See also Bryce, 1888, vol.1, p.614; Ford, 1904; Karl, 1963, p.8.

the results that would have followed from a restriction of the franchise to the propertied classes.

First gropings towards structural reform involved strengthening the powers of the mayor, so adapting the weak mayor–council form of government into the strong mayor–council form.[23] This solution was based on the business model of the lone entrepreneur. The National Municipal League's first model city charter advocated this form of government, but it was quickly seen as a limited improvement not least because no man 'engaged in active business' could grant the 'time' to perform the mayoral duties properly (Goodnow, 1897, p.277).

In 1900 a tidal wave destroyed one-third of the property and one-sixth of the life in Galveston, Texas. It was the most wonderful *deus ex machina* of municipal reform. The 'property owning class' of the city had been 'despairing of ever being able to control' the old mayor–council form of government, but with the breakdown of municipal organisation the businessmen of the city turned to the Texas legislature and called for a new charter that would entrust 'the administration of the city's affairs to a commission of 5 members, 3 appointed by the governor and 2 elected by the citizens of Galveston at large'. MacGregor (1911, pp.35–7) goes on to make it clear that 'it was the deliberate intention of the framers of the Galveston plan to take local government out of the hands of the people. They . . . had lost faith in democracy.' In 1903, against the wishes of the better elements in the city, the charter was amended so that all five commissioners were popularly elected. The commission form of government was born. It may be considered the first major experiment in local government in America, and in the next twenty years it was copied by some 500 cities. The form was favoured because it was seen as businesslike (Dohoney, 1910; Turner, 1906), and 'underlying this thrust for reorganisation was the more important effort to place businessmen in municipal office' (Schiesl, 1972, p.221). MacGregor (1911, p.113) considered that 'the commission form of government will undoubtedly facilitate the election of a higher type of men' because (like our own advocates of reorganisation) he too felt that 'experience clearly demonstrates that small bodies with large powers attract a better class of men than large bodies with small

23 Conkling (1894, p.32) argued that the mayor should have 'absolute sway. He should be the king or monarch of the city.'

Commission form

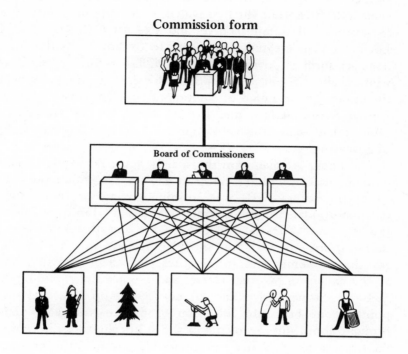

Commission form of government. From Childs, 1952, p.135

powers'. The trouble was that the plan was not seen as very successful in increasing calibre partly because of the heavy time demands on commissioners who were expected both to determine *and* administer policy (Munro, 1913, pp.308–10). The National Municipal League never endorsed the plan. More important, most of the cities that adopted the plan, including Galveston itself, have since abandoned it. In 1974 it was the form of government in less than 3% of American cities.

The businessmen's objective of dominating city government was proving to be illusive. Richard S. Childs (1952, pp.14–15), a wealthy businessman and a major figure in the movement for municipal reform, did not feel that the commission plan was an adequate copy of business practice. Maybe the small commission could be seen as a board of directors, but 'there would have to be a manager put under that board to make it resemble a corporation'. In 1910, Childs learned that the Lockport Board of Trade had created a committee to look into the commission plan. He sent them a draft charter which provided for an appointed city manager to assume all administrative and executive duties. The 1911 Lockport plan created what came to be known as the council—manager form of government. At long last reformers had found a winner, and 'within a generation they had substantially changed the structure and much of the practice of city government in the United States' (Glaab and Brown, 1967, p.167). By 1974 over 60% of American cities with population over 25,000 had this form of government.

The Lockport plan won the speedy approval of local chambers of commerce. Childs (1965, p.7) had no doubt that the plan led to 'better councils'. He was crushingly aware of 'the importance of institutional-structural arrangements . . . [and] he perceived that structure affected "access" to the loci of political power in urban affairs'. In fact, his 'model may have so structured access for the economic and social elites that they tend to dominate to the exclusion of other classes and groups' (East, 1965, pp.163, 144—5). Stone, Price and Stone (1940, pp.238, 194—5, 49) pointed out how 'the adoption of the city manager plan has brought about improvements in the political leadership of municipalities', as in 'previously machine-ridden cities' the new leaders were of 'greater prestige . . . and broader objectives . . . Locally the difference was adequately expressed by the statement that they were businessmen, not politicians.'[24]

It was hardly surprising, then, that the 'new form of government and the city manager himself were popularly identified with businessmen and their motives' and '"money saving and efficiency" were pursued as key objectives under the manager plan'. Childs told the city managers at their fourth annual conference that they could 'unblushingly point with pride' to an average saving of 10% in tax levies in their cities (Holli, 1969, p.179; Weinstein, 1962, pp.172—3). In 1937 the United States Chamber of Commerce questioned some sixty-five local chambers as to their assessment of the working of the council—manager plan in their own city: all replies were favourable. The National Municipal League (1935, p.4; see also 1939, p.17) tersely pointed out that 'local government costs the taxpayer less in cities operating under the council—

24 For detailed work on the change in the class composition of councils under the council—manager plan, see Taft, 1933; Weinstein, 1962.

Council – Manager form

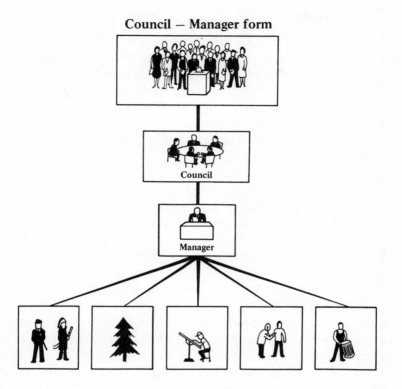

Council–manager form of government. From Childs, 1952, p.142

manager plan than in cities having other forms of government'.[25] In 1967, Lineberry and Fowler made a careful study of taxing and spending in 200 American cities. They found that reformed cities did tend to spend and tax less than unreformed municipalities.

After a lot of trials and many errors, reformers had got the rules—access equation right. In effect they had succeeded in 'shaping the structure of municipal government so that political power would no longer be broadly distributed but would be more centralised in the hands of a relatively small segment of the population' (Hays, 1964, p.167; see also Holli, 1969; Schiesl, 1972, p.319; Lowi, 1964, pp.193—7; Yates, 1973, p.16; Steigman,

---

25 Of course, securing these sorts of gains bore rather heavily on the working classes. Strikes by municipal employees were discouraged, and there was 'constant supervision over men, teams, and service' (Rightor, 1919, p.136; Holli, 1969, p.166).

1967, p.1073). What, then, were the magic rules of the council—manager form of government that led to this result?

First, the very fact that the council—manager form was modelled on business became 'the main plea by which busy and important citizens were induced to run for office' (Stone, Price and Stone, 1940, p.166). Moreover, the appointment of a city manager and the creation of a career civil service reduced the time demands on council men so that 'persons of large private interests can accept the service without serious sacrifice of valuable time' (Childs, 1965, pp.7, 78).

Second, the short ballot principle of fewer elective offices concentrated legislative power into a very much smaller city council that was elected for longer terms. Munro (1913, p.309) regarded it as 'a commonplace of political experience that the calibre of men in public office is closely related to the amount of power and authority which they exercise'.

Third, whereas large councils tended to be elected on a ward basis, the introduction of a small council facilitated at-large city-wide elections for the entire city. This was a crucial structural change limiting working class representation. Reformers and experts were all agreed that election by wards led to a 'dismal mediocrity of council membership' (Childs, 1952, p.179; see also Goodnow, 1897, pp.151–2; Munro, 1913, pp.308–9; White, 1890, p.369; Wilcox, 1897, p.151; Webb, 1898, p.139). Gosnell (1948, p.172) pointed out that 'especially in the larger cities the contrast between the results obtained in the large and small districts stands out' and he noted how 'better results' were obtained with at-large elections in both Detroit and New York City. At-large elections hit working class and minority candidates because they involved a more expensive city-wide campaign, and they knocked out the political feasibility of particularistic and class-based demands in favour of those geared to the 'interests of the city as a whole' which, in the nature of things, tended to go soft on redistributive policies grounded in an open expression of class conflict. Equally, this sort of election smiled on those candidates of standing in the city even though they might lack any solid base of local support. The change in the rules meant that the working class politician or the ethnic representative who served his inner city ward well would find his support diluted. He would be swamped, and come out second best, when pitted against a prominent businessman who could look to hard financial support from boosting economic concerns and soft support from the newer and expanding suburban areas that were increasingly under-represented in the old ward system. Let no one forget that in the 1917 election in Dayton (the first large city to adopt the council–manager form) 'the socialists cast 43% of the votes . . . and yet they did not succeed in securing a representative' (Rightor, 1919, p.28). Similarly, it was recognised by Cincinnati reformers in the 1920s 'that strong candidates who would have little chance in a ward election might well be carried into office if running at large', and Straetz (1958, pp.53–4) goes on to point out that 'the general experience of at-large elections has been that this system has improved the calibre of local representation'.

Fourth, 'the non-partisan ballot, a feature of most commission and manager plans, and widely heralded as a great advance in democracy, also tended to operate against minority groups' (Weinstein, 1962, p.177). Nearly two-thirds of America's cities use the non-partisan ballot to elect local officials (Dye, 1969, p.273). A class based view of politics is caught up in the championing of non-partisanship and so it is not surprising that 'efforts to initiate or to maintain "non-political" operations in municipal government tend to divide communities along class status lines with upper class elements favoring and lower class elements opposing these procedures' (Lockard, 1963, p.247; see also Schnore and Alford, 1963; Kessel, 1962; Sherbenou, 1961). Lineberry and Sharkansky (1974, p.63) argue that 'to a significant degree, the non-partisan ballot fulfills the expectations of its designers' in making for 'better' councils[26] and weakening trade union influence.[27] In Toledo, 'the role of lower income groups has been restricted', and in Oakland, 'the elimination of the partisan ballot in 1911, the creation of at-large elections in 1933, and the political influence of the *Tribune*, have made it nearly impossible for labor, articulate small-business candidates, or representatives of racial minorities to win office. The result is a system of mobilised bias': a system of structured access (Stinchcombe, 1968, p.231; Hayes, 1972, pp.189–90). In addition to all this, 'electoral turnout is significantly lower in non-partisan cities than in partisan cities', and the reduction in the size of the electorate is not random and across the board but is 'concentrated particularly in lower-income

26 See also Adrian, 1952; 1959, p.458; Key, 1949, ch. 14; Salisbury and Black, 1963; Banfield and Wilson, 1963, pp.156–61; Schiesl, 1972, p.319.
27 See also Gray and Greenstone, 1961.

groups who would normally vote Democratic' so still further encouraging the representation of business and Republican interests in the urban political arena (Lineberry and Sharkansky, 1974, p.64; see also Gray, 1971).

Fifth, it is important to consider the implications of the professionalisation and bureaucratisation of municipal government. Reformers had a belief in the power and wisdom of the educated expert. Administration, and even city government itself, were regarded as a science. The amateur's role in government had to be restricted. Maintaining a distinction between policy and administration, and seeing government as a business involving essentially technical problems which admitted of apolitical solutions involving no conflict, did not simply limit the role of those who were elected to government but it also legitimised a major role for the new city managers. Such beliefs paved the way for a merit civil service, and opened the door for the power shift into relatively autonomous, rapidly growing, public service bureaucracies which would tend to see it as appropriate and necessary to operate on the basis of *their* view of problems and solutions unfettered by any raucous intrusion from public service recipients. The intellectual soil of local government has been well-prepared for this by reformers in both Britain and America. Nowadays, technocratic considerations can easily be seen as the only basis for decision-making because we accept this ideology and choose to deny that local government is about politics, conflict and values, so tamely accepting the values and interests caught up in dominant ideologies as inevitable and necessary for the public good.

In America, reformers 'may have lost most of their battles for power [but] they have in the main won their war for the adoption of particular measures of structural . . . change' (Banfield and Wilson, 1963, p.148). Changing the rules of the local government game helped to ease businessmen back into power, if not by the formal front door of elections, then by the equally legitimate side door of appointed experts sensitive to their needs. Reformers have not simply done much to change the structure of city government, they have also provided us with a language of governmental discourse that restricts the nature of the political debate. Although this language helps to police and contain dissent, it does not compensate for the fact that established modes of government are not nearly as well-equipped as were the machines and the bosses to prevent and manage conflict and dissent. The machines gave business a measure of governmental power *and* a vehicle for social control. More direct and effective governmental power has been paid for at the price of less effective social control, and so there is now something of 'a political crisis of control for urban authorities'. Katznelson and Kesselman (1975, p.421) are referring to the problem of governing American cities, but when we in Britain are told that we too have an 'urban crisis' let no one doubt that there is a similar perception of the problem of control and order. I will be dealing with this in the next chapter.

9

A Political Perspective on the Contemporary Reorganisation of British Local Government

The mastery of any field of political science involves some knowledge of institutional history.
(Munro, 1913, p.1)

The careful student of history must seek the explanation of the forms and changes of political institutions in the social and economic forces that determine them.
(Turner, 1920, p.243)

Capital accumulation requires urbanization but urbanization requires investment, consumption and expense outlays which market exchange cannot handle. This dramatically increases the role of state enterprise in the economy, but the structure of state production, *particularly at the local level of government*, is only partially complementary to private accumulation.
(Hill, 1977, pp.89—90, italics mine)

1. Beyond Councillor Calibre

The call for economy in local administration is incessant and clamorous. It is sometimes anonymous, frequently it is unintelligent, and generally it is linked with a criticism of local administration.
(Wetherall, 1933, p.157)

Why should certain people persistently worry about 'declining' councillor calibre? Why, that is, should they worry about who governs at the local level, and about the changes that have occurred in the last century or so in the class composition of many local councils — and why should they want to effect a change in this through reorganisation?

This is the only question I am addressing myself to in this concluding chapter, and I will endeavour to answer it by situating the anxiety (and the political reality behind it) in the sort of context which serves to give it harder meaning and significance.

It might still be suggested that the anxiety, and therefore the question itself, is trivial. This is not the case. At its very gut the anxiety about declining councillor calibre pushes beyond the mere personnel of government to deal with what the fundamental relationship is, and should be, between dominant interests and the interventions of the local representative bodies of the state. Reorganisation has long been seen as urgent because of an implicit conception of the *necessity* for dominant interests controlling local government more directly. Moreover, reorganisation has held out the *possibility* that changing facets of the local government apparatus could actually achieve this result. A number of other issues are also involved. We are forced to consider the implications of universal suffrage and the rise of the Labour Party. We have to pay particular attention to the impact of state intervention and public expenditure on dominant interests. Finally, we must have regard to the constraints on that intervention — constraints that tend to manifest themselves in particular moments of economic (and therefore, typically, political) crisis, even though we must recognise that the problem of state intervention and public expenditure is built into the system. Not all these points will be discussed (and none will be discussed fully) but all need to be taken into account in any future work on local government and its reorganisation.

'The capitalist class, as a class, does not actually "govern". One must go back to isolated instances of the early history of capitalism . . . to discover direct and sovereign rule by businessmen' (Miliband, 1969, p.55). Indeed, economic and political power are formally separated in capitalist economies, and there is a distinction between public and private property. With the development of the market economy and the liberal individualist society, a non-arbitrary system of government was needed that would be responsive to the choices of the men of substance. Initially, there was nothing necessarily democratic about the politics of competition and the responsible party system. 'However, the market society did produce, after a time, a pressure for democracy which became irresistible . . . So finally the democratic franchise was introduced into the liberal state' (Macpherson, 1966, p.9). The growth of universal suffrage has been a crucially important development, and today it is 'the typical institution of a state which has gained autonomy from the economic'. The fact that 'the capitalist type of state . . . presents a relative autonomy vis-à-vis the dominant classes and fractions' and one consequence of the 'separation' between the economic and the political is that 'one cannot conclude from the existence of a "requirement of the economy" that the state will meet this requirement' (Poulantzas, 1973, pp.230, 256; Holloway, 1977, p.28). The state does not respond automatically to the requirements and *logic* of *capital*. It does not even inevitably respond to the direct *orders* of the *capitalist class*. It responds instead, and reacts to, a complex of political processes through which conflicting class interests are mediated and advanced. At one level the state is 'the place of confrontation between classes with antagonistic interests' (Lojkine, 1977, p.19), and dominant classes have to pursue their own interests in the face of working class pressure. Therefore the relations of political domination are inevitably and unavoidably complex, unstable, and problematic, and in continual need of reorganisation. Miliband (1977, p.67) is right to remind us that 'the relation between the "ruling class" and the state is a problem which cannot be assumed away'. In fact, the anxiety about declining councillor calibre is born out of a keen recognition of *precisely* the problem posed by Miliband — a problem which is often glossed over by Marxists in their recent concern to study British local government.

Bennington's observation (1975, p.3) that although 'there are a number of theoretical studies of the role of the state in advanced capitalist societies . . . there seems to have been much less critical study of the functions and operations of local government as an entity within the state apparatus' is rapidly becoming out of date. There is now a crop of British work in progress on 'the local state', and an emerging view tends to present local government as a simple instrument lacking any real autonomy. If it is not presented as the instrument of business, then it is presented as the instrument, or agent, of the central state.

The idea that local government is the instrument of business is most forcefully expressed in studies of local planning where particular attention centres on the interest and impact of commercial capital. Monahan's (1976, pp.180—1) study of the redevelopment of Covent Garden pointed to the 'collusion of public and private sectors' so that 'in the end the planners were no more than agents for the developers, and their job was merely to control some of the more gross manifestations of greed'. In a similar vein, Ambrose (1976, p.5), in his study of housing in Brighton, points out that it is becoming 'increasingly difficult to distinguish between local authorities and developers', and Ambrose and Colenutt

(1975, pp.63, 67) note, not just that 'the developer is . . . in a very strong position compared with the planners or the public', but that 'the main beneficiaries of the [present planning] system are not the public or the local authorities but the development industry'. Slightly softer in its implications is that work which, although not seeing local government as the instrument *of* business, nevertheless sees its interventions as directly functional *for* business. For example, the *Final Report* of Coventry CDP (1975, pp.55—6) noted how the local authority 'provided big business for a limited number of building and civil engineering firms' and 'performed a number of active functions on behalf of the engineering industry'. This general pattern of instrumental, or functional, politics is usually explained by pointing to the petty bourgeois composition of many local councils; the close relationship between business and local government even without direct business representation on the local council, be it formal and open or the result of friendship and corruption ('very different from . . . the consultation with the public'); and by noting how 'not only are the members of each political party circumscribed by the conditions in which they have to work, i.e. by market forces, but also by the permanent staff of the various authorities' (CIS, 1973, p.60).

The idea that local authorities are mere agents of the central government has a long history in the orthodox literature of local government studies where there is entrenched an explanation which centres on the fact that he who pays the piper calls the tune (for a critique, see Dearlove, 1973, pp.11—21). A Marxist tendency to see the state as a 'centralised unity' so that 'there is no question of there being separate "pieces" of the state' (Poulantzas, 1973, p.303; 1975, p.164) has meant that emerging tradition of local political economy has chosen to accept the cogency of the orthodox description and explanation, although it is now given a harder edge with talk of increasing local fiscal dependency. A CIS/CDP (1975, p.25) report tersely noted how 'the whole myth behind local government is that it should be based on local democracy', but it went on to note that 'in practice central government has a very firm grip on how it operates'. Broadbent (1977, p.138) went further, considering that 'the total picture does seem to support the idea of the local state as an agent of central government'. Cockburn (1977, pp.42—6, 71, 65), in an extremely important study centring on the London

Borough of Lambeth, argues not just that 'the state in capitalism is an instrument of class domination' which 'responds to and serves capital', but also that local government itself 'is only a small part of a large state structure' as local councils 'are, and under capitalism have always been, subject to central government' so that they perform as 'local agencies of the state'.

Both these sorts of view contain important elements of truth, and the crude idea of the local state as a simple instrument provides a better *starting* point for understanding and explanation than do those accounts which talk limply of a healthy local democracy and which grumble about the democratic implications of 'too much' central control. I say this because the instrumental emphasis recognises the need to situate local government and politics within the context of the encompassing political economy. All too often 'studies of municipal politics and administration have almost universally sought to isolate cities as independent objects of inquiry' and have treated them as 'self-sufficient and . . . assumed that attention could appropriately be confined to actors and issues within the city's geographic boundaries' (Kirlin and Erie, 1972, p.182; Kesselman, 1972, p.10). At its best, the perspective of political economy involves a keen recognition that the urban 'system' is not self-contained and, in consequence, is not amenable to study simply on the basis of locally focused case studies. Such a recognition poses a challenge to a key and emerging thrust of urban political science. It also challenges the un-thought-out tendency to see local government as neutral and *completely* autonomous — as somehow suspended in mid air, *above* the local economy and responding to the needs of the local 'community' and the political demands of 'citizens', and *below* (potentially at least) the unwarranted intrusions of the central government. But for all this, to see local government as an instrument embodies an economism that makes local government unproblematic and so renders any detailed study of it almost superfluous. More important, it actually provides a perspective that is inadequate in the face of the complex and contradictory reality of local government in its relations to class and state. Because of this it cannot see what I will later go on to define as the particular problem of local government. The Edinburgh CSE Group (1977, p.28) is right: 'existing marxist accounts of the restructurings of the local state are, as yet, unsatisfactory'.

Let me, then, return to the issue of declining councillor calibre, and quickly admit that it need not necessarily pose any sort of problem for dominant interests. The class composition of many local authorities may have changed but dominant interests may not need to rule directly, and there are those who maintain that it is actually best if they do take a political back seat (Poulantzas, 1969, pp.73–4). We clearly should not forget that 'there are many ways for a ruling class to exercise and maintain its rule, other than by supplying, from its own ranks, the political personnel' (Therborn, 1976, p.5), and so we need to spend some little time exploring what these ways might be.

There are a number of related approaches to this. Miliband (1969, p.146) highlights the importance of business as a pressure group, in the broad meaning of that term, maintaining that it 'enjoys a massive superiority outside the state system . . . in terms of the immensely stronger pressures which, as compared with labour and any other interest, it is able to exercise in the pursuit of its purposes'. This may well be so, but it is not necessarily the most important point, and to assess the political weight of various interests solely on the basis of a study of their overt activity in the making of governmental decisions involves 'taking over and reproducing the bias of the system' you are studying (Lukes, 1974, p.36). It ignores the less visible face of power whereby dominant interests may be able to inhibit potential issues from emerging fully onto the political stage, so confining the scope of public action to issues which do not touch on the 'private' power of their interest (Bachrach and Baratz, 1962, 1963). Issues may even be kept out of politics without action or conflict. Crenson's study of action on air pollution makes the point that the issue was not raised in Gary, Indiana, because US Steel had a 'reputation for power' and this alone was sufficient for it to influence 'the content of the pollution ordinance without taking any action on it' (1971, pp.124, 69). This highlights the importance of our looking at any political system and inferring the existence of power by judging from the consequences or outputs of the policy process whose interests and priorities have been served by that process – 'in a word, who benefitted?' (Hayes, 1972, p.x). Of course, this is not totally accurate as subordinate interests may have a false picture of the potential power of those who are inactive, only to find that they subsequently intervene more directly to reverse whatever policies may have been developed against them (Painter,

1969). There are those who would claim that none of this goes far enough in dealing with the relation between dominant interests and the state.

From Gramsci's perspective it is important to understand the subtle but pervasive forms of ideological control and manipulation that serve to perpetuate all repressive structures. His concept of hegemony goes beyond ideology and deals with the permeation throughout civil society of an entire system of values, attitudes, and beliefs, that in one way or another is supportive of the established order and the class interests that dominate it. In this situation a given form of domination is in practice *internalised*, so transforming the whole question of class rule and of opposition to it (Boggs, 1976, ch.2; Williams, 1977, ch.6). Although those familiar with the literature on non-decisions and non-protest (Dunleavy, 1977) can sense the importance of this contribution, it is clear that it opens up a whole range of wider issues and problems.[1]

From a rather different perspective, Poulantzas (1969, pp.70−3) also claims that 'direct participation of members of the capitalist class in the state apparatus and in government, even where it exists, is not the important side of the matter'. Such a conception, which involves a focus on 'inter-personal relations', derives from 'a problematic of the subject'. This problematic, in not 'comprehending social classes and the State as objective structures', inevitably fails to see that 'the relation between the bourgeois class and the State is an objective relation' of which 'men' are but the 'bearers'. Poulantzas (1973, pp.256, 284−5, 190) rightly rejects 'a simplistic and vulgarised conception which sees in the state the tool or the instrument of the dominant class', stressing instead that 'the capitalist type of state . . . presents a relative autonomy *vis-à-vis* the dominant classes or fractions'. Having said that, he makes what I consider to be a highly contentious point when he asserts that precisely *because* of that, the capitalist state 'takes charge . . . of the bourgeoisie's political interests and realises the function of political hegemony which the bourgeoisie is unable to achieve'. This may involve both 'compromises *vis-à-vis* the dominated classes' (and 'guarantees which may even be contrary to the short term economic interests of the dominant classes'), and

---

1 For a useful attempt to deal empirically with a facet of this perspective in the urban context, see CDP, 1977, ch. 7.

interventions 'against the long-term economic interests of one or other fraction of the dominant class'. But, in spite of this, Poulantzas (1976, p.72) considers that 'the (capitalist) State, in the long run can only correspond to the political interests of the dominant class or classes'.

I think Miliband (1970, p.57) is broadly right in his claim that Poulantzas' 'exclusive stress on "objective relations" suggests . . . that what the state does is . . . wholly determined by these "objective relations"': in other words, that the structural constraints of the system are so absolutely compelling as to turn those who run the state into the merest functionaries and executants of policies imposed upon them by 'the system'. Poulantzas may push an instrumentalist conception out of the front door, but he seems to introduce it through the back door, by stressing 'objective relations' when he says: 'the state is not "manipulated" by the ruling class into doing its bidding: it does so autonomously but totally because of the "objective relations" imposed upon it by the system'. Miliband maintains that to conceive of the state—class relationship as purely objective one leads to a 'structural determinism' which prevents us establishing the relative autonomy of the capitalist state that is such a crucial facet of Poulantzas' problematic (Miliband, 1973, p.87). Moreover, it also tends to assume away the very problem of the relation between the ruling class and the state and renders naive and irrelevant those questions which ask *how* dominant interests rule and the sorts of *limits* that may impinge on them in the context of bourgeois democracy.

Notwithstanding the heat of the Poulantzas—Miliband debate, we must surely recognise that the implied dichotomy between, on the one hand, objective relations and structural determinism, and, on the other, the problematic of the subject and an emphasis upon the personnel of the state and interpersonal and interorganisational relations, is ultimately a false and fruitless one. It only makes sense to situate your enquiry and analysis exclusively within the 'objective relations' camp if you are prepared to argue, both that the political sphere is so constrained as to be robbed of *any* autonomy, and that the constraints somehow operate *outside* politics and the (unpredictable and uncertain) relations of struggle and compromise. Social formations may have considerable stretch to them so that those who run the state machine just cannot be reduced to administrators of policies imposed by the system. At a minimum and at least in the short run, politicians and administrators have some room for manoeuvre, although this will vary depending on the form of the state. It will also vary at different points in time; with respect to different aspects of state intervention; and (crucially important in the context of this particular study) at different levels of the state apparatus. In addition, it must also be recognised that political and governmental processes themselves possess a 'certain internal dynamic' (Hirsch, 1977, p.1) which serves to place them beyond easy 'control' once set in motion, almost regardless of either the state of struggle or the functional needs of capital. All this being the case, and *because* this is the case — precisely because the capitalist state is relatively autonomous in relation to the dominant classes; precisely because economic and political power are formally separated; precisely because the capitalist state responds to political forces and not to objective necessities; and precisely because the relation of the 'ruling class' to the state is always and in all circumstances bound to be problematic, an interest in political (and even governmental) processes and in those who occupy the seats of governmental power cannot be reduced to a crass concern of empirical social science. It is possible to go 'too far in dismissing the nature of the state elite as of altogether no account' (Miliband, 1970, p.57), and this must be recognised, as must the importance of studying political and governmental processes. Having said that, it is also clear that we must study personnel and politics within a *context* which involves the exploration of those factors which have some sort of ultimate bearing on the limits of state intervention.

We have come full circle and are back to the anxiety about councillor calibre. Because local government cannot be regarded as the simple instrument of either the central state or dominant interests (and therefore because local authorities do have room for political manoeuvre) the issue of declining councillor calibre is likely to be seen as a problem, although it will be seen as *more* than a problem about the quality of the personnel of local government alone. There *are* a variety of ways in which dominant interests may assert their rule without direct involvement in government, and, in itself and taken on its own, the question of who actually governs is *not* really very important. However, declining councillor calibre has been correctly seen as relating to, and even *causing*, problems with respect to the scale of local public expenditure and the scope and direction of the interventions of local government. Before I deal with these more fundamental problems of local government — problems which take us beyond councillor calibre — it is important to orient ourselves by first dealing with the general problem of state intervention and public expenditure.

2. The General Problem of State Intervention and Public Expenditure

Session after session we are amplifying the province of the Legislature, and asserting its moral prerogatives. Parliament aspires to be the *pater patriae*, and is laying aside the policeman, the gaoler, and the executioner, in exchange for the more kindly and dignified functions of the father, the schoolmaster and the friend.
(*The Times*, 4 May 1847)

I believe . . . that an increase of taxation in present conditions which fell on industry would be the last straw. Schemes involving heavy expenditure, however desirable they may be, will have to wait until prosperity returns.
(The Chancellor of the Exchequer to the House of Commons, 11 February 1931)

Whatever the short term constraints, we must protect and improve the industrial capability which will be essential for our economic growth in the longer term . . . I now turn to the cuts in public expenditure which have become inevitable.
(The Chancellor of the Exchequer to the House of Commons, 15 April 1975)

During the early period of capitalist development the role of the state was facilitative and limited to the provision of some material infrastructure and the enforcement of a legal framework necessary for the market to function. The liberal state guaranteed freedom of contract and trade, and dismantled the restrictive apparatus of the feudal economy. Over the years there have been important changes in the British economy and in the general role of the state, and nowadays the scale and pervasiveness of state intervention is immeasurably greater than ever before. In addition to social policy and the whole apparatus of the welfare state, there is increased involvement in the monetary and fiscal management of the economy (as well as more direct interventions at the level of the firm); greatly increased infrastructure support; and increased involvement in the regulation of conflict between wage labour and capital. Part of these developments has been an increase in public expenditure and an increase in the numbers employed in the public sector. The ratio of public expenditure to gross domestic product has risen from 14.4% in 1900 to 39% in 1950, and to 60% in 1976. In similar vein, 5.8% of the working population were employed by the public sector in 1901, but by 1975 some 25.8% of the working population were in this position.[2]

We need to ask a number of questions about these developments. First, how can we explain the growth of the interventionist state? Second, how can we best categorise the essential nature of state activity: what part does it all play in the life of society; what interests benefit from the various interventions; and have they (taken together) effected a fundamental change in the essentials of the capitalist system? Finally, and of particular importance in the context of this study, what are the problems of state intervention and public expenditure as defined by certain interests, and what, therefore, are the limits which they might seek to impose in order to make it more functional for their interest at particular moments? There are a number of perspectives on these problems.

The predominant view has tended to regard state intervention as the enlightened and humanitarian response to the miseries created by the rapidity of nineteenth-century industrialisation and the harshness of cyclical depression. Welfare provision and economic management are seen as having effectively harnessed, controlled, and tempered the play of market forces so as to change the system in the interests of all citizens. Nowadays, however, there is a keener recognition of the limits of this perspective, and Hay (1975, p.62) makes the point that 'humanitarian opinion, by itself, seems to have achieved less than an earlier generation of historians believed'.

A functionalist stream of sociological writing tends to be inattentive to the morality of those involved in reform, choosing instead to emphasise how the unplanned development of any industrial society throws up new problems and new needs which are inevitable and unavoidable. Because established forms of voluntary provision have generally been inadequate it has been 'necessary' for the state in all industrial countries to extend the scope of public provision.[3] More recently, this kind of work has

2 Figures from Peacock and Wiseman, 1961, p.166; *Public Expenditure to 1979—80*, 1976, p.1; Abramovitz and Eliasberg, 1957, p.25; Department of Employment, *British Labour Statistics*, 1975, pp.216, 121.
3 See, for example, Wilensky and Lebaux, 1958; and Kerr, Dunlop, Harbison, and Myers, 1962. For a brief critique, see Wedderburn, 1965, esp. pp.137—9.

been given a harder edge by 'marxist functionalism' (Corrigan, 1977, p.88). Instead of operating on the basis of a consensual view of society, and instead of pointing to the impact of the needs and problems of all interests on state provision, those in this tradition point to the continuance of *laissez faire* as posing particular, and politically significant, problems for capital. The actions of individual competing capitals have been seen as in sharp contradiction to the needs of the system of production as a whole, because the competitive struggle compels them to take certain courses of action which, if allowed to continue unchecked, would be disastrous for the continued dominance of the overall system within which they are the major beneficiaries. In these circumstances, state intervention has come to involve more than just repression. It also provides the general conditions for production, and it is seen as assuming a particularly important role in *repro*ducing the conditions of production, a task that involves it in reproducing labour power and the relations of production (Althusser, 1971, pp.121—73; Lefebvre, 1976). Attention has often centred on the particular needs of monopoly capital in relation to the problem of underconsumption, where state expenditure (especially on armaments) is seen as functioning to offset the lack of demand elsewhere in the economy (Sweezy, 1942; Kidron, 1970). But, more generally, those who choose to operate within this functional, or capital-logic, problematic rarely tell us how instances of intervention are developed and implemented, and work out in practice; they do not dwell on the differences in the provision of welfare services in different capitalist countries; and they point to the persistence of poverty and inequality as proof of the absence of any fundamental change (Offe, 1972, pp.480—1). Moreover, their formulation, which suggests that state intervention is functional for capital as a whole and in the long run, not only raises the question of what exactly is the long run, but also begs the question of the sort of analysis that is appropriate to the shorter run. A perspective which so easily dismisses reformism can easily arrive at a political position which is 'purely negative and utopian' (Corrigan, 1977, p.88), and at an analysis of capitalism which is static and inattentive to the implications and significance of politics and struggle (Clarke, 1977). If those who operate within this problematic do not go so far as to see class struggle itself as functional for capital (Altvater, 1973, p.103), then they either minimise the role of such struggle in leading to state intervention (which they see as occurring without controversy), or else they see it as easily contained within the logic of established relations by a series of mere palliatives that serve both to effect social control and to enlarge the social base of the ruling class (Müller and Neusüss, 1975; Piven and Cloward, 1972).

'Against this functional approach may be set those who emphasize the role of class struggle in the development particularly of social services since the Second World War' (Gough, 1975, p.57). Instead of just pointing to similarities with respect to welfare provision, there is a concern to 'explain some of the important differences which exist between different capitalist countries' and a recognition that in order to do this 'we have to examine political forces' (Wedderburn, 1965, p.142). There is no denial of the social control functions of certain state interventions (it would be quite impossible to sustain such a position),[4] and there is no presumption that all interventions have occurred as a response to an actual or potential threat from below. However, there is a keen perception that public policies are developed in relation to and in the 'presence' of the working class. This means, at a very minimum, that the actual 'social expenses'[5] which the state chooses (but somehow has) to incur to legitimise and sustain its rule are partly determined by the form and organisation of that presence, which may be such as to wrest 'concessions from the state over and above what it would wish to have granted', with Gough (1975, p.75) going on to claim that 'the strength of working class pressure can roughly be gauged by the comprehensiveness and the level of social benefits'. A key feature of the capitalist state is the extent to which this threat has been recognised and entrenched in, at the same time as it has been legitimised through, the extension of the franchise. In spite of delaying tactics, 'in the long run, given the working class majority among the electorate, both Tories and Liberals were forced to adapt themselves to the political demands of this new audience' (Saville, 1975, p.61). This is not to say that the extension of the franchise caused

4 Numerous writers attest to the fact that 'social policy . . . was used as means of avoiding social revolution' (Fraser, 1973, p.8); Balfour, Gladstone, and Chamberlain (among others) have made it clear that certain of their policies were developed in response to and as a counter to demands from below; and there are studies which highlight the social control dimension of certain welfare policies (see esp. Piven and Cloward, 1972).

5 O'Connor (1973, p.7) sees social expenses consisting of 'projects and services which are required to maintain social harmony — to fulfil the state's "legitimation" function'. See esp. ch. 6.

the development of the welfare and regulatory state, but it did
'provide constitutional channels for popular pressures' whereby
the working classes 'might attempt to control the state' (Macpherson, 1966, pp.10—11; Briggs, 1961, p.239).

That the Industrial Revolution created, and had an effect on the
consciousness of, the working class cannot be doubted in the face
of the problems which it created and aggravated. Both the Labour
Party and the Trades Union Congress had extensive social reform
programmes by the early 1900s, and it is doubtful how far their
measures on unemployment, health and education were based on
an acceptance of middle class values. 'There is a wide measure of
agreement among historians and social scientists that political
pressure from the working class was one of the main reasons for
the origins of social reform', and although it is probably 'im-
plausible . . . to assert that the social reform of the period 1906
to 1914 was simply the inevitable result of working class pressure
through the ballot box, or by direct action or the threat of it, this
does not mean that such pressures were not important or non-
existent' (Hay, 1975, pp.25, 29). Barratt Brown (1972, pp.12,
16, 151) has no doubt that the power of private capital can be
challenged by labour. He sees the 'political and economic settlement after 1945 . . . [as] a tacit bargain between the representatives
of Capital and Labour' which was such as to 'assure a real improvement in the whole quality of life of the British working people',
and he considers that 'the social services in Britain, despite all
their weaknesses, are a tribute to the social demands of the Labour
Movement'.

It makes little sense to see the welfare state and state intervention
as an all-of-a-piece, uncomplicated lump. If it is silly to define it
as socialism, or as some sort of fundamental change in the essentials
of the capitalist social formation, then it is equally silly to define
it all as the bald defence of the status quo in a way which is
unambiguously functional for capital as a whole. The truth of the
matter is that none of the perspectives that I have discussed can,
on their own, adequately grasp the essential reality of the welfare
state and state intervention. They cannot do this precisely because
state intervention in contemporary capitalism is a contradictory
reality which is ambiguous in terms of the interests it advances.
It takes this form because of the social reality it confronts — a
reality made up of classes in conflict, but still with certain interests

in common. So, it is simultaneously the social wage — a means of securing social needs, of developing the powers of the individual, and of exerting some control over an anarchic market — *and* a means of muting civil disorder, enforcing work norms, and of reproducing labour.[6] It is important in aiding and abetting the accumulation of capital, in reproducing capitalist relations, and in legitimising many of the essentials of the established order by both solving and mystifying the problems it throws up. But is is also susceptible to pressure from below, and facets of the welfare state constitute a working class gain, both directly and in terms of the grudging entrenchment of an ideology of provision based on need rather than on cash payment which raises expectations and serves as a pointer to better things. The welfare state is a battle-ground and we should not forget that intended vehicles of working class incorporation are also tokens of bourgeois defeat which serve as double-edged weapons, the effect and implications of which cannot easily be predicted.

If it is important to distinguish the positive and progressive elements of state intervention from the negative and regressive aspects, and if we must begin this task by categorising the nature of state intervention and state *expenditure*,[7] then it is equally important to deal with the sources of state *finance*. There is substantial debate as to whether taxes fall on the working class or on capital, with some maintaining that 'the incidence of taxation is an empirical question that cannot be answered on an *a priori* basis' (Gough, forthcoming; see also Fine and Harris, 1976, p.106; Bullock and Yaffe, 1975, p.31). Regardless of the state of debate on either the incidence of taxation, or the interests served by state intervention there is, and has long been, a perception that there exists a clash between private accumulation and taxing — a clash between capitalism and an extensive public sector. At root this can best be seen as the embodiment of the nineteenth-century fear of the implications of democracy for private property, but in the twentieth century the concern about public expenditure has surfaced at certain moments with a particular virulence.

This is not a study of the state of the British economy. At the same time, some brief consideration of its development since the

6 For a much more extensive development of these sort of points see Gough (forth-coming).
7 O' Connor (1973) is an important contribution to this. See also Semmler, 1977.

Second World War and of the problems it has been facing since the 1960s cannot be avoided. It is relevant to the general problem of state intervention and public expenditure and it also has a direct bearing on local government reorganisation itself, providing the context which gives it meaning at the moment when it occurred.

Notwithstanding the long-term problem of the international competitiveness of British industry, rearmament and then the war eliminated unemployment by 1941. The capitalist system in the post-war period experienced an unprecedented expansion and Britain shared in this. Investment became profitable. The reconstruction of the international monetary system was important. There was also the appearance of new fields for investment (notably in cars and construction) that raised productivity and yielded high returns. Besides low wage costs, the supply of raw materials and primary products was cheapened as the terms of trade moved in favour of the industrialised countries from the 1950s. No account of the factors sustaining (and eventually rendering problematic) the long post-war boom would be complete if it were to ignore the crucial part played by the state. In a variety of ways state spending socialised the costs of production by raising productivity and lowering labour costs. In addition, undoubtedly prompted by 'the pressure of labour movements pressing for policies of full employment' (Barratt Brown, 1972, p.225), the state also came to assume more a role in economic management. There was a recognition that 'public investment can . . . be used more directly as an instrument of employment policy' (*Employment Policy*, 1944, p.21), and public expenditure was a general stimulus to private investment (so inhibiting the tendency to stagnation) and a specific means of regulating and sustaining effective demand (so smoothing out the trade cycle). The problem was that the seeds of later destruction were contained in this activity. State intervention and expenditure, and the inflation that was an inevitable part of it (Gamble and Walton, 1976, p.32), was a means of postponing slump and depression (Mattick, 1971): it was a means of postponing the necessity for a fundamental restructuring of British industry that would at some point become inevitable in the light of changed world conditions and general competitive struggle. Full employment not only involved depleting the reserve army of labour (so eliminating an automatic regulator of the capitalist economy), but it was also a factor increasing the power and expectations of labour, so strengthening 'a trend

towards labour taking a growing share of the national income'
(Glyn and Sutcliffe, 1972, p.32).

Unemployment has been on an upward climb since 1966,
and by the 1970s the British economy was experiencing its worst
crisis since the war. Britain has not been alone, but even so there
has been a steady worsening of our performance on the world
market. The obvious reason for the poor British performance in
world trade has been its high and rapidly rising prices in the face
of more productive competitors. In Glyn and Sutcliffe's (1972,
p.10) opinion, the 'crisis has developed because mounting demands
from the working class for a faster growth in living standards has
coincided with growing competition between capitalist countries.
This competition . . . has prevented British capitalism from simply
accommodating successful wage demands by pushing up prices
correspondingly.' The combined effect of pressure at home on
the wages front[8] and in resistance to measures which might have
increased productivity, and from the growing competition of
other capitalist countries, has made it increasingly difficult for
British industry to obtain profits. The share of profits in company
net output has fallen from 25.2% in 1950–4 to 21.2% in 1964 and
12.1% in 1970. Moreover, the rate of profit fell in much the same
way as the share of profits, with the pre-tax rate declining from
16.5% in 1950–4 to 9.7% in 1970 and 5% in 1974 (Glyn and
Sutcliffe, 1972, pp.58, 55; Gough, 1975, p.89). Not surprisingly
the squeeze on profits has made it increasingly difficult to generate
investment and so keep economic growth going.

The situation of 'stagflation' presents a problem whereby the
state's role in economic management demands that it try and face
both ways at once. To 'solve' stagnation and maintain full employment (to assure victory at the polls), the government needs to
reflate the economy by increasing public expenditure. But to curb
inflation and improve the competitive position of British goods on
the international market, the government needs to decrease public
expenditure. Government expenditure may socialise industrial
costs and provide conditions for growth and expansion, but 'their
extension to the degree that it requires further taxation is a burden
that the bourgeoisie is increasingly reluctant to shoulder' (Bullock
and Yaffe, 1975, p.33). State intervention which helped to provide
a bedrock for post-war accumulation now threatens the con-

8 For a critique of this position see Yaffe, 1973.

tinuance of accumulation itself. There is a growing consensus, both inside and outside the state apparatus, that the public sector and public expenditure is a major part of our problem. This assessment is made up of the idea that increasing employment in the state sector reduces the supply of labour available to the private sector at times of expansion, but more fundamentally it is caught up in the thesis which suggests that public expenditure crowds out the opportunities for private profit, so contributing to a process of deindustrialisation. Bacon and Eltis (1976, pp.13—14) point out 'how growth in public expenditure has contributed to Britain's difficulties', noting that 'higher state consumption must squeeze net-of-tax profits or wages and salaries as a share of marketed output. In so far as it squeezes profits, and this is perhaps what it is now most likely to squeeze in many countries, it will also squeeze investment . . . [and] inadequate investment can easily lead to structural employment.' They are not alone in this view. The Government's white paper on *An Approach to Industrial Strategy* (1975, p.5) also made the point that part of the problem experienced by manufacturing industry lay in the fact that government had been involved in the 'pre-emption of resources by the public sector . . . to the detriment of industry's investment and export performance'. The CBI (1976, pp.34, 31) is also clear that 'the public sector has pre-empted the resources needed for exports, import substitution and investment' and it regarded it as 'crucial that over the next few years the scale of public expenditure is reduced to allow the wealth producing sectors to flourish'.

Notwithstanding the fact that cuts in public expenditure are not unambiguous in their implications for profitability (because they damp down demand for products from the private sector), and notwithstanding the fact that a variety of factors may make it difficult for the state to effect cutbacks, it is clear that we are pressing up against very particular limits of state intervention. I say this, not so much because we can point to the *objective* necessity for constraints on the relative autonomy of the capitalist state, but because there is *political organisation* against public expenditure and certain facets of state intervention. This is expressed above all in terms of a critique of the welfare state, a critique which is itself grounded in a particular view of society and its problems and in the presentation of the contemporary situation as one that admits of no policy choice. It is not too surprising, therefore, that from the mid 1970s there have been cut-backs in public expenditure. In May and December 1973 it was announced that £1,700 million would be cut from expenditure in 1974—5, and in April 1975 the Chancellor of the Exchequer announced a further cut in planned expenditure of £1,100 million for 1976—7. But this is not all. Contemporary orthodoxy sees it as equally important to *redirect* the scope of the public sector so as to 'functionalise' it to the needs of capital in its effort to restructure in the face of changes in the competitive position. The government has made it clear that 'within total expenditure, a higher priority is being given to expenditure which is designed to maintain or improve our industrial capability' (*Public Expenditure to 1979—80*, 1976, p.2). Plans for this were laid out in the white paper on *An Approach to Industrial Strategy* (1975) which the CBI (1976, p.54) regarded as 'a step in the right direction'.

It should be obvious that the general state of the British economy and the proposals to cut back and redirect the public sector must have profound implications for local government. Indeed, 'reorganisation represents an important adjustment in the state apparatus at the local level; adjustments which are a response to important developments within the British economy' (Bennington, 1975, p.3). Reorganisation can scarcely be understood outside a context which pays attention to the general problem of state intervention and public expenditure — a problem which becomes acute at certain moments even though facets of it are caught up in the system on a continuing basis and are acutely focused at the local level.

3. The Particular Problem of Local Government

. . . at the local level, relatively smaller size and geographical
proximity mean that government power is potentially more ac-
cessible and — in theory — responsible to the working population.
In fact, many [American] cities in the late 19th and 20th centuries
were ruled by political organisations solidly rooted on the immigrants who were flowing into Eastern cities.
(Markusen, 1976, p.56)

Biarez *et al*. note that a large proportion of local authorities in
France are today controlled by parties representing nonhegemonic,
or dominated classes, thus presenting a potential challenge to the
identification of the general interest with the economic interests of
the hegemonic fraction.   (Pickvance, 1977, p.231)

The general problem of state intervention and public expenditure has been particularly focused at the local level.

While total public spending has risen as a proportion of GNP, local government spending has done so even faster. In 1890 local government expenditure in the United Kingdom was 3.4% of GNP, by 1963 it was 8.9%, and by 1974 it stood at 12.4%. Between 1963 and 1973 local authority expenditure in England and Wales rose from £3,647 million to £13,472 million. In 1971, the government admitted that 'on present trends there will continue to be a gap between the amount required to finance a programme of development of local authority services and the yield of the local revenue on which the provision of such services depends' (*The Future Shape of Local Government Finance*, 1971, p.2). This gap (termed by O'Connor (1973) 'The fiscal crisis of the state') has been reflected in, and filled by, an increased reliance upon central government grants and an increased level of local authority indebtedness. In 1949–50 government grants amounted to 34% of the current income of local authorities in Great Britain, but by 1973–4 the figure stood at 45%. Over the same period, the gross debt of local authorities in England and Wales increased ten-fold. In 1949–50 loan charges amounted to 12% of their current expenditure but by 1973–4 the figure stood at 19%. The various trends with respect to local government expenditure are reflected in figures for local government employment. In 1891, 1.2% of the total working population were employed in this sector; by 1952 this figure was 6.2%; and by 1975 it had increased to 11.3%. In fact, the actual numbers employed in local government more than doubled between 1949 and 1975, rising from 1.4 million to some 3 million, an increase greater than the increase in total public sector employment over the same period.[9]

Local government is overwhelmingly concerned with 'social consumption'[10] — it is critically concerned, that is, with expenditure on goods and services that are consumed collectively and which contribute to the reproduction and extended reproduction

9 Figures from Peacock and Wiseman, 1961, p.107; Committee of Inquiry into Local Government Finance, 1976, pp.384, 388, 381; Department of the Environment, *Local Government Financial Statistics: England and Wales, 1973–4*, pp.8–9; Abramovitz and Eliasberg, 1957, p.25; Department of Employment, *British Labour Statistics Yearbook*, 1969, 1975.
10 See O'Connor, 1973, ch. 5. Castells (1977) calls much the same thing 'collective consumption'.

of labour power. Education dominates local spending and has grown massively since the war. Housing expenditure has also increased. Together they amounted to 27.9% of the current expenditure and 73.4% of the capital expenditure of local authorities in England and Wales in 1947—8; these figures stood at 54% and 44% respectively in 1972—3 (Broadbent, 1977, figure 24, p.131). In addition to expenditure on law, order and protective services, local authorities are also critically involved in the provision of health and personal social services, and in the provision of a variety of leisure and cultural amenities. It is precisely the sorts of services provided by local government that can be seen as an integral part of the social wage; it is these services that are especially ambiguous in terms of the interests they advance; and it is these services around which are focused conflicts as to the levels and inclusiveness at which they should be provided.

So, at one level, the problem of local government is essentially a problem of its scale and scope. It is a problem that is clearly seen to have increased in magnitude in the recent past and we are now witnessing an attempt to set new limits on the nature of its services and interventions. But having said that, the *particular* and special problem of local government is about *more* than that. Moreover, even the problem of its scale and scope is not a new problem since nineteenth-century commentators were mindful of the fact that 'the total burden of local taxation is increasing at an alarming rate' (Phillips, 1882, p.466). This being the case, to look for an explanation of the roots of the problem *solely* in terms of the contemporary state of the British economy and the needs of business is inadequate. Clearly demographic changes have been of importance in prompting an increase in local public expenditure, and this *has* posed a particularly acute difficulty when looked at in conjunction with problems of profitability and inflation. However, any explanation must also have regard to the personnel and politics of local government, and must go back to consider the problematic implications of nineteenth-century reorganisation.

When local government was democratised it was clearly designed to provide a vehicle for popular participation in government, but at a level where the then range of functions was neither particularly extensive nor such as to touch on issues of redistribution which might adversely affect the propertied classes who provided the finance. Local self-government was to socialise and mobilise the

population at large into a broad acceptance of the emerging
political economy that was to lie beyond popular control.[11] It
was also seen as providing a more specific political training ground
for the few who might go on to serve in more important governmental posts at the national level (see Bentham, cited in Mac-
Kenzie, 1961, p.13). Brodrick (1875, pp.94—5) saw all this as
providing 'the permanent bulwark of social order', since by
'accustoming representatives of all classes to work together daily
for public but non-political objects, they would strike at the root
of . . . class prejudices' and help in 'building up conservative
barriers or breakwaters against revolutionary floodwaves'. What
was hoped for from the democratisation of local government, and
what might actually result, are two very different matters. Democratic local government became more vulnerable to working class
demands and even to direct working class control. It also posed a
particular problem for the direct representation of business
interests. More than this, the democratisation of local government
strengthened an ideology of local self-government which inhibited
the political feasibility of extending central control. Let me now
deal briefly with each of these three points in turn, since they are
at the core of the particular problem of local government.

The growth of government activity cannot be understood in terms
of the impact of economic forces alone. The political and
ideological environment of the nineteenth century tended to check
the expansion of governmental activity and so 'the full impact
of many problems which appeared before 1900 was not felt until
the present century. One retarding factor was the distribution of
political power' (Abramovitz and Eliasberg, 1957, pp.19—20).
However,

> after 1880 annual workers increasingly claimed the right to be town
> councillors . . . True, J. S. Mill and his disciples had acknowledged
> the right of all sorts of groups to participate in municipal adminis-
> tration. But participation was one thing, domination was another
> . . . [M]any of those who were prepared for a working class presence
> strongly repudiated the *policy implications of working class*

---

11 *The Radical Programme* of 1885 considered that local government 'has proved itself
an educational agency of the highest value' (Chamberlain, 1885, p.235). When the
President of the Local Government Board introduced the Local Government of
England and Wales Bill in 1893 he quoted sections from the work of J. S. Mill and De
Tocqueville on the educative value of local representative assemblies, making it clear
that 'we believe that these institutions are not only good for the purpose for which
they are devised but good for the state' (Hansard, 21 March 1893, col. 701—2).

domination . . . Workingmen tended to demand more collective
provision and give less scope to private enterprise.

(Hennock, 1973, pp.326—7, my italics)

This has continued to be reflected in patterns of spending by local
authorities. Boaden and Alford (1969, p.203) noted that 'there are
sources of diversity in the decisions of English local authorities
which cannot be explained by differences in their legal powers',
and, in a later study, Boaden (1971, p.112) showed that

> Labour councils were more active in services with a significant impact
> on the overall role of government. They were bigger spenders on the
> bigger services. In addition, they were more active where the service
> appeared to benefit sections of the community supporting them.
> Even where these two factors were less operative, there was a
> tendency for Labour to favour higher standards in the broadest
> sense. Our evidence suggests very clearly that party affects priorities
> established between services. At the same time, the data on grammar
> schools, especially when taken with earlier work on comprehensives,
> and the data on council rents, suggest that party may affect priorities
> within services as well.

In a similar vein, Alt (1971, pp.61, 49) showed that 'population
and wealth do not explain away the effects of party control'
as 'the presence of greater Labour representation on councils is
associated in such areas as housing, education, and local health
with higher levels and in the case of the police service with lower
levels of expenditure'. Davies, Barton and McMillan (1972,
p.110), in their study of variations in children's services, recognised
that spending levels were influenced by a number of variables,
but, even so, they argued that 'the political balance of the authority
. . . had an impact on the spending level of the authority as a
whole: Labour is the spending party'. More than this, they also
recognised that 'the greater was Labour representation the more
authorities appeared to display behaviour towards children in their
care that was protective'. Other studies also have a bearing on this
question (Danziger, 1974; Ashford, 1975B; Oliver and Stanyer,
1969; King, 1973), and although we should probably be a little
wary of all this it clearly raises questions that demand further
exploration.

Even if you choose to dismiss the policy implications of party
control of local government you still have to pay attention to the
significance of what has come to be called 'community action'
or the 'urban social movement'. These working class struggles are
best seen as a response to a process of inner city industrial decline
that accelerated in the 1960s, squeezing both jobs and housing —

the more so as the process of industrial change occurred alongside massive schemes of public and private urban redevelopment (CDP, 1977A; CIS, 1973). For a variety of reasons (some of which bear on the nature of the Labour Party (Hindess, 1971), some on the general health of local democracy) this activity has tended to occur outside the framework of party politics and the established and respectable channels of pressure group access. It does, however, focus on the local authority and it embodies demands that centre on a range of services that collectively constitute a key facet of the social wage. These demands not only constitute direct pressure for an increase in social consumption outlays, but they may also force a situation in which an increase in social expenses may be politically necessary in order to contain it. The implications and significance of this activity, and of the local authority response to it, are by no means simple. One way or another it again reveals and suggests the vulnerability of local government to subordinate classes.

Much of the activity represents a general challenge to the *system* of local government itself, and it nearly always poses a very direct challenge to an established pattern of local public policy. Because of this it is tempting for any local authority to deny, delay, or destroy the demands of these groups and this is probably the usual response. But there is a danger in this. The liberal ideology of representative and responsible government is strongly entrenched at the local level, *but* it is also particularly vulnerable to challenge and contradiction at that level. In other words, if demands are denied then this may serve to highlight the false promises contained within that ideology for subordinate classes. To the extent that this occurs, then the legitimacy of the system will be undermined, so heaping up larger political problems of control and management for the future. In Chapter 2 I pointed to the apathy and ignorance surrounding local government, but I did not dwell on the public dissatisfaction and distrust which provides the fertile soil within which a legitimacy crisis may flower. The Committee on the Management of Local Government (1967, vol.1, pp.94, 92) regarded it as 'a matter for concern that there should be an indefinable gulf between local authorities and the communities which they serve', revealed especially in the finding that 'nearly a quarter of the Survey's[12] informants suggest

12 See Committee on the Management of Local Government, 1967, vol.3.

that they have a feeling of "alienation" from the local authority in the sense that the members do not care about the electorate or are not known to it, or that the electorate is not told enough about what is going on'. Two years later the Royal Commission on Local Government in England (1969, vol.1, p.28) still found that 'the relationship between local authorities and the public is not satisfactory . . . and indeed it is not uncommon to find contempt expressed'. A survey undertaken for *The Times* (6 August 1973) revealed a 'widespread lack of public confidence' and the leading article warned that unless the central government took action 'they will be condemning local government to an era of public distrust'. Confirmation of these findings was contained in the Prime Minister's Committee on Local Government Rules of Conduct (1974, pp.3, 35), which recognised that 'there is at present a great deal of disquiet about conduct in local government' and, therefore, the need to 'secure public confidence' from what a wider ranging government investigation into the same problems termed a 'grudging electorate' (Royal Commission on Standards in Public Life, 1976, p.117). Further evidence of public distrust *and* governmental concern was provided by the Committee on Financial Aid to Political Parties (1976), and in a survey undertaken for the Royal Commission on the Constitution (1973, pp.18—21), which pointed to a '"we" and "they" situation' and a 'sense of grievance' in which 'people tended to feel powerless in the face of government and cut off from it' — especially if they come from 'working class households'. In the light of both survey evidence *and* the harder reality of community action, I do not think it an exaggeration to suggest that part of the problem of local government is the crisis of local representative democracy itself.

Notwithstanding the possible significance of this activity for the legitimacy of local government, it is tempting to dismiss its political impact. If groups urging change and innovation on local authorities do not fail and fold up, then their survival is maintained in the face of a number of hostile local authority strategies, and at the cost of their downscaling their demands; turning to self-help activities; developing a social welfare role; or involving themselves in assisting the individual to fit into, and gain rights within, the established order. Groups which originally sought to challenge established authorities and policies frequently finish up supporting the very things which they sought to change. Moreover, in so far as radical community action survives and sustains itself then it is likely to be incorporated through its institutionalisation in some sort of controlled participatory exercise (Dearlove, 1974). This sort of assessment may be correct at the level of detail, but it has to be regarded as incomplete. First, although incorporation through controlled participation may work at particular moments and in particular cases, it is a potential trojan horse, the future implications of which cannot be so easily anticipated or dismissed no matter what the current state of play may be. Second, to measure success solely on the basis of a one-to-one relationship between particular campaigns and demands and particular governmental responses is to ignore the significance of the cumulative, or drip, effect of all this activity. This is perhaps best revealed in the changing agenda of politics. This agenda is now forced to confront the needs that are associated with 'the "rediscovery" of urban poverty' (Cockburn, 1977, p.18). Moreover, because the dominant ideology surrounding the welfare state promised the solution of these problems, their rediscovery poses a demand on the system that cannot easily be dismissed as beyond the proper scope of public concern and action. This poses yet another problem, however, in that the demand cannot be fully met within the confines of the established system. Leaving that aside, part of all this is the widespread perception that we are experiencing an 'urban crisis' in the inner cities. The term itself tends to mystify the nature of the crisis by viewing it solely in spatial terms. But one thing is clear. The urban crisis is about more than unemployment and low incomes, inadequate schools, bad housing, poor transport, crime, and the dogged entrenchment of racism. It is about more than the technical problem of public service delivery. It takes us beyond the gap between social problems and public resources. That a variety of social and economic problems are now defined as *political* problems derives from the fact that the problems have been thrust up politically and some sort of response has been demanded, because at its root the urban crisis poses nothing less than a crisis of order, social control, and political stability. The current Labour Government is well aware that

> the inner parts of our cities ought not to be left to decay. It would mean leaving large numbers of people to face a future of declining job opportunities, a squalid environment, deteriorating housing and declining public services. But without effective action, that could

be the future for those who live in inner areas, bringing with it
mounting social bitterness and an increasing sense of alienation.

(*Policy for the Inner Cities*, 1977, p.5)

Similarly, the Conservative Political Centre (1974, p.5) has noted
how 'concentrating resources on geographical areas where the
causes and symptoms of social stress are present in combination
is the only way to avoid social breakdown on a very serious scale'.
At the 1969 Ditchley Park Conference, called to discuss the CDP
and the Inner Area Studies in the light of the American Poverty
Programme's experience, the Chief Inspector of the Children's
Department at the Home Office readily admitted that in the
variety of initiatives being taken by the government 'there appeared
to be an element of looking for a new method of social control'.
The Report of the Conference continued:

> Mr. Smith (West Riding, EPA Research Officer) also emphasised
> the control aspects of the programmes . . . He was quite certain
> that social administrators saw social action priority areas as
> 'problems', in other words areas which were in need of additional
> control, and not as areas in which they were under some moral
> obligation to enhance the opportunities of the less privileged.
>
> (Report of the Anglo-American Conference held at
> Ditchley Park, Oxfordshire, 1969, pp.38–9)

It is precisely this awareness that the urban crisis is partly a crisis
of social control that throws us back to my earlier point about
community action posing a challenge to the legitimacy of the
system itself. Indeed, at the Ditchley Park Conference, Derek
Morell, the civil servant who devised CDP, recognised that 'the
general context [of the discussion] was ←. . . the liberal-democratic
process', and he was mindful that 'today's problem was not
success, rather that consent might be withheld, because of
accumulating evidence of failure' (cited in CDP, 1977, p.56).

The democratisation of local government has, at the same time as
it has facilitated working class access to local government, also
increased the difficulty of dominant interests securing the kind of
easy and *direct* control of local government which they enjoyed
in the nineteenth century. This problem has been exacerbated by
the evolving nature and form of much of business. Those sectors
of the economy where businesses are small and numerous and
usually run by the owners and their families are clearly still in a
position where they do enjoy direct representation on many local

authorities.[13] On the other hand, the organisation of production in ever larger plants to reap economies of scale has produced a corporate sector accounting for a growing proportion of total production and employment which is very much less grounded in any one locality. Financial control is increasingly centralised in the hands of holding companies, multinationals and conglomerates of all kinds, and so ownership and control are no longer fused in the hands of a locally resident and politically active bourgeoisie. It is little wonder that Freeman (1976, p.27) bemoans the fact that 'big business above all is conspicuous by its absence' from the council chamber.

It might be suggested that much of business has been content to withdraw from direct involvement in local government, either because local government is no longer so relevant to their interest; or because they can rule without direct involvement; or because they can rely on the central state to control and manage local government to their advantage. There is a certain amount of truth in all these bald assertions, but no more than that, and to agree fully with them would mean ignoring a key facet of the particular problem of local government. Let us explore each of these arguments in turn.

Local government has long been relevant to the business interest, and continues to be so, both because of the financial demands which local government makes and because of the services it provides. The fact that industry was derated by 75% in 1929 clearly relieved them of a certain financial burden, but since 1963, all derating has been abolished,[14] and every class of property is assessed at current rental values. This has meant 'the decline in domestic rates as a proportion of total rates' and 'the increase in the size of rate demands on industry and commerce in recent years has been more than on domestic properties and that of other taxes on business. The increase has occurred in the period when the profitability of business in general has been declining' (Committee of Inquiry into the Impact of Rates on Households, 1965, p.25; Committee of Inquiry into Local Government Finance, 1976, p.259). In 1938—9 domestic ratepayers in England and Wales contributed 57.4% of rate income but by 1975—6 they were

13 Committee on the Management of Local Government, 1967, vol.2; Committee of Inquiry into the System of Remuneration of Members of Local Authorities, 1977, vol.2.
14 Except agriculture which is 100% derated, and charities which enjoy 50% derating. The 1973 revaluation hit commercial property especially hard (Ilersic, 1975).

contributing only 38.8% of rate income.[15] The CBI (1975, p.3; 1976, p.46) pointed out that 'between the financial years 1973/74 and 1974/75 industrial rates will have risen by about 40%', and so it is little wonder that they 'conclude that the government's aim should be to reduce the rate contribution by industry and commerce'. Aims of Industry's evidence to the Royal Commission on Local Government in England (1969, *Written Evidence of Commercial, Industrial, and Political Organisations*, p.1) highlighted just how 'British industry has a direct and vital interest in local government'. After first noting that industry is a major source of local government finance they went on:

> Secondly, industry is a major consumer of local government services, and in some cases is vitally dependent on them for its efficient functioning. Thirdly, local government is a major user of men and resources . . . which are frequently in short supply and are largely similar to those on which industry draws and depends. Fourthly, local government is an important customer of industry . . . Lastly, local government increasingly appears as industry's direct competitor.

In the first section of this chapter I recognised that dominant interests might well benefit from the actions of governments without their needing to be directly involved in government or the making of political decisions. That this is so has not altered the fact that much of industry and commerce expresses concern about its lack of effective access to, and influence over, local government. It considers itself to be 'virtually disenfranchised' at that level, and this at a time when the changes in the mode and scale of business organisation have probably eased their way into an ever more effective rapport with the institutions that focus on and around the central state. Not surprisingly, then, business groups have often pointed to the need for some form of '*direct* industrial representation . . . on the local governing bodies' which may involve 'an element of bicameralism', the 'inclusion of co-opted or nominated representatives drawn from industry' or the establishment of 'statutory consultation with manufacturing industry'.[16]

15 Committee of Inquiry into the Impact of Rates on Households, 1965, table 51(b); Department of the Environment and Welsh Office, *Rates and Rateable Values in England and Wales*, 1975–6, p.5, table 2.
16 See Committee of Inquiry into Local Government Finance, 1976, Appendix 4; Royal Commission on Local Government in Scotland, 1968, *Written Evidence 9*; Royal Commission on Local Government in England, 1969, *Written Evidence of Commercial, Industrial and Political Organisations*.

The suggestion that business controls local government through the central state is part of a larger argument about the impact of central control to which I must now turn.

The simple assertion that local authorities are agents of the central government lacking any real autonomy and held in that situation because of their constitutional position, a public desire for uniform services, and an increased dependence upon central government grants, is wrong, and it therefore ignores a facet of the problem of local government. Not only does such a formulation ignore the differences between the interventions of the various central government departments concerned with local government (Griffith, 1966) and the different responses of local authorities to central direction, but it also underestimates the vast differences which exist between the same services in different areas and fails to recognise that 'the degree of dependence upon Government for revenue does not . . . determine the extent to which local autonomy is impaired by central regulation' (Davey, 1971, p.50). Ashford (1974, pp.318—20), in his analysis of the effects of central finance over the period 1949—67, has noted that 'though central spending for localities has increased over sixfold in the past twenty years, and has risen from about 40 to 60 per cent of current revenues, the control exercised over localities by the complex financial structure is minimal'. He concludes that 'several of the more emotional arguments about central dominance of local affairs are exaggerated if not totally incorrect'. Far from central government grants facilitating the control of local government and its expenditure there are those who maintain — probably correctly — that 'perhaps the most serious objection to increased state subventions to local authorities is that they tend to lead to increased expenditure' (Departmental Committee on Local Taxation, 1914, p.18; see also Committee of Inquiry into Local Government Finance, 1976, p.11). My critique of the orthodoxies surrounding arguments about central control does not mean that I am asserting that local authorities are completely autonomous — far from it — but I am saying that we need an analysis which is sensitive to the limits of that control and to the problems of its assertion. For example, we must be alive to the fact that although 'the Government have formal powers to approve borrowing by local authorities which provide an effective means of regulating capital expenditure within narrow limits . . . [they] have no similar powers over the level and distribution of local authority current expenditure, nor can they control the income raised through rates' (*The Government's Expenditure Plans*, 1977, p.8). Its main coercive weapon, the Rate Support Grant, was designed to help poorer local authorities. It was not intended to serve as an instrument of control, and its method of calculation may well serve to encourage local authorities to spend more while penalising those who reduce their expenditure. In addition, we cannot ignore the potentially crippling implications of the ideology, and grudging reality, of democratic local self-government. The *Written Evidence of H.M. Treasury* to the Royal Commission on Local Government in England (1969, pp.4—5) was well aware of the fact that expenditure by local authorities formed a major part of total public expenditure. It regarded it as 'therefore inescapable that the central government, and in particular the Treasury, should be increasingly concerned with the need for forward planning and effective control of the movement of local authority expenditure as a whole'. However, it also recognised that

> on the other hand . . . it has been a declared objective of successive governments, based on the view that local authorities are responsible bodies competent to discharge their own functions and to exercise responsibilities in their own right, to simplify and reduce detailed Departmental control, while at the same time providing them collectively with ever increasing financial help.

Not surprisingly the Treasury drew the correct conclusion that the 'need to exercise closer control over the expenditure of local authorities as a whole is not easily reconciled with the need to give them greater individual freedom to determine both their total expenditure and its distribution between services'. The current Labour Government is aware that 'the dilemma which faces central government is to secure and promote an effective local democracy with genuine political choice and at the same time fulfil their responsibilities for the management of the economy and for the standard of public services' (*Local Government Finance*, 1977, p.3). In this situation it is surely right to recognise that 'the ability of the Government to regulate, within a reasonable margin, the total of local authority expenditure (both capital and current) depends essentially on the cooperation which they receive from local government' (*The Government's Expenditure Plans*, 1977, p.8). Where effective central control has to depend on cooperation with local authorities then the 'calibre' of councillors and officers can assume a crushing relevance: Poplar and Clay Cross are expensive reminders of that.

The information and ideas that I have been setting down in this chapter and in this section should enable us to form a crisper appreciation of the general problem of the public sector and the particular problem of local government that the drive for reorganisation has continually sought to confront and solve. It should also enable us to be alive to the implications of the setting of the contemporary economic situation within which extensive reorganisation has occurred. In addition, I have also pointed to other problems that impinge on the possibility of actually solving the more particular problem of local government.

At the most general level, the problem of local government can be seen as an aspect of the overall problem of the public sector in a capitalist economy. This is a problem that centres on the sources of state revenue and the scale of public expenditure, and on the scope and direction of state intervention. It is a problem that becomes acute at certain moments. The simple problem of local government would appear to be its long-standing fiscal crisis — the tendency for local government expenditure to outpace locally generated income, especially in the metropolitan areas (Simon, 1938, pp.421—2; AMA, 1976). However, it is clear that the problem of local government is more than just a problem of local authority income, and it is not, therefore, a problem of the rates to be solved by the introduction of some new and buoyant sources of local income. In its most *immediate* form, the problem of local government is a problem of the scale of its expenditure and the nature of its interventions. More fundamentally, however, the problem of local government goes beyond this. It derives from the fact that local government is neither an instrument of business nor a mere agent of the central state. This does not mean that it is completely autonomous and neutral as some might maintain. But the *particular and enduring* problem of local government in all of this century has been one that transcends the immediate moment of any economic crisis. Moreover, it could also be argued that this problem has, in some small degree, actually increased the severity of the fiscal crisis in certain localities. In my view the particular problem of local government centres on its relative autonomy from both the concerns of the central state and the impact of dominant classes. Related to this, local government is especially vulnerable to working class demands, pressures, and even control. The relative autonomy of local government has both 'allowed' the decline in councillor calibre to occur, and has made that decline a problem that goes beyond any simple anxiety about the personnel of local government alone. Although any explanation for all this must centre on a consideration of trends with respect to business organisation and the organisation and activity of the working class in relation to these developments, the nineteenth-century democratisation of local government has had a certain significance in exacerbating and giving political form to these underlying trends

Anxiety about declining councillor calibre is a crude but direct way of highlighting the relative autonomy of local government. The persistent concern to increase councillor calibre through reorganisation makes it equally clear that the essential object of reorganisation has been to make local government more functional for dominant interests, by restructuring it so as to facilitate their direct control of its expenditure and interventions. The study of the reorganisation of British local government has to be undertaken as a study of the struggle to counter its relative autonomy from dominant interests and the state in order that closer links might be reasserted between economic and governmental power. This has a relevance beyond the immediate moment of any economic crisis, although there is no doubt that crisis gives the particular problem the sharper and more insistent edge that overcomes opposition and forces change.

4.   Solving the Problem of Local Government?

At both local and national level growing state expenditures have
. . . led to important shifts in the institutions and processes of
bourgeois democracy.   (Gough, 1975, p.85)

. . . as soon as democracy shows the tendency to negate its class
character and become transformed into an instrument of the real
interests of the population, the democratic forms are sacrificed by
the bourgeoisie and by its state representatives.
                                                (Luxemburg, 1908, p.56)

At the present time, and at certain other moments, making local government conform more closely to the requirements of dominant interests tends to involve two things. First, it involves escaping from the fiscal crisis by cutting the scale of local public spending.

Second, it involves the redirection of the thrust of local government activity towards the more direct support of business.

In 1932 the Chancellor of the Exchequer wrote to local authority associations inviting them to 'combine in the appointment of a committee to consider the whole field of local expenditure and make recommendations at the earliest possible date for ensuring reductions in such expenditure'. The Committee itself was of 'the opinion that economy in national and local expenditure, if it results as it should result, in reduction of the burden of rates and taxes, will not only set money free for the redevelopment of trade and industry, but by removing the anxiety lest even greater burdens should be imposed, will also stimulate business enterprise'. Given this sort of assessment of the needs of the situation, it was not surprising that the Committee set about its task with a will, estimating that if all their proposals were put into effect then within three years local government expenditure would be reduced some 15—18% below that for the financial year 1929—30 (Committee on Local Expenditure, 1932, pp.8, 11, 20). The Annual Report of the Minister of Health for the year 1931—2 pointed to a 'striking diminution in the amount of loans sanctioned to local authorities during the year in comparison with the amount sanctioned in the previous year': the amount was cut by some 28% (p.161). The crude and general cutting of local public expenditure was not the only response to the economic crisis of that time. In 1928,

> as a result of a careful review of the difficultues of productive
> industry the Government have, as local authorities are aware, come
> to the conclusion that the basis of rating of agricultural, industrial
> and transport properties needs to be revised; and they have adopted
> a plan which they believe will . . . contribute to the revival of agri-
> culture and the basic industries.

This plan involved the total derating of agriculture and the 75% derating of freight transport and industry. The effect of this was that local authorities lost some 15% of their total rate income (*Proposals for the Reform in Local Government and in the Financial Relations Between the Exchequer and Local Authorities*, 1928, pp.3—4).

In 1966, the government correctly noted that 'local expenditure can only be reduced significantly either by cutting services or by transferring the responsibility for particular services from local to central government'. At this time it was 'convinced that the need

is not to lower present standards of service but to raise them'
(*Local Government Finance: England and Wales*, p.5). In 1969,
the Royal Commission on Local Government in England (vol.1,
p.13) pointed out that 'as local government expenditure is now
increasing at a faster rate than the gross national product, we do
not imagine that the trends can be accepted without some modification for very much longer'. By 1971, the government was
also aware that 'local government expenditure is absorbing an
increasing share of national resources', and it felt that 'one
possibility would be to cut back . . . the rate at which local
authority expenditure is growing', noting that 'there remains the
question how fast we can afford to improve standards' (*The
Future Shape of Local Government Finance*, pp.2–3). In his
budget statement of 12 November 1974, the Chancellor of the
Exchequer said that the need to give priority to investment and
the balance of payments had important implications for public
expenditure. Although he was alive to the fact that local authority
expenditure 'presented a special problem', local authorities 'would
be expected to play their part in the achievement of national
objectives by limiting the rise in their expenditure, other than
that due to inflation, to what was absolutely inescapable' (Department of the Environment Circular, 17/74, p.2). By 1977, the
government was able to announce that although 'local authority
expenditure has increased faster than public expenditure
programmes as a whole . . . During the past two years . . . it has
declined slightly both in absolute terms and as a proportion of
public spending' (*The Government's Expenditure Plans*, p.7).

Those who advocate the cutting of local public spending also
tend to advocate the following. First, there is an insistence upon
charging for local government services. At present local authorities
finance about 13% of their total revenue expenditure from rents,
fees and charges. The Committee of Inquiry into Local Government Finance (1976) thought it possible for charges to play a
bigger part in the financing of local services, and they therefore
recommended that there should be a joint review of central and
local government's policies towards charging for local services.
The Labour Government accepted the Committee's proposal
(*Local Government Finance*, 1977, pp.20–1; see also Harris and
Seldon, 1976; Maynard and King, 1974; Wright and Hobhouse,
1884, p.103; Lee, 1932, p.50). Second, it is argued that local
authorities should increase their 'efficiency'. Larger local auth-

Public Expenditure by local authorities (Great Britain)
£ million at 1976 survey prices

	1974—5	1975—6	1976—7	1977—8	1978—9
Current	10,284	10,736	11,015	11,031	10,959
Capital	5,076	4,520	3,792	2,873	2,702
Total	15,360	15,256	14,807	13,904	13,661
As percentage of all public expenditure programmes	30.2	29.4	28.5	28.1	27.4

Source: The Government's Expenditure Plans, 1977, table 3.

orities have long been advocated as a means to secure the economies of scale that would facilitate the attainment of this objective. Some of the problems of increasing efficiency were set down in Chapter 3. State production is not under competitive pressure to reduce costs; many local authority services are produced under constant cost conditions; and the significance of public sector unions cannot be ignored. Third, there is the view that there is a 'need not only for economy in the use of manpower but for a flexible approach towards staffing matters' (Committee on the Staffing of Local Government, 1967, p.69). Finally, it is recognised that cutting local public expenditure must have implications for the quality and availability of the services provided by local government.

A related, but slightly different, aspect of the concern to decrease the *scale* of local government and effect cutbacks in local public expenditure is the concern to change the *scope* of local government as well. The current 'need' for this is most clearly revealed in the Department of the Environment's circulars to local authorities explaining the implications of the government's 'Approach to Industrial Strategy'. In Circular 71/77,

> the Secretaries of State wish to emphasise how important to the health and confidence of industry are the attitudes, policies and decisions of local authorities throughout the country . . . This circular is concerned with action that can be taken in respect of both the immediate needs of industry and of foreseeable future requirements. Above all, it is concerned to encourage local authorities to

develop and maintain a close awareness of the problems and difficulties that industrial undertakings face, to give help whenever it
is practicable to do so, to deal speedily with applications and
requests for information, and to ensure that full account is taken of
industrial needs in reaching decisions . . . [They] ask authorities to
take stock of their attitude towards industry, and to see whether
more can be done.

In the paragraphs which followed they suggested 'ways in which
local authorities can improve the general conditions for industrial
confidence and growth and then make specific proposals within
the fields of local government planning, housing, and transport
responsibilities'. In a later circular it was again pointed out that
'there are close inter-relationships between the policies of local
authorities and the well-being of firms', and although it was noted
that 'much is already being done . . . The Secretary of State now
asks authorities . . . to consider whether more can be done' (Welsh
Office, 118/77). I made clear in my last section that certain
problems are acutely focused on the central city. The government
is well aware of this. In their *Policy for the Inner Cities* (1977,
p.9), they have pointed out how 'local authorities now need . . .
to stimulate investment by the private sector, by firms and by
individuals, in industry, in commerce and in housing'. The Inner
Urban Areas Bill was designed to give powers to inner city local
authorities to support the creation of new employment opportunities and improve the environment in industrial areas. To this
end, local authorities (initially in seven 'partnership areas') would
be enabled to make interest-free loans to firms for land purchase
and preparation in inner cities, and to declare industrial improvement areas. The Bill also simplified certain planning procedures
to avoid delay in taking action, and empowered local authorities
to give grants towards rent.

Setting down the immediate ends of public policy towards local
authorities at the present time does not tell us *how* these ends
are to be attained. In addition, it does not focus on the particular
and enduring problem of local government and the possible
solutions to that — solutions which would also serve as the means
towards the attainment of the immediate ends themselves. What,
then, are the orthodox solutions to the problems of local government?

First, increasing councillor calibre has long been seen as of
importance. In the body of my text I chose to emphasise this,

not just because it has been a long-established strategy within the debates about the need for boundary change and internal reorgan- isation, but because it provides a gross confirmation of the orthodox concern to counter the relative autonomy of local government from dominant interests. I have already mentioned some of the problems of changing the class composition of local authorities. But the process of gentrification in some of the poorer inner city residential areas, in changing the social base of an area, may well have an immediate effect on planning priorities (Pitt, 1977, p.3), as well as a longer-term effect on the class (and possibly the party) composition of local authorities. Certainly Castells (1972, p.107) has noted how in Paris urban renewal itself has extended the 'spontaneous' trend whereby workers were being replaced by 'executives' in the inner city. This attacks the fact that 'the municipal councils are in the hands of the working classes and their representatives, or in those of the traditional bourgeoisie and petite-bourgeoisie' and facilitates the 'reconquest of Paris'. Even so, a major obstacle to any strategy which seeks to increase councillor calibre is the fact of universal suffrage.

Second, and not surprisingly, there have as a result been attacks on the principle of universal suffrage. In Chapter 8 I noted how this was seen as an ultimate solution to the problem of city govern- ment in America. In nineteenth-century Britain the propertied classes feared the policy implications of one man one vote, and in the twentieth century there have been attempts to push back the democratic clock. For example, Deacon and Briggs (1973, pp.349, 364) point out that in the 1920s the

> success of persons ideologically committed to a policy of generous
> relief in first securing election as Guardians and then fulfilling their
> election pledges at the expense of local manufacturers and the more
> conservative and wealthy Unions brought the question of the local
> franchise to the forefront of British social politics . . . [The] Cabinet
> came within a hair's breadth of disenfranchising hundreds of
> thousands of its citizens, and each time it only drew back for fear
> of the political repercussions.

Third, and growing out of the problem of limiting the franchise, there has been a tendency for certain services to be removed from the control of local government and placed in the hands of appointed institutions at the local, regional, or national level. In the 1930s the creation of the Unemployment Assistance Board removed local authorities from the administration of unemploy- ment assistance (Briggs and Deacon, 1973). In the 1940s the hospital service was lost to appointed Regional Hospital Boards and Hospital Management Committees, and a number of municipal utilities were nationalised. In the 1960s the regional apparatus of the state was developed and, to a degree, the purpose of the Regional Economic Planning Councils and Boards 'was clearly to bypass local power structures by a territorial central state apparatus more functional to the class interests represented by the central state' (Geddes, 1978, p.5). In the 1970s, the creation of Area Health Authorities and Regional Water Authorities are foremost among structural innovations that have implications for the scope of local government. Notwithstanding these changes, we should not exaggerate the loss of municipal functions. Local authorities are still critically involved in important and fast-growing sectors of social provision, and so local government, in continuing to be relevant, continues to be problematic.

Fourth, over the years a variety of factors have probably conspired to increase the influence of the non-elected permanent officials within local authority deliberations. The attempt to introduce corporate planning into local government has probably served to strengthen the hand of those officers who are less intimately involved in the direct provision of services to the public and so are more able to take those decisions which are defined as being in the interest of the 'community' as a whole and in the long run. In addition, a key thrust of contemporary reorgan-isation has been the quite overt concern to 'close up' local authority decision-making to public intervention. The Committee on the Management of Local Government (1967, vol.1, p.48) pointed out that 'a systematic approach is required to ensure that the component parts of the organisation are not distracted by the pressure of current problems'. The more recent Working Group on Local Authority Management Structures (1972, p.12) recognised that 'some policy changes will inevitably be in the nature of a reaction to outside events', but it deplored this and believed that 'essentially, policy decisions should be based on planning and analysis of objectives and the means of attaining them'.

Fifth, from the mid 1960s onwards, in the wake of the rediscovery of poverty and a whole clutch of urban problems, the central government has itself taken a variety of initiatives within spheres of concern that have traditionally been more within the province of local government. Of particular importance have been the action and research projects centred on 'areas of special need' since they have frequently involved extensive co-operation between local and central government. In 1968, the DES introduced its Educational Priority Areas Programme, and in 1969 the Home Office announced its two-part Urban Programme centring on the National Community Development Project and the Urban Aid Programme. In addition to these specific initiatives, over the course of this century there have been attempts to assert more direct central control over the activities, and especially the expenditure, of local authorities. All this can best be seen as a response to the particular problem of local government.

> In 1815 there was no Local Government Board or Ministry of Health, and the Home Office only required an establishment of 18 clerks. Indeed, it has been cynically said that at this time, central control was politically unnecessary, seeing that the class which sat in Parliament was identical with the class which ruled the counties and controlled municipal government.   (Jarratt, 1930, p.59)

In a similar sort of vein, Rothwell (1928, p.106) has pondered the question as to whether it was 'practical politics to build up a system by which local authorities could develop a satisfactory standard of efficiency from within, either as an alternative to control or in justification of some relaxation of such control'. In a word, the recognition of the inevitability of increased central control as a response to counter 'declining' councillor calibre and continued 'inefficiency' is yet another veiled way of suggesting that local government may be out of step with the needs and interests of dominant classes and the state. In my last section I pointed to some of the obstacles which lay in the way of increasing central control. But in spite of these, the government has recently been involved in giving local authorities 'detailed advice, service by service, in the type of action that should be taken' to effect public expenditure cutbacks (DOE Circular, 88/75). In addition, 'the Government have been impressed by the way in which local authorities have sought to bring their budgets into line with the Government's public expenditure policies' (*Local Government Finance*, 1977, p.24). However, despite the tough attitude, repeated circulars urging restraint, and thinly veiled threats from ministers, the imposition of 'cash limits' in 1975 for the financial year 1976–7 did not stop local authority expenditure exceeding the planned amount. In fact, the government is well aware that 'under the present statutory arrangements, local authority current expenditure cannot be directly controlled by central Government' (*Cash Limits on Public Expenditure*, 1976, p.3). Moreover, there are dangers in even attempting to increase central control in order to make local government more functional for dominant interests, since orthodoxy asserts that 'if the nature of central government controls is such as to suggest that local authorities are not competent . . . it is hardly likely that people of calibre, either officers or members, will regard local government services as attractive' (Committee on the Management of Local Government, 1967, vol.1, p.83).

The capacity to effect cutbacks and redirect local government, and the capacity to counter its relative autonomy, are also limited' by the necessity of confronting the rediscovery of urban poverty and the legitimacy crisis of local representative democracy.

First, the rediscovery of urban poverty and the increased insistency of new demands could not have come at a worse time. The pressing reality of the local fiscal crisis has meant that it is less possible to incorporate the political expression of the urban crisis through service provision, even though it is now more necessary to do so. In this sort of 'Catch 22' situation local government has been forced to move beyond the attainment of mere 'efficiency' with respect to an established package of services in order to reach 'effectiveness' in confronting the new configuration of social problems with more limited resources. Nowadays 'realists' in government talk more about the 'management' of problems than their solution. Cockburn (1977, p.65) is, therefore, quite right to see corporate management as 'a response to these two problems. On the one hand the growing need to keep down costs, to manage scarce resources as fears grew about the level of public spending. On the other the apparently undiminishing problem of deprivation, the shame of urban poverty in what was supposed to be a thriving and exemplary capitalist society.' Advocates of the new systems admit as much themselves. When Rose (1969, p.11) asks 'why has PPBS been introduced?' he can answer simply that 'generally, the search for improved methods of budgeting arises from the inevitable shortage of resources in relation to demands which are made upon them'. Similarly, at a discussion on 'Corporate Management in the '70s', D. B. Harrison, the Chief Executive of Sheffield, had no doubt that

> these changes towards corporate planning are being forced on us to some extent, are they not, by a growing realisation that we have limited resources to do an ever expanding task? In the past local

> government had a rather more liberal attitude to the spending of
> money ... But now we are deeply conscious that, if one draws too
> much out of the bucket for one service, the other services suffer.
> Isn't that what has caused us to say: 'Let us look at the bucket as
> a whole'?   (cited in Cossey, 1971, p.29)

(See also Eddison, 1973, pp.88–9.) The 'traditional' committee
system had long been under attack because it was seen as 'inimical
to proper financial control' and was said to have disastrous implications for the calibre of both councillors and officers (Committee
on the Management of Local Government, 1967, vol.1, p.35;
RIPA Conference, 1967, p.10; Gibbon and Bell, 1939, p.662;
Knowles, 1971, p.19; Marshall, 1965, p.17; and see above, Chapter
5, Section 2). It is the contemporary economic situation that has
forced the essential changes that have been advocated for years.
But, as I made clear in Chapter 7, it is not possible to implement
the corporate approach in the form in which it is presented to us
by those who reject muddling through. Moreover, the demands
associated with the rediscovery of urban poverty set a limit on
the extent to which local public expenditure can be cut back and
redirected.

Second, the legitimacy crisis of local representative democracy
can only be further aggravated by a reorganisation which has been
designed to enable dominant interests to rule more directly in
their interest. Unless the true intent of that reorganisation can
somehow be concealed, then the probable loss of mass loyalty
must place a limit on any attempt to counter the relative autonomy
of local government. Three developments have been of significance
in facilitating the public acceptability of the overall thrust of
reorganisation. First, the fact that social scientists have been
prepared to present reorganisation as apolitical reform in the
simple interest of good government has set the seal of scientific
approval on a limited presentation and consideration of reorganisation that does not even admit the possibility of asking questions
about who rules and for whom. Second, reorganisation tends to
be seen as an inevitable and necessary response to technical
problems of government which admit no choice. The organisational
experts concerned to introduce the corporate approach speak a
language which hides the ultimate meaning of their actions from
ordinary citizens at the same time as it places them beyond easy
critique. There is the presumption that knowledge, information
and experts can transcend ideology and interests. Politics is
depoliticised; opposition is reduced to stupidity or ignorance;

and political conflicts are defined as social problems. The firm entrenchment of this perspective on reorganisation is crisply situated within the prevailing ideology of science and technology. To the extent that this ideology admits no rivals, then it holds the stage in legitimising the contemporary politics of management, administration, and problem-solving that is no longer sanctioned by the liberal-democratic process itself. Such an ideology also legitimises the increased political role of those trained professionals who are left unkissed by the rude, but legitimising intrusions of the ballot box. Third, alongside the dominant thrust of reorganisation there has been the encouragement of public participation. The Ministry of Housing and Local Government, in a circular to local authorities on the Public Bodies (Admission to Meetings) Act, 1960, pointed out that local authorities 'may sometimes have to take unpopular decisions, even decisions to which there is strong local opposition. It is the more important that they should be seen to have acted in the knowledge of public opinion and that reasons for their action should be fully understood' (MHLG Circular, 21/61). Moves to extend public participation in local government have tended to focus on planning. The Planning Advisory Group (1965, para. 7.43) felt sure that their 'new system . . . should provide a real stimulus to public interest in the work of local planning authorities and provide those authorities with a new opportunity for winning public support for their proposals'. The Committee on Public Participation in Planning (1969, p.5) recognised that public participation could increase delay, but it considered that 'the expenditure of time and effort will be justified if it produces an understanding, co-operative public and planning better geared to public opinion. If objections can be anticipated or eliminated the formal stage of public inquiry will be smoother, less contentious and speedier.' In effect, there was a recognition that if 'plans are to be understood and generally accepted, and if the proposals in them are to be implemented successfully, [then] the authorities must carry the public with them' (DOE Circular, 52/72). It is little wonder that Rein (1969, p.240) can regard the direct participation of local citizens as a strategy of legitimacy for city planners. Professionals can preserve their institutional power and autonomy if they can co-opt their challengers (Haug and Sussman, 1969, p.153). Cockburn (1977, pp.2, 37) is, therefore, right to see the whole 'community approach' as the tender aspect of contemporary reorganisation designed to provide a basis for collecting facts, implementing policies, and legitimising a system of rule that is being increasingly distanced from the possibility of effective popular control.

This has been a study of the contemporary reorganisation of British local government. In it I have sought to challenge the adequacy of that understanding which is situated within the framework of old orthodoxies. I have also sought to offer a political perspective on reorganisation that is sensitive both to the particular and enduring problem of local government, and to those additional problems which place a limit on any attempt to counter the problem of its relative autonomy from dominant interests and the state. The overall problem of local government is but a facet of the general problem which requires the capitalist state to fulfil the two basic and often mutually contradictory functions of accumulation and legitimisation. As O'Connor (1973, p.6) puts it,

> the state must try to maintain or create the conditions in which profitable capital accumulation is possible. However, the state also must try to maintain or create the conditions of social harmony. A capitalist state that openly uses its coercive forces to help one class accumulate capital at the expense of other classes loses its legitimacy and hence undermines the basis of its loyalty and support. But a state that ignores the necessity of assisting the process of capital accumulation risks drying up the source of its own power, the economy's surplus production capacity and the taxes drawn from this surplus.

In this situation the relations of political domination are inevitably complex and unstable and in continual need of reorganisation, and there is a continuing tension between capitalism and democracy. The contemporary reorganisation of British local government both reflects that tension and tries to resolve it in a certain direction. The ultimate stability of that resolution is an open question.

Appendix 2
A Brief Note on Policy Analysis

> The great failing of a policy science approach is that it has not
> recognised that the price of rapid professionalism and integration
> is high.   (Horowitz, 1967, p.373)

> [Technocrats] usually ideologise their work as being independent
> and rational: a neutral power committed to progress. At the same
> time they tend to see the state as an agency independent of cor-
> porate power which mediates the divergent interests of a pluralist
> society.   (Dreitzel, 1972, p.177)

In America, advocates of PPBS bounced back in the face of
criticism. Their perception that political obstacles lay in the way
of implementation led them to offer 'policy analysis' to politicians
as to the practical 'feasibility' of particular reorganisation and
policy proposals (Meltsner, 1972; Dror, 1967).

Similar moves are afoot in the world of British local government, where the problem of implementing the corporate approach
has not been totally ignored by its advocates.[1] Having said that,
there is no real appreciation of the problem and the inevitable
obstacles it faces. We are told that the problem can be solved,
with McKinsey and Co. (1969, p.15) taking the view that a
new management system can be made 'fully operational [in]
approximately four months'.[2] More to the point, there is a keen
commitment to solving the problem and advice abounds as to the
necessary prerequisites for the successful introduction of corporate planning.[3]

1 The rather dismal fate of earlier proposals for reorganisation made sure that the
problem would not be totally ignored. See, for example, Page, 1936; Ripley, 1970,
p.40; Friend and Jessop, 1969, p.245; Elliott, 1971.
2 For comments in a similar vein, see Amos, 1974, p.8; Skitt, 1975, p.191; IMTA,
1971, p.21; Cossey, 1971, p.30; Butt, 1970A.
3 Lothian Region have helped us all in providing a list of 'seven important rules [for]
introducing policy or corporate planning in local government: keep it simple; one
chief officer must assume responsibility for its implementation; the concept must be
presented positively to the elected member; all officers must be informed and in-

It is one thing for management consultants and those in local government to concern themselves with *solving* this problem. It is surely quite another matter when we find academics involving themselves in solving the problems of government and limply defining themselves as the servants of power. Those academics who know the most about corporate planning have an institutional and professional stake in its success, and so are more committed to solving and even minimising the problems than they are to subjecting them to serious study.

Professor John Stewart from the Institute of Local Government Studies has deplored 'the tendency for research to be carried out *into* rather than *for* local government'. As he saw it the Institute was 'beginning to provide an academic focus of attention that corresponds more to the perceived needs of local government', and in his inaugural lecture he talked of the 'capacity to develop the knowledge required by local authorities and other agencies for the purposes of urban government — to move to the development of urban policy science'. At a more general level he has even argued that 'public administration could perhaps develop towards that policy science advocated in the writings of Yehezkel Dror' (Stewart, 1972C, pp.10—11; 1973, p.15; 1971D, p.42). Stewart is by no means alone in expressing these views. Parris (1969) and Marshall (1965) say much the same thing and Tony Eddison, the director of the recently created School for Advanced Urban Studies at Bristol University, wrote to *The Times Higher Education Supplement* (25 February 1977) of the need for 'increasing the working contacts between government and the academic world'. A position statement issued by the School in 1977 pointed to the necessity of it 'becoming established in the eyes of government' and noted that 'all our research work to date . . . involved working with local authorities, government departments or both'. The Corporate Planning Unit of the Management Centre at Bradford University has pointed out that the 'research of the Bradford group is aimed at assessing in the first instance the feasibility of a truly corporate approach in local government, and secondly how in a practical manner this may be introduced'.

volved; time scales, responsibilities and resources must be established; tangible results must start to be apparent quickly; build flexibility into planning' (cited in Young, 1977, p.129).

This practical and relevant orientation to those in power has meant that all these institutions have tended to engage in a special *kind* of research which, because of its starting brief and assumptions, is objectively deficient and ideological. In addition to 'policy analysis', 'policy studies', and studies of 'feasibility', these institutions have also been involved in selling systems of corporate planning through the provision of training courses designed to overcome the 'comprehension gap' and break down the last vestiges of old-fashioned and bigoted resistance to the kinds of rational change that these institutions have chosen to define as in the interests of the whole community.

References and Author Index

Figures in italics are page references to this book.

Abramovitz, M., and Eliasberg, V. F. (1957), *The Growth of Public Employment in Great Britain* (Princeton, Princeton University Press). *223n, 232n, 234*

Ackoff, R. L. (1970). *A Concept of Corporate Planning* (New York, Wiley). *145n*

Adrian, C. R. (1952). 'Some general characteristics of non-partisan elections', *American Political Science Reveiw*, 46, pp.766—76. *209n*

(1959). 'A typology for non-partisan elections', *Western Political Quarterly*, 12, pp.449—58. *209n*

(1961). 'Metropology: folklore and field research', *Public Administration Review*, 21, pp.148—57. *17, 108*

Alford, R. R. (1967). 'The comparative study of urban politics', in L. F. Schnore and H. Fagin (eds.), *Urban Research and Policy Making* (Beverley Hills, Sage), pp.263—302. *16n*

Allinson, E. P. (1887). *The City Government of Philadephia* (Baltimore, Johns Hopkins Studies in Historical and Political Science, vol.5). *194, 199, 203*

Allison, G. (1969). 'Conceptual models and the Cuban missile crisis', *American Political Science Review*, 63, pp.689—718. *179n*

(1971). *The Essence of Decision* (Boston, Little Brown). *179n*

Alt, J. (1971). 'Some social and political correlates of county borough expenditure', *British Journal of Political Science*, 1, pp.49—62. *235*

Althusser, L. (1971). *Lenin and Philosophy and Other Essays* (London, NLB). *224*

Altshuler, A. A. (1970). *Community Control* (New York, Bobbs-Merrill). *12, 110*

Altvater, E. (1973). 'Notes on some problems of state interventionism', *Kapitalistate*, 1, pp. 96—108; 2, pp.76—83. *224*

AMA (1976). *Cities in Decline* (London, AMA). *244*

Ambrose, P. (1976). *Who Plans Brighton's Housing Crisis?* (London, Shelter). *215*

Ambrose, P., and Colenutt, B. (1973). *The Property Machine* (Harmondsworth, Penguin). *48n*

American Political Science Association, Committee on Political Parties (1950). 'Toward a more responsible two party system', *American Political Science Review*, supplement, 44. *38n*

Amos, F. (1970). 'Systematic local government: some implications of PPBS for local government', Public Works and Municipal Services Congress. *143n, 145n*

(1972). 'Management in the new local authorities', *Surveyor*, 30 June, pp.18—20. *138*

Amos, F. *et al.* (1974). *Corporate Management in Action* (London, Brown, Knight and Truscott). *257n*

An Approach to Industrial Strategy (1975). Cmnd 6315 (London, HMSO). *230, 231, 248*

Anderson, W. (1925). *American City Government* (New York, Holt). *192*
　(1945). *The Units of Government in the United States* (Chicago, Public Administration Service). *107*

Andreski, S. (1974). *Social Sciences as Sorcery* (Harmondsworth, Penguin). *9*

Ansoff, H. I. (1965). *Corporate Strategy: An Analytical Approach to Business Policy for Growth and Expansion* (New York, McGraw-Hill). *145n*

Anthony, R. N. (1965). *Planning and Control Systems: A Framework for Analysis* (Cambridge, Mass., Harvard University Press). *139n*

Argyriades, D. (1965). 'Some aspects of civil service reorganisation in Greece', *International Review of Administrative Sciences*, 31, pp.297—309. *176n*

Armstrong, R. H. R. (1969). 'The approach to planning, programming, budgeting systems in local government', *Local Government Finance*, November, pp.454—66. *141*
　(1973). 'Program budgeting in English local government', in D. Novick (ed.), *Current Practice in Program Budgeting* (London, Heinemann), pp.105—10. *124, 142, 165*

Ashford, D. E. (1973). 'National parties and local political participation in British local government', Paper prepared for delivery at the 1973 annual meeting of the American Political Science Association, Jung Hotel, New Orleans, 4—8 September. *39n*
　(1974). 'The effects of central finance on the British local government system', *British Journal of Political Science*, 4, pp.305—22. *242*
　(1975). 'Theories of local government: Some comparative considerations', *Comparative Political Studies*, 8, pp.90—107. *16n*
　(1975A). 'Parties and participation in British local government and some American parallels', *Urban Affairs Quarterly*, 11, pp.58—81. *16n*
　(1973B). 'Resources, spending and party politics in British local government', *Administration and Society*, 7, pp.286—311. *235*

Ashton, T. S. (1948). *The Industrial Revolution: 1760—1830* (London, Oxford University Press). *85*

Astor, Lord, Simon, E. D., and Burgess, A. W. S. (n.d.). *Local Government Areas: The Boundary Commission — Problems and Opportunities* (London, Argus Press). *60n, 68*

Atlee, C. R., and Robson, W. A. (1925). *The Town Councillor* (London, Labour Publishing Company). *31*

Bachrach, P., and Baratz, M. S. (1962). 'The two faces of power', *American Political Science Review*, 56, pp.947—52. *218*
　(1963). 'Decisions and nondecisions: an analytical framework', *American Political Science Review*, 57, pp. 641—51. *218*

Bacon, R., and Eltis, W. (1976). 'How growth in public expenditure has contributed to Britain's difficulties', in R. Bacon *et al.*, *The Dilemmas of Government Expenditure* (London, IEA), pp.1—21. *230*

Bailey, J. (1975). *Social Theory for Planning* (London, Routledge and Kegan Paul). *4, 9*

Bailey, J. J., and O'Connor, R. J. (1975). 'Operationalising incrementalism: measuring the muddles', *Public Administration Review*, 35, pp.60—6. *179*

Bailey, S. D. (1959). *British Parliamentary Democracy* (London, Harrap).*133*

Baker, C. A. (1910). 'Population and costs in rleation to city management', *Journal of the Royal Statistical Society*, 74, pp.73—9. *64*

Baker, J., and Young, M. (1971). *The Hornsey Plan — A Role for Neighbourhood Councils in the New Local Government*, 3rd edn (London, Association for Neighbourhood Councils). *34n*

Banerjee, A. M. (1963). 'Fifteen years of administrative reforms: an overview', *Indian Journal of Public Administration*, 9, pp.441—56. *159*

Banfield, E. C., and Grodzins, M. (1958). *Government and Housing in Metropolitan Areas* (New York, McGraw-Hill). *108*

Banfield, E. C., and Wilson, J. Q. (1963). *City Politics* (Cambridge, Mass., Harvard University Press). *209n, 210*

Banwell, H. (1963). 'The machinery of local government: the creaks', *Public Administration*, 41, pp.335—44. *41n, 136, 186n, 188*

Barber, J. D. (1966). *Power in Committees* (Chicago, Rand McNally). *179n*

Baritz, L. (1960). *Servants of Power: A History of Social Science in American Industry* (Middleton, Conn., Wesleyan University Press). *158*

Barnett, H. O. (1921). *Canon Barnett: His Life, Work and Friends* (London, John Murray). *95*

Barr, J. (1968). 'The amenity protesters', *New Society*, 1 August, pp.152—3. *49n*

Barratt Brown, M. (1972). *From Labourism to Socialism* (Nottingham, Spokesman). *226, 228*

'The Basildon Experiment' (1966). *Public Administration*, 44, pp.213—25. *127, 186n*

Bassett, R. (1935). *The Essentials of Parliamentary Democracy* (London, Macmillan). *37*

Batley, R., O'Brien, O., and Parris, H. (1970). *Going Comprehensive: Educational Policy-making in Two County Boroughs* (London, Routledge and Kegan Paul). *54n*

Bay, C. (1972). 'Thoughts on the purposes of political science education', in G. J. Graham and G. W. Carey (eds.), *The Post-Behavioural Era: Perspectives on Political Science* (New York, David McKay), pp.88—99. *4n*

Bayliss, R. (1958). 'Tell the people', *Public Administration*, 36, pp.83—5. *45n*

Baynes, P. (1973). *Case Studies in Corporate Planning* (London, Pitman). *145n*

Bealey, F., and Bartholomew, D. J. (1962). 'The local elections in Newcastle-Under Lyme: May 1958', *British Journal of Sociology*, 13, pp.273—85, 350—68. *40n*

Bealey, F., Blondel, J., and McCann, W. P. (1965). *Constituency Politics* (London, Faber). *40n, 42, 48n, 54n, 83*

Beckman, M. J. (1960). 'Some aspects of returns to scale in business administration', *Quarterly Journal of Economics*, 74, pp.464—71. *113n*

Beer, S. H. (1965). *Modern British Politics* (London, Faber). *45*

Beloff, M. (1971). 'Introduction', in I. B. Rees, *Government by Community* (London, Charles Knight). *72*

Benemy, F. W. G. (1960). *Whitehall, Townhall* (London, Harrap). *120*

Bennett, A. E. (1972). 'Policy planning: determination of needs (management)', *Local Government Chronicle*, 17 March, p.452. *114n*

Bennington, J. (1973). 'Focus on government', *Municipal Journal*, 81 (30 March), pp.465—9. *53n*

(1975). *Local Government Becomes Big Business* (London, CDP Occasional Paper no. 11). *177n, 215, 231*

Bevan, A. (1952). *In Place of Fear* (London, Heinemann). *51*

Bickner, R. E. (1971). 'I don't know PPB at all', *Policy Sciences*, 2, pp.301–4. *115n*

Birch, A. H. (1950). 'The habit of voting', *The Manchester School of Economics and Social Studies*, 18, pp.75–82. *39n*
    (1959). *Small Town Politics* (London, Oxford University Press). *40n, 45*, 60n, *82, 89, 186n*

Birch, A. H., and Campbell, P. (1950). 'Voting behaviour in a Lancashire constituency', *British Journal of Sociology*, 1, pp.197–208. *39n*

Birley, D. (1970). *The Education Officer and His World* (London, Routledge). *54n*

Bish, R. L., and Warren, R. (1972). 'Scale and monopoly problems in urban government services', *Urban Affairs Quarterly*, 8, pp.97–122. *77n*

Blackburn, R. (1972). *Ideology in Social Science* (London, Fontana/Collins). *8*

Bliss, W. D. P. (1897). *The Encyclopedia of Social Reforms* (New York, Funk and Wagnalls). *194n*

Boaden, N. (1970). 'Central departments and local authorities: the relationship re-examined', *Political Studies*, 18, pp.175–86. *27*
    (1971). *Urban Policy-Making* (London, Cambridge University Press). *235*

Boaden, N., and Alford, R. R. (1969). 'Sources of diversity in English local government decisions', *Public Administration*, 47, pp.203–23. *190n, 235*

Board, W. J. (1925). 'The qualifications, recruitment, training and official organisation of local government officers', *Public Administration*, 3, pp.398–405. *127n*

Bochel, J. M., and Denver, D. T. (1971). 'Canvassing, turnout, and party support: an experiment', *British Journal of Political Science*, 1, pp.257–70. *39n*
    (1972). 'The impact of the campaign on the results of local government elections', *British Journal of Political Science*, 2, pp.239–43. *39n*

Boggs, C. (1976). *Gramsci's Marxism* (London, Pluto). *219*

Bollens, J. C., and Schmandt, H. J. (1970). *The Metropolis*, 2nd edn (New York, Harper and Row). *108, 110*

Bonnor, J. (1954). 'Public interest in local government', *Public Administration*, 32, pp.425–8. *40n*

Booz-Allen and Hamilton (1969). *London Borough of Islington: Reorganisation of the Committee System* (London, Booz-Allen and Hamilton). *156n*
    (1970). *Departmental Organisation in Local Government: A Survey of London and County Boroughs* (London, Booz-Allen and Hamilton). *165n*
    (1971). *County Borough of Stockport: Progress Report and Review of Present Organisation* (London, Booz-Allen and Hamilton). *128n*

Botner, S. B. (1970). 'Four years of PPBS: An appraisal', *Public Administration Review*, 30. pp.423–32. *176, 178*
    (1972). 'PPB under Nixon', *Public Administration Review*, 32, pp.254–5. *176*

Boyden, H. J. (1961). *Councils and their Public*, Fabian Research Series 221 (London, Fabian Society). *30, 45n*

Brace, C. L. (1872). *The Dangerous Classes of New York* (New York, Wynkoop and Hallenbeck). *197*

Bradford, G. (1893). 'Our failures in municipal government' *Annals of the American Academy of Political and Social Science*, 3, pp.691—702.

Bradley, D. S., and Zald, M. N. (1965). 'From commercial elite to political administrator: the rectuitment of the mayors of Chicago', *American Journal of Sociology*, 71, pp.153—67. *196*

Brand, J. (1974). *Local Government Reform in England: 1888—1974* (London, Croom Helm). *1, 36n*

Braverman, H. (1974). *Labor and Monopoly Capital* (New York, Monthly Review Press). *85, 158*

Braybrooke, D., and Lindblom, C. E. (1963). *A Strategy of Decision* (Glencoe, Ill., Free Press). *179n*

Brech, E. F. L. (1965). *Organisation: The Framework of Management*, 2nd edn (London, Longmans). *152*

Brennan, T., Cooney, E. W., and Pollins, H. (1954). 'Party politics and local government in Western South Wales', *Political Quarterly*, 25, pp.76—84. *35, 39n*

(1954A). *Social Change in South-West Wales* (London, Watts). *89*

Bridgeman, J. M. (1973). 'Planning-programming-budgeting in the United Kingdom central government', in D. Novick (ed.), *Current Practice in Program Budgeting* (London, Heinemann), pp.89—95. *141*

Brier, A. P., and Dowse, R. E. (1966). 'The amateur activists', *New Society*, 29 December, pp.975—6. *49n*

Brierley, J. D. (1973). 'Programme budgeting in education in the United Kingdom', in D. Novick (ed.), *Current Practice in Program Budgeting* (London, Heinemann), pp.97—103. *141n*

Briggs, A. (1950). 'Social structure and politics in Birmingham and Lyons, 1825—1848', *British Journal of Sociology*, 1, pp.67—80. *88, 94*

(1952). 'The background of the parliamentary reform movement in three English cities, 1830—2', *Cambridge Historical Journal*, X, 3, pp.293—317. *88*

(1961). 'The welfare state in historical perspective', *Archives Européenes de Sociologie*, 2, pp.221—58. *226*

Briggs, E., and Deacon, A. (1973). 'The creation of the Unemployment Assistance Board', *Policy and Politics*, 2, pp.43—62. *250*

Bristow, S. (1972). 'The criteria for local government reorganisation and local authority autonomy', *Policy and Politics*, 1, pp.143—62. *27*

Broadbent, T. A. (1977). *Planning and Profit in the Urban Economy* (London, Methuen). *216, 233*

Brodrick, G. (1875). 'Local government in England', in J. W. Probyn (ed.), *Local Government and Taxation* (London, Cassell, Petter, and Galpin), pp.1—96. *62n, 91, 95n, 96, 102n, 234*

Brown, D. M. (1974). *Introduction to Urban Economics* (New York, Academic Press). *74*

Brown, J. A. C. *et al.* (1953). 'A comment on a criterion of efficiency in local administration', *Journal of the Royal Statistical Society*, Series A, 116, pp.406—7. *64*

Brown, J. C. (1958). 'Local party efficiency as a factor in the outcome of British elections', *Political Studies*, 6, pp.174—8. *39n*

Brown, R. G. S. (1976). 'Structure and local policy-making in the reorganised NHS', *PA Bulletin*, 20, pp.9—19. *182n*

Brown, R. G. S., Griffin, S., and Haywood, S. C. (1975). *New Bottles: Old Wine?* (Institute for Health Studies, University of Hull). *182n*

Bryce, J. (1888). *The American Commonwealth*, 2nd edn (2 vols., London, Macmillan). *191–2, 196, 203n*

(1921). *Modern Democracies* (2 vols., London, Macmillan). *192*

Buenker, J. D. (1973). *Urban Liberalism and Progressive Reform* (New York, Scribner's). *195n*

Budge, I. (1965). 'Electors' attitudes to local government', *Political Studies*, 13, pp.386–92. *40n*

Budge, I., Brand, J. A., Margolis, M., and Smith, A. L. M. (1972). *Political Stratification and Democracy* (London, Macmillan). *40n, 53n*

Bugbee, J. M. (1887). *The City Government of Boston* (Baltimore, Johns Hopkins University Studies in Historical and Political Science, vol.5). *195*

Bullock, P., and Yaffe, D. (1975). 'Inflation, the crisis and the Post War boom', *Revolutionary Communist*, 3/4, pp.5–45. *227, 229*

Bulpitt, J. G. (1963). 'Party systems in local government', *Political Studies*, 11, pp.11–35. *35, 39n*

(1967). *Party Politics in English Local Government* (London, Longmans). *36n, 39n, 188n*

(1972). 'Participation and local government: territorial democracy', in G. Parry (ed.), *Participation in Politics* (Manchester, Manchester University Press). pp.281–302. *1, 28, 34, 56*

Bunbury, H. N. (1930). 'Rationalisation and the process of administration', *Public Administration*, 8, pp.275–82. *155*

Bunce, J. T. (1882). 'Municipal boroughs and urban districts', in J. W. Probyn (ed.). *Local Government and Taxation in the United Kingdom* (London, Cassell, Petter, and Galpin), pp.271–318. *102n*

Burke, T. J. *et al.* (1971). *New Directions for Local Government* (London, McKinsey and Co.). *131n, 133n*

Burn, D. (1972). *Rent Strike: St Pancras 1960* (London, Pluto). *49n*

Burns, T., and Stalker, G. M. (1961). *The Management of Innovation* (London, Tavistock). *183n*

Burridge, M. E. (1974). 'Corporate Planning – an approach to community planning', *London Review of Public Administration*, 5, pp.20–5. *139n*

Busteed, M. A. (1975). *Geography and Voting Behaviour* (London, Oxford University Press). *103*

Butani, K. N. (1966). 'Implementing administrative innovations and reforms', *Indian Journal of Public Administration*, 12, pp.612–17. *162*

Butler, D. E. (1953). 'Local government in Parliament', *Public Administration*, 31, pp.46–7. *50n*

Butler, D. E. and Stokes, D. (1969). *Political Change in Britain* (London, Macmillan). *40n*

Butt, R. (1970). 'PPBS in British local government', *PAC Bulletin*, 9, pp.43–50. *139*

(1970A). 'Programme budgeting survey', *Local Government Finance*, August, pp.292–7. *141, 257n*

Butterworth, R. (1966). 'Islington Borough Council: some aspects of single-party rule', *Politics*, 1, pp.21–31. *39*

Buxton, R. (1973). *Local Government*, 2nd edn (Harmondsworth, Penguin). *6n, 35, 37, 40n, 50n, 51n, 53, 61*

Caiden, G. E. (1970). *Administrative Reform* (London, Allen Lane). *114, 116, 146, 161, 176n*

(1973). 'Development, administrative capacity and administrative reform', *International Review of Administrative Sciences*, 39, pp.327—44. *176n*

Caiden, G. E. and Wildavsky, A. (1974). *A Constant Quantity of Tears: Planning and Budgeting in Poor Countries* (New York, Wiley). *182n*

Cairncross, A. (1960). *Introduction to Economics*, 3rd edn (London, Butterworth). *113n*

Callow, A. B. (1969). *American Urban History* (New York, Oxford University Press). *193n*

Campbell, A. K. and Sacks, S. (1964). 'Administering the spread city', *Public Administration Review*, 24, pp.141—52. *107*

Cartwright, J. (1975). 'The corporate plan's the thing', *Municipal Review*, December, p.269. *118n, 124*

Cash Limits on Public Expenditure (1976). Cmnd 6440 (London, HMSO). *252*

Castells, M. (1972). 'Urban renewal and social conflict in Paris', *Social Science Information*, 11, pp.93—124. *250*

(1976). 'The wild city', *Kapitalistate*, 4/5, pp.2—30. *109*

(1977). *The Urban Question* (London, Edward Arnold). *109, 232n*

CBI (1975). *Evidence to the Committee of Inquiry into Local Government Finance* (London, CBI). *241*

(1976). *The Road to Recovery* (London, CBI). *230, 241*

CDP (1977). *Gilding the Ghetto* (London, CDP). *219n, 239*

(1977A(. *The Costs of Industrial Change* (London CDP). *236*

Chalklin, C. W. (1974). *The Provincial Towns of Georgian England* (London, Edward Arnold). *84*

Chaloner, W. H. (1950). *The Social and Economic Development of Crawe* (Manchester, Manchester University Press). *10, 45n, 90*

Chamberlain, J., *et al.* (1885). *The Radical Programme* (Brighton, Harvester Press, 1971). *21, 60n, 234n*

Chambers, J. D. (1968). *The Workshop of the World*, 2nd edn (London, Oxford University Press). *86*

Chandler, A. D. (1951—4). 'The origins of progressive leadership' in E. E. Morrison (ed.), *The Letters of Theodore Roosevelt* (8 vols., Cambridge, Mass., Harvard University Press), vol.8, appendix 3, pp.1462—4. *194n*

Chapeltown News (1975). *Planning to Deceive*, Pamphlet no. 1 (Leeds). *49n*

Checkland, S. G., and Checkland, E. O. A. (eds) (1974). *The Poor Law Report of 1834* (Harmondsworth, Penguin). *62, 65, 67n*

Chenery, H. B. (1949). 'Engineering production functions', *Quarterly Journal of Economics*, 63, pp.507—31. *74n*

Chester, D. N. (1950). 'Development of the cabinet', in G. Campion *et al.*, *British Government Since 1918* (London, George Allen and Unwin), pp.31—55. *174*

(1951). *Central and Local Government* (London, Macmillan). *30, 31*

(1954). *Local Government and its Critics* (Warburton Lecture, University of Manchester). *2, 125n, 188n*

(1954A) 'Council and committee meetings in county boroughs', *Public Administration*, 32, pp.429—31. *186n*

(1968). 'Local democracy and the internal organisation of local authorities', *Public Administration*, 46, pp.287—98. *133, 134n*

Chester, D. N., and Willson, F. M. G. (1968). *The Organisation of British Central Government: 1914—64*, 2nd edn (London, George Allen and Unwin). *173, 174*

Childs, R. S. (1914). *The Story of the Short Ballot Cities* (New York, National Short Ballot Organisation). *199*

(1952). *Civic Victories* (New York, Harper). *199, 205, 207, 208*

(1954). 'Citizen organisation for control of government', *Annals of the American Academy of Political and Social Science*, 292, pp.129—35. *192*

(1965). *The First Fifty Years of the Council-Manager Plan of Municipal Government* (New York, National Municipal League). *206, 208*

Chorley, K. (1950). *Manchester Made Them* (London, Faber and Faber). *96*

Churchman, C. W., and Schainblatt, A. H. (1969). 'PPB: how can it be implemented?, *Public Administration Review*, 29, pp.178—88. *176n*

CIS (1973). *The Recurrent Crisis of London* (London, CIS). *48n, 216, 236*

CIS/CDP (1975). *Cutting the Welfare State (Who Profits?)* (London, CIS/ CDP). *216*

Civic Trust (1976). *The Local Amenity Movement* (London, Civic Trust). *45n, 49n*

Clark, D. M. (1973). *Greater Manchester Votes* (Newcastle-Upon-Tyne, Redrose Publications). *102*

Clark, K. B., and Hopkins, J. (1969). *A Relevant War Against Poverty* (New York, Harper and Row). *49n*

Clarke, J. J. (1939). *The Local Government of the United Kingdom*, 12th edn (London, Pitman). *21, 30, 38n, 102n*

Clarke, S. (1977). 'Marxism, sociology and Poulantzas' theory of the state', *Capital and Class*, 2, pp.1—31. *224*

Clements, R. V. (1969). *Local Notables and the City Council* (London, Macmillan). *82n, 186, 188n, 189, 190n*

Coates, K., and Silburn, R. (1970). *Poverty: the Forgotten Englishman* (Harmondsworth, Penguin). *49n*

Cockburn, C. (1977). *The Local State* (London, Pluto). *104, 164, 189n, 216, 238, 253, 255*

Coker, F. W. (1922). 'Dogmas of administrative reform', *American Political Science Review*, 16, pp.399—411. *158n*

Cole, G. D. H. (1921). *The Future of Local Government* (London, Cassell). *75n*

(1947). *Local and Regional Government* (London, Cassell). *38n*

(1955). *Studies in Class Structure* (London Routledge and Kegan Paul). *86*

Cole, M. (1956). *Servant of the Country* (London, Dobson). *32, 37, 38n, 120*

Collins, N., Hinings, C. R., and Walsh, K. (1976). 'The best politician in town', Institute of Local Government Studies, University of Birmingham, mimeo. *53*

Committee for Economic Development (1966). *Modernizing Local Government* (New York, CED). *107*

Committee on Financial Aid to Political Parties (1976). *Report*, Cmnd 6601 (London, HMSO). *237*

Committee of Inquiry into the Civil Service (1968). *Report*, Cmnd 3638 (London, HMSO). *154*

Committee of Inquiry into the Impact of Rates on Households (1965). *Report*. Cmnd 2582 (London, HMSO). *240, 241n*

Committee on Inquiry into Local Government Finance (1976). *Report*. Cmnd 6453 (London HMSO). *6n, 12, 30, 40n, 74, 98n, 232n, 240, 241n, 242, 247*

Committee of Inquiry on Small Firms (1971). *Report*, Cmnd 4811 (London, HMSO). *74n*

Committee of Inquiry into the System of Remuneration of Members of Local Authorities (1977). *Remuneration of Councillors*, vol.2, *The Surveys of Councillors and Local Authorities* (London, HMSO). *189, 240n*

Committee on Local Authority and Allied Personal Social Services (1968). *Report*. Cmnd 3703 (London, HMSO). *125n, 127*

Committee on Local Expenditure (England and Wales) (1932). *Report*, Cmd 4200 (London, HMSO). *246*

Committee on the Management of Local Government (1967); vol.1, *Report*; vol.2, *The Local Government Councillor*; vol.3, *The Local Government Elector*; vol.4, *Local Government Administration Abroad*; vol.5, *Local Government Administration in England and Wales* (London, HMSO). *27n, 28, 35, 36, 40–5 passim, 49n, 51–3 passim, 80, 101, 121, 123n, 126–30 passim, 132, 134–6 passim, 148, 185–9 passim, 236, 240n, 251, 253, 254*

Committee on Public Participation in Planning (1969). *People and Planning* (London, HMSO). *255*

Committee on the Staffing of Local Government (1967). *Report* (London, HMSO). *70, 248*

Conkling, A. R. (1894). *City Government in the United States* (New York, D. Appleton and Co.). *191, 197n, 202, 203, 204n*

Connelly, D. (1970). 'The councillor and his environment' (University of Sussex, BA dissertation). *52n*

Connolly, W. E. (1967). *Political Science and Ideology* (New York, Atherton Press). *9, 11*

Conservative Political Centre (1974). *More Help for the Cities* (London, CPC). *239*

Conservative Research Department (1971). *Notes on Current Politics: Local Government* (London, CPC). *61n*

Consultative Committee on Publicity for Local Government (1947). *Interim Report* (London, HMSO). *41n*

Cornford, J. (1963). 'The transformation of Conservatism in the late-nineteenth century', *Victorian Studies*, 7, pp.36–66. *88, 91, 103n*

Corrigan, P. (1977). 'The welfare state as an arena of class struggle', *Marxism Today*, 21, pp.87–93. *224*

Cossey, C. J. (ed.) (1971). *Corporate Management in the 1970s* (London Municipal Journal). *130, 133n, 138, 254, 257n*

Cousins, P. F. (1973). 'Voluntary organisations as local pressure groups: 1. The general context: 2, The situation in Bromley', *London Review of Public Administration*, 3 April, pp.22–30; October, pp.17–26. *46*

    (1974). 'Voluntary organisations and local government in three South London Boroughs' (London University, PhD thesis). *46*

    (1976). 'Voluntary organisations and local government in three South London Boroughs', *Public Administration*, 54, pp.63–81. *48*

    (1977). 'Theories of democracy and local government', *PA Bulletin*, 23, pp.40–53. *46*

Coventry CDP (1975). *Final Report, Part I* (London, CDP). *216*

Cox, K. R. (1968). 'Suburbia and voting behaviour in the London metropolitan area', *Annals of the Association of American Geographers*, 58, pp.111–27. *103n*

(1973). *Conflict, Power and Politics in the City: A Geographic View* (New York, McGraw-Hill). *103n*

Cox, W. H. (1976). *Cities: The Public Dimension* (Harmondsworth, Penguin). *7, 14, 53, 54n, 130*

Cranston, D. G. *et al.* (1969). *Programme Budgeting.* A Midland Associates Study Group Report (London IMTA). *124n, 127n, 141, 145n*

Crecine, J. P. (1969). *Governmental Problem Solving* (Chicago, Rand McNally). *179n*

Crenson, M. A. (1971). *The Unpolitics of Air Pollution* (Baltimore, Johns Hopkins University Press). *218*

Crick, B. (1970). 'Foreword', in W. Hampton, *Democracy and Community* (London, Oxford University Press). *46*

Crooks, J. B. (1968). *Politics and Progress: The Rise of Urban Progressivism in Baltimore, 1895 to 1911* (Baton Rouge, Lousiana State University Press). *194, 253*

Crossman, R. H. S. (1975). *The Diaries of a Cabinet Minister*, vol.1, *Minister of Housing, 1964–66* (London, Hamish Hamilton and Jonathan Cape). *1, 100*

Cuckney, J. G. (1974). 'The Commercial approach to government operations', *Management Services in Government*, XXIX, 3, pp.121–9. *76n*

Cullingworth, J. B. (1967). *Town and Country Planning in England and Wales* (London, George Allen and Unwin). *79*

Cumming, C. (1971). *Studies in Educational Costs* (Edinburgh, Scottish Academic Press). *70n*

Cyert, R. M., and March, J. G. (1963). *A Behavioral Theory of the Firm* (Englewood Cliffs, NJ, Prentice-Hall). *76n, 179n*

Daalder, H. (1964). *Cabinet Reform in Britain: 1914–63* (Stanford, Stanford University Press). *173–4, 175n*

Dahl, R. A. (1961). *Who Governs?* (New Haven, Yale University Press). *196*
    (1967). 'The city in the future of democracy', *American Political Science Review*, 61, pp.953–70. *106*

Dahl, R. A., and Lindblom, C. E. (1953). *Politics, Economics and Welfare* (New York, Harper and Row). *179n*

Dahl, R. A., and Tufte, E. R. (1974). *Size and Democracy* (London, Oxford University Press). *32*

Daland, R. T. (1957). 'Political science and the study of urbanism', *American Political Science Review*, 51, pp.491–509. *17*

Danielson, M. N. (ed.) (1971). *Metropolitan Politics: A Reader*, 2nd edn (Boston, Little Brown). *107*

Danziger, J. N. (1974). 'Budget-making and expenditure variations in English county boroughs' (University of Stanford, PhD thesis). *147, 179, 235*
    (1976). 'Assessing incrementalism in British municipal budgeting', *British Journal of Political Science*, 6, pp.335–50. *179*

Davey, K. J. (1971). 'Local autonomy and independent revenues', *Public Administration*, 49, pp.45–50. *242*
    (1972). *Programme Budgeting for East Africa* (East African Staff College). *140n*

Davies, B. (1969). 'Local authority size: some associations with standards of performance of services for deprived children and old people', *Public Administration*, 47, pp.225–48. *64, 68*

Davies, B., and Barton, A. (1974). 'Area and authority determinants of the calibre of junior administrators', *Policy and Politics*, 3, pp.71–89. *70n*

Davies, B., Barton, A., and McMillan, I. (1972). *Variations in Children's Services among British Urban Authorities* (London, Bell). *70n, 235*

Davies, B., Barton, A., McMillan, I., and Williamson, V. (1971). *Variations in Services for the Aged* (London, Bell). *70n, 75n*

Davies, C. J. (1973). 'Managing the new local authorities: the Bains Report', *London Review of Public Administration*, 3, pp.1–14. *148, 156n*

Davies, J. G. (1972). *The Evangelistic Bureaucrat* (London, Tavistock). *49n, 53, 125*

Davies, P., and Newton, K. (1974). 'An aggregate data analysis of turnout and party voting in local elections', *Sociology*, 8, pp.213–31. *39n*

Davis, J. W. (ed.) (1969). *Politics, Programs, and Budgets* (Englewood Cliffs, NJ, Prentice-Hall). *139n*

Davis, O. A., Dempster, M., and Wildavsky, A. (1966). 'A theory of the budgetary process', *American Political Science Review*, 60, pp.529–47. *178*

Deacon, A., and Briggs, E. (1973). 'Local democracy and central policy. The issue of pauper votes in the 1920's', *Policy and Politics*, 2, pp.347–64. *250*

Dearlove, J. (1973). *The Politics of Policy in Local Government* (London, Cambridge University Press). *25n, 38, 47, 49n, 51n, 52n, 149, 180, 216*
(1974). 'The control of change and the regulation of community action', in D. Jones and M. Mayo (eds), *Community Work One* (London, Routledge and Kegan Paul), pp.22–43. *49n, 238*

Dell, E. (1960). 'Labour and local government', *Political Quarterly*, 31, pp.333–47. *30n, 31, 41n*

Dennis, N. (1970). *People and Planning* (London, Faber and Faber). *49n*
(1972). *Public Participation and Planners' Blight* (London, Faber and Faber). *49n, 54n*

Denver, D. T., and Hands, G. (1972). 'Turnout and marginality in local elections: a comment', *British Journal of Political Science*, 2, pp. 513–15. *39n*

Department of Education and Science (1970). *Output Budgeting for the Department of Education and Science* (London, HMSO). *141n*

Departmental Committee on Local Taxation (1914). *Final Report*, Cd 7315 (London, HMSO). *242*

Devlin, T. C. (1896). *Municipal Reform in the United States* (New York, Putnam). *202*

Devons, E. (1950). *Planning in Practice (Cambridge, Cambridge University Press). 183*

Dewitt, B. P. (1915). *The Progressive Movement* (Seattle, University of Washington Press, 1968). *193*

Dohoney, C. (1910). 'Commission Government and democracy', *American City*, 2, pp.76–8. *204*

Donnison, D. (1973). 'Micro-politics of the city', in D. Donnison and D. Eversley (eds.), *London: Urban Patterns, Problems, and Polities* (London, Heinemann), pp.383–404. *45n, 48n*

Drain, G. (1966). *The Organisation and Practice of Local Government* (London, Heinemann). *120, 148n, 164*

Dreitzel, H. P. (1972). 'Social science and the problem of rationality. Notes on the sociology of technocrats', *Politics and society*, 2, pp.165–82. *257*

Dror, Y. (1964). 'Muddling through — "science" or inertia?', *Public Administration Review*, 24, pp.153–7. *179*

(1967). 'Policy analysis: A new professional role in government service', *Public Administration Review*, 27, pp.197—203. *257*

Dunleavy, P. (1977). 'Protest and quiescence in urban politics: a critique of some pluralist and structuralist myths', *International Journal of Urban and Regional Research*, 1, pp.193—218. *219*

Dunsire, A. (1956). 'Accountability in local government', *Administration (Dublin)*, 4, pp.80—8. *37*

Dye, T. R. (1969). *Politics in States and Communities* (Englewood Cliffs, NJ, Prentice-Hall). *209*

Dyos, H. J. (1961). *Victorian Suburb* (Leicester, Leicester University Press). *93, 94, 103n*

East, J. P. (1965). *Council-Manager Government* (Chapel Hill, University of North Carolina Press). *194n, 206*

Ebner, M. H. (1973). *The New Urban History: Bibliography on Methodology and Historiography* (Illinois, Council of Planning Librarians Exchange Bibliography, no. 445). *193*

Eddison, T. (1973). *Local Government: Management and Corporate Planning* (Aylesbury, Leonard Hill). *115, 117, 124n, 139, 141, 143, 254*

(1974). 'The advantages and limitations of corporate planning', *London Review of Public Administration*, 5, pp.12—19. *137*

Edinburgh CSE Group (1977). 'State, restructuring, local state', CSE Conference Paper, Bradford. *217*

Editorial (1969). 'The future of English local government', *Public Administration*, 47, pp.411—19. *57*

'Efficiency' (1948). *Encyclopedia of the Social Sciences* (15 vols., New York, Macmillan), vol.5, pp.437—9. *77*

Elden, J. M. (1971). 'Radical politics and the future of public administration in the post industrial era', in D. Waldo (ed.), *Public Administration in a Time of Turbulence* (Scranton, Chandler), pp.19—42. *161*

Elkin, S. L. (1974). *Politics and Land Use Planning: the London Experience* (London, Cambridge University Press). *54n*

Elliott, J. (1971). 'The Harris experiment in Newcastle-Upon-Tyne', *Public Administration*, 49, pp.149—62. *257n*

Emmerich, H. (1950). *Essays on Federal Reorganisation* (Alabama, University of Alabama Press). *154n*

Employment Policy (1944). Cmd 6257 (London HMSO). *228*

Engels, F. (1892). *The Condition of the Working Class in England* (Moscow, Progress Publishers, 1973). *88, 94, 95*

Erie, S. P., Kirlin, J. J., and Rabinovitz, F. F. (1972). 'Can something be done? Propositions on the performance of metropolitan institutions', in L. Wingo (ed.), *The Government of Metropolitan Regions: Reform of Metropolitan Governments* (London, Johns Hopkins University Press), pp.7—41. *110*

Erwin, R. (1973). 'Reform from below', *Politics and Society*, 3, pp.463—71. *8*

Etherton, G. H. (1924). 'Employment and organisation of committees in local government', *Public Administration*, 2, pp.389—98. *126n, 131n, 132, 186n*

Etzioni, A. (1967). 'Mixed scanning: a "third" approach to decision-making', *Public Administration Review*, 17, pp.385—92. *179*

Everest, E. P. (1925). 'The areas of local authorities in relation to their duties', *Public Administration*, 3, pp. 320—37. *34n*

Eversley, D. (1973). 'Problems of social planning in inner London', in D.

Donnison and D. Eversley (eds.), *London: Urban Patterns, Problems and Policies* (London, Heinemann), pp.1—50. *139n*

(1974). 'Britain and Germany: Local Government in perspective', in R. Rose (ed.). *The Management of Urban Change in Britain and Germany* (London, Sage), pp.227—67. *102n*

Fainstein, S. S., and Fainstein, N. (1972). *The View From Below: Urban Politics and Social Policy* (Boston, Little Brown). *8*

Fairlie, J. H. (1904). 'American municipal councils', *Political Science Quarterly*, 19, pp.234—51. *195, 196*

Fantini, M., Gittell, M., and Magat, R. (1970). *Community Control and the Urban School* (New York, Praeger). *110*

Faulkner, H. U. (1931). *The Quest for Social Justice* (Chicago, Quadrangle, 1971). *197*

(1959). *Politics, Reform and Expansion* (New York, Harper and Row). *194n*

Fayol, H. (1916). *General and Industrial Management*, with a foreword by L. Urwick (London, Pitman, 1949). *152—4 passim*

Fenno, R. (1966). *The Power of the Purse* (Boston, Little Brown). *179n*

(1968). 'The impact of PPBS on the Congressional appropriations process', in R. Chartrand *et al.* (eds.), *Information Support, Program Budgeting, and the Congress* (New York, Spartan Books). *177n*

Fesler, J. (1949). *Area and Administration* (Montgomery, University of Alabama Press). *107*

(1957). 'Administrative literature and the Second Hoover Commission Reports', *American Political Science Review*, 51, pp.135—57. *10, 158n*

Filler, L. (1961). *Crusaders for American Liberalism* (New York, Crowell-Collier). *193*

Fine, B., and Harris, L. (1976). '"State expenditure in advanced capitalism": a critique', *New Left Review*, 98, pp.97—112. *227*

Finer, H. (1943). 'The case for local self-government', *Public Administration Review*, 3, pp.51—8. *30n*

(1945). *English Local Government*. 2nd edn (London, Methuen). *27n, 120, 127—34 passim, 155*

Finer, S. E. (1950). *A Primer of Public Administration* (London, Frederick Muller). *30n, 31, 33, 64, 67n*

(1956). 'In defence of pressure groups', *The Listener*, 7 June, pp.751—2. *45*

First Report from the Select Committee on Procedure (1968—9). HC 410 1969

Fiske, D. (1975). 'Education: the cuckoo in the local government nest', The Lady Simon of Wythenshawe Memorial Lecture, Manchester. *173n*

Fletcher, P. (1967). 'The results analysed', in L. J. Sharpe (ed.), *Voting in Cities* (London, Macmillan), pp.290—328. *39n, 40n*

(1969). 'An explanation of variations in turnout in local elections', *Political Studies*, 17, pp.495—502. *39n*

Flinn, T. A. (1970). *Local Government and Politics* (Glenview, Ill., Scott Foresman). *108*

Florence, P. S. (1933). *The Logic of Industrial Organisation* (London, Kegan and Paul). *76*

(1969). *Economics and Sociology of Industry*, 2nd edn (London, C. A. Watts). *76*

Foley, D. L. (1972). *Governing the London Region: Reorganisation and Planning in the 1960's* (Berkeley, University of California Press). *6n*

Ford, H. T. (1904). 'Principles of municipal organisation', *Annals of the American Academy of Political and Social Science*, 23, pp.195ff. *203n*

Fordham, H. G. (1911). 'Local government as a school of citizenship', in G. M. Harris (ed.), *Problems of Local Government* (London, P. S. King), pp.404–11. *34n, 63, 102n*

Foster, J. (1974). *Class Struggle and the Industrial Revolution* (London, Weidenfeld and Nicolson). *83n, 85, 89*

Fox, D. M. (1973). 'The president's proposals for executive reorganisation: a critique', *Public Administration Review*, 33, pp.401–6. *175, 176n*

Fox, D. R. (1919). *The Decline of Aristocracy in the Politics of New York: 1801–1840* (New York, Harper and Row, 1965). *196*

Frank, A. G. (1963–4). 'Administrative role definition and social change', *Human Organisation*, 22, pp.239–42. *176n*

Fraser, D. (1973). *The Evolution of the British Welfare State* (London, Macmillan). *225n*

    (1976). *Urban Politics in Victorian England* (Leicester, Leicester University Press). *36n, 45n, 82, 88, 103n*

Freeman, R. (1976). 'Industry and local government', *CBI Review*, 21, pp. 21–8. *99, 240*

Freeman, T. W. (1959). *The Conurbations of Great Britain* (Manchester, Manchester University Press). *79*

    (1968). *Geography and Regional Administration: England and Wales, 1830–1968* (London, Hutchinson). *79*

Friend, J. K., and Jessop, W. N. (1969). *Local Government and Strategic Choice* (London, Tavistock). *121, 122, 125, 135, 136, 139, 257n*

Friend, J. K., Power, J. M. and Yewlett, C. J. L. (1974). *Public Planning: The Intercorporate Dimension* (London, Tavistock). *139*

Friend, J. K. and Yewlett, C. J. L. (1971). 'Inter-agency decision processes: practice and prospect', Conference paper, Royal Society of Arts, 6 December. *139*

Friesma, P. (1969). 'Black control of central cities: the hollow prize', *Journal of the American Institute of Planners*, 35, pp.75–9. *109*

Frisch, M. H. (1969). 'The community elite and the emergence of urban politics: Springfield, Mass. 1840–80', in S. Thernstrom and R. Sennett (eds.), *Nineteenth Century Cities* (New Haven, Yale University Press), pp.277–96. *195, 196*

Fulmer, R. M. (1974). *The New Management* (London, Collier-Macmillan). *145n*

The Future Shape of Local Government Finance (1971). Cmnd 4741 (London, HMSO). *232, 247*

Gamble, A., and Walton, P. (1976). *Capitalism in Crisis* (London, Macmillan). *228*

Garner, J. F. (1960). 'Administration in a small authority', *Public Administration*, 38, pp.227–34. *33*

Geddes, M. (1978). 'Crisis, cuts, regional problems, regional policy and planning', Paper prepared for CSE working group on state expenditure, London, February. *251*

Gibbon, I. G. (1928). 'Types of administrative organisation in local government', *Public Administration*, 6, pp.204–10. *120, 187n*

    (1931). 'Some problems of local government', *Public Administration*, 9, pp.99–119. *34, 127, 128n, 130n, 134*

    (1932). 'Co-ordination', *Public Administration*, 10, pp.53–7. *127*

(1937). 'The party system in government', *Public Administration*, 15, pp.10—19. *36n, 38n*

Gibbon, I. G., and Bell, R. W. (1939). *History of the London County Council: 1889—1939* (London, Macmillan). *127n, 254*

Gilbert, A. B. (1919). *American Cities: Their Methods of Business* (New York, Macmillan). *197*

Gill, H. S. (1973). 'Behavioural science and the Bains Report', *Local Government Studies*, 6, pp.35—43. *125*

del Giudice, D., and Warren, C. (1971). *Reorganisation by Presidential Plan: Three Case Studies* (Washington, National Academy of Public Administration). *175n*

Glaab, C. N., and Brown, A. T. (1967). *A History of Urban America* (New York, Macmillan). *196, 206*

Glassberg, A. (1973). 'The linkage between urban policy outputs and voting behaviour: New York and London', *British Journal of Political Science*, 3, pp.341—61. *38*

Glendinning, J. W., and Bullock, R. E. (1973). *Management by Objectives in Local Government* (London, Charles Knight). *138, 156*

Clyn, A., and Sutcliffe, B. (1972). *British Capitalism, Workers and the Profits Squeeze* (Harmondsworth, Penguin). *229*

Godkin, E. L. (1898). *Problems of Modern Democracy*, 3rd edn (New York, Scribner's). *196, 198, 201*

Goodnow, F. J. (1897). *Municipal Problems* (New York, published for Columbia University Press by Macmillan). *201, 204, 208*

(1910). *Municipal Government* (New York, The Century Co.). *197, 201, 202*

Gordon, D. N. (ed.) (1973). *Social Change and Urban Politics: Readings* (Englewood Cliffs, NJ, Prentice-Hall). *193n, 194n*

Gorham, W. (1968). 'Sharpening the knife that cuts the public pie', *Public Administration Review*, 28, pp.236—41. *178*

Gosnell, H. F. (1948). *Democracy and the Threshold of Freedom* (New York, The Ronald Press Co.). *208*

Gough, I. (1975). 'State expenditure in advanced capitalism', *New Left Review*, 92, pp.53—92. *225, 229, 245*

(forthcoming). *The Welfare State Under Capitalism* (London, Macmillan). *227*

The Government's Expenditure Plans (1977). Cmnd 6721—I (London, HMSO). *243, 247, 248*

Gowan, I. (1957). *New Look for Local Government* (London, CPC). *61*

Grant, W. P. (1971). ' "Local" parties in British local politics: a framework for empirical analysis', *Political Studies*, 19, pp.201—12. *36n*

(1972). 'Non partisanship in British local politics', *Policy and Politics*, 1, pp.241—54. *36n*

Gray, C. V. (1971). 'Political and social structures as determinants of voter participation: a comparative study of American cities' (University of Massachussetts, PhD thesis). *210*

Gray, K. E. and Greenstone, D. (1961). 'Organised labor in city politics', in E. C. Banfield (ed.), *Urban Government* (New York, Free Press), pp.368—79. *209n*

Greater London Council (1970). *PPBS: A General Introduction to the Greater London Council's Planning-Programming-Budgeting System* (London, GLC). *143n*

(1972). *PPBS: Some Questions and their Answers on the Greater London Council's Planning-Programming-Budgeting System* (London, GLC). *139n, 140n*

Green, B. S. R. (1968). 'Community decision-making in Georgian city' (Bath University of Technology, PhD thesis). *83*

Green, G. (1974). 'Politics, local government and the community', *Local Government Studies*, 8, pp.5—16. *49*

Green, L. P. (1959). *Provincial Metropolis* (London, George Allen and Unwin). *61n, 62, 79, 101n*

Greenleaf, W. H. (1975). 'Toulmin-Smith and the British political tradition', *Public Administration*, 53, pp.25—44. *6, 28n*

Greenstein, F. L. (1964). 'The changing apttern of urban party politics', *Annals of the American Academy of Political and Social Science*, 353, pp.1—13. *196*

Greenwood, R., Hinings, C. R., and Ranson, S. (1975). 'Contingency theory and the organisation of local authorities: Part I. Differentiation and integration', *Public Administration*, 53, pp.1—23. *167n*

(1977). 'The politics of the budgetary process in English local government', *Political Studies*, 25, pp.25—47. *179*

Greenwood, R. Hinings, C. R., Ranson, S., and Walsh, K. (1976). *In Pursuit of Corporate Rationality* (University of Birmingham, Institute of Local Government Studies). *113, 118n, 169n, 170n, 184*

Greenwood, R. Lomer, M. A., Hinings, C. R., and Ranson, S. (1975). *The Organisation of Local Authorities in England and Wales, 1967—75*, Discussion paper, series L, no. 5 (University of Birmingham, Institute of Local Government Studies). *165, 167n*

Greenwood, R., Norton, A. L., and Stewart, J. D. (1969). *Recent Reforms in the Management Arrangements of County Boroughs in England and Wales*. Occasional paper no. 1, Series A (University of Birmingham, Institute of Local Government Studies). *165n*

(1969A). *Recent Reforms in the Management Structure of Local Authorities — The London Boroughs*, Occasional paper no. 2, Series A (University of Birmingham, Institute of Local Government Studies). *165n*

(1969B). *Recent Reforms in the Management Structure of Local Authorities — The County Councils*, Occasional paper no. 3, Series A (University of Birmingham, Institute of Local Government Studies). *165n, 189*

(1969C). 'Local government management reform', *Local Government Chronicle*, 19 July, pp.1339—40. *165n*

Greenwood, R., Smith, A. D., and Stewart, J. D. (1971). 'Corporate planning and the chief executive's group', *Local Government Studies*, 1, pp.5—17. *118n, 124, 145n*

(1971A). *New Patterns of Local Government Organisation*, Occasional paper no. 5, Series A (University of Birmingham, Institute of Local Government Studies). *139n, 165, 169n*

(1972). 'The local government councillor', *Local Government Studies*, 2, pp.77—80. *169n*

Greenwood, R., and Stewart, J. D. (1972). 'Corporate planning and management organisation', *Local Government Studies*, 3, pp.25—40. *145n, 183*

(1973). 'Towards a typology of English local authorities', *Political Studies*, 21, pp.64—9. *169*

(1974). *Corporate Planning in English Local Government* (London, Charles Knight). *138, 139, 143*

Greenwood, R., Stewart, J. D., and Smith, A. D. (1972). 'The policy committee in English local government', *Public Administration*, 50, pp.157—66. *165n*

Greer, S. (1963). *Metropolis* (New York, Wiley). *108*

Gregory, R. (1967). 'The Minister's Line: or the M.4 comes to Berkshire', *Public Administration*, 45, pp.113—28, 269—86. *49n*

(1969). 'Local elections and the "rule of anticipated reactions"', *Political Studies*, 17, pp.31—47. *51n*

Grierson, A. (1928). 'Internal organisation of local authorities', *Public Administration*, 6, pp.211—20. *125n, 127n, 128, 129, 132n, 186n*

Griffith, J. A. G. (1963). 'Local democracy: a sorry state?', *New Society*, 14 February, pp.15—17. *39n, 41*

(1966). *Central Departments and Local Authorities* (London, George Allen and Unwin). *63, 64, 242*

(1969A). 'The traditional pattern reconsidered', *Political Quarterly*, 37, pp.139—48. *60n, 68, 133n*

(1969). 'Maud — off the target', *New Statesman*, 20 June, p.866. *23n*

Grodzins, M. (1951). 'Public administration and the science of human relations', *Public Administration Review*, 11, pp.88—102. *108, 159*

Gross, B. M. (1969). 'The new systems budgeting', *Public Administration Review*, 29, pp.113—37. *139n, 143*

Grundy, J. (1950). 'Non-voting in an urban district', *Manchester School of Economics and Social Studies*, 18, pp.83—99. *40n, 41*

Guetzkow, H. (1965). 'The creative person in organisations', in G. A. Steiner (ed.). *The Creative Organisation* (Chicago, University of Chicago Press). pp.35—45. *183n*

Gutman, H. (1959). 'An iron workers' strike in the Ohio Valley, 1873—74', *Ohio Historical Quarterly*, 68, pp.353—70. *197n*

Gyford, J. (1976). *Local Politics in Britain* (London, Croom Helm). *7, 39n, 53n, 104, 120*

Hadfield, E., and MacColl, J. E. (1948). *British Local Government* (London, Hutchinson). *66, 67*

Haldi, J., and Whitcomb, D. (1967). 'Economies of scale in industrial plants', *Journal of Political Economy*, 75, pp.373—85. *74n*

Hall, P., Gracey, H., Drewett, R., and Thomas, R., *et al.* (1973). *The Containment of Urban England* (2 vols., London, PEP and George Allen and Unwin). *93, 96n*

Hall, P. F. (1906). *Immigration and its Effects upon the United States* (New York, Henry Holt). *202*

Hallows, D. A. (1974). 'The treasurer's role in corporate management' (Lecture to the London Students Society of CIPFA, 7 February). *124n*

Hammond, J. L. (1935). 'The social background, 1835—1935', in H. J. Laski, W. I. Jennings, and W. A. Robson (eds.), *A Century of Municipal Progress: 1835—1935* (London, George Allen and Unwin), pp.37—54. *21*

Hammond, J. L., and Hammond, B. (1966). *The Rise of Modern Industry*, 9th edn (London, Methuen). *86*

Hampton, W. (1969). 'Local government and community', *Political Quarterly*, 40, pp.151—62. *47*

(1970). *Democracy and Community* (London, Oxford University Press). *34n, 39, 51n, 52n, 81n, 83n*

(1972). 'Political attitudes to changes in city council administration', *Local Government Studies*, 2, pp.23—35. *173n, 190n*

Handlin, O. (1973). *The Uprooted*, 2nd edn (Boston, Little Brown). *195*

Hanham, H. (1959). *Elections and Party Management: Politicians in the Time of Disraeli and Gladstone* (London, Longmans). *36n*

Hansen, P. (1974). 'Interorganisational programme planning and coordination: prior consultations in the UN system', *International Review of Administrative Sciences*, 40, pp.216—26. *140n*

Harris, G. M. (1911). *Problems of Local Government* (London, P. S. King(. *59*

(1939). 'Cooperation between local authorities and the electorate', *Public Administration*, 17, pp.395—413. *27n*

(1939A). *Municipal Self-Government in Britain* (London, P. S. King). *36n, 39n, 41n, 44n, 120, 126n, 127, 128, 130n, 134n, 135, 139n*

Harris, N. (1974). 'Urban England', *Economy and Society*, 3, pp.346—54. *92*

Harris, R., and Seldon, A. (1976). *Pricing or Taxing?* (London, IEA). *247*

Harris, W. F. (1966). 'Local government — in transition?', *Westminster Bank Review*, August, pp.37—48. *119, 129, 131n, 187n*

Harrison, W. (1952) *The Government of Britain*, 2nd edn (London, Hutchinson). *162*

Hart, W. (1965). 'Some administrative problems of local government' (Paper delivered at IMTA Eastbourne Conference, 10 June). *114, 118n, 119, 120, 130n, 132n, 135*

(1968). *Local Government and Administration*, 8th edn (London, Butterworth). *35, 119, 120, 127n, 130n, 147, 148n*

(1968A). 'Great metropolitan giant of London', *Municipal Journal*, 16 February. *6n*

Hartley, O. A. (1971). 'The relationship between central and local authorities', *Public Administration*, 49, pp.439—56. *23n, 28n*

Harvey, D. (1973). *Social Justice and the City* (London, Edward Arnold). *4n, 109*

Hasluck, E. L. (1936). *Local Government in England* (Cambridge, Cambridge University Press). *15, 36, 61n, 73, 100, 119, 128, 186*

Haug, M. R., and Sussman, M. B. (1969). 'Professional autonomy and the revolt of the client', *Social Problems*, 17, pp.153—61. *255*

Haward, H. (1932). *The LCC from Within* (London, Chapman and Hall). *125n*

Hawkins, B. (1966). *Nashville Metro: the Politics of City-County Consolidation* (Nashville, Tennessee, Vanderbilt University Press). *108*

Hawley, W. D., and Rogers, D. (eds.) (1974). *Improving the Quality of Urban Management* (Beverly Hills, Sage). *140*

Hay, J. R. (1975). *The Origins of the Liberal Welfare Reforms 1906—14* (London, Macmillan). *223, 226*

Hayes, E. C. (1972). *Power Structure and Urban Policy* (New York, McGraw-Hill). *194n, 209, 218*

Hays, S. P. (1964). 'The politics of reform in municipal government in the Progressive Era', *Pacific Northwest Quarterly*, 55, pp.157—69. *79, 193n, 194, 195, 207*

Headley, J. T. (1873). *The Great Riots of New York, 1712—1873* (New York, Dover Publications, 1971). *197*

Headrick, T. E. (1962). *The Town Clerk in English Local Government* (London, George Allen and Unwin). *123, 125n, 126n, 129, 130, 134*

Heath, P. M. (1925). 'The areas of local authorities in relation to their duties', *Public Administration*, 3, pp.309—19. *63n, 66*

Heclo, H. H. (1969). 'The councillor's job', *Public Administration*, 47, pp. 185—202. *53n*

Hennock, E. P. (1973). *Fit and Proper Persons* (London, Edward Arnold). *14, 36n, 53, 80, 82, 83, 90n, 92, 97, 100, 102, 186, 235*

Herman, H. (1963). *New York State and the Metropolitan Problem* (Philadelphia, University of Pennsylvania Press). *107*

Herson, L. J. R. (1957). 'The lost world of municipal government', *American Political Science Review*, 51, pp.330—45. *17*

Higgins, G. M., and Richardson, J. J. (1971). 'Local government and public participation', *Local Government Studies*, 1, October, pp.19—31. *53n*

Hilary, H. O. (1929). 'The position and function of committees in local administration', *Public Administration*, 7, pp.276—86. *127n, 187n*

Hill, D. M. (1970). *Participating in Local Affairs* (Harmondsworth, Penguin). *31, 40n, 42, 45n, 46, 49*

———— (1974). *Democratic Theory and Local Government* (London, George Allen and Unwin). *28, 48n, 54n, 104*

Hill, I. (1973). *Corporate Planning: Revolution through Evolution* (Paisley College of Technology. Local Government Research Unit, Occasional Paper no. 2). *42n, 115n, 124, 130n, 144*

Hill, R. C. (1976). 'Fiscal crisis and political struggle in the decaying US central city', *Kapitalistate*, 4/5, pp.31—49. *109*

———— (1977). 'State capitalism and the urban fiscal crisis in the United States', *International Journal of Urban and Regional Research*, 1, pp.76—100. *213*

Hindes, B. (1971). *The Decline of Working Class Politics* (London, MacGibbon and Kee). *236*

Hinings, C. R., and Greenwood, R. (1973). 'Research into local government reorganisation', *PA Bulletin*, 15, pp.21—38. *160*

Hinings, C. R., Greenwood, R., and Ranson, S. (1975). 'Contingency theory and the organisation of local authorities: Part II. Contingencies and structure', *Public Administration*, 53, pp.169—90. *167n*

Hinings, C. R., Ranson, S., and Greenwood, R. (1974). 'The organisation of metropolitan government: the impact of Bains', *Local Government Studies*, 9, pp.47—54. *167n*

Hirsch, J. (1977), 'What is the fiscal crisis of the state? On the political function of the fiscal crisis', Paper delivered at the CSE Conference, Bradford. *221*

Hirsch, W. Z. (1959). 'Expenditure implications of metropolitan growth and consolidation', *Review of Economics and Statistics*, 41, pp.232—41. *106*

———— (1967). *About the Supply of Urban Public Services* (Los Angeles, Institute of Government and Public Affairs, University of California). *76*

———— (1970). *The Economics of State and Local Government* (New York, McGraw-Hill). *73n, 74*

———— (1973). 'Program budgeting in the UK', *Public Administration Review*, 33, pp.120—8. *141*

Hobhouse, H. (1911). 'Local government and state bureaucracy in Great Britain', in G. M. Harris (ed.), *Problems of Local Government* (London, P. S. King), pp.396—403. *34n, 63*

Hobsbawn, E. J. (1973). *The Age of Revolution* (London, Sphere Books). *85, 86, 87*

Hobson, J. A. (1926). *The Evolution of Modern Capitalism*, rev. edn (London, George Allen and Unwin). *86, 87n*

Hofstadter, R. (1955). *The Age of Reform* (New York, Vintage Books). *192, 194*

Holi, M. G. (1969). *Reform in Detroit* (New York, Oxford University Press). *113, 206, 207*

Holloway, J. (1977). 'State expenditure cuts', CSE working group paper. *215*

Holman, R. (1972). *Power for the Powerless: The Role of Community Action* (London, British Council of Churches). *45n*

Hookham, M. (1948). 'A plea for local government', *Political Quarterly*, 19, pp.244—53. *44*

Hoos, I. R. (1972). *Systems Analysis in Public Policy: A Critique* (Berkeley, University of California Press). *117n, 176, 177*

Hornsby, P. R. G. (1957). 'Party politics and local government in Hampshire', (University of Southampton, MSc (Econ.) thesis). *38n, 81*

Horowitz, I. L. (1967). 'Social science and the public policy: implications of modern research', in I. L. Horowitz (ed.), *The Rise and Fall of Project Camelot* (Cambridge, Mass., MIT Press), pp.339—76. *257*

Howe, F. C. (1907). *The British City: The Beginnings of Democracy* (London, T. Fisher Unwin). *14, 44n, 92*

Hughes, J. T. (1967). 'Economic aspects of local government reform', *Scottish Journal of Political Economy*, 14, pp.118—37. *67, 70n*

Hugins, W. (1960). *Jacksonian Democracy and the Working Class: A Study of the New York Workingmen's Movement 1829—1837* (Stanford, Stanford University Press). *198*

Hutchmacher, J. (1962). 'Urban liberalism and the age of reform', *Mississippi Valley Historical Review*, 49, pp.231—41. *195n*

Hyneman, C. S. (1939). 'Administrative reorganisation: an adventure into science and theology', *Journal of Politics*, 1, pp.62—75. *158n*

Ilersic, A. R. (1975). *Local Government at the Crossroads* (London, Aims of Industry). *240n*

IMTA (1970). *Programme Budgeting: Concept and Application* (London, IMTA). *118n, 141, 142*

   (1971). *Programme Budgeting: Some Practical Problems of Implementation* (London, IMTA). *257n*

   (1971A). *Programme Budgeting: The Approach* (London, IMTA). *141*

Ingham, G. K. (1970). *Size of Industrial Organisation and Worker Behaviour* (Cambridge, Cambridge University Press). *73n*

Interdepartmental Committee (1947). *Expenses for Members of Local Authorities*, Cmd 7126 (London, HMSO). *90*

International Union of Local Authorities (1953). *The Large Town and the Small Municipality: Their Strength and Weakness* (The Hague, IULA). *32, 67n*

Isaac-Henry, K. (1975). 'Local authority associations and local government reform', *Local Government Studies*, I, 3, pp.1—12. *1*

Jackson, R. M. (1965). *The Machinery of Local Government*, 2nd edn (London, Macmillan). *64, 66n, 147*

Jackson, W. E. (1963). *Local Government in England and Wales* (Harmondsworth, Penguin). *62*

Jacobs, S. (1975). 'Rehousing in Glasgow: reform through community action', in D. Jones and M. Mayo (eds.), *Community Work Two* (London, Routledge and Kegan Paul), pp.55—71. *49n, 53n*

James, E. (1966) 'Frontiers in the welfare state', *Public Administration*, 44, pp.447—71. *64, 68*

James, R. (1973). 'Is there a case for local authority planning? Corporate management, the use of business management models and the allocation of resources in local government', *Public Administration*, 51, pp.147—63. *116, 127n*

Jaques, E. (1972). 'Grading and management organisation in the civil service', *O and M Bulletin*, 27, pp.116—23. *175n*

Jarratt, E. (1930). 'Changes of relations between local authorities and central departments', *Public Administration*, 8, pp.56—66. *252*

Jennings, R. E. (1975). 'Political perspectives on local government reorganisation', *Local Government Studies*, 1, pp.21—37. *104*

Jennings, W. I. (1947). *Principles of Local Government Law*, 3rd edn (London, University of London Press). *29, 32, 35*

Jernberg, J. E. (1969). 'Information change and Congressional behaviour: a caveat for PPB reformers', *Journal of Politics*, 31, pp.722—40. *178*

Jessup, F. C. (1949). *Problems of Local Government in England and Wales* (London, Cambridge University Press). *34n, 36, 41n, 44n, 53, 185*

Jewell, R. E. C. (1975). *Local Government Administrative Practice* (London, Charles Knight). *119*

Jha, C. (1957). 'The committees system in British and Indian local authorities' (University of London, LSE, PhD thesis). *119*

Johnson, A. W. (1963). 'Efficiency in government and business', *Canadian Public Administration*, 6, pp.245—60. *76n*

(1973). 'Planning, programming, and budgeting in Canada', *Public Administration Review*, 33, pp.23—31. *140n*

Jones, A. (1968). *Local Governors at Work* (London, CPC). *187n*

Jones, G. S. (1971). *Outcast London* (Oxford, Clarendon Press). *88, 93—6 passim*

Jones, G. W. (1969). *Borough Politics* (London, Macmillan). *14, 38, 83, 91, 103n*

(1969A). 'The Redcliffe-Maud report: the implications for local democracy', *PAC Bulletin*, 7, December, pp.3—20. *42n, 190*

(1973). 'The functions and organisation of councillors', *Public Administration*, 51, pp.135—46. *135*

Jones, J. H. (1933). *Economics of Private Enterprise* (London, Pitman). *113n*

Jones, V. (1942). *Metropolitan Government* (Chicago, University of Chicago Press). *107, 108*

Julian, G. H. (1878). 'Pending ordeals of democracy', *International Review*, 5, pp.734—53. *201*

Kantor, P. (1974). 'The governable city: islands of power and political parties in London', *Polity*, 7, pp.4—31. *16n, 39, 51n*

Karl, B. D. (1963). *Executive Reorganisation and Reform in the New Deal* (Cambridge, Mass., Harvard University Press). *203n*

Kasperson, R. E. (1965). 'Toward a geography of urban politics: Chicago, a case study', *Economic Geography*, 41, pp.95—107. *103n*

(1969). 'On suburbia and voting behavior', *Annals of the Association of American Geographers*, 59, pp.405—11. *103n*

Kasson, J. A. (1883). 'Municipal reform', *North American Review*, 137, pp.218—30. *196n, 202*

Katznelson, I., and Kesselman, M. (1975). *The Politics of Power* (New York, Harcourt Brace Jovanovich). *108, 200, 211*

Keith, H. S. (1928). 'Internal organisation of local authorities', *Public Administration*, 6, pp.221—32. *127n, 186n*

Keith-Lucas, B. (1952). *The English Local Government Franchise: A Short History* (Oxford, Basil Blackwell). *1, 13, 90*

  (1955). 'Local government in Parliament', *Public Administration*, 33, pp.207—10. *50n*

  (1961). *The Councils, the Press and the People* (London, CPC). *36, 80n, 101*

  (1977). 'Book review of "History of Kent County Council 1889—1974" ', *Local Government Studies*, III, 2, pp.78—9. *81*

Kennedy, D. M. (ed.) (1971). *Progressivism: The Critical Issues* (Boston, Little Brown). *193n*

Kerr, C., Dunlop, J. T., Harbison, F. H., and Myers, C.A. (1962). *Industrialism and Industrial Man* (London, Heinemann). *223n*

Kessel, J. H. (1962). 'Governmental structure and political environment: a statistical note about American cities', *American Political Science Review*, 56, pp.615—20. *209*

Kesselman, M. (1970). 'Research choices in comparative local politics', *The New Atlantis*, 1, pp.48—64. *16n*

  (1972). 'Research perspectives in comparative local politics: pitfalls and prospects', *Comparative Urban Research*, 1, pp.10—30. *217*

Key, V. O. (1949). *Southern Politics in State and Nation* (New York, Knopf). *209n*

Kidron, M. (1970). *Western Capitalism Since the War* (Harmondsworth, Penguin). *224*

Kimber, R., and Richardson, J. J. (1977). 'The integration of groups in the policy process: a case study', *Local Government Studies*, 3, pp.31—47. *49n*

King, D. N. (1973) 'Why do local authority rate poundages differ? *Public Administration*, 51, pp.165—73. *235, 247*

Kingdon, J. W. (1967). 'Politicians' beliefs about voters', *American Political Science Review*, 61, pp.137—45. *51n*

Kirlin, J. J., and Erie, S. P. (1972). 'The study of city governance and public policy making: a critical appraisal'. *Public Administration Review*, 32, pp.173—84. *217*

Klein, R. (1972). 'The politics of PPB', *Political Quarterly*, 43, pp.270—81. *141*

Knowles, R. S. B. (1971). *Modern Management in Local Government* (London, Butterworth). *114n, 118, 120, 121, 124n, 125n, 127n, 128n, 131n, 156, 254*

Kogan, M., and van der Eyken, W. (1973). *County Hall* (Harmondsworth, Penguin). *54n*

Kohn, P. D. (1976). 'The environment of decision-makers: an examination of elected representatives and decisionl premises in an English local authority' (University of Birmingham, MSocSc thesis). *53n, 54*

Kolko, G. (1967). *The Triumph of Conservatism* (Chicago, Quadrangle Books). *194n*

Labour Party (1942). *The Future of Local Government: The Labour Party's Post-War Policy* (London, Labour Party). *62*

  (1977). *Regional Authorities and Local Government Reform* (London, Labour Party). *6n*

LAMSAC (1972). *A Review of the Theory of Planned Programme Budgeting* (London, LAMSAC). *114n, 118n, 126n, 127n, 130n, 139, 142, 143n, 144*

Landau, M. (1969). 'Redundancy, Rationality and the problem of duplication and overlap', *Public Administration Review*, 29, pp.346–58. *157n, 176n*

Langrod, G. (1953). 'Local government and democracy', *Public Administration*, 31, pp.25–34. *28n*

Langton, J. (1975). 'Residential patterns in pre-industrial cities: some case studies from 17th century Britain', *Institute of British Geographers: Transactions*, 65, pp.1–27. *93*

Larkin, S. (1932). 'Co-ordination', *Public Administration*, 10, pp.58–67. *119, 126n*

Larkin, S., and Ralph, H. R. (1929). 'The essentials of an efficient promotion system', *Public Administration*, 7, pp.143–52. *119, 155*

Laski, H. J. (1935). 'The committee system in local government', in H. J. Laski, W. I. Jennings, and W. A. Robson (eds.), *A Century of Municipal Progress* (London, George Allen and Unwin), pp.82–108. *38n, 44n, 127*

—— (1950). *A Grammar of Politics*, 4th edn (London, George Allen and Unwin). *27, 30, 91n*

Lawrence, D. A. E. (1975–6). 'The role of management services in local government decision making', *London Review of Public Administration*, 8, pp.1–7. *165*

Lee, H. (1932). 'Economy in the local government services', *Public Administration*, 10, pp.44–51. *247*

Lee, J. M. (1963). *Social Leaders and Public Persons* (Oxford, Clarendon Press). *54n, 81*

Lee, J. M. Wood, B., Solomon, B. W., and Walters, P. (1974). *The Scope of Local Initiative* (London, Martin Robertson). *6n, 189n*

Lefebvre, H. (1976). *The Survival of Capitalism* (London, Allison and Busby). *224*

Leiserson, A. (1947). 'Political limitations of executive reorganisation', *American Political Science Review*, 41, pp.68–84. *160, 175*

Leonard, P. (ed.) (1975). *The Sociology of Community Action* (University of Keele; Sociological Review Monograph, no. 21). *49n*

Levermore, C. H. (1886). *The Town and City Government of New Haven* (Baltimore, Johns Hopkins Studies in Historical and Political Science). *196*

Lewis, J. (1975). 'Variations in service provision: politics at the lay–professional interface', in K. Young (ed.), *Essays on the Study of Urban Politics* (London, Macmillan), pp.52–77. *53n*

Liebenow, G. J. (1957). 'Some problems of introducing local government reforms in Tanganyika', *International Review of Administrative Sciences*, 23, p.107. *176n*

Lindblom, C. E. (1958). 'Policy analysis', *American Economic Review*, 48, pp.298–312. *179n*

—— (1959). 'The science of "muddling through"', *Public Administration Review*, 19, pp.79–88. *178*

—— (1965). *The Intelligence of Democracy* (New York, Free Press). *179n*

Lineberry, R. L., and Fowler, E. P. (1967). 'Reformism and public policies in American cities', *American Political Science Review*, 61, pp.701–16. *207*

Lineberry, R. L., and Sharkansky, I. (1974). *Urban Politics and Public Policy*, 2nd edn (New York, Harper and Row). *209, 210*

Lipman, V. D. (1949). *Local Government Areas, 1834–1945* (Oxford, Basil Blackwell). *1, 60n*

Local Government: Areas and Status of Local Authorities in England and Wales (1956). Cmd 9831 (London, HMSO). *62n*

Local Government Boundary Commission (1947). *Report for the Year 1947* (London, HMSO). *60n, 65, 66, 68*

Local Government Commission for England (1961). *Report and Proposals for the West Midlands Special Review Area* (London, HMSO). *34n, 44n, 60n, 98*

——— (1964). *Report and Proposals for the West Yorks Special Review Area* (London, HMSO). *68n*

——— (1964A). *Report and Proposals for the York and North Midlands General Review Area* (London, HMSO). *98*

Local Government Commission for Wales (1963). *Report and Proposals for Wales* (London, HMSO). *33, 62n, 64, 65, 67n, 68*

Local Government in England: Government Proposals for Reorganisation (1971). Cmnd 4584 (London, HMSO). *34n, 60n, 62n*

Local Government in England and Wales During the Period of Reconstruction (1945). Cmd 6579 (London, HMSO). *62*

Local Government Finance (1977). Cmnd 6813 (London, HMSO). *243, 247, 252*

Local Government Finance: England and Wales (1966). Cmnd 2923 (London, HMSO). *247*

Local Government: Functions of County Councils and County District Councils in England and Wales (1957). Cmnd 161 (London, HMSO). *34n*

Local Government Manpower Committee (1951). *Second Report*, Cmd 8421 (London, HMSO). *136n, 155*

Local Government in Wales (1967). Cmnd 3340 (London, HMSO). *58, 62n, 68*

Lockard, D. (1963). *The Politics of State and Local Government*, 2nd edn 1969 (New York, Macmillan). *209*

Lojkine, J. (1977). 'L'analyse Marxiste de L'Etat', *International Journal of Urban and Regional Research*, 1, pp.19–23. *215*

Lomax, K. S. (1943). 'The relationship between expenditure per head and size of population of country boroughs in England and Wales', *Journal of the Royal Statistical Society*, 106, pp.51–9. *64n*

——— (1952). 'A criterion of efficiency in local administration', *Journal of the Royal Statistical Society*, Series A. 115, pp.521–3. *64n*

Long, B. E. (1964). 'A study of the membership of selected local authorities with specific reference to social and political change' (University of Nottingham, MA thesis). *81*

Long, J. (1975). 'The impact of scale on management structures and processes'. *Local Government Studies*, 1, April, pp.45–59. *114*

Long, J., and Norton, A. (1972). *Setting up the New Authorities* (London, Charles Knight). *114n*

Long, N. E. (1967). 'Political science and the city', in L. F. Schnore and H. Fagin (eds.), *Urban Research and Policy Planning* (Beverly Hills, Sage), pp.243–62. *17*

Loomis, M. E. (1939). 'Some random comments on British local government', *Public Administrations*, 17, pp.365–72. *125n*

Lowell, A. L. (1908). *The Government of England* (2 vols., London, Macmillan). *61, 80*

Lowi, T. J. (1964). *At the Pleasure of the Mayor* (New York, Free Press). *194n, 196, 207*

(1972). 'The politics of higher education: political science as a case study', in G. J. Graham and G. W. Carey (eds.). *The Post-Behavioral Era: Perspectives on Political Science* (New York, David McKay), pp.11–36. *5n*

Luckling, R. C., Greenwood, M. J., and Howard, K. (1974). 'Corporate planning and management: a review of their application in English local government', *Town Planning Review*, 45, pp.131–45. *115n, 118n, 120, 124n, 139n, 167n*

Lukes, S. (1974). *Power: A Radical View* (London, Macmillan). *218*

Luxemburg, R. (1908). *Reform or Revolution* in M. A. Waters (ed.), *Rosa Luxemburg Speaks* (New York, Pathfinder Press, 1970). *245*

Lyden, F. J., and Miller, E. G. (eds.) (1972). *Planning-Programming-Budgeting: A Systems Approach to Management*, (2nd edn (Chicago, Markham). *139n*

Lynd, R. S. (1939). *Knowledge for What?* (Princeton, Princeton University Press). *vi, 4*

McCarthy, M. P. (1970). 'Businessmen and professionals in municipal reform: the Chicago experience 1887–1920' (Northwestern University, PhD thesis). *194*

MacColl, J. E. (1949). 'The party system in English local government', *Public Administration*, 27, pp.69–75. *36, 38n*

(1951). *Some Management Problems in Local Government* (London, British Institute of Management, Occasional Papers no. 5). *60n, 118n, 120, 124, 127n, 130n, 134n, 146, 187*

McGrath, J. C. (1925). 'The areas of local authorities as in relation to their duties', *Public Administration*, 3, pp.300–8. *63*

MacGregor, F. H. (1911). *City Government by Commission* (Madison, Bulletin of the University of Wisconsin no. 423). *199, 202, 203, 204*

McGuire, J. W. (1964). *Theories of Business Behavior* (Englewood Cliffs, NJ Prentice-Hall). *76n*

Mchinery of Government Committee (1918). *Report*, Cd 9230 (London, HMSO). *133, 154*

McKenzie, R. T. (1958). 'Parties, pressure groups and the British political process', *Political Quarterly*, 29, pp.5–16. *45*

MacKenzie, W. J. M. (1950). 'The structure of central administration', in G. Campion *et al.*, *British Government Since 1918* (London, George Allen and Unwin), pp.56–84. *173, 174, 175n*

(1951). 'The conventions of local government', *Public Administration*, 29, pp.345–56. *50n, 147n*

(1953). 'Committees in administration', *Public Administration*, 31, pp. 235–44. *147n*

(1954). 'Local government in parliament', *Public Administration*, 32, pp.409–23. *50n*

(1961). *Theories of Local Government*, Greater London Papers no. 2 (London, London School of Economics and Political Science). *4, 27, 28, 234*

MacKenzie, W. J. M., and Grove, J. W. (1957). *Central Administration in Britain* (London, Longmans). *175*

McKinsey, J. O. (1922). *Budgetary Control* (New York, Ronald Press). *139n*

McKinsey and Co. Inc. (1969). *A New Management System for the Liverpool Corporation* (London, McKinsey). *257*
    (1971). *Hull – A Turning Point* (London, McKinsey). *120, 125n, 127n, 129, 131n, 151*
Mackintosh, J. P. (1968). *The Devolution of Power* (Harmondsworth, Penguin). *34n, 41n, 43, 68n*
    (1968A). *The British Cabinet*, 2nd edn (London, Methuen). *133*
Macpherson, C. B. (1966). *The Real World of Democracy* (Oxford, Clarendon Press). *214, 226*
Maddick, H. (1963). *Democracy, Decentralisation and Development* (Bombay, Asia Publishing House). *28n, 30n, 60n, 65*
Maddick, H., and Pritchard, E. P. (1958). 'The conventions of local authorities in the West Midlands: Part I. County borough councils', *Public Administration*, 36, pp.145–55. *121, 127, 130n*
    (1959). 'The conventions of local authorities in the West Midlands: Part II. District councils', *Public Administration*, 37, pp.135–43
Mansfield, H. C. (1969). 'Federal executive reorganisation: 30 years of experience', *Public Administration Review*, 29, pp.332–45. *175n, 176*
March, J. G., and Simon, H. A. (1958). *Organisations* (New York, Wiley). *152, 160n, 161*
Marini, F. (ed.) (1971). *Toward a New Public Administration* (Scranton, Chandler). *162n*
Markusen, A. R. (1976). 'Class and urban social expenditures; a local theory of the state', *Kapitalstate*, 4/5, pp.50–65. *110, 111, 231*
Marshall, A. H. (1960). *Financial Administration in Local Government* (London, George Allen and Unwin). *32*
    (1965). *Local Government in the Modern World* (London, University of London, Athlone Press). *120, 131n, 132n, 133n, 187, 254, 258*
Marshall, D. (1973). *Industrial England, 1776–1851* (London, Routledge and Kegan Paul). *87, 94*
Marshall, D. R. (1972). 'Metropolitan government: views of minorities', in L. Wingo (ed.), *The Governance of Metropolitan Regions: Minority Perspectives* (Baltimore, Johns Hopkins University Press). pp.9–30. *21, 108, 109*
Martin, C. (1960). 'In praise of political apathy', *The Listener*, 63, pp.1079–80. *43n*
Mason, T. (1977). 'Community action and the local authority: a study n the incorporation of protest' (Centre for Environmental Studies, Urban Change and Conflict Conference, York). *49n*
Massie, J. L. (1965). 'Management theory', in J. G. March (ed.). *Handbook of Organisations* (Chicago, Rand McNally), pp.387–422. *153, 154, 159, 160n*
Masterman, C. F. (1910). *The Condition of England*, 4th edn (London, Methuen). *94*
Matthews, N. (1895). *The City Government of Boston* (Boston, Rockwell and Churchill). *196, 202*
Mattick, P. (1971). *Marx to Keynes* (London, Merlin). *228*
Maud, J. (1932). *Local Government in Modern England* (London, Thornton, Butterworth). *35, 40, 119, 126, 127, 135*
Maud, J., and Finer, S. E. (1960). *Local Government in England and Wales* (London, Oxford University Press). *35, 40*

Maynard, A. K. and King, D. N. (1974). *Rates or Prices?* (London, IEA). *247*

Meghen, P. J. (1964). 'Why local government?', *Administration (Dublin)*, 12, pp.190—206. *28*

Melanson, P. H. (1972). 'The political science profession, political knowledge and public policy', *Politics and Society*, 2, pp.489ff. *7n*

Mellors, C. (1974). 'Local government in Parliament — 20 years on', *Public Administration*, 52, pp.223—9. *50n*

Meltsner, A. J. (1972). 'Political feasibility and policy analysis', *Public Administration Review*, 32, pp.859—67. *257*

Merewitz, L., and Sosnick, S. H. (1971). *The Budget's New Clothes: A Critique of Planning-Programming-Budgeting and Benefit Cost Analysis* (Chicago, Markham). *139n, 142, 177*

Meriam, L., and Schmeckebier, L. F. (1939). *Reorganisation of the National Government: What Does it Involve?* (Washington, Brookings). *175*

Merkle, J. A. (1968). 'The Taylor strategy: organisational innovation and class structure', *Berkeley Journal of Sociology*, 8, pp.59—81. *158n*

Meynaud, J. (ed.) (1963). *Social Change and Economic Development* (Paris, UNESCO). *4*

Miliband, R. (1969). *The State in Capitalist Society* (London, Weidenfeld and Nicolson). *214, 218*

(1970). 'The capitalist state: reply to Nicos Poulantzas', *New Left Review*, 59, pp.53—60. *220, 221*

(1973). 'Poulantzas and the capitalist state', *New Left Review*, 82, pp. 82—92. *220*

(1977). *Marxism and Politics* (London, Oxford University Press). *215*

Mill, J. S. (1861). 'Considerations on Representative Government', in *Utilitarianism, Liberty and Representative Government* (London, Everyman's Library, 1964). *24n, 27n, 80*

Miller, D. (1970). *International Community Power Structures* (Bloomington, Indiana University Press). *16n, 48n*

Miller, E. G. (1968). 'Implementing PPBS: Problems and prospects', *Public Administration Review*, 28, pp.467—8. *176n*

Millington, H. A. (1928). 'Internal organisation of local authorities', *Public Administration*, 6, pp.233—40. *127n*

Mills, C. Wright (1967). *Power, Politics and People: The Collected Essays of C. Wright Mills*, I. L. Horowitz (ed.) (New York, Oxford University Press). *4, 12*

(1970). *The Sociological Imagination* (Harmondsworth, Penguin). *5, 10*

Millward, R. E. (1968). 'PPBS: problems of implementation', *Journal of the American Institute of Planners*, 34, pp.88—94. *176n*

Ministry of Health (1924). *Fifth Annual Report: 1923—4*, Cmd 2218 (London, HMSO). *131n*

(1928). *Ninth Annual Report: 1927—8*, Cmd 3185 (London, HMSO). *139n*

(1932). *Thirteenth Annual Report: 1931—2*, Cmd 4113 (London, HMSO). *246*

(1934). Departmental Committee. *Qualifications, Recruitment, Training and Promotion of Local Government Officers* (London, HMSO). *155*

(1939). Committee of Enquiry into the Anti-Tuberculosis Service in Wales and Monmouthshire, *Report* (London, HMSO). *63*

Ministry of Housing and Local Government (1965). *The Report of the Bognor Regis Enquiry* (London, HMSO). *32*

Minshull, F. C. (1929). 'The departmental organisation of the work of local authorities', *Public Administration*, 7, pp.296—303. *128n, 129n*

Minshull, H. O. (1929). 'The position and functions of committees in local administration', *Public Administration*, 7, pp.278—86

Mitchell, G. D. (1951). 'The parish council and the local community', *Public Administration*, 29, pp.393—401. *81, 88n*

Mohr, L. B. (1969). 'Determinants of innovation in organisations', *American Political Science Review*, 63, pp.111—26. *183n*

Monahan, J. (1976). 'Up against the planners in Covent Garden', in P. Hain (ed.), *Community Politics* (London, John Calder), pp.175—92. *215*

Money, W. J. (1973). 'The need to sustain a viable system of local democracy', *Urban Studies*, 10, pp.319—33. *23n, 28, 34n*

Moodie, G. C. (1971). *The Government of Great Britain*, 3rd edn (London, Methuen). *133*

Moorhouse, H., Wilson, M., and Chamberlain, C. (1972). 'Rent strikes — direct action and the working class', in R. Miliband and J. Saville (eds.), *The Socialist Register, 1972* (London, Merlin), pp.135—56. *45n*

Moorhouse, H. F. (1973). 'The political incorporation of the British working class: an interpretation', *Sociology*, 7, pp.341—59. *90*

Morrell, J. B., and Watson, A. G. (eds) (1928). *How York Governs Itself* (London, George Allen and Unwin). *120, 126n*

Morris, D. S., and Newton, K. (1970). 'Profile of a local political elite: businessmen as community decision-makers in Birmingham, 1838—1966', *The New Atlantis*, no. 2, pp.111—23. *81n, 83, 91, 97, 104*

 (1971). 'Marginal wards and social class', *British Journal of Political Science*, 1, pp.503—7. *39n*

Morris, J. H. (1960). *Local Government Areas* (London, Shaw). *33, 64, 125n*

Morris-Jones, W. H. (1954). 'In defence of apathy: some doubts on the duty to vote', *Political Studies*, 2, pp.25—37. *43n*

Morrison, H. (1931). *How Greater London is Governed* (London, Lovat Dickson and Thompson). *37*

Morton, J. (1970). *The Best Laid Schemes? A Cool Look at Local Government Reform* (London, Charles Knight). *2, 65, 71*

Mosher, F. (1954). *Program-Budgeting: Theory and Practice with Particular Reference to the US Department of the Army* (New York, American Book—Stratford Press). *139n*

 (1965). 'Some notes on reorganisations in public agencies', in R. C. Martin (ed.), *Public Administration and Democracy* (Syracuse, Syracuse University Press), pp.129—50. *114*

 (1967). 'Communications', *Public Administration Review*, 27, pp.67—71. *115n*

 (1967A). *Governmental Reorganisations: Cases and Commentary* (Indianapolis, Bobbs-Merrill). *175n*

 (1969). 'Limitations and problems of PPBS in the states', *Public Administration Review*, 29, pp.160—7. *177*

Moulin, L. (1954). 'Local self-government as a basis for democracy: a further comment', *Public Administration*, 32, pp.433—7. *28n*

Mouzelis, N. P. (1975). *Organisation and Bureaucracy* (London, Routledge and Kegan Paul). *153*

Mowry, G. E. (1951). *The California Progressives* (Berkeley, University of California Press). *194n*

Moynihan, D. P. (1970). 'Policy vs program in the 70's', *Public Interest*, 20, pp.90—100. *177*

Muchnick, D. M. (1970). *Urban Renewal in Liverpool* (London, Bell). *54n*

Mueller, C. (1973). *The Politics of Communication* (New York, Oxford University Press). *8*

Muir, R. (1907). *A History of Liverpool* (Liverpool, Liverpool University Press). *36n*

Müller, W., and Neusüss, C. (1975). 'The illusion of state socialism', *Telos*, 25, pp.13–90. *225*

'Municipal Management' (1949). *Public Administration*, 27, pp.241–2. *129n, 130n*

Munro, W. B. (1913). *The Government of American Cities* (New York, Macmillan). *195, 197, 203, 205, 208, 213*

(1926). 4th edn of Munro, 1913. *191, 192, 202*

Mushkin, S. J. (1969). 'PPB in cities', *Public Administration Review*, 29, pp.167–78. *140*

Myrdal, G. (1957). *Economic Theory and Underdeveloped Regions* (London, Duckworths). *11*

NALGO Reconstruction Committee (1945). *Report on Relations Between Local Government and the Community* (London, NALGO). *40n, 44n, 45, 62n*

National Advisory Council on Civil Disorders (1967). *Report* (Washington, DC, Government Printing Office). *200n*

National Board for Prices and Incomes (1967). *The Pay and Conditions of Manual Workers in Local Authorities, the NHS, Gas and Water Supply*, Report no. 29, Cmnd 3230 (London, HMSO). *134n*

National Municipal League (1935). *Council-Manager Cities During the Depression* (New York, NML). *206*

(1939). *Forms of Municipal Government: How Have They Worked* (New York, NML). *206*

(1974). *Questions and Answers About the Council-Manager Plan* (New York, NML). *192*

Newton, K. (1969). 'City politics in Britain and the United States', *Political Studies*, 17, pp.208–18. *16n*

(1972). 'Turnout and marginality in local elections', *British Journal of Political Science*, 2, pp.251–5. *39n*

(1972A). 'Rejoinder', *British Journal of Political Science*, 2, pp.515–16. *39n*

(1975). 'Community politics and decision-making: the American experience and its lessons', in K. Young (ed.), *Essays on the Study of Urban Politics* (London, Macmillan), pp.1–24. *16n*

(1976). *Second City Politics* (Oxford, Clarendon Press). *13, 39, 40n, 45–52 passim, 54, 149*

Newton, K., and Morris, D. S. (1975). 'British interest group theory reexamined: the politics of 4,000 voluntary organisations in a British city', *Comparative Politics*, 7, pp.577–95. *48n*

Newton, R. (1968). *Victorian Exeter* (Leicester, Leicester University Press). *36n, 79, 82, 95*

New Towns Committee (1946). *Final Report*, Cmd 6876 (London, HMSO). *134n*

Nicholson, R. J., and Topham, N. (1972). 'Investment decisions and the size of local authorities', *Policy and Politics*, 1, pp.23–44. *70n*

Novick, D. (1954). *Efficiency and Economy in Government Through New Budgetary and Accounting Procedures* (Santa Monica, The Rand Corporation). *139n*

(1973). *Current Practice in Program Budgeting (PPBS)* (London, Heinemann). *140n*

Nye, R. B. (1959). *Midwestern Progressive Politics* (London, Angus and Robertson). *200n*

O'Connor, J. (1973). *The Fiscal Crisis of the State* (New York, St Martin's Press). *225n, 227n, 232, 256*

Offe, C. (1972). 'Advanced capitalism and the welfare state', *Politics and Society*, 2, pp.479—88. *224*

Oliver, F. R., and Stanyer, J. (1969). 'Some aspects of the financial behaviour of county boroughs', *Public Administration*, 47, pp.169—84. *235*

O'Malley, J. (1977). *The Politics of Community Action* (Nottingham, Spokesman). *48n*

Ostrogorski, M. (1902). *Democracy and the Organisation of Political Parties* (2 vols., London, Macmillan). *80, 91*

Overly, D. H. (1967). 'Decision making in city government: a proposal', *Urban Affairs Quarterly*, 3, pp.41—53. *140*

P.A. Management Consultants (1969). *The London Borough of Brent: Management in the 1970s* (London, P.A.). *123, 151, 156n*

P-E Consulting Group (1970). Report no. 1. *Borough of Swindon: Organisation and Staffing* (Egham, Surrey). *156*

Page, C. H. (1946—7). 'Bureaucracy's other face', *Social Forces*, 25, pp.88—94. *159*

Page, H. R. (1936). *Coordination and Planning in the Local Authority* (Manchester, Manchester University Press). *126, 127, 128n, 130n, 134n, 135, 155, 187n, 257n*

Pahl, R. (1970). *Patterns of Urban Life* (London, Longmans). *49n*

Painter, M. (1969). 'Decision making and change in a local council: the case of "overspill" development in Newmarket' (University of Sussex, MA thesis). *51n, 218*

Panter-Brick, K. (1953). 'Local government and democracy — a rejoinder', *Public Administration*, 31, pp.344—8. *28n*

(1954). 'Local self-government as a basis for democracy: a rejoinder', *Public Administration*, 32, pp.438—40. *28n*

Parkin, F. (1974). 'Strategies of social closure in class formation', in F. Parkin, *The Social Analysis of Class Structure* (London, Tavistock), pp.1—18. *49n*

Parkman, F. (1878). 'The failure of universal suffrage', *North American Review*, 127, pp.1—20. *196*

Parris, H. (1969). 'Local government research in the universities', *Studies in Comparative Local Government*, 3, pp.45—54. *258*

Patton, C. W. (1940). *The Battle for Municipal Reform* (Washington, American Council on Public Affairs). *191, 202*

Peacock, A. T., and Wiseman, J. (1961). *The Growth of Public Expenditure in the United Kingdom* (London, Oxford University Press). *223n, 232n*

Pelling, H. (1967). *Social Geography of British Elections* (London, Macmillan). *103n*

Perry, P. J. (1975). *A Geography of Nineteenth Century Britain* (London, Batsford). *79*

Peschek, D., and Brand, J. (1966). *Policies and Politics in Secondary Education*, Greater London Papers no. 11 (London, London School of Economics and Political Science). *54n*

Pfiffner, J. M., and Sherwood, F. P. (1960). *Administrative Organisation* (Englewood Cliffs, N. J. Prentice-Hall). *158*

Phillips, J. C. (1935). *Operation of the Council-Manager Plan of Government in Oklahoma Cities* (Philadelphia). *194n*

Phillips, J. R. (1882). 'Local Taxation in England and Wales', in J. W. Probyn (ed.), *Local Government and Taxation in the UK* (London, Cassell, Petter, Galpin), pp.465—506. *233*

Picken, R. M. F. (1934). 'On the report of the departmental committee on qualifications, recruitment, training and promotion of local government officers', *Public Administration*, 12, pp.222—8. *127n*

Pickvance, C. G. (1977). 'Marxist approaches to the study of urban politics: divergencies among some recent French studies', *International Journal or Urban and Regional Research*, 1, pp.219—55. *231*

Pile, W. (1974). 'Corporate planning for education in the Department of Education and Science', *Public Administration*, 52, pp.13—25. *141n*

Pimlott, B. (1972). 'Does local party organisation matter?', *British Journal of Political Science*, 2, pp.381—3. *39n*

  (1973). 'Local party organisation: turnout and marginality', *British Journal of Political Science*, 3, pp.252—5. *39n*

Pitt, J. (1977). *Centrification in Islington* (London, Barnsbury Peoples Forum). *250*

Piven, F. P., and Cloward, R. A. (1967). 'Black control of cities: heading it of by metropolitan government', *New Republic*, 30 September and 7 October. *109*

  (1972). *Regulating the Poor* (London, Tavistock). *225*

Planning Advisory Group (1965). *The Future of Development Plans* (London, HMSO). *255*

Platt, C. (1976). *The English Medieval Town* (London, Secker and Warburg). *92*

Plummer, D. (1969). 'GLC introduces PPBS', *Studies in Comparative Local Government*, 3, pp.39—40. *141*

Polenberg, R. (1966). *Reorganising Roosevelt's Government: The Controversy Over Executive Reorganisation, 1936—1939* (Cambridge, Mass., Harvard University Press). *175*

Policy Advisory Committee (1954). 'Coventry and organisation and methods', *Public Administration*, 32, pp.52—94. *120, 125n, 126, 127n, 129*

Policy for the Inner Cities (1977). Cmnd 6845 (London, HMSO). *239, 249*

Political and Economic Planning (1947). 'Active democracy — a local election', *Planning*, 261, 24 January, pp.1—20. *26, 41n, 52n, 82n*

  (1948). 'Local elections: How many vote?', *Planning*, 291, 29 November, pp.163—78. *39n*

  (1955). 'Voting for local councils', *Planning*, 379, 9 May, pp.49—64. *39n, 43n*

Pollard, S. (1959). *A History of Labour in Sheffield* (Liverpool, Liverpool University Press). *83n*

Poulantzas, N. (1969). 'The problem of the capitalist state', *New Left Review*, 58, pp.67—78. *218, 219*

  (1973). *Political Power and Social Classes* (London, NLB). *215, 216, 219*

  (1975). *Classes in Contemporary Capitalism* (London, NLB). *216*

  (1976). 'The capitalist state: a reply to Miliband and Laelau', *New Left Review*, 95, pp.63—83. *220*

Poulantzas, N. M. (1960). 'Centralization and decentralization in the local government', *Revue Hellenique de Droit International*, 13, pp.254—88. *63n*

Powell, B. M. (1958). 'A study of the change in social origins, political affiliations and length of service of members of the Leeds city council, 1888–1953' (University of Leeds, MA thesis). *82*

Pratten, C., Dean, R. M., and Silbertson, A. (1965). *The Economics of Large-Scale Production in British Industry: An Introductory Study* (Cambridge, Cambridge University Press). *74n, 113n*

Prescott, J. R. V. (1972). *Political Geography* (London, Methuen). *103n*

Pressman, J. L., and Wildavsky, A. (1973). *Implementation* (Berkeley, University of California Press). *113, 182n*

Price, D. K. (1941). 'The promotion of the city manager plan', *Public Opinion Quarterly*, 5, pp.563–78. *195*

Prime Minister's Committee on Local Government Rules of Conduct (1974). *Report*, Cmnd 5236 (London, HMSO). *37, 237*

Pritchard, R. M. (1976). *Housing and the Spatial Structure of the City* (Cambridge, Cambridge University Press). *93, 94*

Proposals for Reform of Local Government and in the Financial Relations Between the Exchequer and Local Authorities (1928) Cmd 3134 (London, HMSO). *246*

Public Expenditure to 1979–80 (1976). Cmnd 6393 (London, HMSO). *223n, 231*

Rae, D. W. (1971). *The Political Consequences of Electoral Laws*, Rev. edn (New Haven, Yale University Press). *13*

Raine, W. (1928). 'Internal organisation of local authorities', *Public Administration*, 6, pp.241–50. *126n*

Ranney, A. (1962). *The Doctrine of Responsible Party Government* (Urbana, University of Illinois Press). *38n*

Rathbone, E. (1905). *William Rathbone* (London, Macmillan). *93*

Redcliffe-Maud, Lord (1967). 'Local governors at work: could they do better?', *Public Administration*, 45, pp.347–52. *2, 3, 4, 124, 133n, 185*

Redcliffe-Maud, Lord, and Wood, B. (1974). *English Local Government Reformed* (London, Oxford University Press). *6n, 30, 31, 39n, 41n, 44n, 62n, 72*

Redlich, J. (1903). *Local Government in England*, edited and with additions by F. W. Hirst (2 vols., London, Macmillan). *1, 21, 29, 31, 41, 60, 61, 91, 127n*

Reed, T. H. (1934). *Municipal Government in the United States*, rev. edn (New York, D. Appleton-Century Co.). *191, 192*

Rees, A. (1968). 'Democracy in local government', in B. Lapping and G. Radice (eds.), *More Power to the People* (London, Longmans), pp. 119–42. *14, 40n, 44, 47, 50, 60n*

Rees, A., and Smith, T. (1964). *Town Councillors: A Study of Barking* (London, Acton Society Trust). *52n, 105*

Rees, I. B. (1969). 'Local government in Switzerland', *Public Administration*, 47, pp.421–9. *64*

    (1971). *Government by Community* (London, Charles Knight). *3n, 60, 70, 72, 75*

Reform of Local Government in England (1970). Cmnd 4276 (London, HMSO). *23*

Reid, J., and Richmond, S. (1974). *The Democratic Charade Exposed* (Croydon, Suburban Press). *53n*

Rein, M. (1969). 'Social planning: the search for legitimacy', *Journal of the American Institute of Planners*, 35, pp.233–44. *255*

Report of the Anglo-American Conference Held at Ditchley Park, Oxford-shire (1969). *Experiments in Social Policy and Administration*. *239*

Rex, J., and Moore, R. (1967). *Race, Community and Conflit* (London, Oxford University Press). *96n*

Reynolds, G. W. (1971). *The Councillor's Work* (London, Charles Knight). *32*

Rhodes, G. (1970). *The Government of London: the Struggle for Reform* (London, Weidenfeld and Nicolson). *100*

(ed.) (1972). *The New Government of London: The First Five Years* (London, Weidenfeld and Nicolson). *6n, 104n*

Rhodes, R. A. W. (1973). 'The politics of policy', *Local Government Chronicle*, 28 September, pp.1026—7. *180*

(1975). 'The lost world of British local politics', *Local Government Studies*, 1, pp.39—59. *7, 53*

(1976). *Current Developments in the Study of Public Administration in the United States* (University of Birmingham, Institute of Local Government Studies). *161n*

Richards, A. R. (1954). 'Local government research; a partial evaluation', *Public Administration Review*, 14, pp.271—7. *17*

Richards, P. G. (1968). *The New Local Government System* (London, George Allen and Unwin). *27, 38n, 40n, 45n, 46*

(1973). *The Reformed Local Government System* (London, George Allen and Unwin). *3, 59, 65, 133, 147n*

(1975), 2nd edn of Richards, 1973. *37, 42, 54n, 61*

Richardson, H. W. (1972). *Regional Economics* (London, Weidenfeld and Nicolson). *106*

(1973). *The Economics of Urban Size* (Westmead, Farnborough, Saxon House). *70n, 74, 75n*

Ridley, F. F. (1972). 'Public administration: cause for discontent', *Public Administration*, 50, pp.65—77. *161n*

Rightor, C. E. (1919). *City Manager in Dayton* (New York, Macmillan). *195, 197n, 202, 207n, 209*

RIPA Conference (1967). *Management of Local Government: the Maud Report* (London, RIPA). *155, 188, 254*

(1973). *Creating the New Local Government* (London, RIPA). *155*

Ripley, B. J. (1970). *Administration in Local Authorities* (London, Butter-worths). *114n, 120, 124n, 125n, 126, 128, 129, 157, 165, 257n*

Rivlin, A. M. (1971). *Systematic Thinking for Social Action* (Washington, Brookings). *143*

Roberts, H. (1951). 'The domestic procedure of the LCC', *Public Administration*, 29, pp.113—25. *129n*

(1954). 'Common services in local government', *Public Administration*, 32, pp.264—73. *128*

Roberts, J. R. H. (1929). 'The professional expert and administrative control', *Public Administration*, 7, pp.247—59. *125n, 127n*

Robinson, E. A. G. (1931). *The Structure of Competitive Industry* (London, Nisbet). *113n*

Robson, W. A. (1931). *The Development of Local Government* (London, George Allen and Unwin). *75*

(1937). 'London and the LCC election', *Political Quarterly*, 8, pp.194—203. *38n*

(1945). 'Local government in occupied Germany', *Political Quarterly*, 16, pp.277—87. *60n*

(1948). *The Government and Misgovernment of London*, 2nd edn (London, George Allen and Unwin). *65*

(1954). 3rd edn of Robson, 1931. *62n, 64, 66*

(1961). 'The reform of London government', *Public Administration*, 39, pp.59—71. *27n, 67n*

(1966). *Local Government in Crisis* (London, George Allen and Unwin). *27n, 62n*

(1972). 'The great city of today', in W. A. Robson and D. E. Regan (eds.), *Great Cities of the World*, 3rd edn (2 vols., London, George Allen and Unwin), vol. 1, pp.23—127. *34n, 35, 36n, 42n, 65, 75n, 96*

Rogers, J. M. (1968). *Management and Management Techniques with Particular Reference to Local Government* (London, IMTA). *130n, 136n*

Roosevelt, T. (1885). 'Phases of state legislation', *Century*, 7, pp.820ff. *198*

Rose, B. (1970). *England Looks at Maud* (London, Justice of the Peace Ltd)

Rose, K. E. (1969). *Towards Multi-Purpose Budgeting in Local Government* (London, IMTA). *115, 142, 253*

(1970). 'Planning and PPBS with particular reference to local government', *Environment and Planning*, 2, pp.203—10. *118, 139, 143*

Rothwell, J. H. (1928). 'Efficiency as an alternative to control', *Public Administration*, 6, pp.106—111. *252*

Rowan, P. (1977). 'Beleaguered by Bains and bureaucrats', and 'When did you last see your chief education officer?' *The Times Higher Educational Supplement*, 18 March and 25 March. *173n*

Rowbottom, R., Hey, A., and Bliss, D. (1974). *Social Services Departments* (London, Heinemann). *182*

Rowley, G. (1971). 'The GLC elections of 1964 and 1967: a study in electoral geography', *Transactions: Institute of British Geographers*, 53, pp. 117—31. *103n*

Royal Commission on the Constitution (1973). Research Papers 7, 'Devolution and other aspects of government: an attitudes survey' (London, HMSO). *237*

Royal Commission on the Distribution of the Industrial Population (1940). Cmd 6153 (London, HMSO). *102n*

Royal Commission on Local Government (1925). *First Report*, Cmd 2506 (London, HMSO). *63n*

(1928). *Second Report*, Cmd 3213 (London, HMSO). *63n*

(1929). *Final Report*, Cmd 3436 (London, HMSO). *63n, 127n, 129, 131n, 139n*

Royal Commission on Local Government in England (1969). *Short Version*, Cmnd 4039; vol. 1, *Report*, Cmnd 4040; vol. 2, *Memorandum of Dissent by Mr Derek Senior*, Cmnd 4040—I; vol. 3, *Research Appendices*, Cmnd 4040—II; Research Study 1, *Local Government in South East England*; Research Study 2, *Lessons of the London Government Reforms*; Research Study 3, *Economies of Scale in Local Government Services*; Research Study 4, *Performance and the Size of Local Education Authorities*; Research Study 5, *Local Authority Services and the Characteristics of Administrative Areas*; Research Study 7, *Aspects of Administration in a Large Authority*; Research Study 9, *Community Attitudes Survey: England*; Research Study 10, *Administration in a Large Local Authority: A Comparison with Other County Boroughs*; *Written Evidence of Commercial, Industrial and Political Organisations*; *Written Evidence of the Ministry of Housing and Local Government*; *Written Evidence of H. M. Treasury* (London, HMSO). *2, 6n, 27n,*

30n, 31, 32, 34, 39, 40, 44, 45, 46, 59, 61n, 62n, 65–72 passim, 74n, 75n, 79, 98n, 101n, 102n, 114n, 132, 133n, 137, 160, 186, 190n, 237, 241, 243, 247

Royal Commission on Local Government in Greater London (1960). *Report*; Cmnd 1164 (London, HMSO). *15, 23n, 27, 28, 31, 33, 35, 44, 67, 70, 102n*

Royal Commission on Local Government in Scotland (1969). *Report*, Cmnd 4150; *Written Evidence* 9 (Edinburgh, HMSO). *80n, 98n, 241n*

Royal Commission on London Government (1923). *Report*, Cmd 1830 (London, HMSO). *61n, 102n*

Royal Commission on the Police (1962). *Final Report*, Cmnd 1728 (London, HMSO). *62n*

Royal Commission on Standards in Public Life (1976). *Report*, Cmnd 6524 (London, HMSO). *237*

Rubinstein, W. D. (1977). 'Wealth, elites and the class structure of modern Britain', *Past and Present*, 76, pp.99–126. *83n, 91*

Rudd, N. B. (1933). 'Some aspects of coordination', *Public Administration*, 11, pp.209–14. *126n, 130n*

Salisbury, R., and Black, G. (1963). 'Class and party in non-partisan elections: the case of Des Moines', *American Political Science Review*, 57, pp. 584–92. *209n*

Sancton, A. (1976). 'British socialist theories of the division of power by area', *Political Studies*, 24, pp.158–70. *4, 28*

Saran, R. (1973). *Policy Making in Secondary Education: A Case Study* (Oxford, Clarendon Press). *54n*

Saunders, P. (1975). 'They make the rules: political routines and the generation of political bias', *Policy and Politics*, 4, pp.31–58. *49, 50*

(1975A). 'Who runs Croydon?' (University of London, PhD thesis). *83*

(1978). 'Urban managers, community power and the "local state"', Paper delivered at the Institute of Local Government Policy Studies Conference, Birmingham University. *83*

Saville, J. (1975). 'The welfare state: an historical approach', in E. Butterworth and R. Holman (eds.), *Social Welfare in Modern Britain* (London, Fontana), pp.56–69. *225*

Savitch, H. V., and Adler, M. (1974). *Decentralisation at the Grass Roots: Political Innovation in New York and London* (Beverly Hills, Sage). *16n*

Sayre, W. S., and Polsby, N. W. (1965), 'American political science and the study of urbanisation', in P. M. Hauser and L. F. Schnore (eds.), *The Study of Urbanisation* (New York, Wiley), pp.115–56. *17, 193*

Schaffer, B. B. (1973). *The Administrative Factor* (London, Frank Cass). *160, 173*

(1976). 'The rise and fall of the Royal Commission on Australian Government Administration: reflections from participation in administrative reform', Paper delivered to the European Group of Public Administration, Tampere, Finland. *160, 161, 183n*

Schattschneider, E. E. (1960). *The Semi-Sovereign People* (New York, Holt). *49*

Schick, A. (1966). 'The road to PPB; the stages of budget reform', *Public Administration Review*, 26, pp.243–58. *139n*

(1969). 'Systems politics and systems budgeting', *Public Administration Review*, 29, pp.137–51. *142*

(1973). 'A death in the bureaucracy: the demise of Federal PPB', *Public Administration Review*, 33, pp.146–56. *176, 178*

Schiesl, M. J. (1972). 'The politics of efficiency' (SUNY Buffalo, PhD thesis). *194n, 198, 203*

Schiff, A. L. (1966). 'Innovation and Administrative decision making: the conservation of land resources', *Administrative Science Quarterly*, 11, pp.1—30. *183n*

Schnore, L. F., and Alford, R. R. (1963). 'Forms of government and socio-economic characteristics of suburbs', *Administrative Science Quarterly*, 8, pp.1—17. *209*

Schultze, C. L. (1968). *The Politics and Economics of Public Spending* (Washington, Brookings). *139n, 143*

Scott, J. C. (1969). 'Corruption, machine politics and political change', *American Political Science Review*, 63, pp.1142—58. *200*

Scottish Development Department (1974). *Community Councils* (Edinburgh, HMSO). *34n*

Seidman, D. R. (1970). 'PPB in HEW: Some management issues', *Journal of the American Institute of Planners*, 36, pp.168—78

Seidman, H. (1975). *Politics, Position and Power: the Dynamics of Federal Organisation*, 2nd edn (New York, Oxford University Press). *177n*

Self, P. J. O. (1961). *Cities in Flood*, 2nd edn (London, Faber). *79*

    (1962). 'The Herbert Report and the values of local government', *Political Studies*, 10, pp.146—62. *3, 27n, 65*

    (1971). 'Elected representatives and management in local government: an alternative analysis', *Public Administration*, 49, pp.269—77. *4, 71, 190n*

    (1972). *Administrative Theories and Politics* (London, George Allen and Unwin). *151n, 154, 162*

Semmler, W. (1977). 'Private production and the public sector', Paper delivered at the CSE Conference, Bradford. *227n*

Shani, M. (1976). 'Will a reduction in the number of ministries lead to better government?', *Israel Annual of Public Administration and Public Policy*, 15, pp.15—34. *154n, 176n*

Shapero, A. (1969). 'Planning, programming, budgeting systems (PPBS)', *Local Government Finance*, April, pp.154—9. *141, 143n*

Sharkansky, I. (1968). 'Agency requests, gubernatorial support and budget success in state legislatures', *American Political Science Review*, 62, pp.1220—31. *179n*

Sharp, E. (1962). 'The future of local government', *Public Administration*, 40, pp.375—86. *60, 62n, 63, 68n, 102, 125n, 186n*

    (1969). *The Ministry of Housing and Local Government* (London, George Allen and Unwin). *1, 2, 65*

Sharpe, L. J. (1960). 'The Politics of local government in Greater London', *Public Administration*, 38, pp.157—72. *39n, 43n*

    (1962). 'Elected representatives in local government', *British Journal of Sociology*, 13, pp.189—209. *14, 81n*

    (1962A). *A Metropolis Votes*, Greater London Papers no. 8 (London, London School of Economics and Political Science). *40n, 41, 81n*

(1965). *Why Local Democracy?* Fabian Tract no. 361 (London, Fabian Society). *1, 28, 32, 62n, 65, 67, 68*

    (1966). 'Leadership and representation in local government', *Political Quarterly*, 37, pp.149—58. *96n*

    (1967). 'In defence of local politics', in L. J. Sharpe (ed.), *Voting in Cities* (London, Macmillan), pp.1—14. *45*

(1970). 'Theories and values of local government', *Political Studies*, 18, pp.153—74. *4, 26n, 28, 32*

(forthcoming). 'Reforming the grass roots: an alternative analysis', in D. Butler (ed.), *Politics, Administration and Policy* (London, Macmillan). *6n*

Shaw, A. (1907). *Political Problems of American Development* (New York, Columbia University Press). *202*

Shelley, A. N. C. (1939). *The Councillor* (London, Nelson). *31*

Shepherd, J., Westaway, J., and Lee, T. (1974). *A Social Atlas of London* (Oxford, Clarendon Press). *103n*

Shepherd, W. G. (1967—8). 'What does the survival technique show about economies of scale?' *Southern Economic Journal*, 34, pp.113—22. *74n*

Sherbenou, E. L. (1961). 'Class participation and the council—manager plan', *Public Administration Review*, 21, pp.131—5. *209*

Sherman, A. (1970). *Local Government Reorganisation and Industry* (London, Aims of Industry). *73, 99*

(1974). *Bigger Will Mean Dearer* (London, Aims of Industry)

Sills, P. (1976). 'Voluntary initiative and statutory reaction: a study in the political control of social reform', *Community Development Journal*, 11, pp.120—5. *49*

Simey, M. B. (1951). *Charitable Effort in Liverpool in the Nineteenth Century* (Liverpool, Liverpool University Press). *87, 93, 95*

Simmie, J. M. (1974). *Citizens in Conflict* (London, Hutchinson). *5*

Simon, E. D. (1926). *A City Council From Within* (London, Longmans and Green). *120, 127, 130n, 134, 188*

(1928). 'Some problems of local government', *Public Administration*, 6, pp.199—203. *37*

(1932). 'The practical working of city government in England', *Public Administration*, 10, pp.278—83. *135, 147n, 187*

(1938). *A Century of City Government: Manchester 1838—1938* (London, George Allen and Unwin). *97, 244*

Simon, H. A. (1957). *Administrative Behavior*, 2nd edn (New York, Free Press). *158*

Sjoberg, J. (1960). *The Pre-Industrial City: Past and Present* (Glencoe, Ill., Free Press). *93*

Skitt, J. (ed.) (1975). *Practical Corporate Planning in Local Government* (Leighton Buzzard, Leonard Hill Books). *141, 142, 144, 151, 257n*

Smallwood, F. (1965). *Greater London: The Politics of Metropolitan Reform* (New York, Bobbs-Merrill). *56, 100*

Smith, B. L. (1969). 'The justification of local government', in L. D. Feldman and M. D. Goldrick (eds.), *Politics and Government of Urban Canada: Selected Readings* (Toronto, Methuen), pp.332—47. *26n, 40n, 50n*

Smith, F. H. (1944). 'The expert in the local government service', *Public Administration*, 22, pp.30—40. *127n*

Smith, T. Dan (1965). 'Local government in Newcastle-Upon-Tyne: the background to some recent developments', *Public Administration*, 43, pp.413—18. *131n, 133n*

Smithies, A. (1955). *The Budgetary Process in the United States* (New York, McGraw-Hill). *139n*

(1965). 'Conceptual framework for the program budget', in D. Novick (ed), *Program Budgeting* (Cambridge, Mass., Harvard University Press), pp.24—60. *139n, 143n*

Snell, Lord (1935). 'The town council', in H. J. Laski, W. I. Jennings, and W. A. Robson (eds.), *A Century of Municipal Progress* (London, George Allen and Unwin), pp.66–81. *30, 42*

Society of Clerks of Urban District Councils (1951). *The Clerk of the Council and His Department. 129*

Southend-on-Sea CBC (1969). *Report on Reorganisation. 156n*

Spann, R. N. (1962). 'Large-scale administration: some "Principles" and problems', *Public Administration (Australia)*, 21, pp.204–17. *74n*

Sparks, F. M. (1916). *Government as a Business* (New York, Rand McNally). *202*

Spencer, P. (1971). 'Party politics and processes of local democracy in an English town council', in A. Richards and A. Kuper (eds.), *Councils in Action* (London, Cambridge University Press), pp.171–201. *29, 38, 40n, 51n*

Stacey, M. (1960). *Tradition and Change* (London, Oxford University Press). *84*

Stacey, M., Batstone, E., Bell, C., and Murlott, A. (1975). *Power, Persistence and Change* (London, Routledge and Kegan Paul)

Stanyer, J. (1967). *County Government in England and Wales* (London, Routledge and Kegan Paul). *7, 120, 125n, 127*

  (1967A). 'The Maud Committee Report', *Social and Economic Administration*, I, 4, pp.3–19. *147*

  (1970). 'The local government commissions', in H. V. Wiseman (ed.), *Local Government in England 1958–69* (London, Routledge and Kegan Paul), pp.15–41. *1, 114n, 134, 147*

  (1970A). 'The Maud Committee Report', in H. V. Wiseman (ed.), *Local Government in England 1958–69* (London, Routledge and Kegan Paul), pp.42–70. *3*

  (1971). 'Elected representatives and management in local government' a case of applied sociology and applied economics', *Public Administration*, 49, pp.73–97. *147, 148, 190*

  (1973). 'The Redcliffe-Maud Royal Commission on Local Government', in R. A. Chapman (ed.), *The Role of Commissions in Policy-Making* (London, George Allen and Unwin), pp.105–42. *3, 71, 72*

  (1976). *Understanding Local Government* (London, Fontana). *52n, 53n, 146, 148*

Steed, M. (1969). 'Politics: more balance?', *New Society*, 19 June, pp.951–2. *102, 103*

Steer, W. S., and Lofts, D. (1970). 'The Mallaby Committee', in H. V. Wiseman (ed.), *Local Government in England 1958–69* (London, Routledge and Kegan Paul), pp.71–95. *148*

Steigman, A. L. (1967). 'Mayor–council government: Yonkers, New York 1908–39 – A study of failure and abandonment' (New York University, DPA thesis). *207*

Steiner, G. Y. (1966). *Metropolitan Government and the Real World: The Case of Chicago* (Chicago, Loyola University). *110*

Sterne, S. (1877). 'The administration of American cities', *International Review*, 4, pp.631–46. *202*

Stewart, F. M. (1950). *A Half Century of Municipal Progress* (Berkeley, University of California Press). *192, 194n, 196, 203*

Stewart, J. D. (1970). *Local Authority Policy Planning* (London, Charles Knight). *118, 123, 130, 137, 141, 145*

  (1970A). 'Programme budgeting and the management of local government in the United Kingdom', in IMTA. *Programme Budgeting: Concept and Application* (London, IMTA), pp.9—11. *142*

(1971). 'Issues of organisational change', *Local Government Finance*, 16 June, pp.1064—5. *71*

(1971A). 'Management process and structure in the new authorities', *Local Government Chronicle*, 29 May, pp.929—20. *114n*

(1971B). *Management in Local Government: A Viewpoint* (London, Charles Knight). *123, 130, 131, 137, 139, 143, 145*

(1971C). 'Corporate planning and structure planning', *Local Government Finance*, LXXV, 5, pp.130—3. *138, 139*

(1971D). 'Public administration and the study of public policy-making', *PAC Bulletin*, 11, pp.42—56. *162, 258*

(1971E). 'Policy planning in the new authorities', *Local Government Chronicle*, 5 June, pp.968—9. *165*

(1972). 'Local government — changing patterns of management', *Education (Supplement)*, 23 May, pp.v—vi. *137, 139*

(1972A). 'From corporate planning to community planning', *Local Government Finance*, May, pp.155—9. *139*

(1972B). 'New separatism or new corporatism', *Local Government Chronicle*, 17 March, pp.450—1. *139*

(1972). 'Research in local government', *SSRC Newsletter*, 17, December, pp.10—11. *258*

(1979). *Management — Local — Environment — Urban — Government: A Few Words Considered*, University of Birmingham, inaugural lecture. *123, 258*

(1973A). 'Developments in corporate planning in British local government: the Bains Report and corporate planning', *Local Government Studies*, 5, pp.13—29. *142*

(1974). *The Responsive Local Authority* (London, Charles Knight). *123, 145, 165*

Stewart, J. D., and Eddison, T. (1971). 'Structure planning and corporate planning', *Journal of the Royal Town Planning Institute*, 57, pp.367—9. *138*

Stinchcombe, J. (1968). *Reform and Reaction* (Belmont, Calif., Wadsworth). *209*

Stone, H. A., Price, D. K., and Stone, K. H. (1940). *City Manager Government in the United States* (Chicago, Public Administration Service). *194, 203, 206, 208*

Straetz, R. A. (1958). *PR Politics in Cincinnati* (New York, New York University Press). *209*

Strauss, A. L. (1967). 'Strategies for discovering urban theory', in L. F. Schnore and H. Fagin (eds.), *Urban Research and Policy Planning* (Beverly Hills, Sage), pp.79—98. *6n*

Studenski, P. (1930). *The Government of Metropolitan Areas* (New York, National Municipal League). *107*

Suthers, R. B. (1905). *Mind Your Own Business* (London, Clarion Press). *30*

Swaffield, J. C. (1960). 'Green fingers in the council chamber', *Public Administration*, 38, pp.131—5. *166n, 186, 188*

Sweezy, P. (1942). *Theory of Capitalist Development* (New York, Monthly Review). *224*

Taft, C. P. (1933). *City Management: The Cincinnati Experiment* (New York, Farrar and Rinehart). *194, 206n*

Taylor, D. H. (1972). 'Local government 1974: The challenge of management', *District Councils Review*, October, pp.251—2. *164*

Taylor, F. W. (1911). *The Principles of Scientific Management* (New York, Harper). *152*

Tee, R. H. (1927). 'The place of finance departments, committees, and officers in administrative control', *Public Administration*, 5, pp.444—53. *127*

Therborn, G. (1976). 'What does the ruling class do when it rules?', *Insurgent Sociologist*, 6, pp.3—16. *218*
   (1977). 'The rule of capital and the rise of democracy', *New Left Review*, 103, pp.3—41. *83n, 90*

Thernstrom, S. (1964). *Poverty and Progress* (Cambridge, Mass., Harvard University Press). *196*

Thernstrom, S., and Sennett, R. (eds.) (1969). *Nineteenth Century Cities* (New Haven, Yale University Press). *193*

Thomas, N., and Blanshard, P. (1932). *What's the Matter with New York?* (New York, Macmillan). *200n*

Thompson, E. P. (1968). *The Making of the English Working Class* (Harmondsworth, Penguin). *86, 87, 93*

Thompson, P. (1967). *Socialists, Liberals and Labour: The Struggle for London, 1885—1924* (London, Routledge and Kegan Paul). *88, 91, 93, 103n*

Thompson, V. A. (1965—6). 'Bureaucracy and innovation', *Administrative Science Quarterly*, 10, pp.1—20. *183n*

Thompson, W. R. (1965). *A Preface to Urban Economics* (Baltimore, Johns Hopkins University Press). *74, 75n, 77n, 106*

Thornhill, W. (1971). *The Growth and Reform of English Local Government* (London, Weidenfeld and Nicolson). *1, 7, 26*

Tillett, N. R. (1949). *Town Hall and Shire Hall* (London, Harrap). *119, 127n*

Tilley, J. (1975). 'Local government councillors and community work', *Community Development Journal*, 10, pp.89—94. *47, 48n*

Town Planning Institute (1968). Memoranda submitted to the Committee on Public Participation in Planning, *Journal of the Town Planning Institute*, 54, pp.343—4. *31*

Tudor, D. (1970). *Planning-Programming-Budgeting Systems* (Council of Planning Librarians, Exchange Bibliography, no. 121). *142*

Tudor, J., and Stanyer, J. (1970). 'Local government from 1945 to 1958', in H. V. Wiseman (ed.), *Local Government in England, 1958—1969* (London, Routledge and Kegan Paul), pp.1—14. *114*

Turner, F. J. (1920). *The Frontier in American History* (New York, Henry Holt). *197, 213*

Turner, G. K. (1906). 'Galveston: A business corporation', *McClure's*, 27 October. *204*

Urwick, L. (1937). 'Organisation as a technical problem', in L. Gulick and L. Urwick (eds.), *Papers on the Science of Administration* (New York, Institute of Public Administration). *159*
   (1943). *The Elements of Administration*, 2nd edn (London, Pitman, 1947). *152, 153, 154*

Vance, J. E. (1971). 'Land assignment in pre-capitalist, capitalist, and post capitalist cities', *Economic Geography*, 47, pp.101—20. *92*

Waldo, D. (ed.) (1971). *Public Administration in a Time of Turbulence* (Scranton, Chandler). *162n*

Walton, J., and Masotti, L. (1976). *The City in Comparative Perspective* (Beverly Hills, Sage). *16n*

Warburg, O. (1929). 'Some problems of London today', *Public Administration*, 7, pp.20—9. *139n*

Ward, B. (1968). 'Problems of local government', *Marxism Today*, 12, pp. 83—93. *60n*

Ward, R. A. (1970). *Starting Planned Programme Budgeting and Strategic Planning in a Local Authority* (London, Metra Consulting Group). *123*

Warren, J. H. (1950). 'Local self-government: the basis of a democratic state', *Public Administration*, 28, pp.11—16. *32, 120, 127n, 130n*

(1952). 'The party system in local government', in S. D. Bailey (ed.), *The British Party System* (London, Hansard Society), pp.177—92. *32, 36, 37, 100*

(1957). *In Defence of Local Democracy* (London, CPC). *28n, 32, 95n*

(1961). *The English Local Government System*, 6th edn (London, George Allen and Unwin). *32*

Warren, R. O. (1966). *Government in Metropolitan Regions* (University of California, Davis, Institute of Governmental Affairs). *107, 108*

Wasserman, G. J. (1970). 'Planning, programming, budgeting in the police service in England and Wales', *O and M Bulletin*, 25, pp.197—211. *141n*

Watson, R. A., and Romani, J. H. (1961). 'Metropolitan government for Cleveland: an analysis of the voting record', *Midwest Journal of Political Science*, 5, pp.365—90. *108*

Webb, B. (1898). *American Diary 1898*, edited by D. A. Shannon (Madison, University of Wisconsin Press, 1963). *29, 191, 208*

(1948). *Our Partnership* (London, Longmans Green). *21*

Webb, B., and Webb, S. (1920). *A Constitution for the Socialist Commonwealth of Great Britain* (London, Longmans Green). *34, 75n, 91n*

(1932). *Methods of Social Study* (London, Cambridge University Press, 1975). *123, 125n, 126, 127, 130n, 132, 134n, 135*

Weber, A. (1899). *The Growth of Cities in the Nineteenth Century* (New York, Macmillan). *197*

Wedderburn, D. (1965). 'Facts and theories of the welfare state', in R. Miliband and J. Saville (eds.), *The Socialist Register 1965* (London, Merlin). *223n, 225*

Weinstein, J. (1962). 'Organised business and the city commission and manager movements', *Journal of Southern History*, 29, pp.166—82. *194n, 195, 206*

Wells, H. G. (1903). 'A paper on administrative areas read before the Fabian Society', in H. G. Wells, *Mankind in the Making* (London, Chapman and Hall), pp.309—417. *62, 102n*

The West Midland Group (1948). *Conurbation* (London, Architectural Press). *66*

A West Midland Study Group (1956). *Local Government and Central Control* (London, Routledge and Kegan Paul). *14, 30n, 43*

Wetherall, R. A. (1933). 'The report of the committee on local expenditure', *Public Administration*, 11, pp.157—65. *213*

Whalen, H. (1960). 'Democracy and local government', *Canadian Public Administration*, 3, pp.1—13. *34, 50*

(1960A). 'Ideology, democracy, and the foundations of local self-government', *Canadian Journal of Economics and Political Science*, 26, pp.377—95. *28n*

Wheare, K. C. (1955). *Government by Committee* (Oxford, Clarendon Press). *120, 126, 129n, 130*

White, A. D. (1890). 'The government of American cities', *The Forum*, 10, December, pp.357—72. *191, 195, 202, 208*

White, L. D. (1927). *The City Manager* (New York, Greenwood Press). *192, 194*

White, R. G. (1883). 'Class distinctions in the United States', *North American Review*, 137, September, pp.231—46. *197*

Whyte, W. E. (1928). 'Internal organisation of local authorities', *Public Administration*, 6, pp.251—61. *132n*

Wickwar, W. H. (1970). *The Political Theory of Local Government* (Columbia, South Carolina, University of South Carolina Press). *26, 28n, 57*

Wiebe, R. H. (1962). *Businessmen and Reform* (Chicago, Quadrangle Books, 1968). *193*

Wilcox, D. F. (1897). *The Study of City Government* (New York, Macmillan). *191*

(1904). *The American City: A Problem in Democracy* (New York, Macmillan). *196n, 201, 202*

Wildavsky, A. (1964). *The Politics of the Budgetary Process* (Boston, Little Brown). *176—9 passim*

(1966). 'The political economy of efficiency: cost-benefit analysis, systems analysis, and program budgeting', *Public Administration Review*, 26, pp.292—310. *157n, 177n*

(1973). 'If planning is everything, maybe it's nothing', *Policy Sciences*, 4, pp.127—53. *58*

(1975). *Budgeting: A Comparative Theory of Budgetary Processes* (Boston, Little Brown). *139n, 140n, 142, 177, 178*

Wilder, A. P. (1891). *Municipal Problems* (New Haven). *196*

Wilensky, H. L., and Lebaux, C. N. (1958). *Industrial Society and Social Welfare* (New York, Russell Sage Foundation). *223n*

Williams, A. (1966). 'The optimal provision of public goods in a system of local government', *Journal of Political Economy*, 74, pp.18—33. *77n*

(1967). *Output Budgeting and the Contribution of Microeconomics to Efficiency in Government*, CAS Occasional paper no. 4 (London, HMSO). *141n*

Williams, D. (1976). 'Too many managers — a resignation statement', *Education*, CILVIII, 15, October, p.285. *173n*

Williams, J. E. (1955). 'Paternalism and local government in the nineteenth century', *Public Administration*, 33, pp.439—46. *84*

Williams, R. (1977). *Marxism and Literature* (London, Oxford University Press). *219*

Williamson, C. (1960). *American Suffrage: From Property to Democracy, 1760—1860* (Princeton, Princeton University Press). *201*

Williamson, O. E. (1967). 'Hierarchical control and optimum firm size', *Journal of Political Economy*, 75, pp.123—38. *76*

Wilson, C. H. (1948). 'The foundations of local government', in C. H. Wilson (ed.). *Essays on Local Government* (Oxford, Basil Blackwell), pp.1—24. *28*

Wilson, J. Q. (1966). 'Innovation in organisation: Notes toward a theory', in J. D. Thompson (ed.). *Approaches to Organisational Design* (Pittsburgh, University of Pittsburgh Press), pp.193—218. *183n*

(1968). 'The police and the delinquent in two cities', in J. Q. Wilson (ed.), *City Politics and Public Policy* (New York, Wiley), pp.173—95. *58*

Wiseman, H. V. (1963). 'The party caucus in local government', *New Society*, 31 October, pp.9—10. *39n*

(1963A). 'Local government in Leeds', *Public Administration*, 41, pp.51—69, 137—56. *39n*

(1967). *Local Government at Work* (London, Routledge and Kegan Paul). *39n*

Wistrich, E. (1972). *Local Government Reorganisation: The First Years of Camden* (London, London Borough of Camden). *6n, 104*

Wood, B. (1976). *The Process of Local Government Reform* (London, George Allen and Unwin). *5, 60n, 72, 74n, 75, 102*

Woodruff, C. R. (1903). 'An American Municipal Program', *Political Science Quarterly*, 18, pp.47—58. *202*

(1912). 'American Municipal tendencies', *National Municipal Review*, 1, January, pp.3—20

Working Group on Local Authority Management Structures (1972). *The New Local Authorities: Management and Structure* (London, HMSO). *15, 118, 121, 125, 126, 131, 132, 138, 139n, 157, 186, 187n, 188n, 190, 251*

Wright, R. S., and Hobhouse, H. (1884). *An Outline of Local Government and Local Taxation in England and Wales* (London, W. Maxwell and Son). *60n, 61, 247*

Yaffe, D. (1973). 'The crisis of profitability: A critique of the Glyn-Sutcliffe thesis', *New Left Review*, 80, pp.45—62. *229*

Yates, D. (1973). *Neighbourhood Democracy* (Lexington, Mass., Lexington Books). *207*

Young, K. (1975). *Local Politics and the Rise of Party* (Leicester, Leicester University Press). *7, 36*

(1975A) *Essays on the Study of Urban Politics* (London, Macmillan)

Young, R. G. (1972). *Crisis for Democracy* (Paisley College of Technology, Local Government Research Unit). *190n*

(1973). *From Corporate Planning to Community Action* (Paisley College of Technology, Local Government Research Unit). *190n*

(1977). *The Search for Democracy* (Milngavie, Heatherbank Press). *258n*

Subject Index